W9-ARD-580

BRIEF CONTENTS

WITHDRAWN

SEVENTH EDITION

BUSINESS AND GOVERNMENT IN THE GLOBAL MARKETPLACE

Murray L. Weidenbaum

Washington University
St. Louis, Missouri

PEARSON

Prentice
Hall

Upper Saddle River, New Jersey 07458

Library of Congress Cataloging-in-Publication Data

Weidenbaum, Murray L.
  Business and government in the global marketplace / Murray L. Weidenbaum. — 7th ed.
    p.   cm.
  Includes bibliographical references and index.
  ISBN 0-13-049902-1
  1. Industrial policy — United States.   2. Trade regulation — United States.   I. Title.

HD3616.U47W368 2003
338.973—dc21

2003040555

Executive Editor: Rod Banister
Editor-in-Chief: P. J. Boardman
Managing Editor (Editorial): Gladys Soto
Assistant Editor: Marie McHale
Editorial Assistant: Joy Golden
Marketing Manager: Kathleen Mclellan
Marketing Assistant: Christopher Bath
Managing Editor (Production): John Roberts
Production Editor: Renata Butera
Production Assistant: Joe DeProspero
Permissions Coordinator: Suzanne Grappi
Associate Director, Manufacturing: Vincent Scelta
Production Manager: Arnold Vila
Manufacturing Buyer: Michelle Klein
Cover Design: Bruce Kenselaar
Composition: Progressive Information Technologies
Full-Service Project Management: Progressive Publishing Alternatives
Printer/Binder: Courier – Westford

Credits and acknowledgments borrowed from other sources and reproduced, with permission, in this textbook appear on the appropriate page within the text.

Copyright © 2004, 1999, 1995, 1990, 1986 by Pearson Education, Inc., Upper Saddle River, New Jersey, 07458. All rights reserved. Printed in the United States of America. This publication is protected by Copyright and permission should be obtained from the publisher prior to any prohibited reproduction, storage in a retrieval system, or transmission in any form or by any means, electronic, mechanical, photocopying, recording, or likewise. For information regarding permission(s), write to: Rights and Permissions Department.

Pearson Prentice Hall™ is a trademark of Pearson Education, Inc.
Pearson ® is a registered trademark of Pearson plc.
Prentice Hall ® is a registered trademark of Pearson Education, Inc.

Pearson Education LTD.
Pearson Education Australia PTY, Limited
Pearson Education Singapore, Pte. Ltd
Pearson Education North Asia Ltd
Pearson Education, Canada, Ltd
Pearson Educación de Mexico, S.A. de C.V.
Pearson Education – Japan
Pearson Education Malaysia, Pte. Ltd

10 9 8 7 6 5 4 3 2 1
ISBN 0-13-049902-1

CONTENTS

⟞∞⟝

PREFACE

Public policy—especially as shaped by a host of government and interest group interactions—is a pervasive influence on the business firm. This book analyzes both sides of that relationship, covering the many ways in which government policy affects the activities of the modern corporation and the various responses on the part of business.

The purpose of this book is not to indoctrinate the student but to provide a better understanding of the intricate relationship between the public and private sectors—why and how government intervenes in the economy and how business can respond. Thus, quite deliberately, this book does not present an all-embracing theoretical framework to guide the student to the author's personal view of the optimal public policy and the appropriate private response. It is hoped that the tools for that search are provided here, and instructors are free to provide their preferred guidance to the student reader.

This seventh edition represents a continuing effort to meet the changing needs and desires of the two main sets of users: students and faculty in schools of business and departments of economics. As someone who teaches both MBA students and upper-level undergraduate economic students, I have tried out preliminary versions on my students and have benefited from their reactions. This edition adds new sections on globalization, energy policy, reforming corporate governance, and terrorism, while it eliminates older, less relevant material.

Part I is an overview of the tools that government has available to influence business decision making. Part II covers the field of government regulation in both the social and economic areas. Changes have been made to reflect recent developments in public policy. The new chapter on business and terrorism draws on my service in the fall of 2001 on a special task force on terrorism.

Part III begins with a presentation of the pros and cons of globalization. Part IV brings together three important aspects of business–government relations that are often overlooked by researchers in this field: credit programs, the government market for the products of business, and tax policy.

Part V deals with the key responses of business to government influence. Each chapter has been updated to cover recent developments. Part VI contains a thoroughly revised and updated chapter on corporate governance. In the last chapter, which focuses on the future of the business firm, an effort is made to identify the coming changes in government policies affecting private business.

As in the previous editions, the focus of this book is on the future practitioner—the business executive who will be dealing with issues of public policy as a day-to-day aspect of the job. Also, it is hoped that this book will assist present and future government officials and members of interest groups to better appreciate the various consequences of their actions on the business system.

The author would like to acknowledge Alan Hamlin, Southern Utah University, Thomas Lyon, Indiana University, and Donald Hicks, University of Texas at Dallas, for their suggestions on the revision of this text.

The author is indebted to Ryan Argo and David Switzer for extremely helpful research assistance. As she has in the past, Christine Moseley carefully typed the various drafts and helped get the manuscript ready for publication.

I am particularly grateful to my wife, Phyllis, for encouraging me to continue striving to improve communications with the generations that follow us.

Murray L. Weidenbaum
Washington University

ABOUT THE AUTHOR

Murray L. Weidenbaum holds the Mallinckrodt Distinguished University Professorship at Washington University in St. Louis, where he also serves as honorary chairman of the university's Weidenbaum Center on the Economy, Government, and Public Policy (founded as the Center for the Study of American Business). For 25 years, he has been teaching a popular course on business and government.

In 1981–1982, Dr. Weidenbaum served as President Reagan's first Chairman of the Council of Economic Advisers. In that capacity, he played a major role in formulating the economic policy of the Reagan administration and was a major spokesman for that administration on economic and business issues, both domestic and international. In 1999–2000, he chaired the Congressional Commission on the Trade Deficit.

Dr. Weidenbaum has held a variety of business, government, and academic positions. He was the first Assistant Secretary of the Treasury for Economic Policy and served earlier as Fiscal Economist in the U.S. Bureau of the Budget and as the Corporate Economist at the Boeing Company. He has been a member of the board of directors of corporations ranging from *Fortune* 100 giants to small service companies.

Dr. Weidenbaum is known for his research on business–government issues, taxes, regulation, and international trade. He is the author of seven books and has written several hundred articles in publications ranging from the *American Economic Review* to the *New York Times*.

Dr. Weidenbaum received his Ph.D. from Princeton University. He has received the Distinguished Writers Award from the Center for Strategic and International Studies, the Alexander Hamilton Medal "in recognition of distinguished leadership in the Department of the Treasury," the Leavey Prize for excellence in private enterprise education from the Freedoms Foundation, and the Adam Smith Award from the Association of Private Enterprise Education. In 1992, the Association of American Publishers honored Dr. Weidenbaum as author of the economics book of the year. In 1997, he was a finalist in the global competition for business book of the year.

PART I

SETTING THE FRAMEWORK

A central issue facing contemporary society is how to deal constructively with the dynamic tension between the public and private sectors. This uneasy relationship is evidenced by the continuing interaction between government and business, where government, on occasion, is both the unwelcome regulator and the most welcome customer, and business is simultaneously the suspicious recipient of subsidy and the mechanism for producing food, clothing, shelter, and carrying out other important societal activities.

A fundamental challenge is how to harness the innovative power and motivating incentive of the business enterprise so that it can contribute to the well-being of the overall society without weakening its positive and unique characteristics. Surely there is no invariant set of answers suitable for all circumstances. Grappling with these issues is the continuing responsibility of decision makers in both the public and private sectors. Meanwhile, it is helpful to raise the information level available and to improve the techniques for analyzing and evaluating these issues. That is the task on which we now embark.

The substantial arsenals of power that reside in both the public and the private sectors of a modern society generate numerous changes in the complex relationships between business and government. Part I examines the instruments through which government power is exerted. Such basic knowledge is essential to understand the impacts of government on business and to evaluate the responses of business, which are the tasks of the later parts of this book.

1

THE POWERS OF GOVERNMENT AND BUSINESS

The chairman of the board of Globally Diversified Enterprises (GDE) has just summoned the board's secretary (a bright, young MBA fresh from a tour of duty in Singapore with an international management consulting firm). The purpose of the meeting is to review the agenda for the upcoming meeting of the company's board of directors.

PREPARING FOR THE BOARD MEETING OF GLOBALLY DIVERSIFIED ENTERPRISES

Aside from the usual committee reports—audit, finance, executive compensation, and governance—the GDE board meeting will focus on the chairman's quarterly review of operations. The current year is progressing better than the previous one but is falling substantially short of the objectives set at the board's summer planning session. A longer-than-usual list of problems has arisen that the chairman wants to discuss with the board.

- The Industrial Machinery Division is behind schedule on its new factory. The division president is flying in from his headquarters in Frankfurt to explain the unexpected changes in the European Union's approval procedures.
- The Consumer Products Division has been turned down again by U.S. government regulators on key new products it has developed. Two chemical compounds have failed to receive clearance by the Environmental Protection Agency, and the division's marketing subsidiary in Amsterdam is anxious to move ahead with them on its own.
- The Government Products Division is pressing for a larger capital budget. Its military order backlog is rising once again. The division is also competing for a new generation of weapon systems geared to fighting terrorism.
- The Farm Equipment Division has reported an unexpected decline in sales, resulting from the loss of some overseas markets, especially in Asia. The division's management and the general counsel are urging the company to take a more active role in the national debate on maintaining open markets to international commerce.
- The treasurer has deferred the bond issue scheduled for this month in view of the unexplained gyrations in foreign exchange markets. Renewed economic growth has fueled speculation about the Federal Reserve raising interest rates.
- The senior vice president for human resources has been spending most of her time in Washington, trying to settle a class action suit instituted by the Equal

Employment Opportunity Commission. The company has been receiving unfavorable national publicity for its alleged reluctance to promote recovering alcoholics to supervisory positions.

- The vice president for labor relations has begun preliminary negotiations with the International Association of Machinists on a major labor contract that is about to expire. Because GDE is in a pace-setting industry, the Secretary of Labor has publicly urged the company to take an "enlightened" attitude in dealing with union demands for enhanced job security.
- The vice chairman of the board has been meeting with representatives of the New York State Employees' Pension Fund, a major holder of the company's stock, on the fund's opposition to the proposed reelection of several members of the board of directors because of their board service with several companies that have recently gone bankrupt.
- The executive board of the National Association of Manufacturers has asked for a go-ahead to nominate GDE's CEO as the next chairman of that broad-based business association.

The list goes on, but the chairman is reluctant to raise more of these nonbusiness, or at least nontraditional, issues with the board all in one meeting. He wonders out loud whether Globally Diversified Enterprises is properly staffed and organized to handle this variety of matters. The secretary suggests bringing in some high-powered consultants to advise the company. This, the chairman objects, would at best be a quick fix, a short-term solution. Similar matters would likely come up the following year.

The secretary asks if some of these oddball problems have arisen or at least worsened because GDE's managers are not sufficiently trained or experienced to deal with them. "Exactly," replies the chairman. At this point, the company's director of stockholder relations calls with a report that several influential analysts are seriously questioning the data in the company's latest quarterly report.

This scenario, of course, is hypothetical and simplified. However, problems like these regularly arise in modern corporations. The need to help the current as well as the future generation of managers to understand and to deal with such problems is widespread. This book is a response to that need.

The public sector influences private-sector decision making in a great variety of ways—and of course the private sector responds. Most analyses of the interaction between business and government focus on the pros and cons of public-policy actions. This book turns the tables on that conventional approach. Rather than just attempting to play public policy maker, we will also examine the interactions between business and government from the vantage point of the private business firm and its management.

The contemporary corporation is undergoing a fundamental transition from a business serving the home market to a transnational enterprise. This transition is far from complete, and many companies have only begun the change. Even the smallest firm, however, is subject to powerful indirect influences of the global marketplace. In large measure, this development is driven by economic and market factors. In a considerable variety of cases, however, these changes in business decision making are the direct result of domestic and foreign governmental policies.

THE POWER OF BUSINESS

The government agency and the business enterprise are two of the most powerful institutions in modern society. The shifting and complicated relationships between them exert great influence on the performance of the economy and on the lives of citizens. These relationships range from cooperative to competitive, from friendly to hostile. Fundamentally, it is an uneasy relationship, each side possessing certain powers and each having an important need for the other. In virtually every modern industrialized society, the result is a mixed economy in which the public and the private sectors interact in many ways.

The basic power of the business firm lies in the widespread recognition that it is a fundamental mechanism for achieving human progress. Especially in the United States and other Western nations, the public's strong belief in the role of private markets, competition, and the independent business firm ultimately limits the ability of government to dominate the economy and to intervene in the operation of private enterprise.

In turn, its substantial resources enhance the ability of business to respond to government and to influence public policy. As shown in Part V, corporations are among the largest donors to election campaigns and also finance a variety of advocacy groups and public policy research organizations. These powers of private enterprises, as we will see, have not prevented government from exercising very substantial authority over business policy matters.

As will be shown in great detail in the chapters that follow, governments at all levels are involved in business decision making. However, before we examine that aspect of the business–government relationship, it is useful to understand the underpinnings for continuing public support of the private enterprise system.

A brief reconnaissance of national experiences in modern times reveals that capitalistic economies generally have performed much better than those with a much larger governmental presence, while providing their citizens with more personal freedom. This contrast has been most notable in societies ruled by communist and socialist governments.

INTERNATIONAL COMPARISONS

History shows us that superior economic performance is not necessarily a question of natural resources, inherited wealth, culture, or geography. Looking at the developed nations of Europe—which have similar levels of resources and culture—it is clear that the capitalist countries of the West outperformed the communist economies of the East and the latter are now moving—albeit with fits and starts—toward some variation of the Western economic pattern. In Asia, the nations with a large and vibrant private business sector—Taiwan, South Korea, and Singapore, for example—outperform the communist economies of North Korea and Myanmar.

As for resources and inherited wealth, Spain and Great Britain present a striking contrast. Despite the hoards of gold and silver Spain received from the Americas in the early stages of modern economic experience, its highly controlled economy remained for centuries at a relatively primitive level of development. The initially far more modest but also far more open economy of England, especially in the postmercantilist era, led the economic development of the globe for long periods. In our own time, a nation with few natural endowments—Japan—was the economic pacesetter for much of the post–World War II era, although it more recently has been suffering from a variety of public policy shortcomings.

What common characteristics do the successful economies have? A cluster of key economic institutions stands out: a strong private business sector, primary reliance on competition and decision making in the marketplace to allocate resources, protection of private property, freedom of exchange, and the resultant decentralization of power (see Figure 1.1).[1] The countries with a large and strong private sector tend to be those that provide their citizens with a large degree of individual liberty. On reflection, that is not coincidental. The decentralization of power that is essential for capitalism to prosper is also the basic way of avoiding a totalitarian society.

Because the modern industrial society rests on the foundations of capitalism as well as of democracy, we inevitably encounter tensions and uneasy compromises. As individuals, we attach different weights to the two sets of values, and we reach different conclusions on particular policy issues that define the scope of the marketplace and the limits of the political process.

At least implicitly in most public policy debates, citizens rely on some unifying principles that promote consensus. Thus, we recognize that the government needs a strong private enterprise system for two reasons: as a support and as a counterweight. As a support for government in a capitalistic system, the business sector is the goose that lays the golden eggs. The marketplace finances the public efforts to educate our youth, aid the poor, and provide for the national defense. To be crass but accurate, the material resources required to fulfill the objectives of the public sector come from the tax base provided by a healthy private sector.

A private enterprise economy is characterized by a great number of competing firms and thus economic power is decentralized. That tendency offsets the greater centralization of power in the public sector and thus contributes to the survival of democracy. It is a remarkable uniformity of history that a fully collectivized economy has never produced a single free election or one free press. Some analysts are quite adamant on this point. Historian Arthur Schlesinger, Jr., contends that democracy is

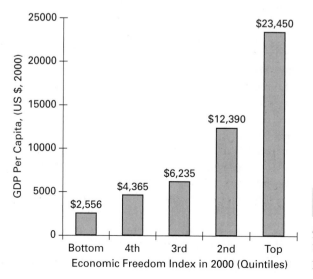

FIGURE 1.1   Economic Freedom and Per-Capita Income

Source: James Gwartney and Robert Lawson, *Economic Freedom of the World,* 2002 Annual Report (Vancouver, B.C.: Fraser Institute, 2002).

impossible without private property because the presence of resources beyond the arbitrary reach of government provides the only secure basis for political opposition and intellectual freedom.[2]

Turning to the other side of the coin, the success of the private enterprise system depends critically on the government and the exercise of its legal powers. It is almost a paradox to note that the most basic attributes of a market economy—the value of contracts, promises to pay, and money itself—all stem from the power of politicians and bureaucrats to penalize violators of the rules of the marketplace.[3] In enforcing such restraints, society draws a line between liberty and license, and between legitimate access and trespass. The United States is a cogent case in point. The high degree of economic freedom enjoyed by the private sector, and the rules defining the specific nature of that freedom, has extensive constitutional underpinnings.

THE U.S. CONSTITUTION AND ECONOMIC FREEDOM

The delegates at Philadelphia more than two centuries ago were acutely aware that an economic system organized primarily along the lines of private enterprise was a necessary precondition to national strength and the preservation of a democratic political system. A similar high priority was assigned to the protection of private property rights. As a result, the Constitution of the United States contains many provisions designed to preserve commercial freedoms.

The Fifth Amendment (of the original Bill of Rights) states in part, "nor shall private property be taken for public use, without just compensation." This is generally referred to as the *takings clause*. Rooted in English common law, the takings clause recognizes that property rights can be invaded for public, but not for private, purposes. Government may exercise the power of *eminent domain* to take private property for some public purpose, such as building a highway. The normal expectation, however, is that the owner of property ceded through the eminent-domain process will be fairly recompensed by the government. In 1987, the Supreme Court held that a property owner is entitled to payment of just compensation when land-use regulations deny reasonable use of property, even though the owner retains the nominal right of ownership. That landmark decision established a limit on government power to control the use of private-sector resources.

The Founding Fathers understood very well that basic to the functioning of the private enterprise system is the right to enter into binding contracts. They wished to provide a stable environment for business, conducive to trade and investment and protected from excessive political manipulation. In that spirit, Article I, Section 10, of the Constitution states, "No State . . . shall pass any Law impairing the Obligation of Contracts."

That is amplified in the Fourteenth Amendment, which states, "nor shall any State deprive any person of life, liberty, or property, without due process of law . . ." The national government thus established the "rules of the game," in the form of restraints on the exercise of government power, a basic precondition to the effective functioning of private markets.

In retrospect, as a result of key constitutional provisions, the United States became one of the earliest common markets in the global economy. Under the earlier Articles of Confederation, in contrast, the individual states—which continue to be sovereign in our federal system—imposed taxes, quotas, and other barriers on interstate commerce. Recognizing that an economic system based on private enterprise depends on the free flow of goods and services, Article 1, Section 9, provides that "no Tax or Duty shall be laid on Articles exported from any State. No preference shall be given by any Regulation of Commerce or Revenue to the Ports of one State over those of another; nor shall Vessels bound to, or from, one State, be obliged to enter, clear, or pay Duties in another." It is unlikely that the high degree of prosperity achieved by the American economy could have been achieved without this constitutional creation of the American "common market."

However, Article 1, Section 8, of the Constitution gives the Congress the power "to regulate Commerce with foreign Nations and among the several States." This "commerce clause" has been the fundamental legal basis for expanded federal government regulation of the economy.

The reconciliation between the pressures of the private marketplace and the demands of the public sector requires careful balance. Before discussing where that balance should be, it is helpful to analyze the reasons for the relative success of capitalistic systems. Reliance on private enterprise to produce and distribute goods and services is not a matter of blindly accepting a "black box" whose workings we cannot fathom.

THE BASIS FOR THE SUPERIORITY OF THE MARKETPLACE

In this age of information, we need to remind ourselves of the basics. For centuries, the competitive marketplace has generated volumes of vital information beyond the capability of the most sophisticated central planning authority. By using the price system, the marketplace transmits signals to many thousands of producers that reflect the values of hundreds of millions of consumers, offering profits for the production of those goods whose value to consumers exceeds their costs to producers. The much-maligned, but universally used, influence of profits serves as the magnet that pulls resources into their most productive use. The paradox of Adam Smith's "invisible hand" continues to be pertinent in the modern economy. In the competitive market-place, economic self-interest serves as the primary engine of social welfare—although it simultaneously generates pressures for governmental intervention.

Often we take this process for granted. However, it contrasts so vividly with the inefficiencies of the communist system. In the former Soviet Union, in the absence of the signaling mechanism of competitive price setting, surpluses of components frequently developed in one factory, while shortages of other components kept the supply of the end product far below consumer desires. Competition can create values for the consumer far greater than the wealth it bestows on successful entrepreneurs and their financial backers—and those consumer benefits are widely distributed. Clearly, an enormous social surplus was created by the dramatic transformation of energy use masterminded by Thomas Edison.

But maintaining a competitive economy does not come easily, nor does the price system solve all social problems. The favorable implications of Smith's invisible hand are undermined by monopoly. Monopoly is the very antithesis of competition. It imposes a logic of scarcity rather than productivity. It enforces rigidity rather than responsiveness, consumer exploitation rather than consumer sovereignty.

Visions of monopoly conjure up big businesses swallowing small businesses. However, in practice, a competitive marketplace generates new businesses more rapidly than old businesses can take them over. In fact, often those new businesses elbow out established larger firms from their dominant positions in major markets. This point is underscored by comparing the listing of the largest U.S. corporations today with those of a generation ago. Wal-Mart, Hewlett-Packard, Verizon, SBC Communications, and American International Group, for example, have replaced Mobil, Swift, Gulf Oil, Bethlehem Steel, and Armour.

The truth is that the typical cases of monopoly arise from the actions of government. The postal monopoly did not arise from the overpowering success of a single large enterprise, but rather from the government's unwillingness to let new enterprises enter this market. Visions of David and Goliath come to mind, but with a less happy ending. From time to time, the U.S. Postal Service takes to court a few youngsters who offer to deliver Christmas mail more efficiently or more cheaply than the government's own postal monopoly. Invariably, Goliath wins: The government's monopoly over the delivery of first-class mail and the use of the homeowners' mailbox is absolute.

In other instances, government awards monopoly power to private companies, notably in the areas of transportation, communication, and utilities. Curbing that use of the government's power to create private monopolies can reduce costs and result in a more efficient economic system. However, as we will see in later chapters, the transition from monopoly to competition is not always a simple or painless matter.

Assessing the role of private enterprise in a democratic society is not a simple choice among polar alternatives. Friedrich Hayek explained that point clearly in his *Constitution of Liberty:*

> A functioning market economy presupposes certain activities on the part of the state; there are some other such activities by which its functioning will be assisted; and it can tolerate many more, provided that they are of the kind which are compatible with a functioning market. . . . The range and variety of government action that is, at least in principle, reconcilable with a free market system is thus considerable.[4]

In practice, the democratic capitalistic nations are not uniform in the relative size of their market economies. Each draws the line between the public and private sectors at a different point. Moreover, that point varies over time, as would be expected in a free society. It seems quite clear, however, that in the case of the more successful societies—successful in both economic production and personal liberty—the bulk of economic activity is performed in the market economy.

We will first examine the types of actions government takes that can affect the business firm. Then we will see how these actions influence business decision making.

THE POLICY TOOLS AVAILABLE TO GOVERNMENT

Government possesses many mechanisms that it can use directly or indirectly to influence actions in the private sector. Some impacts on the business firm are ancillary to achieving government objectives, whereas others may be unintentional. In the aggregate, the typical business firm faces an impressive array of government powers.

GOVERNMENT PAYROLLS (GOVERNMENT AS PAYMASTER)

The oldest policy tool available to government is to hire people and put them on the government's payroll. Government employees represent such diverse professions as teachers, foresters, and revenue agents. Payrolls provide a cadre of public officials whose actions can then be controlled in terms of their influence on the rest of society. This is the tip of the proverbial iceberg because small proportions of government resources are devoted to compensation of government employees.

At first blush, direct government hiring seems to have little impact on business, but often government sets the standards in the United States. The now prevailing eight-hour day began in the federal government. Wage restraint in the private sector in recent years followed President Reagan's actions in 1981 in breaking the strike of the government's air traffic controllers. In specific personnel categories, such as secretaries and teachers, government hiring patterns influence the entire labor market. In 2001, federal, state, and local governments combined had an aggregate payroll of $946 billion.

In the personnel area, the president's appointment power is pervasive. The Congress has delegated substantial amounts of discretion and decision-making authority to such presidentially appointed officials as the administrator of the Environmental Protection Agency, the director of the Internal Revenue Service, and the members of the board of governors of the Federal Reserve System. The constitutional checks and balances give the Senate power to approve or reject these appointments.

GOVERNMENT PURCHASES

Substantial portions of government budgets are devoted to ordering goods and services produced in the private sector. Products purchased range from high-tech space exploration vehicles to standard off-the-shelf pens and pencils. The importance of the government market is obvious to key defense-oriented industries, such as aerospace, electronics, ordnance, and shipbuilding. In addition, public-sector buyers—from national, state, county, and municipal agencies—purchase items from virtually every industry. Government procurement can be the difference between a good year and a mediocre year for many companies. Thus, many businesses have a strong incentive to influence government actions (a subject that Part V covers in detail).

Although the size of the government market is large ($893 billion in 2001), the magnitude is considerably smaller than the more frequently encountered measure of "government purchases of goods and services" (see Table 1.1). Government purchases from the private sector exclude several important categories of public-sector outlays: compensation of government employees, transfer payments, interest, and subsidies.

TABLE 1.1   Derivation of the Size of the Government Market in 2001

Derivation of Market Size	Billions of Dollars
Government purchases of goods and services*	1,839
Less: Compensation of government employees	946
Equals: Government purchases from the private sector	893

*"Government consumption expenditures and gross investment" on a national income and product accounts basis.

At the national level, military contracts to private industry continue to be the major category of purchases from business. State and local government agencies, in contrast, contract mainly for roads and school buildings and various categories of office supplies. As we will see in Chapter 15, the government procurement process is an important way in which government influences private-sector actions. The public sector's methods of doing business are very different from standard commercial operations. Moreover, for the companies that produce primarily for military and space markets, the government is virtually a monopoly buyer. It exerts powerful control over the contractors' internal operations by forcing them to act in many ways like a government agency and also to be "socially responsible." Requirements imposed by government on private industry range from hiring and training minority groups to adopting federally set wage and hour standards.

A trend toward privatization (or rather the private performance) of some traditional government functions, begun in the 1980s, has increased the size of the public-sector market for which business firms can compete. Many municipalities now contract out solid-waste collection and disposal and depend on private companies for towing and storing illegally parked automobiles. However, the extent of privatization of government activity in the United States is quite limited. Only a few localities contract out airport operations or the delivery of services for the elderly and handicapped.

TRANSFER PAYMENTS

A third policy tool available to government is to provide money to individuals—what economists call transfer payments and what the public at large may refer to less euphemistically as handouts. The key example is the monthly Social Security check sent to senior citizens. Here the impacts are more indirect than in the case of government procurement. Such expenditures strongly influence the amount of consumption by the recipients and thus affect the size and composition of consumer markets available to business.

Government spending for transfer payments, most of which are labeled entitlements, has become so massive in recent years that trends in that category can be a significant factor in the entire business outlook and especially influence the prospects for balancing government budgets. In 2001, government transfer payments in the United States totaled $1,149 billion, mainly for Social Security and medical care programs, such as Medicare.

GOVERNMENT SUBSIDIES

Government subsidizes private activity in many ways. By absorbing a portion of the cost of private production, subsidies raise the demand for the subsidized products in relation to other items. For example, subsidies to the mining industry can mean the difference between continuing to operate and closing down a titanium mine. Generous subsidies are provided to many sectors of the economy—and sometimes are referred to pejoratively as *business welfare:* agriculture (farm price supports), fishing (financing for new vessels), nuclear energy (government payments for developing new products), transportation (aid to urban mass transit), housing (low-rent public housing), and mining (special tax benefits). Subsidies are also received by a variety of special clienteles, such as minority enterprises.

Subsidies often contain a regulatory component. For example, government subsidies to shipbuilders can be vital in decisions to build ships in domestic yards rather than overseas. But to qualify for federal subsidies, the ships must incorporate specific national-defense and safety features spelled out by the government. These added features raise both acquisition and operating costs.

Government can be foe as well as friend to private business. In many ways, government is a competitor for funds or influence. Thus, the Tennessee Valley Authority competes with private utilities, the Government Printing Office with commercial publishers (especially mapmakers such as Rand McNally), and the U.S. Postal Service with private parcel delivery services (United Parcel Service and Federal Express, most notably). Government enterprises also compete with private enterprises in the large markets represented by the government's own purchases. This competition between the public and private sectors is more visible at state and local levels, in such areas as health, recreation, trash collection, and neighborhood and building security services.

GOVERNMENT LOANS

The government also acts as a banker, lending money to private firms and individuals as well as to many other categories of borrowers. The gamut of federal lending extends to exporters (Export-Import Bank), farmers (Farmers Home Administration), real estate developers (Federal Housing Administration), and small enterprises (Small Business Administration). Sometimes low interest rate government loans merely substitute for available private funds. But, more frequently, the government credit is provided for projects whose expected returns are so low that private markets will not finance them. As we will see in Chapter 14, government loans are anything but the proverbial free lunch.

GOVERNMENT CREDIT PROGRAMS (GOVERNMENT AS UNDERWRITER)

Even without spending its own money or establishing rules on private conduct, government can strongly influence private economic activity. One way the public sector does that is by use of its credit power. The method used most frequently is the guarantee of private loans, as in the dramatic case of Chrysler and the less well-known but more frequent guarantees of new ship construction and exports. Because much of the risk is shifted from the private lender to the government, borrowers who are not considered creditworthy by normal commercial standards are given access to funds. Also, the government fosters the creation of quasi-government credit corporations, such as in the agricultural and housing credit areas (the farm credit banks and the federal home loan banks). As shown in Chapter 14, the use of the government's credit alters the flow of funds in the economy and thus strongly influences which companies and which individuals gain access to the resources of the economy.

Because they do not seem to require (at least initially) the direct expenditure of government money, loan guarantees have been proliferating, as have other uses of the government's credit. In 2001, all of the non-Treasury borrowing under federal auspices came to $679 billion. As seen in the bailouts of insured but failed savings and loan associations, the government's contingent liability can at times be converted to direct expenditure—and in very substantial amounts.

GOVERNMENT REGULATION

A major area of government involvement in business is the use of the regulatory power. The alphabet soup of regulatory agencies has become well known to many business executives and often to the public at large: CFTC, CPSC, EEOC, EPA, FAA, FDA, FEC, FERC, FMC, FTC, ITC, MSHA, NLRB, NRC, NTSB, OSHA, SEC, TSA, and on and on (see the List of Acronyms at the end of this chapter). Regulations range from broad-gauged requirements for pollution control to rules on the sales of lemons in a given month, from wide-ranging rules on worker health and safety to specialized restrictions on transactions in futures markets. Aside from the limited use of government personnel to design and enforce regulations, the bulk of the costs generated is "off budget" because the expenses incurred are mainly for compliance by private companies and individuals being regulated. Such outlays do not show up in the government's budget; thus, regulation has become especially popular during periods of budgetary restraint. The cumulative effects of regulation on business performance—and on consumers—are pervasive (see Part II).

Attention in recent years has focused on efforts to reduce the burdens of government rule making by relying more heavily on economic incentives to achieve social objectives. Simultaneously, however, support continues for more extensive social regulation, especially in the area of the environment. The rising concern about terrorism has generated a new wave of government activity (see Chapter 9).

TAXATION

The governmental tax collector does more than share profits with the owners of companies. Tax considerations are a major influence on business decision making. For example, the liberality of depreciation provisions and the level of marginal tax rates affect the threshold for making new investments. In contrast to these across-the-board provisions, many sections of the internal revenue code are aimed at promoting—or inhibiting—very specific sectors of business (such as real estate, new energy sources, and overseas activities).

Government regularly employs its tax power to provide incentives for designated private activities. Dangling the carrot of tax incentives, governments often coax what they consider to be greater social responsibility out of business. In the United States, specific internal revenue provisions include tax credits for hiring certain categories of people (minority groups) and tax deferrals for income from exports. The latter is an example of the complex interaction between tax policy and other governmental activities; the European Community regularly objects to what it considers to be unfair U.S. subsidies to exports by means of the tax system.

At times, there is a direct link between taxes and controls. For a company's retirement contributions to qualify as a federal tax deduction, a pension program must meet detailed requirements spelled out in regulations issued under the Employee Retirement Income Security Act. As shown in Chapter 16, business has an important stake in the various proposals for comprehensive tax reform.

GOVERNMENT AS BUSINESS PARTNER

In addition to affecting business practices through policy or legislative mandates, governments sometimes manipulate the private sector directly by entering into partnerships with business enterprises. The involvement of government in the ownership of business is common in less developed countries or in nations with a history of public control of business. In a few cases, the federal government has purchased equity positions in small but vital defense contractors that lack adequate financial resources to meet the military's production needs.

As businesses become more global in their operations by expanding into foreign markets, they often establish joint ventures and other associations with their host governments. For instance, McDonald's became the first U.S. firm to penetrate the Russian economy when it opened a restaurant in Moscow in 1990. The restaurant, located near the Kremlin, is a joint venture with the Moscow City Council.

Joint relationships between private and public enterprises are also common in Asia, particularly China, where the government owns a great variety of businesses. The close connection between the public and private sectors in China is illustrated by the Wuhan No. 2 Printing and Dyeing Company, which is jointly owned by Hongtex Development Company, a Hong Kong firm, and the city of Wuhan.

MONETARY POLICY (GOVERNMENT AS REGULATOR OF THE ECONOMY)

The conduct of monetary policy by central banks such as the Federal Reserve System is a prime example of government actions that profoundly affect business but are not normally considered an aspect of business–government relations. The Federal Reserve strongly influences interest rates, the flows of money and credit, inflation rates, and the overall level of business activity in the economy. The Fed is a creature of the Congress and, although technically independent of the executive branch, often responds to presidential leadership. The power of the Federal Reserve System via its purchases and sales of treasury securities and its setting of discount rates and bank reserve requirements greatly affects the economic and financial environment in which companies operate.

The cost and availability of credit can be key influences on the performance and at times the very existence of business firms. A company's board of directors may spend almost as much time discussing the outlook for the prime rate as the finance committee's report. During wartime and under other emergency conditions, governments often augment indirect monetary (and fiscal) instruments with direct controls over wages, prices, and the use of materials.

MORAL SUASION (GOVERNMENT AS LEADER)

From time to time, leaders of every nation call on their people to take actions on a voluntary basis. Especially when an activist president occupies the White House, the U.S. government tries to persuade (or "jawbone") the private sector to support it on specific issues. Several modern presidents have called on business to do such "patriotic" things as limit wage and price increases or eliminate discrimination in the workplace. Such displays of presidential leadership can be compelling because of the vast array of government powers—the proverbial "stick in the closet"—available to reinforce the "request" for voluntary action.

In 1990, following the Iraqi invasion of Kuwait, President George H. W. Bush jawboned the oil companies not to raise prices too much. The large producers promptly complied. Ironically, the result was to squeeze the high-cost, smaller "independent" dealers who found it more difficult to absorb the higher cost of crude oil as established in world markets.

In that same year, Health and Human Services Secretary Louis Sullivan criticized RJ Reynolds for marketing a new brand of cigarettes aimed at African-American consumers. As an African-American physician, he possessed a great deal of moral authority. Within 24 hours, RJR canceled plans to test-market the new product. A year later, some members of Congress objected vociferously to the plan of Japan's Fanuc Ltd. to buy 40 percent of a Connecticut machine tool builder that helps to make nuclear weapons. Although the legal authority to reject foreign purchases of American companies on national security grounds had lapsed, Fanuc backed off.

In 1993, then-Senator Paul Simon (D-IL) warned producers of television programs and TV networks to take aggressive action to curb violence on television or face congressional intervention. In response to earlier Senate hearings, the networks had already agreed to issue warnings to audiences prior to showing programs with substantial amounts of violence. In late 1996, after further public criticism, the major television networks established a voluntary system of describing the content of various categories of programs.

More recently, in 1998, the Department of Defense requested that aerospace giant Lockheed Martin not acquire Northrop Grumman, another large aerospace company (the Department of Justice also indicated its potential opposition). Even though the shareholders of both companies had approved the merger, these important defense contractors yielded to the wishes of their major customer. The merger was aborted.

In every administration, corporate leaders are very susceptible to presidential suasion, especially when they are called into the Oval Office in small groups. In the author's personal experience, the toughest executives often melt like butter when the President personally smiles at them.

IMPACTS ON THE BUSINESS FIRM

If one side of the business–government coin is the proliferation of government power to accomplish a variety of public purposes, the other side is the extent to which government pervades internal business decision making. An examination of business–government relations from the business executive's viewpoint shows a considerable public presence in what historically have been private matters.

Government is a continuing presence and often one of increasing influence in business decision making. As pointed out in the literature on public choice, government officials are motivated by incentives that often may be closer to their own needs and desires than to broad principles of public interest. In this view, as expressed most forcefully by Nobel Prize–winner James Buchanan, "Bureaucrats could no longer be labeled 'economic eunuchs.'"[5] The mythology of the faceless bureaucrat following orders from above is thus replaced by the notion of government employees who make their own policy choices as well as carry out the decisions of others (e.g., voters).

Government influences business decision making of all types: planning, research and development, production, marketing, personnel, finance, facilities, and so forth. The organizational chart of a hypothetical industrial firm, shown in Figure 1.2, conveys graphically the diverse nature of federal government involvement in many aspects of business. For each position on the company's organizational chart, there is an overlay of regulatory agencies that influence or even direct decision making in that area of business. To compound the problem, in reality there is a multiplicity of such overlays, representing state and local governments and the corresponding array of governments in each of the nations in which the company does business. Additional overlays are needed for international governmental organizations, such as the United Nations and the European Union. In practice, the precise nature of business–government relationships will vary by industry, size of firm, location, type of product, and markets served.

The modern array of government intervention affects management at all levels—from the board of directors to new employees on the production floor. The reach of government action extends to business managers with both line and staff responsibility, and it embraces the most senior executives, middle management, and first-line supervision.

No company, large or small, can operate without obeying a myriad of government rules and restrictions. Entrepreneurial decisions fundamental to the functioning of the enterprise are subject to government influence, review, and control. Decisions such as what lines of business to go into—in the case of utilities—are subject to approval by state public service commissions. The choice of products and services to produce, in the case of pharmaceuticals, is subject to the decision making of the Food and

FIGURE 1.2   Hypothetical Industrial Corporation and U.S. Government Relations

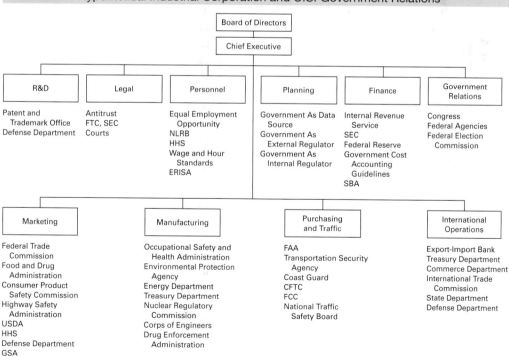

Drug Administration. Which investments can be financed is determined, especially for new enterprises, by the Small Business Administration. The Occupational Safety and Health Administration strongly influences how to produce goods and services. The costs to meet Environmental Protection Agency requirements have a major influence on where companies choose to make those products. Federal Trade Commission decisions on advertising affect marketing strategies. The Internal Revenue Service has a large say in what profits a firm can keep.

Virtually every major department of a typical company in today's economy has one or more counterparts in a government agency that controls or strongly influences its internal decision making. Much of the work of scientists in corporate research laboratories is aimed at ensuring that the products they develop are not rejected by lawyers in regulatory agencies. Engineers in manufacturing departments must make sure that the equipment they specify or design meets the standards promulgated by Labor Department authorities.

Marketing staffs must follow procedures set by government administrators in product safety agencies. The location of business facilities must conform with a host of environmental statutes. The activities of personnel staffs are geared to meet the standards for hiring, promotion, pay, and retirement set by the Department of Labor and the Equal Employment Opportunity Commission. Finance departments often bear the brunt of the paperwork burden imposed on business by government agencies. In short, few aspects of business activities escape some type of government review or influence.

Moreover, the scope of governmental involvement in business operations can multiply by several orders of magnitude if the enterprise has facilities in foreign markets. For a variety of political reasons—mainly to "protect" home industry owners, managers, and employees, but sometimes on ostensibly national security grounds—governments often erect barriers to international commerce that business enterprises must expend substantial resources to overcome. Businesses are often forced to choose second-best strategies when dealing with foreign governments. For instance, some host governments, such as Indonesia, restrict foreign ownership of local manufacturing facilities to minority shares only, forcing outside companies to enter into joint arrangements with native individuals, businesses, or governmental agencies.

ROLE OF CITIZEN GROUPS

A major expansion of government involvement in private industry in the United States has been underway for four decades (in other nations, nationalization of enterprises often took the place of regulation of private business activity). Continued impetus for this expanded government participation comes from a variety of consumer groups, labor unions, environmentalists, civil rights advocates, and other citizen organizations. Underlying support is provided by the belief that the private sector itself is responsible, at least in part, for many of the problems facing society. Concerns generating pressure for government involvement in business cover such social issues as pollution, discrimination in employment, unsafe products, unhealthy working environments, and misleading financial reporting.

Government looms large between business and its customers, its employees, its shareholders, and the public. Ralph Nader has noted on many occasions that business, too, has its power, and that is true. Actions by multibillion-dollar corporations can have strong positive or negative effects on a community or an entire region of a country. Companies can shift their operations—and jobs—from one region (or nation) to another. Although such moves are not costless to the enterprises involved, even the threat to do so can exert significant impact on governmental decision makers. Money can be a very useful and also a corrupting influence in the political process. Yet the contrast between government and business power is striking. The largest company cannot tax you; the smallest unit of government can. The most profitable corporation cannot throw you in jail; the smallest municipality can.

Conclusions

Let us try to summarize the highlights of the relationship between business and government in a modern society. Government exercises a variety of important powers in dealing with the individual private enterprise, ranging from taxation to regulation. Business, in turn, relies on constitutional protections and its substantial financial resources as well as on public support of its basic role in creating income, employment, and material standards of living. The business–government relationship in a dynamic society is constantly changing. The line between the public and private sectors frequently shifts.

In a global economy, that line is especially difficult to define. As we will see throughout this book, the strategies and issues discussed apply, with perhaps minor variations, to most governments and businesses around the world. Nevertheless, examples, illustrations, and discussions are taken in large measure from the experiences of firms headquartered in the United States—although increasingly they do business in many nations on several continents.

LIST OF ACRONYMS—OR THE BUREAUCRAT'S ALPHABET SOUP

ABC	American Business Conference
ATSB	Air Transportation Stabilization Board
BLS	Bureau of Labor Statistics
BRAC	Business Research Advisory Council
CAB	Civil Aeronautics Board
CFA	Consumer Federation of America
CFTC	Commodity Futures Trading Commission
CPSC	Consumer Product Safety Commission
DOD	Department of Defense
DOT	Department of Transportation
ED	Environmental Defense (formerly, Environmental Defense Fund)
EEOC	Equal Employment Opportunity Commission
EPA	Environmental Protection Agency
ERISA	Employee Retirement Income Security Act
EU	European Union
FAA	Federal Aviation Administration
FAO	Food and Agricultural Organization
FCC	Federal Communications Commission
FDA	Food and Drug Administration
FDIC	Federal Deposit Insurance Corporation
FEC	Federal Election Commission
FERC	Federal Energy Regulatory Commission
FHA	Federal Housing Administration
FMC	Federal Maritime Commission
FTC	Federal Trade Commission

IAC	Industry Advisory Council
ILO	International Labor Organization
IOCU	International Organization of Consumers Unions
IRA	Independent Retirement Account
ITC	International Trade Commission
MNC	Multinational Corporation
NAAG	National Association of Attorneys General
NAD	National Advertising Division
NARB	National Advertising Review Board
NHTSA	National Highway Traffic Safety Administration
NIH	National Institutes of Health
NIOSH	National Institute of Occupational Safety and Health
NLRB	National Labor Relations Board
NRC	Nuclear Regulatory Commission
OECD	Organization for Economic Cooperation and Development
OFCC	Office of Federal Contract Compliance
OMA	Orderly Marketing Agreement
OMB	Office of Management and Budget
OSHA	Occupational Safety and Health Administration
PAC	Political Action Committee
PBGC	Pension Benefit Guaranty Corporation
RFC	Reconstruction Finance Corporation
SARA	Superfund Amendments and Reauthorization Act
SEC	Securities and Exchange Commission
TSA	Transportation Security Agency
TSCA	Toxic Substances Control Act
USDA	United States Department of Agriculture
VAT	Value-Added Tax
VER	Voluntary Export Restraint
WHO	World Health Organization
WTO	World Trade Organization

Notes

1. See James Gwartney and Robert Lawson, *Economic Freedom of the World,* Annual Report 2002 (Vancouver, B.C.: Fraser Institute, 2002), p. 11; Gerald P. O'Driscoll, Jr., Kim R. Holmes, and Melanie Kirkpatrick, *2001 Index of Economic Freedom* (Washington, DC: Heritage Foundation, 2001). See also Douglass C. North, *Institutions, Institutional Change and Economic Performance* (Cambridge, UK: Cambridge University Press, 1990).

2. Arthur Schlesinger, Jr., "Has Democracy a Future?" *Foreign Affairs,* September/October 1997, p. 7.

3. John McMillan, *Reinventing the Bazaar: A Natural History of Markets* (New York: W.W. Norton, 2002); see also William Baumol, *The Free-Market Innovation Machine* (Princeton, NJ: Princeton University Press, 2002).

4. F. A. Hayek, *The Constitution of Liberty* (Chicago: University of Chicago Press, 1960), pp. 224–225.

5. James M. Buchanan, "The Economic Theory of Politics Reborn," *Challenge,* March–April 1988, p. 5.

PART II

GOVERNMENT REGULATION OF BUSINESS

Of all the powers that government exerts on private business, regulation is the most pervasive—and often the least understood. Part II is devoted to a detailed examination of the many forms that regulation takes and the various impacts of those government actions on the rest of the society. The nature and composition of regulation are changing rapidly. There is more environmental and other social regulation simultaneous with reforms and curtailments of traditional economic regulation. In the newer regulatory areas, economic incentives and market choices often replace conventional command-and-control techniques.

2

THE RATIONALE
FOR REGULATION

A basic way that government exerts its power over business is to issue regulations governing private sector behavior. The use of regulatory power has grown in the United States, especially in recent decades. Many rationales have been put forth to justify this type of government intervention in the economy, notably the failure of private markets to work well.

Government regulation of private economic activity is as old as human history. In the Old Testament of the Bible, the Book of Deuteronomy commands, "Thou shalt not lend upon usury to thy brother." The ancient Babylonian Code of Hammurabi established uniform weights and measures and limited the rate of interest. The prohibition of usury was included in medieval theology, along with the notion of a "just price." Modern regulation is often far more pervasive and requires an analysis of its theoretical underpinnings.

THEORIES OF REGULATION

Why do governments want to regulate private economic activity? The question is not easy to answer. Competitive markets, under the right circumstances, result in an efficient allocation of resources. At least in theory, the firms competing in such markets only produce those goods and services that consumers value most highly, in the quantities they are willing to purchase, and by methods that minimize the costs of production.

In practice, however, the economic system also produces many cases of *market failure*—a technical term referring to situations where competitive or market forces do not operate effectively. These market failures come in many forms, and government regulation is a frequent response. Let us examine the major justifications for such public-sector involvement in what are essentially private-sector activities.

RESPONDING TO NATURAL MONOPOLY CONDITIONS

The classic case for regulation is natural monopoly. A market controlled by one supplier is considered "natural" where economies associated with large-scale production make it inefficient for more than one firm to operate. In those industries, cost per unit of output becomes so low that the most efficient firm produces all of the industry's output. In technical terms, a natural monopoly exists when the production of a commodity is characterized by increasing returns to scale. That is, per-unit production costs decrease as the firm becomes larger. Consequently, the largest firm in the industry is also the most efficient; it has the lowest cost per unit of output. Such a company has the ability to underprice competitors and drive them out of business or to deter them from entering the market in the first place. The smaller firms, as a practical matter, cannot compete and are forced to close down. In the absence of regulation, the monopolist company is then free to reduce output and to charge higher prices.

 20

Traditional policy toward natural monopoly has been to retain the single large firm in a given sector of the economy, but to use regulation to prevent monopolistic exploitation. The idea is that regulating a natural monopoly will allow society to reap the benefits of economies of large-scale production without the burden of monopolistic prices and without resorting to splitting the monopolist into smaller firms that would produce the same or less output at higher prices.

Local utilities are prime examples of such monopolies. State "public-service" commissions regulating entry, prices, and profits are the most widely encountered governmental response. The fundamental rationale for this traditional style of economic regulation is that parallel and competing electric, gas, water, and local telephone systems would entail wasteful duplication and higher costs to consumers. The main examples of regulation at the federal level that is justified by the natural monopoly argument are oil and gas pipelines, and interstate transmission of electricity. State or local governments regulate local utilities as well as cable television.

Unregulated monopolies can cause social losses because they restrict production and raise prices. Such monopoly prices will enrich producers at the expense of consumers. Thus, decreasing cost industries present society with a dilemma. Competition in such industries is likely to be unstable and inefficient, but unregulated monopoly can result in high prices and discrimination among customers. The regulatory response typically involves setting rates (prices) for the monopoly firm and restricting or eliminating entry by potential competitors.

However, a natural monopoly is only natural in a given technological or economic environment. With market growth or engineering advances, competition may develop automatically. For example, when rail regulation began in 1887, competition possibilities were very limited in most markets. Natural monopoly in the railroad industry was one of the stated justifications for railroad regulation. Although the opportunities for competition in that industry are still limited, railroads face intense competition from trucks and inland waterway barges on most of the freight they haul. That competition ensures that, on most routes and for most commodities, no monopoly of any significance exists for the railroads today; consequently, Congress has abolished the Interstate Commerce Commission. Thus, yesterday's natural monopoly can become today's workably competitive industry.

Conversely, in the early 1900s, more than half the electric power used by industry was self-generated (or, in today's terminology, *cogenerated*) and regulation of electric utilities was far from universal. The term *cogeneration* describes the process in which useful thermal energy (usually steam) and electricity are produced in sequence from a single fuel source. However, as the availability of power supplied by the public utility companies increased, and the unit prices declined, most of the early cogenerators abandoned their on-site power systems. Local electric utilities developed monopoly positions, and state governments became prone to regulate their prices and rates of return.

In this industry, the tide is turning again. Small but growing numbers of industrial firms have responded to the combined effects of long-term increases in energy prices and a more permissive regulatory environment by returning to cogeneration. Thus, the monopoly position of electric utilities may be weakened in those regions where industrial customers increasingly generate their own electrical energy (see Chapter 7 for a variety of recent developments affecting electric utilities).

ENCOURAGING SENSIBLE USE OF NATURAL RESOURCES

Regulation or other controls may be appropriate where a common resource must be allocated rationally or where there is no incentive to conserve natural resources. The electromagnetic spectrum is a good example of a resource owned by society as a whole. If everyone were allowed full use and access, chaos would result. Broadcasters using the same frequency would interfere with one another. Reception of signals would be poor or impossible. Some sort of government intervention to allocate spectrum use is necessary.

When many producers draw from a common pool of resources—such as a petroleum reservoir or a fish supply—no one will have economic incentive to conserve; if one person or organization holds back, the balance will simply be taken over by others. Under American law, oil or gas belongs to whoever brings it to the surface on his or her own land. However, the oil or gas in a pool can flow underground, and the ownership of these pools is often fragmented. In the absence of regulation, property owners race to get the oil or gas out before the neighbors take it all. In responding to such a problem of the commons, government intervention in the form of regulation can avoid wasting valuable nonreproducible resources.

REQUIRING PRODUCERS AND CONSUMERS TO TAKE ACCOUNT OF EXTERNAL COSTS ("EXTERNALITIES")

Regulation—or another form of governmental intervention—can be a means to compel individuals or organizations to take account of *external costs* or *spillover effects,* the costs they impose on other people. Environmental pollution, for example, imposes substantial costs that—owing to the present system of property rights—may not be borne by the person or organization generating them. (See box, "Private Property Rights.")

As shown in Figure 2.1, if some of the costs of producing a good or service are external to the firm, the firm's pricing actions will not reflect these costs. Thus, the private cost curve (C_{PR}) will understate society's true cost curve $(C_{PR} + C_{PU})$, which includes the externality of costs imposed on the public. As a result, the market price (P_1) will be lower than if it reflected the society's total costs (P_2). A larger amount of this good or service will be produced (Q_2) than would be the case if the firm's cost of production were to include the external effects (Q_1).

For example, a steel mill that produces smoke and soot imposes costs on its neighbors in the form of polluted air, bad health, and ugly surroundings. In the absence of controls, since these costs do not fall primarily on the mill, its management may choose to ignore them. On the other hand, if these "external" costs fell on the polluting firm, it would attempt to minimize them. Moreover, if these environmental costs were borne by the firm, they would be reflected in its product prices. Consumers would be encouraged to avoid such pollution-intensive products.

Externalities can be produced by government agencies as well as by business firms. Upstream municipalities dumping inadequately treated sewage into a river can impose substantial cleanup costs (or polluted waters) on the people living downstream from them. Ironically, over a century ago, English common law rejected a potential private solution to the issue of externalities. When legal actions were brought against polluters, they were dismissed. General nuisances, such as factory smokestacks, were found to

BOX 2-1

PRIVATE PROPERTY RIGHTS

Understanding the role of property rights sets the stage for private action and public policy in a variety of regulatory areas, especially when the environment is involved. Within the framework of existing legislation, the courts determine private property rights, and executive branch agencies are responsible for enforcing those rights.

For example, a cigarette smoker and a nonsmoker are seated next to each other in a crowded subway car. Assuming an agreement could be reached, should the smoker compensate the nonsmoker for having to breathe the secondhand smoke, or should the nonsmoker compensate the smoker for not being able to enjoy a cigarette? It depends on who has what property rights: whether the smoker has the right to dissipate smoke into the environment or whether the nonsmoker has the right to breathe clean air. Different rulings on this issue have resulted from the rulings of various state courts as well as from state legislatures. In recent years, victims of secondhand smoke are increasingly protected by governmental law and regulatory action restricting smoking in public places.

Consider another example of the general principle: a copper-smelting plant located on Commencement Bay in Tacoma, Washington. Some years ago, high levels of lead were discovered in the children of families who lived near the plant. One by-product of the smelting of copper is arsenic, which is used in the manufacture of computer chips. Another by-product is lead, emitted into the air through one huge smokestack at the Commencement Bay plant. Is the air a common property resource, in which case factory management has the right to use it for waste disposal? Or do the people living in the area have a right to a healthy environment, free from such hazards as lead in the atmosphere? The case went to the courts to determine the property rights of the two parties.

In this instance, the rights of the families prevailed. The courts determined that the smelting plant must reduce the levels of lead emitted to be within federal standards. The owners determined that the installation of smokestack scrubbers, the only resolution to the problem, would not be cost effective; thus, the plant closed down, putting a large number of men and women out of work. This action also decreased the amount of arsenic available to the producers of computer chips, somewhat increasing their costs and so slightly reducing their availability.

As seen in this case, externalities can be internalized to the extent that private property rights are clearly defined and effectively enforced. Both costs and benefits may be generated in the process.

cause no *particular* harm to the plaintiffs—everybody was being polluted. Also, the courts reasoned that the polluters were operating within their statutory authority and that producing goods served a public interest. If the decisions had gone the other way, we might now have class action suits instead of detailed government regulation of emissions into the environment.

In the absence of government intervention—and given the current regime of property rights—voluntary action to deal with environmental wastes places a firm under a competitive disadvantage. The specific company attempting to reduce the external costs imposed on the public would bear the full costs, while the benefits of the improvement would be widely dispersed in the society. "Free riders," or firms that do not make the expensive changes, nevertheless keep prices lower and share in the benefits. An example of this situation is provided by the regulation of pollution standards for motor vehicles. The basic justification given by government for setting

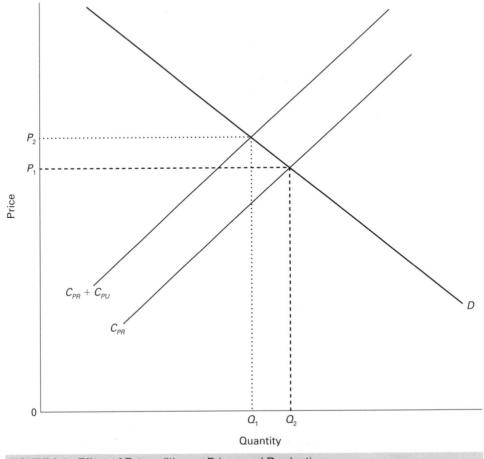

FIGURE 2.1   Effect of Externalities on Prices and Production

such standards was clearly stated by a senior executive of a major automotive manufacturer:

> [A] large part of the public will not voluntarily spend extra money to install emission control systems which help clean the air. Any manufacturer who installs and charges for such equipment while his competition doesn't soon finds he is losing sales and customers. In cases like this, a government standard requiring everyone to have such equipment is the only way to protect both the public and the manufacturer.[1]

A similar argument relates to safety measures in the workplace. Because market incentives for voluntary health and safety programs by employers may be insufficient in some instances, regulation can be used to force employers to "internalize" the costs associated with job hazards to their employees.

The economic justification for regulation of nuclear power is similar but a bit more complex. The external costs of nuclear power generation are not observable. They take the form of risk of bodily harm and property damage. The possibility of a nuclear mishap imposes a cost on all those it might injure. In technical terms, that cost is the expected value of the damage produced by a nuclear accident—the probability of an accident multiplied by the amount of the injury inflicted. Well-designed government standards would reduce the hazard and, in the process, the firm would internalize some of these external costs. The price of nuclear power would rise to reflect those costs.

Federal law (the Price–Anderson Act) limits the total liability of the firms involved and provides that the government will indemnify them for some of the liabilities should a nuclear accident occur. Because such limitation of liability reduces the incentive to reduce risks, it provides a justification for safety regulation by the Nuclear Regulatory Commission.

INADEQUATE INFORMATION

Another case of market failure arises where individuals are not sufficiently informed to make sensible decisions in the marketplace. Much product information is difficult or expensive to obtain. For example, in regulating the use of certain chemicals in the treatment of baby clothes, the Consumer Product Safety Commission has sought to mitigate any harm that might come to the children exposed to that hazard. The rationale for government action in such a situation is that consumers lack knowledge of either the chemicals with which the clothing is treated or the hazards that they give rise to. The justification underlying much of the health, safety, and consumer protection regulation is that producers provide inadequate information about the products they sell.

Many companies have little incentive to make safety information on their products freely available. As a result, the marketplace may not provide enough information for the consumer to know which product contains cancer-causing additives, which device is defective, or what health hazards exist in a particular workplace. Some producers and employers may view it in their interests to provide inaccurate or at least incomplete information.

Regulation in this area can take two basic forms, depending largely on the knowledge of those affected. In areas where it is relatively easy or inexpensive for consumers to evaluate accurate information, the regulatory response may be to require accurate labeling and to prohibit misleading promotional statements. The Food and Drug Administration, for example, requires informational labeling telling consumers about the fat, protein, carbohydrate, and calorie content of certain foods.

However, the problem of imperfect knowledge is not solved in all cases simply by providing more information. When it is very difficult for the people using the product to understand and act on the technical data involved, it makes sense for the government to establish and enforce standards or even to license producers. For example, consumers cannot generally be expected to acquire the expertise or resources needed to evaluate various prescription drugs. As a result, the Food and Drug Administration sets standards and approves specific products before they can be marketed to the general public. In the case of certain dangerous or highly addictive drugs, banning them may be the preferred solution to protect the public welfare.

As another example, it hardly would make sense for the passengers to have to inspect the qualifications of pilots or safety of the equipment on airplanes on which they fly. The Federal Aviation Administration exercises this responsibility, licensing pilots, prescribing aircraft standards, and specifying flight procedures.

On the other hand, some governmental regulation reduces the amount of product information available to consumers. This is the case where government either restricts or outright bans types of advertising, which is an underestimated form of information.

For example, the FDA regulations at times discourage prescription drug ads from being shown on television, a major source of information for many consumers, because of the amount of technical material required to be included in the commercial.

The result is just the opposite of what the FDA wants to achieve. Due to the restraint on advertising, consumers may not be aware that a treatment exists for a certain condition, and so they will not consult a physician. In other circumstances, consumers may suffer some symptoms (e.g., thirst) without realizing that these are symptoms of a treatable disease (e.g., diabetes). Alternatively, a new remedy with reduced side effects may become available, but patients are not aware of it and do not visit their physicians to obtain a prescription.[2] Because consumers must obtain a prescription from a physician in order to acquire prescription drugs, there is less reason to fear deception in advertising in this market than in others.

AVOIDING PHONY JUSTIFICATIONS

Given the power of the regulatory process, it is not surprising that many interests have cloaked their pleas for special treatment with a reference to some broader public purpose. One justification sometimes offered is that, in the absence of regulation, competition would be "destructive." That is, without controls, some industries might operate at a loss for long periods of time. In theory, this could occur in companies where large proportions of costs are fixed and where the resources employed are immobile. Agriculture and mining may at times provide pertinent examples.

Studies of the subject, however, generally conclude that destructive competition is more a fear than a reality. In most of these cases, government intervention disrupts the normal movement of labor and other resources from industries with excess supply to expanding industries that could put those resources to more productive use. After all, not all losses and bankruptcies are bad. They weed out higher-cost producers and force companies to adopt more efficient techniques of production.

Outside the realm of market failures, it is often claimed that *distributive justice,* or concern with political and social equity, is a reason for government intervention. In other words, the government's involvement is seen primarily as a way of bringing about the transfer of income or wealth to a worthy segment of society. In practice, however, a small group (i.e., a special interest) often benefits at the expense of the mass of consumers. Regulation has been used in this way to redistribute income among the regions of the nation, to promote one industry at the expense of others, to provide services for small communities, and to give special protection to those deemed particularly worthy (usually, that translates as being politically powerful).

Until deregulation, interstate trucking was a pertinent example of using government power to protect the "ins." Regulation of this industry merely insulated existing trucking firms and their employees from competition created by new trucking companies that had not received the approval of a regulatory agency (the Interstate Commerce Commission, or ICC) to enter the business. The redistribution of income in this case was from consumers in general to the owners, managers, and employees of the regulated industry. The elimination of ICC regulation has also resulted in substantial transfers of income and wealth, but this time it has been from the regulated portion of the industry to new entrants or what had been the unregulated part of the trucking industry (see Chapter 8).

The "property rights" acquired by regulation—such as radio and television broadcasting licenses—are often valuable. Reducing regulation, therefore, can result in capital losses for some. When the Securities and Exchange Commission required negotiated brokerage rates, the value of seats on the New York Stock Exchange (NYSE) was drastically lowered. But the overall benefits to consumers–investors were far greater. As more people became investors, an upward trend in the price of an NYSE seat soon began.

Assuring service to particular groups or communities is a frequent motivation for regulatory controls on rates, entry, and type of service. Of necessity, that entails cross-subsidies: transferring income from profitable business activities to less remunerative areas as a result of regulatory action. The result is higher prices for some in order to support otherwise uneconomical service for others. The issue of cross-subsidization frequently arises in the case of service to small or rural communities. The real and often obscured issues, however, are "service at what price?" or "who should pay?" Prior to the breakup of AT&T, higher charges for long-distance calls helped erase losses in providing household service, especially to sparsely populated areas. Under such circumstances, controls on entry of new competition are used to protect the profits necessary to finance the cross-subsidized service.

Once established, regulation spawns and then protects certain groups, which subsequently have a vested interest in its continuation. The "grandfather" clauses in many regulatory systems tend to confer "squatters' rights" on existing production facilities, compared to new ventures. For example, in "nonattainment" areas under the clean air statute, potential new sources not only need to meet more stringent standards, they also need to arrange for and finance offsets: actual reductions for the same pollutant in the same area from other sources.

Investment and modernization that could result in improved productivity are discouraged by pollution-abatement costs that are higher in newly built facilities than for older factories. Thus, existing facilities are given a degree of protection from competition by virtue of strict new source requirements. Older, less efficient, and more heavily polluting plants tend to be kept in operation longer and used more intensively, which can lead to pollution levels that are higher than if the regulatory hurdle for new investment were lower.

The application of more stringent requirements to new production processes or products than to those already in existence extends to water-pollution abatement, auto safety and fuel-economy rules, and controls over the safety and effectiveness of drugs. Investment and development of new products have accordingly been discouraged.[3] Thus, "protecting" existing firms from new competition via regulation generates pressures to continue the status quo. (See the box, "Taking Regulation for Granite.")

Although regulation is often used by government as a means of correcting market failures, regulatory actions are not the only means available. Consumers can educate themselves and seek product information when they are making large purchases. Responding to normal economic stimuli, firms and their employees can be made more aware of on-the-job hazards. Workers can then bargain for improved working conditions or for higher pay as compensation for the risks. Alternatively, taxes can be levied on polluters and subsidies can be paid to those unfairly harmed by pollution to compensate them for the cleanup burden imposed on them. Regulations represent a

<BOX 2-2>

TAKING REGULATION FOR GRANITE

Vulcan Materials Co. dominates the unglamorous business of crushed stone. The company earns a profit of nearly 10 percent of sales, making it one of the more profitable industrial companies. Vulcan's president explained one of the reasons: "Back in the sixties you used to worry about who was going to open up a quarry right down the road, but now we never concern ourselves about that; problems with zoning and the EPA are so monumental. That gives us an ability to price our product that we didn't have before."

SOURCE: *Regulation*, March–April 1982, p. 12.

halfway house between methods that involve more direct control, such as the nationalization of an industry, and those that involve the use of indirect control mechanisms, such as taxes or subsidies.

GOVERNMENT FAILURE

Most of the discussions of the need for government regulation—especially to deal with the various types of market failure—are based on several very important but usually unstated assumptions. First of all, many proponents of regulation seem to believe that the process of government intervention is costless or, at least implicitly, that the benefits exceed the costs.

Of perhaps even greater importance, many advocates of regulation ignore what can be called *government failure,* the shortcomings in the operation of public-sector agencies.[4] Specifically, the incentives influencing individual government bureaus or officials may not lead them to take actions to attain socially desired results. Believing strongly in their mission, regulators may try to maximize the size of their efforts (and, indirectly, the size of their personal financial and psychic rewards) when the optimal amount of regulation might be substantially less. The economist's notion of diminishing returns often conflicts with the enthusiast's belief that, if something such as regulation is good, then more is always better than less.

Without forgetting the shortcomings of the marketplace (as described previously), it is useful to recognize that regulation may also fall short of perfection. Like most government activities, regulation is generally not connected with any bottom line comparable to the profit-and-loss statement of business for evaluating performance. Moreover, experience shows that there is no reliable mechanism in the public sector for terminating governmental efforts if they are unsuccessful.[5]

Thus, the identification of inadequacies or "failure" in the marketplace may be a necessary but hardly a sufficient criterion for governmental intervention in private economic activity. The inadequacies or "failure" in the public-sector response may be even greater. Or, as the layperson might accurately say, the cure may be worse than the disease. The analyst can respond that there is no need to guess at or assume whether market failure is greater than government failure. Rather, under these circumstances, the need for analysis of the advantages and disadvantages of the proposed public-sector action is compelling. (Chapter 10 examines the methodologies that can be used.)

THE GROWTH OF REGULATION

The development of regulation in the United States has been a gradual process. For the most part, regulatory activities began with the individual states that rely primarily on their "police" power to protect public health and safety. In the landmark decision *Munn* v. *Illinois* (1876), the Supreme Court ruled that the Illinois legislature could set a maximum charge for storing grain in warehouses. "When private property is devoted to a public use, it is subject to public regulation," the Court ruled.

In 1887, Congress—relying on the "commerce" clause of the Constitution—established the Interstate Commerce Commission, the granddaddy of federal rule-making agencies, to regulate railroad rates and routes. In 1996, Congress acknowledged the substantial deregulation of surface transportation that had occurred by closing down the ICC and transferring its residual functions to the Department of Transportation.

In the first century of the Republic, the growth of federal regulatory activity was very slow. The twentieth century witnessed a series of rapid expansions. The Antitrust Division of the Justice Department was set up in 1903 to prosecute violators of the Sherman Antitrust Act. In 1913, the Federal Reserve System was established to oversee the commercial banking system. In the following year, the Federal Trade Commission was created to carry out the Clayton Act, designed to promote competitive behavior. The Federal Power Commission (now the Federal Energy Regulatory Commission) was established in 1920, covering the interstate transmission of electricity and other forms of energy.

The New Deal of the 1930s led to a burst of new government agencies, such as the Securities and Exchange Commission, the Federal Deposit Insurance Corporation, the Federal Maritime Commission, the Federal Communications Commission, the National Labor Relations Board, and the Civil Aeronautics Board (which ceased functioning in 1985).

Government intervention in economic activity expanded rapidly in the 1960s and 1970s (see Figure 2.2). Examples of the newer regulatory agencies include the Environmental Protection Agency, the Consumer Product Safety Commission, the Occupational Safety and Health Administration, and the Equal Employment Opportunity Commission. A few small agencies were eliminated at the beginning of the Reagan administration, notably the Council on Wage and Price Stability, which had promulgated voluntary wage and price standards. In late 2001, Congress established the new Transportation Security Agency to respond to the continuing threat of terrorism in aviation and other forms of transportation (see Chapter 9 for detail).

The direct costs of regulatory activities to the taxpayers are substantial. The operating expenses for the 55 major federal regulatory agencies came to almost $29 billion in fiscal year 2003—approximately twice the amount spent a decade previously

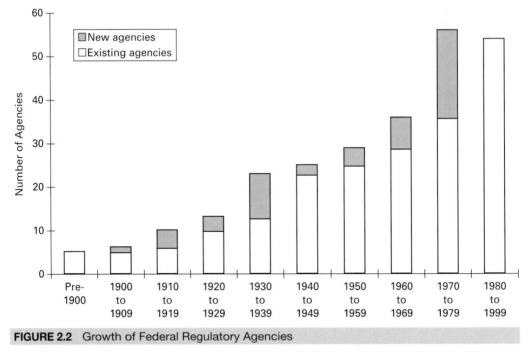

FIGURE 2.2   Growth of Federal Regulatory Agencies

Source: Weidenbaum Center on the Economy, Government, and Public Policy, Washington University, 2002.

(see Table 2.1). In real terms (adjusted for inflation), federal regulatory budgets, after declining slightly from 1980 to 1985, have risen steadily since, with a surge occurring after the terrorist attacks of September 11, 2001.

The biggest regulatory budgets are not those of the traditional economic regulatory agencies, such as the FCC and other industry-specific commissions. Rather, the largest proportion of the funds is devoted to the broader, social regulatory activities, such as environmental regulation by the EPA and consumer product regulation by the Department of Agriculture and the Department of Transportation.

At first glance, government imposition of socially desirable requirements on business appears to be an inexpensive way of achieving national objectives. It seems to cost the government little (aside from the usually overlooked expenses of the regulatory agencies themselves) and therefore is not recognized as much of a burden on the taxpayer. There are obvious political attractions of such an activity whereby government can appear to do good without either levying taxes or increasing its debt.

On reflection, it can be seen that the public does not escape paying the full cost imposed by regulation. For example, when the Occupational Safety and Health Administration imposes on business a more expensive method of production, the cost of the resultant product necessarily will rise. Every time the Consumer Product Safety Commission imposes a standard that is more costly to attain, some product expenses will increase. The same holds true for the activities of the Environmental Protection Agency, the Food and Drug Administration, and so forth.

The point being made here should not be misunderstood. What is at issue is not the worthiness of the objectives of these agencies. Rather, the point is that the public does not get a "free lunch" by imposing public requirements on private industry. Although

TABLE 2.1   Administrative Costs of Federal Regulatory Activities (Fiscal Years, in Millions)

Area of Regulation	1960	1970	1980	1990	2000	2003
Social Regulation						
Consumer safety and health	$250	$ 710	$2,349	$ 3,795	$ 7,123	$15,933
Job safety and other working conditions	35	128	753	1,002	1,450	1,702
Environment	21	214	1,651	4,164	5,396	5,640
Energy	12	64	550	464	501	631
Total Social Regulation	$318	$1,116	$5,303	$ 9,425	$14,470	$23,906
Economic Regulation						
Finance and banking	$ 30	$ 86	$ 362	$ 1,080	$ 1,693	$ 1,808
Industry-specific regulation	49	91	279	320	515	639
General business	47	115	355	743	1,717	2,479
Total Economic Regulation	$126	$ 292	$ 996	$ 2,143	$ 3,925	$ 4,926
Grand Total	$444	$1,408	$6,299	$11,568	$18,395	$28,832

Source: Weidenbaum Center on the Economy, Government, and Public Policy, Washington University, 2002.

the costs of government regulation are not borne by taxpayers directly, in large measure they show up in higher prices of the goods and services that consumers buy. These higher prices represent the "hidden tax" of regulation, which is shifted from the taxpayer to the consumer. Moreover, to the extent that government-mandated requirements impose similar costs (e.g., a catalytic converter on automobiles) on all price categories of a given product, this hidden tax will tend to be more regressive than the federal income tax. That is, the costs may place a heavier relative burden on lower-income groups than on higher-income groups.

Table 2.2 provides another way of looking at the trend of the federal government's regulatory activities, examining the changing size of the total workforce of the regulatory agencies. It shows the rapid growth in the 1970s (a 74 percent rise from 1970 to 1980), the cresting of that regulatory wave in the 1980s and 1990s, and a renewed expansion in the early twenty-first century. The 6 percent decline in the staffing of these activities from 1980 to 1990 reflected the cutbacks during the initial burst of regulatory reform set in motion by President Reagan. A significant upturn has occurred since. The regulatory head count of 176,826 in 2003, an all-time high, demonstrates the continuing ability on the part of government to issue more rules, conduct more inspections, and otherwise impose additional requirements on private business.

TABLE 2.2   Personnel of Federal Regulatory Agencies (Fiscal Years, Full-Time Equivalent Employment)

Area of Regulation	1970	1980	1990	2000	2003
Social regulation	52,500	95,448	87,303	96,700	149,194
Economic regulation	17,253	26,258	27,289	29,155	27,632
Total	69,753	121,706	114,592	125,855	176,826

Source: Weidenbaum Center on the Economy, Government, and Public Policy, Washington University, 2002.

THE CONDUCT OF REGULATION

Government agencies use two methods to carry out laws: *rule making* and *adjudication*. Through rule making, agencies issue general policy statements as well as detailed requirements. In contrast, through adjudication, the agencies enforce these regulations by means of specific orders backed by civil or criminal penalties. Generally, rule making is described as the agencies' "legislative" function, and adjudication as their "judicial" function.

RULE MAKING

Rules, or regulations, are agency statements that implement, interpret, or prescribe a law or policy. Rules may be generated to carry out a new law or to modify procedures under an older law. For example, after Congress passed the Clean Air Act Amendments of 1990, the Environmental Protection Agency (EPA) was required to issue a host of new regulations as well as revisions of rules promulgated under the earlier laws that the new statute amended.

Often, legislation contains specific directions for agencies to follow while allowing them to maintain some discretion. Through the revised Clean Air Act, Congress requires many service and industrial firms to obtain permits to continue operating. The EPA determines specific industry-by-industry standards for the reduction of toxic air pollutants.

Uniform procedures for rule making allow the public to participate in the process. Under the Administrative Procedures Act at the federal level, an agency generally publishes a notice of proposed rule making in the *Federal Register,* announcing the rule it intends to put into effect and soliciting public comments. These responses may address a specific provision in the proposal or the entire proposed rule. To use the Clean Air Act example again, the EPA has offered companies and others an opportunity to comment on each of the proposed standards.

Occasionally, agencies conduct public hearings and invite parties to present their views to the staff or heads of the agency. Rules are based on conclusions drawn from facts the agency gathers from its own research and from information provided by the public. For example, various company and trade association executives have consulted with agency representatives to help them formulate specific rules on issuing corporate securities and reporting financial results.

Each agency is required to consider all comments it receives and other data it has on an issue before promulgating a final rule. Such a rule establishes a policy deemed to best serve the public interest and is enforceable as law. It usually becomes effective 30 days after it is printed in the *Federal Register*. This entire rule-making process can take from a few months to several years. In certain cases, if an agency's rule results only in minor changes to existing law, the final rule may be published without prior notice.

In most cases, publishing a final rule in the *Federal Register* is considered sufficient to alert the public of a change in law, with no other notification of affected parties being necessary. These rules are incorporated into the *Code of Federal Regulations,* which contains the current regulations for all federal agencies. Implementing a single statute may require many such actions and involve more than one agency. Congress typically specifies deadlines for issuance of rules, with different dates for various provisions.

ADJUDICATION

Adjudication is the regulatory agency's process for formulating an order. An *order* is any final disposition other than rule making. Adjudication can be formal or informal. The formal agency process is known as a hearing, which is similar to a trial. If a company is charged with violating a law or regulation, it may defend itself before the administrative law judges of the agency bringing the charges.

Informal procedures constitute the bulk of administrative adjudication. During informal adjudication, an agency determines the rights or liabilities of specific parties in a proceeding other than a formal hearing. Setting rates, awarding licenses or permits, and both civil and criminal law enforcement are all examples of this phase of regulation. The owner or operator of a hazardous-waste storage facility seeking an operating permit would participate in adjudication.

THE CHANGING NATURE OF REGULATION

The industries subject to traditional economic regulation by federal and state agencies represent only one-tenth of the gross domestic product. Through the 1950s, most sectors—accounting for the great bulk of economic activity—remained relatively unregulated, except for certain general standards of business conduct, such as the antitrust laws and the exercise of state and local government "police powers" over public health. But that situation began to change fundamentally in the 1960s with the advent of social regulation, which now extends to virtually the entire American economy.

Social regulation is characterized by the use of agencies organized along functional or issue lines rather than industry categories. Many of the new-style regulatory agencies have power to regulate across all industries, although their jurisdiction is limited to one aspect of business activity. Examples include the Equal Employment Opportunity Commission (EEOC), the Environmental Protection Agency (EPA), and the Occupational Safety and Health Administration (OSHA). Others are more specialized, such as those charged with protecting consumers against unsafe products. The National Highway Traffic Safety Administration (NHTSA) covers automobiles and trucks. The jurisdiction of the Food and Drug Administration (FDA) extends to medical devices and cosmetics, in addition to food and drugs. The Consumer Product Safety Commission (CPSC) has a broad mandate, extending to most other consumer products with a few key exclusions—notably, alcoholic beverages, motor vehicles, tobacco products, and firearms.

Social regulation did not emerge suddenly. However, the early social statutes were usually limited to one specialized area of business activity. For example, one of the first major pieces of federal regulatory legislation was the Animal and Plant Health Inspection Act of 1884.[6]

The recent wave of social regulatory agencies (EPA, OSHA, EEOC, and CPSC) has not been merely an intensification of traditional activities (see Appendix at the end of this chapter). In good measure, it has been a new departure. The standard theory of government regulation of business, which previously dominated thinking on the subject, is based on the model of the now-defunct Interstate Commerce Commission (ICC). Under this approach, a federal commission is established to regulate a specific industry, with the related concern of promoting the well-being of that industry. Often, the public or consumer interest is viewed as subordinate, or is even ignored, since the agency focuses on the needs and concerns of the industry it is regulating.[7]

This specialized focus can acquire curious features. In some cases—because of the unique expertise possessed by the members of the industry or because of job entice-ments for regulators who leave government employment—the regulatory commission can become a "captive" of the industry it is supposed to regulate. This is still a widely held view of the development of the regulatory process.

Regulatory agencies now have rules that restrict the private employment of former employees. Federal law forbids former federal officials from participating in a matter in which they were involved while in government service for at least one year after leaving the government. Some agencies have even more stringent restrictions. The Federal Energy Regulatory Commission (FERC) will not permit a former employee ever to appear in a case before the commission if he or she participated in the case while working for the agency. The Federal Trade Commission (FTC) is even more strict; it bars any previous employee from participating in a proceeding pending while that person was employed by the FTC.

In any event, industries often become so accustomed to living with some types of government regulations that they fight efforts to reduce or eliminate them, even if they opposed the original imposition of the government intervention. Knowing how to comply with regulations provides an advantage to existing firms in the industry, dis-couraging potential new entrants. For example, an attempt by the Treasury Department to deregulate the alcoholic beverage industry was abandoned in the face of sustained opposition from the industry itself. Thus, the Bureau of Alcohol, Tobacco, and Firearms continues to administer provisions of the Federal Alcohol Administration Act such as prohibiting suppliers from providing retailers with paid advertising, signs, fixtures, or other promotional aids.

Economists have developed a more general theory of the regulatory process. This theory pictures the process as the arena in which various interest groups invest their resources in order to effect an outcome more to their liking. The newer version of the *capture theory* is seen in terms of the dominance of a small group with a relatively large stake in the affairs of the society as a whole, whose interests are more diffused.[8] For example, the major proponents of job safety regulation are labor unions; these organi-zations have a strong desire to lock into, or capture, the regulatory activities of job safety agencies. The costs of the standards are borne by consumers, generally in the form of higher prices for manufactured goods. The benefits accrue almost exclusively to the special-interest group itself.

A NEW MODEL OF GOVERNMENT REGULATION

Although the traditional type of federal regulation of business continues, the regula-tory efforts established by Congress in recent years follow a fundamentally different pattern. The new federal regulatory agencies have much broader jurisdiction than the ICC model. Simultaneously, however, in important aspects they are far more restricted. This paradox lies at the heart of this new style of rule making.

The changing nature of regulation can be seen in Figure 2.3. The vertical lines show the traditional relationship between the old style of government commission (DOT, NRC, FERC, FCC) and the specific industry it regulates. However, most sectors of the economy—manufacturing, trade, and services—are virtually exempt from that type of intervention.

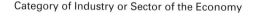

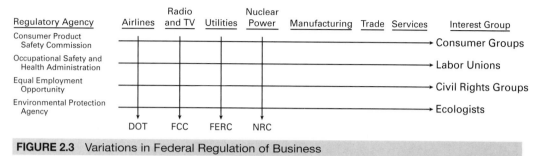

FIGURE 2.3   Variations in Federal Regulation of Business

In contrast, the horizontal lines show the newer breed of regulatory agency (EPA, EEOC, OSHA, CPSC). In the case of each of these relative newcomers to the federal bureaucracy, jurisdiction extends to the great bulk of the private sector, cutting through whole segments of the marketplace. This far-ranging characteristic makes it impractical for any single industry to dominate these regulatory activities in the manner of the traditional model. After all, what specific industry is in a position to capture the EEOC or OSHA, or would have the incentive to do so?

In comparison with the older agencies, however, the new regulators operate in a far narrower range in many important ways. They are not concerned with the totality of a company or industry but only with the one segment of operations that falls under their jurisdiction. The FCC, as an example of a traditional regulator, must pay attention to the basic mission of the telecommunications industry—to provide communications services to the public—as part of its supervision of rates and service in that business. The EPA, on the other hand, is interested almost exclusively in the effect of those operations on the environment. This limitation prevents the newer agency from developing too close a concern with the overall well-being of any company or industry. But it can also result in a lack of awareness or interest in the effects of its actions on any specific company or segment of the economy.

If there is any special interest that comes to dominate such an agency, it is not the industry being regulated but the group that is preoccupied with its specific task: ecologists in the case of environmental cleanup; civil rights, women's, and senior citizens' organizations in the case of elimination of job discrimination; labor unions in the establishment of safer working conditions; and consumer groups in the reduction of product hazards.

Although important benefits may be gained by the newer form of social regulation, limited attention is given by the regulators to the basic mission of the industries they regulate: to provide goods and services to the public. Also ignored or downplayed are crosscutting concerns and matters broader than those dealt with in the specific charter of the regulating agency: productivity, economic growth, employment, cost to the consumer, and overall living standards.

Some important cases blend the old and new forms of regulation. The Securities and Exchange Commission (SEC) is a good example. In one aspect of its activities, it regulates a specific branch of the economy, the securities industry. Yet its rules also influence the way a great many companies prepare their financial statements and reports to shareholders. Economywide regulatory agencies (such as the SEC) are not entirely a recent creation; the FTC has existed since 1914.

Aside from these few hybrid exceptions, the traditional theory of regulation is geared to a world where the regulators, as well as the various private adversaries in the process, are primarily concerned with prices, entry, and profits. In contrast, the new breed of regulators, and the public-interest groups supporting their efforts, are usually oblivious to those economic factors. Many of them condemn as callous or worse any consideration of cost or other business aspects in deliberations on product, worker, or environmental safety. In this fundamental respect, the new wave of government regulation is a markedly different phenomenon than that of the traditional economic regulator.

The results of the new approach in government regulation of business can be the reverse of the traditional capture situation. Rather than being dominated by a given industry, the new type of federal regulatory activity is far more likely to use the resources of various industries, or to ignore their needs, in order to further the specific objectives of the regulatory agency and of its private-sector clientele. Detailed study of the activities of these newer agencies reveals many costs—for business, the economy, and the public—as well as the intended benefits.

Nevertheless, we must recognize that it is difficult to criticize the basic mission of these newer regulatory agencies. Only a Scrooge or a misanthrope would quarrel with the intent of the new wave of government regulation: safer working conditions, better products for the consumer, elimination of discrimination, reduction of pollution, safeguarding the public from terrorist attacks, and so forth. And we must recognize that the programs were deliberately established by Congress in response to a surge of rising public expectations about corporate performance.

Many of these programs have yielded significant benefits to society. In the period 1970 to 2000, emissions of lead in the United States were down a massive 98 percent. The pulp and paper mills of New Hampshire and Maine now pour less than one-tenth of the particulates into the air than they did before 1970. Sulfur dioxide levels in the nation were down 44 percent during the same period. Lake Erie, which once gained notoriety because some of the garbage floating on it caught fire, now attracts hundreds of thousands of fishermen each year.[9] Some companies have found new outlets for their products in the emerging market for pollution-control equipment, while society in general benefits from the social objectives that are achieved. Opening new employment opportunities for minority groups not only eliminates a basic social inequity, it also expands the effective labor force that can produce the goods and services desired by the society.

Even though the results of the new wave of regulation can be the reverse of the capture situation, strange and varying alliances arise in the process of promoting or attempting to reform a given type of regulatory activity. Business firms and labor unions join together to support the traditional, industry-oriented commission to which they have adapted. This often was the case when airline regulation was at its peak. In the area of occupational safety, however, labor unions and consumer groups form alliances to encourage the expansion of regulation, while business groups and economists often oppose such regulation because of excessive costs in relation to the benefits obtained.

Hence, compatriots on one issue find themselves competitors on others. Specific energy regulations for automobiles may be opposed by both unions and companies in the motor vehicle industry, although the two groups differ strongly on job safety standards. Further, labor, management, and local governments may form a coalition when regulations, such as environmental standards, threaten the economy of their community, although some of these groups advocate general ecological advances.

Conclusions

There is little justification for either a general attack by business or other groups on all forms of government regulation or for a blanket endorsement of every instance of government intervention in the economy. Unless we are anarchists, we believe that government should set rules for society. Yet there is no need to jump to the conclusion that each regulation is effective in attaining its stated objective. As with most things in life, the sensible questions are not matters of either — or but of more or less, and how. Thus, we can enthusiastically advocate stringent controls to avoid infant crib deaths without simultaneously supporting a plethora of detailed federal rules and regulations dealing with the color of exit lights and the maintenance of spittoons. Simply put, there are serious questions as to what rules to set, how detailed they should be, and how they should be administered.

Proponents of regulation contend that many of the rules and directives have yielded numerous benefits to the public. The NHTSA claims that seat belts, head restraints, and other mandated safety devices save thousands of lives each year. The EPA notes that because of its controls over industrial discharges, fish and marine life have returned to many rivers and lakes.

However, the regulatory process generates its own set of "externalities." Voters in one congressional district may achieve the bulk of the benefits from a federal regulation, while the costs are borne primarily by citizens in the rest of the nation. For example, regulations making it uneconomical to use low-sulfur (i.e., low-polluting) coal have been supported by those areas producing high-sulfur coal. Consumers generally have borne the costs that result from such special-interest regulation enacted in the guise of environmental improvement.

Because of the very substantial costs and other adverse side effects that government regulation gives rise to, society has begun to take a hard look at the full array of government controls over business. In every recent administration since the presidency of Gerald Ford, Democratic and Republican alike, efforts have been made to eliminate or reassess those rules that generate excessive costs. In theory, government regulation should be carried to the point where the incremental benefits equal the incremental costs. Overregulation — situations where the costs to society exceed the benefits — is thus avoided. In practice, it is difficult to obtain measurements with the necessary precision to make such determinations.

The expansion of regulation also has required a variety of changes in the way companies manage their operations. Complying with government requirements has had the overall effect of pushing companies toward a greater degree of centralization in the areas subject to regulation. The effect is most pronounced in dealing with equal employment and environmental issues. More people are involved in the decision-making network. Prior consultation and multiple reviews are often the order of the day. Authority to take action often moves up the corporate ladder, and the decision-making process slows down.

Thus, productivity can suffer, especially as the costs of legal and other overhead activities rise. Within the company, a counterbureaucracy arises, a cadre of financial, safety, and environmental specialists whose knowledge, training, and narrow responsibilities are characteristic of the regulators themselves. In a wider sense, corporate managers are becoming more sensitive to evolving social demands. Thus, they increasingly understand that responses to at least some of the public's expectations about social performance are a normal aspect of conducting business.

APPENDIX

TABLE 2.3 Major Expansions of Regulation of Business, 1962–2002

Year of Enactment	Name of Law	Purpose and Function of Law
1962	Food, Drug, and Cosmetic Act Amendments	Requires pretesting drugs for safety and effectiveness, and labeling drugs by generic name
1962	Air Pollution Control Act	Provides first modern ecology statute
1963	Equal Pay Act	Eliminates wage differentials based on sex
1964	Civil Rights Act	Creates EEOC to investigate charges of job discrimination
1965	Cigarette Labeling and Advertising Act	Requires warnings on hazards of smoking to be printed on labels
1966	Traffic Safety Act	Provides for a national safety program, including safety standards for motor vehicles
1966	Fair Packaging and Labeling Act	Requires producers to state what a package contains, how much it contains, and who made the product
1966	Child Protection Act	Bans sale of hazardous toys and articles
1966	Coal Mine Safety Amendments	Tightens controls on working conditions
1967	Flammable Fabrics Act	Broadens federal authority to set safety standards for flammable fabrics, including clothing and household products
1967	Age Discrimination in Employment Act	Prohibits job discrimination against individuals aged 40 to 65
1968	Consumer Credit Protection Act (Truth-in-Lending)	Requires full disclosure of terms and conditions of finance charges in credit transactions
1969	National Environmental Policy Act	Requires environmental impact statements for federal agencies and projects
1970	Clean Air Amendments	Provides for setting air-quality standards
1970	Occupational Safety and Health Act	Establishes safety and health standards that must be met by employers
1970	Amendments to Federal Deposit Insurance Act	Prohibits issuance of unsolicited credit cards. Limits customer liability in case of loss or theft to $50. Regulates credit bureaus and provides consumers access to their own files
1970	Securities Investor Protection Act	Provides greater protection for customers of brokers and dealers and members of national securities exchanges
1970	Poison Prevention Packaging Act	Authorizes standards for child-resistant packaging of hazardous substances
1972	Consumer Product Safety Act	Establishes a commission to set safety standards for consumer products and bans products presenting undue risk of injury
1972	Federal Water Pollution Control Act	Establishes national regulation of discharges into navigable waters
1972	Equal Employment Opportunity Act	Gives EEOC the right to sue employers

TABLE 2.3 *(cont.)*

Year of Enactment	Name of Law	Purpose and Function of Law
1972	Noise Pollution and Control Act	Regulates noise limits of products and transportation vehicles
1973	Vocational Rehabilitation Act	Requires federal contractors to take affirmative action on hiring the handicapped
1973	Safe Drinking Water Act	Requires EPA to set national drinking-water regulations
1974	Campaign Finance Amendments	Restricts amounts of political contributions
1974	Employee Retirement Income Security Act	Sets new federal standards for employee pension programs
1974	Hazard Materials Transportation Act	Requires standards for the transportation of hazardous materials
1974	Magnuson–Moss Warranty Improvement Act	Establishes federal standards for consumer product warranties
1976	Hart–Scott–Rodino Antitrust Amendments	Requires large companies to notify the Justice Department of planned mergers and acquisitions
1976	Toxic Substances Control Act	Requires advance testing and restrictions on use of chemical substances
1977	Business Payments Abroad Act	Provides for up to $1 million in penalties for bribing foreign officials
1977	Department of Energy Organization Act	Establishes a permanent department to regulate energy on a continuing basis
1977	Surface Mining Control and Reclamation Act	Regulates strip mining and reclamation of abandoned mines
1977	Fair Labor Standards Amendments	Increases the minimum wage in three increments
1978	Fair Debt Collection Practices Act	Provides for the first nationwide control of collection agencies
1978	Age Discrimination in Employment Act Amendments	Raises the mandatory retirement age from 65 to 70 for most employees
1980	Comprehensive Environmental Response, Compensation, and Liability Act	Creates superfund to pay for cleanup of hazardous chemical spills; taxes petroleum and chemicals
1984	Drug Price Competition and Patent Term Restoration Act	Gives generic drugs more market accessibility and restores some of the patent life lost during the development process
1984	Insider Trading Sanctions Act	Increases sanctions against trading in securities while in possession of material "nonpublic" information
1986	Asbestos Hazard Emergency Response Act	Requires schools to inspect buildings for asbestos-containing materials and submit plans to states to deal with the problem
1986	Superfund Amendments and Reauthorization Act	Requires state and local governments to develop comprehensive emergency response plans; companies that make or use chemicals must report inventories and emissions to the public

Continued

TABLE 2.3 *(cont.)*

Year of Enactment	Name of Law	Purpose and Function of Law
1986	Age Discrimination in Employment Act	Abolishes mandatory retirement, extends protections against discriminatory employment practices to workers over age 70
1988	Employee Polygraph Protection Act	Prohibits use of lie detectors by employers engaged in interstate commerce
1988	Worker Adjustment and Retraining Notification Act	Requires employers to provide 60 days' advance notice of layoffs involving 50 or more workers
1990	Clean Air Act Amendments	Requires many firms to obtain permits to operate; sets industry-by-industry reduction standard for toxic air pollutants
1990	Americans with Disabilities Act	Gives civil rights protections to people with disabilities; requires employers to make "reasonable accommodations"
1990	Nutritional Labeling and Education Act	Requires companies to use approved terms and to list specified information
1990	Oil Pollution Control Act	Includes new liability limits for various classes of vessels as well as double-hull requirements for oil tankers
1991	Civil Rights Act	Reverses several Supreme Court decisions on what constitutes discrimination in employment
1993	Family and Medical Leave Act	Gives employees a legal entitlement to take leave of absence with job reinstatement rights
1995	Lobbying Disclosure Act	Extends disclosure requirements to lobbying executive branch officials and providing more financial data by lobbyists
1995	Private Securities Litigation Reform Act	Limits court action by investors and caps damage awards against companies
1995	Telecommunications Competition and Deregulation Act	Opens telecommunications markets to competition
1996	Food Quality Protection Act	Replaces "zero risk" standard with "negligible risk" requirement
1996	Health Insurance Portability and Accountability Act	Helps maintain health insurance coverage for employees who switch or lose jobs
1997	FDA Modernization Act	Expedites FDA approval process for new pharmaceutical products
2001	USA Patriot Act	Expands Justice Department powers of investigation and surveillance
2001	Aviation and Transportation Security Act	Federal government assumes responsibility for examining luggage and other security matters at airports
2002	Campaign Finance Reform Act	Restricts the use of "soft money" in federal election campaigns and makes other reforms in election campaigns
2002	Corporate Disclosure Act	Regulates auditing activities and establishes responsibility for financial reports

Notes

1. John J. Riccardo, "Regulation: A Threat to Prosperity," *New York Times*, July 20, 1975, p. F12.

2. Murray Weidenbaum, *Restraining Medicine Prices: Controls vs. Competition* (St. Louis, MO: Washington University, Center for the Study of American Business, 1993), p. 21.

3. Marvin H. Kosters, "Government Regulation: Recent Status and Need for Reform," in Michael L. Wachter and Susan M. Wachter, eds., *Toward a New Industrial Policy?* (Philadelphia: University of Pennsylvania Press, 1981), pp. 332–335.

4. See Charles Wolf, Jr., "A Theory of Nonmarket Failure," *Journal of Law and Economics,* April 1979, pp. 107–139.

5. Wolf, p. 114.

6. Bruce Yandle and Elizabeth Young, "Regulating the Function, Not the Industry," *Public Choice* 51, no. 1, 1986, pp. 59–70.

7. See George J. Stigler, *The Citizen and the State: Essays on Regulation* (Chicago: University of Chicago Press, 1975).

8. Sam Peltzman, "Toward a More General Theory of Regulation," *Journal of Law and Economics*, August 1976, pp. 211–240; George J. Stigler, "The Theory of Economic Regulation," in Thomas Ferguson and Joel Rogers, eds., *The Political Economy* (Armonk, NY: M. E. Sharpe, 1984), pp. 67–81.

9. *National Air Quality and Emissions Trends Report, 2000* (Washington, DC: U.S. Environmental Protection Agency, 2000).

3

GOVERNMENT AND
THE CONSUMER

ompetition in the marketplace provides an opportunity to encourage the production of safer products because companies that earn reputations for making unsafe
products face retribution from consumers, just as if they offered unsafe goods (see the
section "Firestone/Bridgestone and Tire Safety" in this chapter). Nevertheless, the public is not content to rely on the marketplace for protection: Government regulation of
consumer product safety takes many forms, ranging from outright bans to requirements for specific types of information on containers to changes in the products themselves. The regulations generate numerous benefits as well as costs, both of which are
ultimately enjoyed or endured by the consumer.

Consumer products are subject to regulation by a great variety of government agencies. In the United States, these public-sector review authorities include the Food and
Drug Administration in the Department of Health and Human Services, the Department
of Agriculture, the Federal Trade Commission, and the Department of Transportation.

However, the Consumer Product Safety Commission (CPSC) has the broadest and
most general responsibility. The Consumer Product Safety Act of 1972 created an independent regulatory agency "to protect the public against unreasonable risks of injury
associated with consumer products." A five-member commission sets safety standards
for consumer products, bans products presenting undue risk of injury, and polices the
consumer product marketing process from manufacture to final sale.

In establishing the commission, Congress adopted a no-fault view of accidental
product injuries. Rather than stressing punitive action against the producers and distributors of unsafe products, the emphasis is on minimizing the likelihood that consumers
will be subjected to product hazards. Under this approach, products are redesigned to
guard against possible consumer misuse and ignorance of proper operation.

The CPSC truly has a broad mandate:

- To work with consumers and businesses to foster voluntary standards for product
  safety.
- To set and enforce mandatory standards.
- To ban unsafe products when a safety standard is not considered to be adequate
  protection for the public.
- To order firms to give public notice of a substantial hazard associated with
  a product and to repair, replace, or refund the price of a product that presents
  a substantial hazard.
- To provide information to help consumers select and use products safely.

Consumers are assured the right to participate in the commission's activities. Any
"interested person" can petition the commission to start a proceeding to issue, amend, or
revoke a consumer product safety rule. Safety standards cover product performance and
contents, as well as composition, design, construction, finish, packaging, and labeling.

Any product representing an unreasonable risk of personal injury or death may, by court order, be seized and condemned. Under the Consumer Product Safety Act, the commission's jurisdiction extends to more than 10,000 products. However, given its modest budget (1.5 percent of that of the Environmental Protection Agency), the CPSC relies primarily on voluntary compliance. Table 3.1 shows the extensive array of the corporate responses.

Congress has excluded from the commission's authority several widely used products that are regulated by other federal agencies. These exclusions cover food, tobacco, drugs, and cosmetics (regulated by the Food and Drug Administration and the Department of Agriculture), pesticides (regulated by the Environmental Protection Agency), firearms and alcohol (subject to some supervision by the Treasury

TABLE 3.1   Voluntary Corrective Actions by Consumer Companies in 2000

Product	Defect or Hazard	Action Taken
Tree lights	Fire hazard	Refund offered
Miniature skateboard keychain	Wheels may come off	Refund offered
Skate brake	Mount could crack	Refit kit provided
Fleece pullover	Zipper may detach	Refund offered
Toddler overalls	Snaps may detach	Refund offered
Lawn mower	Fuel tank may leak	Replacement kit provided
Pull toy	Small parts present choking hazard	Refund or exchange for another toy
Carbon monoxide detector	Alarm may not work	Replacement unit provided
Light fixture	May short-circuit	Item replaced
Extension cord	May overheat	Refund offered
Doll with coverall	Buttons may detach	Refund offered and product discontinued
Battery-operated pump	Potential fire hazard	Retailer repaired product
Go-cart	Clothing may become entangled	Plastic shield provided to cover wheels
Dive computer	May register false depth reading	Dive shops repaired product
Crib	Potential entrapment hazard	Design changed
Home coffee brewer	Handle for glass may break	Replacement pot offered plus $5
Storm door window	Window may fall out	Redesigned replacement window provided
Stroller	Brakes may fail	Free repair kit offered
Electronic skeet shoot	May overheat	Redesigned replacement part provided
Wall thermostat	May not be accurate	Replacement controls provided
Electric saw	Improper wiring	Repair offered
Children's lamp	May catch fire	Refund offered; product discontinued

Source: U.S. Consumer Product Safety Commission.

Department), and automobiles, regulated by the Department of Transportation and the Environmental Protection Agency. (See Appendix to this chapter, "Government and the Automobile.")

THE IMPACT ON CONSUMERS — BENEFITS AND COSTS

Important benefits to the public can be expected from an agency designed to make consumers more aware of product hazards and to require that products likely to cause serious injuries be removed from the market. Simultaneously, such actions also generate substantial costs, which will be borne ultimately by the consumer in the form of higher prices or reduced variety of products. The consumer's total welfare is therefore enhanced by seeking out the most economical and efficient ways of achieving safety objectives. Thus, banning "unsafe" products can be viewed as the most direct way of responding to hazards, but that approach may not always be the most cost-effective one. Other alternatives range from relabeling a container (so that the consumer becomes aware of a previously hidden hazard) to recalling and modifying an existing line of products.

One way of looking at government-mandated product safety requirements is that they constitute a tie-in sale. All consumers, whether they want or need the new layer of protection, have to accept and pay for it. "What is made safe for the village idiot will cost the man of common sense more."[1] At times, higher prices to the consumer result from regulators forcing expensive complexity on the manufacturers of consumer products. Poor and even middle-income families may thus be priced out of some markets for consumer products. All this suggests that when government agencies regulate the safety of consumer products, they should consider a variety of relevant factors.

WHAT IS AN ACCEPTABLE RISK?

Some government regulations aim at eliminating all hazards. For example, the clean water law establishes an ultimate goal of zero discharge of pollutants into the nation's waterways. Prior to its replacement by the Food Quality Protection Act of 1996, the Delaney Amendment to the Food, Drug, and Cosmetic Act prohibited the use of any food additive if it contained the most minute trace of carcinogenic properties.[2] People's personal responses to product hazards are often much more nuanced than regulators' decisions.

For example, most people drink regular "tap" water, rather than buy more expensive—and purer—bottled water. In a similar attitude toward taking risks that they consider worthwhile, families drive on their vacations. They do so because often that is a cheaper and more convenient mode than air travel—even though airline safety records are far superior to those of the average motorist. Likewise, individuals skydive, water ski, or auto race because they willingly undertake the attendant risk in order to enjoy their leisure time. Similarly, some workers seek out employment in hazardous environments, such as commercial deep-sea diving, because, in their view, the rewards are worth the danger involved.

Many people get hurt using the goods they buy. The questions that consumers regularly ask themselves, explicitly or implicitly, is which risks to take and how to minimize the dangers sensibly. Surely that is how individuals tend to make their own decisions. However, as we will see later in this chapter, that is not how the world of government regulation always works. Surely not all hazards are equal. Some useful distinctions can be made among the different types of product hazards.

TYPES OF HAZARDS

If the hazard is *hidden,* the unknowing consumer is denied the freedom of deciding whether to risk using the item. In contrast, the risk in using a sharp knife is visible, and each individual may choose the degree of care in handling the instrument. Thus, there is no demand for regulation of that universal consumer product, which is associated with a variety of injuries. Hazards, however, may be unknown to the consumer—such as the danger of cancer from exposure to asbestos filings which are invisible to the naked eye. Or the risk may be unexpected—for example, the failure of a car's brakes while it is being driven. These hazards are not visible, and consumers have little or no choice in deciding whether or not they will expose themselves to them. As a result, there may be a need for government intervention in the area of hidden risks. The precise nature of that intervention represents another category of decision making that we will take up later.

From the viewpoint of public policy, requiring producers or employers to provide additional information to consumers or workers often constitutes an adequate response. When fully informed of the risks involved, some consumers, but not necessarily all, will reduce their purchases of hazardous products. Employees may insist on a "risk premium" in their pay to agree to work in a hazardous environment. On the other hand, product sales may fall so low, or the risk premium that workers insist on may be so high, that the company is better off redesigning the product or work process to reduce or eliminate the hazard. Often these voluntary responses are superior to government actions to ban products it deems hazardous. That arbitrary approach overlooks the possibility that, for some people, it is beneficial, or at least acceptable, to take the risk and use the item (see Figure 3.1 for an example).

A consumer's choice of a product will also depend on the seriousness of the potential harm (assuming the risk is known). Consumers have unequal tastes for safety as well as for other characteristics of product performance. Particularly where the safety hazard is minor (the occasional blister on a finger), large price increases to pay for eliminating the problem may merely deprive consumers of the use of the product. It is important to consider the cost of correcting safety hazards and to recognize that consumers regularly make trade-offs between safety and other criteria that are important to them.

Consider two similar items: a power tool selling for $100 that cannot be used for much more than an hour without overheating, and one selling for $800 that can be safely used for a much longer period. Some consumers will buy the cheaper model and knowingly take the chance of burning it out. A policy of complete safety would ban the cheaper item, thereby effectively depriving low-income consumers (or thrifty people) from buying a power tool or replacing an old, worn tool produced prior to the establishment of the new standard. If equity is a social goal, then this is an example of increasing safety at the expense of consumer welfare.

One trade-off between safety and other product characteristics can be seen in the following case. About one-fifth of the 16,000 injuries and 500 deaths a year due to

A Letter to the Editor
The Wall Street Journal, July 1, 1975

Your editorial "The Risks of Safety" (June 26) brings back memories.

In 1947 I was in our local sanitarium with service-connected TB. I had tuberculosis not only in the lungs but also in the throat, which was almost always fatal. I could hardly eat and guessed I had maybe two months to go, although I hadn't given up hope.

One day the medical director came to me and said, "Walter, there's a new drug, it may have side effects and it's so new the Vets won't pay for it. I'll let you have it for cost. Do you want to try it?" Of course I did. The drug was streptomycin; the cost was $1 a shot for 360 shots—one every six hours.

I'll never forget the throat specialist, who came up once a month, on his next visit. He looked in my mouth and said, "It's a miracle!" My throat was clear. Six months later I'd gained 70 pounds and was discharged with no side effects and have had no problems since.

If our present regulations concerning the release of new drugs were in effect then, I would have been dead for 28 years.

Walter A. Rothermel

Wyomissing, Pa.

FIGURE 3.1   Taking a Chance

burning clothing are caused by children's sleepwear catching fire. For this reason, the Consumer Product Safety Commission (CPSC) requires children's pajamas to possess a flame-resistant property. But when the National Cancer Institute found that Tris, the major chemical used, can cause cancer, the commission faced the dilemma of reducing the chance of cancer by increasing the chance of injury or death from fire. The commission chose to ban Tris, forcing manufacturers to seek a substitute.

Another example is that of the household ladder. The numerous accidents associated with that product have given rise to pressure for more detailed standards for its design and production. However, industry experts point out that, if a ladder is made too difficult to use or too expensive to buy, many people will wind up climbing on a chair or a table instead—a far more dangerous procedure.

The CPSC mandate for childproof caps for medicines is another instance of the trade-offs involved in complying with regulations governing consumer products. Fewer children have suffered from aspirin poisoning since the requirement was established. But other changes also occurred in the same time period, notably consumer shifts to nonaspirin forms of pain killers. In fact, almost half of all aspirin poisonings are reported to involve bottles that had been left open—an obvious but dangerous way of dealing with difficult-to-open childproof caps.[3] Children are not the only consumers who are affected. Shortly after a heart patient died with an unopened childproof bottle of nitroglycerin tablets, the commission sent a notice to doctors and pharmacists reminding them that childproof containers are not required for nitro tablets.

Personal behavior probably has the most pervasive influence on the risks individuals face. People learn to drive defensively and to lock their doors. The risks that people willingly face—and could choose to avoid—are often much larger than the risks that citizens worry about being obliged to endure. Of those who regularly drive or ride in automobiles, about 2 out of every 10,000 die in car accidents each year, for a total of about 45,000 deaths annually. By comparison, for those who live near municipal solid waste landfills, the mortality risk is substantially less than 1 in 1,000,000 and may be far lower—a minute fraction of the risk of automobile travel, and a risk that shows up (if at all) only decades later in life. Yet, public policy is much more severe on the latter, more remote type of risk.

The *probability of a hazard actually occurring* can be a prime consideration in the risks that we are willing to assume, although statutes limit the ability of regulators to exercise flexibility and judgment. For example, in testing whether trichloroethylene (TCE), a chemical used in decaffeinated coffee, might be a possible cause of cancer, the National Cancer Institute employed a generous dose of the chemical on its test animals—the equivalent of a person drinking 50 million cups of decaffeinated coffee every day for an entire lifetime.[4] Despite the doubtful relevance of this test, the coffee industry quickly changed to the use of a different chemical, fearing a future ban on TCE.

In practice, the public does not support every product ban that a government agency issues in an effort to reduce risk. In this regard, the consumer response to the Food and Drug Administration's attempt to ban saccharin (subsequently postponed by Congress) is instructive. It is readily summed up by a newspaper headline: "A Run on Saccharin Here to Beat Ban."

Also, government agencies do not adopt every proposal from the public to regulate consumer products. For example, the CPSC declined to act favorably on a petition to declare mistletoe hazardous. The commission's research did reveal that 132 "ingestions" of mistletoe were reported in a four-year period and that five of the people involved developed symptoms, two of whom required hospitalization. Although we are left to surmise the reasons for the commission's actions, it is reasonable to assume that the CPSC was wary of creating a field day for cartoonists. It is easy to conjure up illustrations of a couple kissing under a sprig of mistletoe and the accompanying caption reading, "The Federal Government Has Declared This Hazardous to Your Health." In any event, as good bureaucrats, the commission stated that denying the request should not "be construed as endorsement of the complete safety of these plants."[5]

On another occasion, the CPSC denied a petition to regulate pull-tab and pull-off lid containers even though they result in 5,600 emergency room cases a year. It turned out that injuries from conventional metal cans are responsible for over 60,000 emergency hospital visits annually. On yet another occasion, the CPSC promulgated a draft standard on matchbooks to make them more difficult to open. However, it quickly rescinded the standard when it realized, after many industry complaints, that the result often would be opened matchbooks left lying around.

Government experiences great difficulty in choosing the hazards it regulates. Take, for example, the problem of residential fires. The emphasis in public policy to date has been on wiring standards. How important a hazard is household wiring? According to the National Fire Protection Association, only 9 percent of fatal residential fires in the United States in recent years are caused by the electrical distribution system, a category that includes flaws in wiring. The other 91 percent comprises such more important causes as smoking (23 percent), arson (17 percent), heating equipment (14 percent), and children playing (10 percent).

A researcher at the University of Tokyo contends that "dangerousness is a continuum."[6] In that view, it is not possible to establish categories within which substances are uniformly dangerous or uniformly safe. Thus, whiskey will ignite, and large enough doses of sugar (or salt) can kill laboratory animals. Nevertheless, government officials are empowered with the discretion to designate product hazards and to regulate or even ban specific products.

THE EFFECTS ON BUSINESS

Government regulation generates a wide variety of effects on the companies that produce and market to the consumer. The impact on one large industry—automobile manufacturing—is highlighted at the end of the chapter in the Appendix, "Government and the Automobile." For consumer goods generally, the Consumer Product Safety Commission has generated many specific requirements. The paperwork burden on business can be, at times, substantial. The CPSC has called on every manufacturer, distributor, and retailer—upon learning that an item sold "creates a substantial risk of injury"—to inform the commission and provide a wide array of information. The required data include the number of products involved, their model and serial numbers, and a detailed accounting of when and where the items were distributed.

The reporting requirement is not complete until the company submits a final report indicating that the potential hazard has been corrected. Thus, the commission shifts to the company the responsibility and costs of determining and remedying potential defects. Moreover, company decisions on whether or not to report a potentially hazardous product are influenced by the possibility of criminal sanctions should the commission disagree with a company's decision that a given item is not potentially hazardous.

PRODUCT RECALLS

As a result of the expanded role of government regulation of product safety, many corporate marketing departments have developed the capability to handle product recalls. In addition to the highly publicized cases of motor vehicles and tires, various nonautomotive products are recalled from time to time, including adhesives, bicycles, computers, deodorants, drain cleaners, electric shavers, gas ovens, heart monitors, lawn mowers, power drills, safety helmets, television sets, toys, and women's hygienic products.

Voluntary recalls predate the establishment of the Consumer Product Safety Commission. In 1903, the Packard Motor Car Company recalled its Model K when it realized that the car's drive shaft had a habit of popping out of its housing. In the contemporary environment, companies at times have the option of initiating a voluntary recall of a product. This may obviate the need for formal government action and provide more flexibility in dealing with customers. Given the government's "stick in the closet," the voluntary approach provides the benefit of choosing the timing of the recall and minimizing the adverse publicity that may result.

Many companies, especially those catering to consumer markets, have introduced numerous modifications in their operating procedures to reduce the expense and anxiety associated with recalls. A system of coded identification numbers for each product or batch of products is often used to provide an expedited response to product recalls. Computerized information systems keep track of the products throughout the distribution chain. The identification includes the labeling of each package with a code indicating when and where it was produced. Warranty cards are a widely used method of providing the manufacturer with the names and addresses of purchasers of products as well as other details, some of which contribute to market research.

Some manufacturers conduct mock recalls of their products to evaluate the effectiveness of their recall programs. Businesses are devoting considerable attention to preventive action. Some firms have set up special staffs to review consumer complaints that cite specific product defects. Such an approach can be used as evidence of the company's acting in good faith should a product subsequently be declared hazardous.

Responding to recalls can be burdensome. In some cases, the expenses of the recall—locating, removing, and discarding the items—can far exceed the price of the product itself. With product recalls a frequent experience and with high liability judgments, companies have added incentive to produce safer, albeit more expensive, products.

The experience of the Firestone Tire Company illustrates the great stakes involved. After an acrimonious public battle with the National Highway Traffic Safety Administration, the company was forced to recall millions of its tires. The damage to the company's sales and reputation was substantial. Firestone eventually sold out to Bridgestone, a Japanese tire company. Ironically, its successor company subsequently experienced a somewhat similar situation. (For details of this case, see the section "Firestone/Bridgestone and Tire Safety" later in this chapter.)

PACKAGING AND LABELING

Regulators' increasing attention to the role of information has resulted in some of the emphasis in consumer goods packaging being shifted from eye-catching decorative coverings to informational labeling (see Table 3.2). Greater amounts of information have been required on labels (especially for food products), as well as in supporting literature and catalogs. Under the Nutrition Labeling and Education Act of 1990, the FDA and USDA have promulgated a set of nutrition-labeling rules that require food processing companies to adopt uniform labels for hundreds of thousands of products. The purpose is to give consumers more and better information about the nutritional

TABLE 3.2 Authorized Nutrition and Health Claims on Food Packages

Label Claim	Definition (Per Serving)
Calorie free	Less than 5 calories
Low calorie	40 calories or less
Light or lite	1/3 fewer calories or 50 percent less fat
Fat free	Less than 1/2 gram fat
Low fat	3 grams or less fat
Cholesterol free	Less than 2 milligrams cholesterol and 2 grams or less saturated fat
Low cholesterol	20 milligrams or less cholesterol and 2 grams or less saturated fat
Sodium free	Less than 5 milligrams sodium
Low sodium	140 milligrams or less sodium

Source: U.S. Food and Drug Administration.

content of food and to limit the health claims made by manufacturers. Companies must provide information on cholesterol, sodium, carbohydrates, fiber, and fat. To be labeled "low fat," a product must contain no more than three grams of fat per serving. "Light" products must contain 50 percent less fat or one-third fewer calories than standard products.

The Department of Health and Human Services estimated that the changeover cost industry approximately $2 billion but claimed that this one-shot expense was more than offset by reduced health care costs resulting from improved nutrition.

The U.S. Department of Agriculture establishes specific requirements that must be met before an item can be labeled as poultry, hash, pizza, or other food products. At times, the amount of detail becomes humorous. For example, the department issued a regulatory change requiring that every frozen pizza have at least 12 percent cheese topping, with no less than half of that being real cheese. Not all consumers were pleased. One wrote in, urging the USDA to "leave the pizzas just the way they are. . . . My two-and-one-half-year-old son has asthma and allergies. He can't have any milk products. The pizza with fake cheese is a great treat for him."[7] Cartoonists had a field day. (See Figure 3.2 for an example.) To compound the problem, cheese pizza is regulated by the FDA because it contains 2 percent or less meat and poultry products. Sausage and pepperoni pizzas (which contain more than 2 percent meat) are covered by the USDA.

FIGURE 3.2

Source: Washington Post, National Weekly Ed., December 26, 1983. Reprinted by permission of William T. Coulter.

Enforcement of labeling rules can be arbitrary at times. In 1991, the FDA ordered manufacturers of vegetable cooking oils to remove the words "no cholesterol" from their labels. Did the products actually contain cholesterol? No, but the government agency considered the claim "misleading." Consumers, they feared, might mistakenly get the impression that no cholesterol means "no fat" or "no risk of heart disease." In 1997, however, the agency took a more sympathetic attitude. It allowed makers of oatmeal to claim that the product may reduce the risk of heart disease. However, the FDA added a proviso: The claim must also note that the beneficial effect is contingent on the oatmeal being part of a diet low in saturated fat and cholesterol.

ADVERTISING

The government is a substantial influence both in terms of prescribing types of advertising of consumer products and in restricting the claims that are made. Writers of copy are frequently instructed about the liabilities of a product—as well as its attributes. Advertisers and advertising agencies, spurred by federal action, often display awareness of consumer safety in product advertising. Such advertising copy provides tangible benefits, notably enhancing product acceptability and reducing the possibility of unfavorable publicity and safety-related lawsuits.

Some heavy advertisers in consumer markets, or their agencies, have set up formal panels to review the approach to safety in their advertising. These panels include advertiser and agency personnel who have actual experience with the products involved—for example, parents of young children. The National Advertising Review Board, an industry self-regulatory organization, has developed the following checklist for reviewing company advertising to minimize the likelihood of violating federal product safety requirements:

- Is anything shown, described, or claimed in the advertisement that raises questions of consumer safety?
- Is everything known that should be known about the product's performance under both normal and misuse circumstances?
- Is there anything in the advertisement that might prove harmful to children who cannot comprehend the most familiar hazards in consumer products and tend to imitate what they see?
- Is allowance made in advertising for the susceptibility to suggestion of the elderly or the consumer predisposed toward risk taking?

FIRESTONE/BRIDGESTONE AND TIRE SAFETY

A vivid example of the adverse effects on a business that can result from an inadequate response to governmental regulation of the company's product is the experience of the Firestone Tire Company. In 1978, the National Highway Traffic Safety Administration (NHTSA) urged Firestone to recall all 13 million of its Firestone 500 tires, then the company's top-of-the-line, steel-belted radial.

The case against the Firestone 500 rested on evidence that the tire's failure rate and likelihood of causing serious accidents were exceptionally high. Under its statute, the NHTSA is empowered to order recalls of motor vehicles and accessories that either fail to meet its specific standards for design and test performance or exhibit other evidence of a safety-related defect. There was no direct evidence that the 500s violated any specific NHTSA standard. However, they had accident and adjustment rates far greater than those of other tires. By July 1978, the NHTSA had gathered reports of 64 injury-producing accidents and 34 fatalities that involved the Firestone 500. Reports on steel-belted radials sold by Firestone's seven leading competitors showed only 21 fatalities for eight times the number of tires. Furthermore, between 1972 and March 1978, the overall "adjustment" rate for the 500s (the percentage of tires returned by customers and accepted for prorated credit toward new tires) was 17.5 percent, against only 1.7 to 5.3 percent reported by Firestone's leading competitors for their steel-belted radials.

In July, the NHTSA announced an initial determination that the 500s contained a "safety-related defect" and might therefore be subject to recall. Firestone contended that the 500s were safe, dependable, and free of fundamental defects. It argued that the chief cause of failure had been the widespread and persistent tendency of drivers to keep their tires underinflated, thereby irreversibly damaging the tires and making them dangerously susceptible to failure. It discounted the adjustment-rate figures on the grounds that it had been unusually accommodating to customers. Firestone noted that no one had identified any specific defect in the tire and that the tire's reliability, rated in the NHTSA's own test, was "far in excess" of the agency's requirements.

In August 1978, the House of Representatives Commerce Committee issued a report that rebutted many of Firestone's arguments. The committee contended that manufacturers should make tires sufficiently durable to withstand, at least to a reasonable extent, such recognized common abuses as underinflation. For a company to do otherwise, the report suggested, is to produce tires with the expectation of having them fail. Firestone's sales literature and ads had not, up to that time, warned consumers about the critical importance of keeping the 500s properly inflated. More compelling to Firestone was that the steady barrage of unfavorable publicity about the safety of its key product was rapidly eroding its market share.

The company insisted for months that the overall adjustment rate of the 500s was 7.4 percent rather than the actual figure of 17.5 percent. Although the company claimed it had no indication of any safety problems with the 500 until the NHTSA raised the matter, internal company documents released after the signing of the recall show the opposite. A 1972 memo to a Firestone vice president warned that "we are in danger of being cut off by Chevrolet because of separation failures."

Not having access to such evidence at the time, the NHTSA sought an agreement with the company for a voluntary recall. On November 29, 1978, Firestone agreed to recall the Firestone 500. Although less stringent than NHTSA would have liked, the agreement had the advantage of being immune to legal challenge. An estimated 7.5 million 500s sold after September 1, 1975, and manufactured before January 1, 1977, were eligible for free replacement. Although Firestone's legal counsel continued to urge the company to fight the regulatory agency, the top management saw that Firestone was rapidly losing its position in its basic market. The steady public criticism of the safety of the 500 was devastating, and management reluctantly agreed to the recall. However, Firestone never recovered from the loss of consumer confidence in its tires; Bridgestone, the Japanese tire giant, soon after acquired the company.

In an expensive display of irony, in 2000 Bridgestone/Firestone experienced a similar protracted attack on the safety of its tires and ultimately was forced to launch a major product recall. Only after numerous complaints and much embarrassing publicity about the tendency of its tires to shed their treads (especially on the Ford Explorer), the company in August 2000 recalled approximately 6.5 million of its tires. In language reminiscent of the situation two decades earlier, Bridgestone/Firestone firmly stated that it did not know why the specific models of the tires in question were plagued by problems.

This more recent episode was particularly painful because Bridgestone/Firestone had been a key supplier of tires to the Ford Motor Company since early in the Automobile Age when two close friends, Harvey Firestone and Henry Ford, founded those two pioneering companies.

In an unusual display of public acrimony on the part of a company and a major supplier, Ford strongly criticized Bridgestone/Firestone for the failure of Firestone tires on Ford Explorer sport utility vehicles (SUVs), blaming the tires for numerous reported problems with the vehicle. More than 60 percent of the 15-inch, all-terrain Firestone tires recalled during this period had been standard equipment on the Ford SUVs. After Ford replaced Bridgestone/Firestone as its major supplier of tires, the parent Japanese tire company initially lost more than one-half of the market value of its common stock (two years later, Bridgestone stock was still selling at a price substantially lower than the levels experienced in 2000). Once again, the failure to respond quickly and firmly to a public-policy problem proved devastating to the company.

REGULATION AND CONSUMERS

The regulation of consumer products by the Food and Drug Administration (FDA) provides cogent examples of the costs and benefits that flow to the consumer from governmental involvement. The FDA is one of the most wide-ranging governmental agencies, regulating prescription and over-the-counter drugs, biological products, medical devices, cosmetics, and domestic and imported foods. Its consumer protection function includes premarket approval and quality standards for drugs and medical devices, factory inspections, and market surveillance.

The FDA has the power to seize mislabeled or adulterated foods and to take them off the market. The agency also has the authority to seek injunctions in federal courts against producers who manufacture or ship products not meeting its standards of consumer safety. Before a pharmaceutical product or a medical device may be marketed, the company must convince the FDA that it is both safe and effective.

The FDA's drug approval process covers a long development cycle: laboratory and animal studies; clinical analyses including laboratory and field testing for safety and effectiveness; and agency review of pharmaceutical company submissions. It often takes 12 years to complete the entire process of moving a drug from research laboratory to patient use. The cost of developing a new pharmaceutical and carrying it successfully through the entire drug approval process is estimated to exceed $400 million per new drug. On the benefit side, patients in the United States have been spared such horrors as the deformities resulting from use of inadequately tested drugs (except those who smuggled the unapproved drug into the United States). What is not as widely recognized is the cost—both in dollars and lives—of the extra caution.

The full cost of delays in the lengthy approval process is far more than financial. A study of new drugs that were introduced in both the United States and the United

Kingdom in the period 1977 to 1987 reported that far more—114—were first available in Great Britain, compared with only 41 that were first available in the United States. We can understand why FDA reviewers ask for more studies and delay the introduction of new products. Consider the disparate impacts bluntly: If 16 people are harmed by side effects of an approved drug, that becomes front-page news and FDA officials can be expected to have to testify before skeptical congressional committees. On the other hand, if 1,000 people die prematurely because approval of a new drug was delayed, the public is unaware.[8]

Pharmaceutical regulation also provides a cogent example of the positive feedback effect of reports on the shortcomings of regulation. Following studies of regulatory delays and their adverse impacts on patients, in 1992 Congress passed legislation to reduce the lags in the drug review and approval process. It did so by linking reductions in the time taken to approve a proposed pharmaceutical with increases in the FDA's budget. The result of this incentive approach over the following decade was a 50 percent increase in the speed of the reviews.

During the same period, the regulatory authorities of Western European countries took actions that discouraged company investments in developing new pharmaceuticals. Their publicly financed health care systems kept tight ceilings on drug prices. They also banned direct-to-customer advertising. The result of the simultaneous liberalization of U.S. pharmaceutical regulations and intensification of European regulation was a shift in pharmaceutical R&D from Western Europe to the United States. In 1999, Aventis made its Bridgewater, New Jersey, facility its global research headquarters. In 2002, Novartis moved the command center for its worldwide pharmaceutical research from the company's headquarters in Switzerland to Cambridge, Massachusetts.[9]

A relatively new area of controversy involving the FDA is the subject of "genetically engineered" (GE) ingredients or "genetically modified" (GM) foods. So far, the agency has rejected proposals to require the labeling of so-called GE or GM food products. In 2001, the FDA ruled that it found no significant differences between these products and conventional foods. Because in the United States genetically modified crops are not usually segregated from regular crops, labeling would likely involve substantial testing of products. Some retailers of organic foods have benefited from the controversy by selling products with labels that state that the food does not contain genetically modified ingredients.[10]

PRODUCT LIABILITY AND THE COURTS

Even in the absence of regulatory requirements, the product liability system provides substantial incentives for companies to be concerned with the safety of the items they make. Under the U.S. legal system, the primary responsibility for product safety is borne by the manufacturers. To obtain financial compensation, injured consumers must bear the burden of instituting court action on their claims for compensation.

ALTERNATIVE APPROACHES TO LIABILITY

A consumer harmed by a product may sue the manufacturer under one of three legal theories: negligence, breach of implied warranty, or strict liability.[11] Under the traditional *negligence* theory, a manufacturer is liable for the harm caused by its product if the company knew or should have known of the defect that caused the injury. The issue that the court considers is whether a "reasonably prudent" producer under "similar circumstances" would have sold the product. The negligence theory recognizes that mistakes do happen and that the quality control system of a reasonably prudent company may not catch the defect. In such an event, the risk rests on the consumer. Under the theory of *breach of implied warranty,* the manufacturer is responsible for damages if the product is not fit for the purpose for which it is intended or for other reasonably anticipated uses.

The contemporary theory of *strict liability* holds the manufacturer liable for injuries resulting from a defective product that is "unreasonably dangerous," whether or not the company acted unreasonably in setting limitations on implied warranties. The doctrine of strict liability is widely accepted today. The trend toward strict liability has been based on three lines of reasoning: (1) People who are injured by defective products should be compensated, notwithstanding legal niceties of negligence and warranty; (2) the cost of accidents should be spread among those who benefit from the product; and (3) the doctrine of strict liability fosters efficiency because the manufacturer is in the best position to reduce the cost and likelihood of accidents.

Even under strict liability, injured consumers must still meet several specific legal tests. Plaintiffs are required to prove three key facts:

- That the product was in a "defective condition"—that there was something wrong with it.
- That the defect rendered the product "unreasonably dangerous"—that the defect gave rise to dangers of which ordinary consumers were unaware.
- That the defect caused the injuries that gave rise to the suit.

In some cases, manufacturers have been successful in arguing that they should not be liable where a consumer used their product in ways that were unreasonable, negligent, or unforeseeable.[12] In 1988, the bellwether California Supreme Court, ruling in favor of a pharmaceutical company, used rather broad language:

> [I]n accord with almost all our sister states that have considered the issue, we hold that a manufacturer is not strictly liable for injuries caused by a prescription drug so long as the drug was properly prepared and accompanied by warnings of its dangerous propensities that were either known or reasonably scientifically knowable at the time of distribution.[13]

Nevertheless, the product liability process does play an important role in promoting product safety. A survey of 500 chief executive officers revealed that threatened or actual product liability suits caused 36 percent of the surveyed firms to discontinue making specific products. Another 35 percent of the companies reported that their liability experiences had resulted in improving the safety of their products, and 47 percent had improved their product warnings. Product liability costs also were a factor in deciding whether to introduce new products.[14]

High-performance automobiles provide a pertinent case in point. Although the Mercedes-Benz SL roadster made its world debut late in 1988, it was not sold in the United States until the 1991 model year. The reason for the delay was that, if a new product has been in use in Europe for several years and has experienced few problems, it is easier to defend it against liability suits in the United States.

Nevertheless, the mere presence of lawsuits at times is a deterrent to the continued production of some products. In the case of the drug bendectin, prescribed for morning sickness, a series of unsuccessful lawsuits against the manufacturer forced it to abandon production. Even though the company prevailed in each case, the cost of insurance and legal defense almost equaled the profits earned on sales.[15] Unison Industries, Inc., withheld from the market a new and advanced electronic ignition system for light aircraft because of the liability risk that might result from its use. A producer of a pollution-abatement device withdrew that product after failing to obtain liability insurance.

As has been demonstrated in the case of producers of asbestos—such as the Manville Corporation, which declared bankruptcy—very large product risks can create claims far greater than a company's resources. In that particular case, it is unlikely that the full claims for the injuries suffered will be paid. In other cases, court decisions have varied considerably, ranging from upholding consumer claims to denying redress. Here is a sample of how consumer product cases have been handled in recent years:

- A woman suffered a spontaneous abortion and nearly died while wearing a Dalkon shield birth control device. She argued that the device had been defectively designed and had caused an infection. The Colorado Supreme Court upheld a jury verdict of $600,000 in compensatory damages and $6.2 million in punitive damages.
- A child was lifted into a ceiling fan, suffering skull and brain lacerations. The plaintiff argued that the fan's design was defective and that the company should have warned of the danger. The jury found for the company.
- A 16-year-old boy lost an arm when a motorboat ran over the jet ski he was riding. The plaintiff argued that the ski was unstable and difficult to see in waves. The jury ruled that the company should pay $2 million. It then reduced the damages by one-third due to the boy's negligence.

THE CASE OF CIGARETTES

The information route is the one that had been used primarily in the case of one of the most popular consumer products—cigarettes—until the mid-1990s. Since the warning labels were required by Congress in 1966, the courts had ruled in favor of the tobacco companies in almost every case claiming that lung cancer resulted from smoking.[16] The courts said that the label required by the Surgeon General under the Cigarette Labeling and Advertising Act provided adequate warning to smokers.[17]

In a landmark case in 1994, the state of Mississippi sued the tobacco industry to recover its medical costs due to smoking-related illnesses. Several other states filed similar suits and the industry began losing a series of cases in state courts. Meanwhile, tobacco regulation expanded. Most states and many localities restricted smoking in "public places" such as restaurants, public transportation, and workplaces. Beginning in 1995, federal law required state governments to prohibit sales of tobacco to anyone under 18 years of age.

In 1998, the states and the tobacco industry entered into a Master Settlement Agreement. Under the agreement, the companies pay $206 billion to the states over 25 years (about 45 cents a pack) and remove billboard advertisements for cigarettes. A year later, the U.S. Department of Justice sued the industry to recover the federal costs of smoking-related illnesses. The Department of Justice accused the tobacco companies of misleading the public about the risks of smoking.[18]

In early 2002, the federal government indicated that, if it won the prolonged suit, it might seek severe restrictions in marketing cigarettes, including banning the payment of bonuses to retailers who prominently display racks of cigarettes and prohibiting labeling certain blends of tobacco as "light" or "low tar." Earlier, the Surgeon General had encouraged smokers to switch to lower tar cigarettes. However, in November 2001, the National Cancer Institute published a report criticizing the marketing of "light" and "ultralight" cigarettes as deceptive.

In March 2002, the largest tobacco company (Philip Morris) lost a case in Oregon and was assessed $168 million as compensatory damages and $150 million in punitive damages because a woman who smoked low-tar cigarettes died of lung cancer. The jury found the company's product to be "defective and unreasonably dangerous." Earlier appeals often reduced the size of the punitive damage awards in cigarette cases, but they did not eliminate them.[19] Increases in cigarette prices due to regulation and litigation have resulted in a decline in the percentage of people in the United States who smoke. Nevertheless, the production and sale of cigarettes and other tobacco products continue to be an important industry.

Conclusions

Government regulates a great variety of consumer products and in the process influences business decision making in many ways. In some cases, such as prescription drugs, the advance approval of government regulators is required before the item can be marketed. In the case of most consumer products, companies are free to manufacture and sell these items but they are subject to government recalls if they are considered hazardous. Regulatory agencies, in carrying out their mandates, issue a large number of rulings, procedural statements, and instructions.

At times, some of the agencies regulating consumer products rely on the information approach. The Surgeon General (in the Department of Health and Human Services) specifies the warnings that cigarette manufacturers must put on the outside of their packaging (although that has not avoided the litigation described earlier). The CPSC provides consumers with more general information on product safety. The Federal Trade Commission reviews advertising to ensure that consumers are not misled (as might be expected, that function generates lawsuits from time to time).

On occasion, providing pertinent product information can benefit consumers more quickly than regulation. Take the case of three-wheeled, all-terrain vehicles (ATVs). One study showed that they were more dangerous than four-wheeled ATVs. When consumers learned that the four-wheeled version was safer, they ceased buying the three-wheeled models. The Consumer Product Safety Commission did negotiate a virtual ban on three-wheeled ATVs with the industry, but the ban had little effect. Consumers had already ceased buying the three-wheeled variety.[20]

Potentially, market competition can play a key role in reducing injuries from the products consumers use. Information on comparative product safety can provide one firm with a competitive advantage over another. In this way, the market itself would generate pressures to produce safer products. In view of the continuing concerns about product, workplace, and environmental hazards, it is heartening to note the steady increase in life expectancy in the United States, from 47 years for those born in 1900, to 68 years for "the class of 1950," and to 77 years for those born in 1999.[21]

APPENDIX

GOVERNMENT AND THE AUTOMOBILE

Federal regulation of passenger automobiles is the most extensive example of government influence on a consumer product. The regulations issued by a variety of federal agencies cover design, production, and operation of the vehicle. Government is directly involved in setting standards for such basic items as engines, bumpers, headrests, seat belts, door latches, brakes, fuel systems, and windshields, as well as the type of fuel that can be used.

However, there is no provision for coordinating among regulatory agencies and statutes.[22] The law to control emissions also reduces fuel efficiency by about 7.5 percent. The required side-door guard beams, the energy-absorbing steering column, and other safety features have added about 200 pounds to the weight of an automobile, lowering fuel economy and increasing pollution. In turn, fuel-economy standards have forced the manufacture of smaller, lighter cars that are less safe than the cars that would otherwise be produced. When two cars of different sizes collide, the safety advantage lies with the occupants of the heavier vehicle. In fact, the chance of being involved in a fatal accident is about twice as great in a compact as it is in a large automobile. The fuel-efficiency standards applied to cars made in the United States are estimated by the National Academy of Sciences to result in 1,300–2,600 additional traffic deaths each year, even after taking into account the tendency of occupants of smaller cars to use their safety belts more frequently.

Safety and emissions requirements add more than $2,000 to the price of the average new automobile. This higher cost means that many people are driving their old cars longer and thus not getting the intended benefits of the safety–environmental–energy regulations that have been promulgated. Also, drivers are encouraged to use motorcycles and bicycles, which are often cheaper but less safe than conventional motor cars.

Automobile safety regulation in the United States is characterized by great reluctance to interfere directly with individual behavior. The major cause of automobile accidents is driver error, often on the part of drunken motorists. Drunk driving is the leading cause of death for persons in the 15-to-24-year-old age group. In addition, 40 percent of the pedestrians involved in fatal crashes could themselves be considered legally intoxicated. Nevertheless, regulation concentrates on the companies that make the products that people use, rather than on the way people use them. This is evident when we compare the uneven enforcement of statutes on drunk driving with the stringent requirements for safety-related components imposed on manufacturers of motor vehicles.

Because many automobile passengers do not use seat belts, the federal government, after considerable debate, requires the installation of more expensive passive-restraint systems. These systems can be activated without any action by the driver or

TABLE 3.3   Impact of Seat-Belt Use Laws

| Nation | Seat Belt Usage | | Reduction in Fatalities (%) |
	Before Law (%)	After Law (%)	
Australia	30	80	22
Belgium	17	92	39
Canada	21	61	16
France	26	75	22
Great Britain	40	90	24
Sweden	36	79	46
Average	28	80	28

Source: U.S. Department of Transportation.

passengers, most notably the air bags that inflate in a frontal collision. Table 3.3 shows the substantial benefit that results from simply requiring that all occupants of motor vehicles use their seat belts. In contrast, airbags have become controversial. A number of children and adults have been killed by airbags. A much larger number of other people have been saved by the same equipment. The problem arose because at first the government required the bags to have enough force to protect someone not wearing a seat belt. Public outrage forced a modification of this requirement, to reducing the surge of power triggering the use of the airbag.

Economists who have made such comparisons conclude that the costs of existing programs to regulate automobile safety, fuel economy, and emissions are greater than their benefits. As a result, less costly alternatives have been suggested. An incentive-based insurance policy could be developed with fees reflecting the driver's record and the actual "crashworthiness" of the car. Seat belts could greatly reduce fatalities at a low cost if a combination of education and enforcement increased their usage substantially. Stronger enforcement of laws against drunk driving would surely help.

A higher tax on gasoline, proponents contend, would reduce gasoline usage more than the arbitrary corporate average fuel efficiency (CAFE) standards. The CAFE standards mandate the production of motor vehicles that get a stipulated minimum number of miles per gallon of gasoline used. No other major industrialized nation relies on such a command-and-control approach to conserve gasoline. The almost universal practice elsewhere is to use price incentives, such as an increase in the excise tax on gasoline, to achieve the public-policy objective (see Chapter 13).

Another way to reduce the consumption of gasoline, and thus help to achieve national environment and energy objectives, is to accelerate the replacement of old vehicles with high emissions rates and low fuel utilization (the smelly old "klunkers") through retirement bounties or high annual registration fees.[23] At present, public policy operates in the reverse manner—owners of older cars pay lower personal property taxes than the purchasers of newer, more fuel-efficient vehicles.

Notes

1. Walter Guzzardi, Jr., "The Mindless Pursuit of Safety," *Fortune,* April 9, 1979, p. 64.

2. The Delaney Cancer Amendment of 1958 provided that "no additive shall be deemed to be safe if it is found to induce cancer when ingested by man or animal. . . ." The 1996 law substitutes the more realistic standard of "reasonable certainty of no harm."

3. W. Kip Viscusi, "Consumer Behavior and the Safety Effects of Product Safety Regulation," *Journal of Law and Economics,* October 1985, pp. 527–553.

4. U.S. Food and Drug Administration, "Trichloroethylene (TCE) and Coffee," *FDS Talk Paper,* June 27, 1975.

5. *Briefing Paper on Poinsettia Plants and Mistletoe Sprigs* (Washington, DC: U.S. Consumer Product Safety Commission, December 17, 1975).

6. Kazuo Akita, "Handle with Care," *Look Japan,* October 1991, p. 30.

7. Ward Sinclair, "'Truth in Pizza' Rule Draws Crusty Responses," *Washington Post,* National Weekly Ed., December 26, 1983, p. 31.

8. Sam Kazman, "Deadly Overcaution: FDA's Drug Approval Process," *Journal of Regulation and Social Costs,* September 1990; Murray Weidenbaum, *Restraining Medicine Prices* (St. Louis, MO: Washington University, Center for the Study of American Business, 1993).

9. Mary K. Olson, "How Have User Fees Affected the FDA?" *Regulation,* Spring 2002, pp. 20–25; Rick Mullin, "Novartis Shifts Its R&D Headquarters to the U.S.," *Chemical Week,* May 15, 2002, p. 27.

10. Thomas Lee, "Genetically Altered Food Creates Labeling Dilemma for the Industry," *St. Louis Post-Dispatch,* June 16, 2002, p. E1.

11. W. Kip Viscusi, *Regulating Consumer Product Safety* (Washington, DC: American Enterprise Institute, 1984), p. 8.

12. Peter Asch, *Consumer Safety Regulation* (New York: Oxford University Press, 1988), p. 23.

13. *Brown v. Abbott,* Supreme Court of the State of California, March 31, 1988.

14. E. Patrick McGuire, *The Impact of Product Liability* (New York: Conference Board, 1988).

15. Peter W. Huber, "Biotechnology and the Regulation Hydra," *Technology Review,* November–December 1987, p. 64.

16. In one case, a plaintiff was awarded damages on behalf of his late wife, who had started smoking before warning labels were used. "Cracks Seen in Tobacco's Liability Dam," *Wall Street Journal,* June 15, 1988, p. 25.

17. See W. Kip Viscusi, *Smoking: Making the Risk Decision* (New York: Oxford University Press, 1992).

18. Jonathan Gruber, "Tobacco at the Crossroads," *Journal of Economic Perspectives* 15, no. 2, Spring 2001, pp. 193–212; Robert A. Levy, "Battering Big Tobacco," *Regulation,* Summer 1997, pp. 9–10.

19. "Philip Morris Loss in Oregon Court," *Wall Street Journal,* March 25, 2002, p. A17.

20. Paul H. Rubin, "Why Regulate Consumer Product Safety?" *Regulation,* Fall 1991, p. 60.

21. *Life Insurance Fact Book* (Washington, DC: American Council of Life Insurance, 2001).

22. Robert Crandall et al., *Regulating the Automobile* (Washington, DC: The Brookings Institution, 1986); "David Among Goliaths: The Small Car Faces Reality," *Journal of American Insurance,* Spring 1981, p. 2; *Motor Vehicle Regulations* (Washington, DC: General Accounting Office, 1992).

23. Environmental Defense Fund and General Motors, *Mobile Emissions Reduction Crediting* (undated).

4

PROTECTING THE ENVIRONMENT

─────≈ⓔ/ⓔ/ⓔ≈─────

Environmental protection programs are a very large area of government regulation and a major reason for growth of public-sector involvement in private decision making. This growth has coincided with substantial improvement in the quality of the environment. Yet the relationship between the cost of environmental programs and their benefits has not been as straightforward as might be expected. Citizens enthusiastically support environmental activities but are reluctant to pay for them directly, preferring business and/or government to cover the cost.

This chapter undertakes the dual task of examining the gamut of government programs designed to improve the physical environment, and the impact of these efforts on business and the economy. We begin with an economic overview.

THE ECONOMICS OF ENVIRONMENTAL REGULATION

Until relatively recently, air and water (and the environment generally) were viewed as common property, as "free goods." Individuals and organizations, both public and private, used the environment as a convenient dump—which, of course, is the act of polluters polluting. The polluters received private benefits (easy disposal of wastes), but social costs ("externalities") in the form of dirtier air and water resulted. Excessive pollution was encouraged because, although the social costs of polluting often exceeded the social benefits, the private benefits usually exceeded the private costs. People tend to pollute more if they do not have to pay for the cost of cleaning up.

The United States discards over 200 million tons of solid wastes a year, or more than 4 pounds per person a day. Only about one-fourth of this vast amount of discarded material is recycled. Confronting a cleanup challenge of that magnitude is a formidable task. To an economist, the environmental pollution problem is essentially one of altering people's incentives. The basic assumption is that people pollute, not because they enjoy spoiling the environment, but because polluting is cheaper or easier than not polluting. Thus, if the cost of cleaning up had to be borne by the polluters, there is considerable likelihood that they would try to develop forms of production that generate less pollution. Also, they might dispose of their wastes in a less environmentally harmful manner, thereby reducing the cleanup costs that they would be paying. From an economic standpoint, if prices of goods and services would rise to reflect the costs imposed on the environment (perhaps as measured by cleanup costs), some consumers would shift to those less expensive goods and services that embody lower environmental costs.

Figure 4.1 illustrates how the imposition of cleanup costs affects producers and consumers. In this simple example, raising the price of gadgets to cover cleanup costs

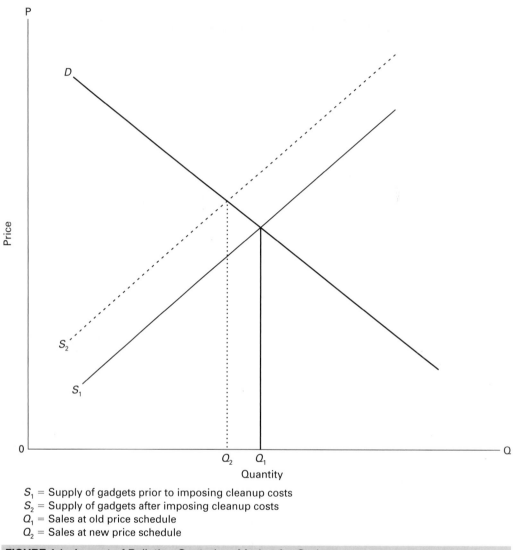

S_1 = Supply of gadgets prior to imposing cleanup costs
S_2 = Supply of gadgets after imposing cleanup costs
Q_1 = Sales at old price schedule
Q_2 = Sales at new price schedule

FIGURE 4.1   Impact of Pollution Control on Market for Gadgets

(perhaps via a pollution tax) results in lower sales—and most likely less pollution. Pollution taxes or effluent charges are tools to correct a serious source of market failure: the absence of a price needed to prevent the careless and excessive use of scarce environmental resources. Although most taxes create harmful side effects on the economy by distorting economic choices, taxes on pollution also have socially beneficial impacts.

There is considerable foreign experience with pollution fees. A cooperative association in Germany's heavily industrialized Ruhr Valley has used a "polluter pays" system since 1913. Fees are based on the amount and quality of the discharger's effluent. The funds generated by the charges help build and operate waste-treatment facilities in the basin. The effectiveness of this strategy in the Ruhr Valley led Germany to pass the Federal Water Act and Effluent Charge Law, establishing a nationwide fee system.[1] The German system delivers cleanup more efficiently than the command-and-control approach used in the United States. However, comparisons of water quality for the Mississippi River and the Ruhr suggest that Germany's fees may be set too low to achieve the water-quality that Americans expect.

France has instituted a system of charges similar to the German program. Fees are used in conjunction with a permit system and primarily raise revenues for administrative costs and specific water-quality projects. Pollution charges are a major, but not dominant, part of the French water-quality program.

In contrast, the Netherlands administers a tougher fee system that encourages dischargers to avoid polluting. Effluent fees in the Netherlands are higher than those in Germany or France. Fees are based on the volume and concentration of a discharger's effluent. Actual discharge levels are used to determine fees for large dischargers, whereas small dischargers pay a fixed fee. As with Germany and France, revenues are used to finance projects to improve water quality. But, in contrast, the Netherlands' effluent fee system has a measurable impact on water quality. Increases in effluent charges are significantly correlated with declines in waterborne pollutants. Between 1976 and 1994, emissions of cadmium, copper, lead, mercury, and zinc plummeted 86 percent or more, primarily because of the charges.[2]

The idea behind pollution fees is not to punish polluters but to get them to change their ways as high-polluting products become more expensive than low-polluting products. Taxation (or an effluent fee) is a basic way of working through the price system. A tax or charge levied on high-polluting products alters relative prices in favor of low-polluting products. A low tax rate (similar to a revenue tariff) does not stop the act of polluting while it mildly discourages the taxed activity, but it does raise the revenue needed to pay for cleaning up. A high enough tax rate (comparable to a protective tariff) would stop the pollution by totally discouraging the purchase of the high-polluting product, although it would not raise revenue.

In practice, we would expect an intermediate result. The pollution tax or effluent fee would shift some, but not all, demand to the lower-priced (and less polluting) alternatives. Some, but not all, producers would have sufficient incentive to reduce the external costs they impose on society by changing to less polluting methods of production and distribution. Thus, producers would have more incentive than they do now to "economize" on pollution—an incentive similar to reducing labor and materials costs. The basic idea is that the price of a product should reflect its costs to, or burden on, the environment.

As an illustration of this proposal, a study of the Delaware estuary shows that effluent fees, set at a high enough level to achieve the desired level of water purity, would cost approximately one-half as much as a conventional regulatory program requiring an equal percentage reduction by all polluters. To achieve the standard of two parts of dissolved oxygen per million, the estimated annual cost comes to $2.4 million via an effluent charge, compared with $5.0 million for treatment of the pollution under a uniform regulation.[3]

Some indication of the practical problems that arise in shifting to an effluent fee system can be obtained from examining Table 4.1. Clearly, it would be less costly to use an effluent fee system to achieve the same amount of pollution cleanup in a 30-mile stretch of the Black Warrior River in Alabama—$1,224 a day compared to $1,839 a day under the existing pollution standards approach. However, three of the seven major

Pollution Source	Daily Cost of Meeting Existing Standards	Daily Cost of Effluent Fees	Gain (+) or Loss (−)
TABLE 4.1 Estimated Cost of Cleanup in a 30-Mile Section of Black Warrior River Under Alternative Approaches			
Empire Coke	$ 116	$ 0	$116
B. F. Goodrich	73	0	73
Gulf State Paper	94	351	−257
Hunt Oil	30	6	24
Reichhold Chemicals	147	228	−81
Warrior Asphalt	16	3	13
City of Northport	122	145	−23
City of Tuscaloosa	1,241	491	750
Total	**$1,839**	**$1,224**	**$615**

Source: Albert H. Link and Frank A. Scott, "Effluent Fees, an Alternative System for Achieving Water Quality: A Case Study," *Water Resources Bulletin,* June 1981.

polluters—Gulf State Paper, Reichhold Chemicals, and the city of Northport—would wind up paying more in pollution fees than their current costs of meeting the standards, and four companies would be better off. The main beneficiary in terms of lower cost would be the city of Tuscaloosa. Thus, support for a shift to effluent fees would not be universal. This pattern of variation would likely be the case in many other regions.

The customary approach that consists of government issuing uniform standards is defended on the grounds of equity: All polluters are treated equally. For example, all cars must meet the same air-pollution rules. However, as a consequence, much of the staff resources of the U.S. Environmental Protection Agency (EPA) have gone into defending the agency against thousands of lawsuits, brought both by environmentalists urging sterner enforcement and by companies seeking relief from what they regard as arbitrary interpretations.

Uniform standards are an expensive regulatory approach. It may cost a great deal to reduce the pollutants from one type of activity and very little from another. For example, it may be cheaper to redesign a new building still on the drafting boards than to totally revamp one that already is standing. Congress has taken an important step in accommodating the economic approach by authorizing "emissions trading" in the acid rain provisions of the Clean Air Act Amendments of 1990, discussed below.

THE DEVELOPMENT OF ENVIRONMENTAL POLICIES

Protecting the environment covers a great variety of concerns—air pollution, water pollution, pesticides, toxic substances, hazardous wastes, unsafe drinking water, ocean dumping, noise emissions, and other adverse impacts on human health and ecological systems. In the United States, the EPA is the main federal organization operating in this area, and it focuses on issuing rules, approving permits, and enforcing its regulations.

Because ecological influences do not always respect national boundaries, these issues increasingly involve the interaction of the public and private sectors of many countries. At times, an agency of the United Nations may provide the forum for inter-governmental actions in this area of policy. As we will see, this is especially so in dealing with the issue of global climate change.

The notion that environmental protection is a proper function of government did not originate in the twentieth century. Nor did a get-tough attitude toward polluters first arise in the United States. More than 600 years before the National Environmental Policy Act of 1969, the king of England proclaimed a no-nonsense pollution-control law, complete with penalties for offenders. As with most congressional action today, the king in 1308 did not consider it necessary to weigh the effectiveness of various deterrents such as fines or emissions fees. Instead, he tried the simple and more straightforward strategy of executing the polluters. However, this stringent level of enforcement did not endure.

Even in the United States, protection of the environment is no newcomer to the realm of government activities. Prior to independence, the Massachusetts Bay Colony enacted regulations to prevent pollution in Boston Harbor. Following the Revolution, most coastal states took some action to ensure that no large floating debris would obstruct navigation of the waterways within their borders.

Throughout the eighteenth and nineteenth centuries and well into the twentieth, local governments bore primary responsibility for the regulation of water and air pollution. However, localities found themselves quite helpless to control water pollution coming from upstream, and a shift in the prevailing winds was apt to make a sleepy hamlet the unwilling recipient of smoky particles from a more industrialized town.

By the end of the nineteenth century, the connections between dirty water and contagious diseases had stimulated most states to enact water pollution laws. These early statutes were concerned with the human health aspects of dirty water rather than with abating pollution that affected ecological systems or that had adverse aesthetic consequences. The result was a tendency for the pollution issues to be buried in public health agencies that largely ignored the problem once a disease had been eradicated.

Federal involvement in the environment during the first half of the twentieth century was piecemeal. Antipollution legislation was aimed primarily at keeping interstate and coastal waterways free from debris to maintain the flow of navigation. The Refuse Act of 1899 forbade dumping into navigable waters without a permit from the Corps of Engineers. The Oil Pollution Act of 1924 banned oil discharges into coastal waters. Otherwise, protecting health and safety was viewed as a function of the states under their police powers.

The first breakthrough in federal pollution legislation was the Water Pollution Control Act of 1948. The law did little more than provide technical and research assistance to the states, but it demonstrated a national responsibility. The Air Pollution Control Act of 1955 very much resembled the 1948 water pollution legislation. Thus, as recently as 1955, a report of a congressional committee stated:

> [I]t is primarily the responsibility of state and local government to prevent
> air pollution. The bill does not propose any exercise of police power by the
> federal government and no provision in it invades the sovereignty of states,
> counties or cities. There is no attempt to impose standards of purity.[4]

During the 1970s, legislation progressively enlarged the role of the federal government in regulating the environment and committing the nation to ambitious goals. The

EPA was established in 1970 to pull together a variety of scattered activities and develop a unified ecological policy at the national level. The EPA now administers programs dealing with air pollution, water pollution, toxic substances, waste disposal, pesticides, and environmental radiation. The agency possesses an impressive arsenal of powers and duties, buttressed by strong public support. When asked whether they would be willing to protect the environment even if it meant losing jobs in their community, 57 percent of a sample queried by the *New York Times* replied in the affirmative, and only 32 percent replied in the negative (the remaining 11 percent answered "don't know").[5]

THE RANGE OF NATIONAL ENVIRONMENTAL REGULATION

After Congress enacts environmental legislation, the focus of attention shifts to the executive branch agencies charged with carrying out the statutes. Activities of the EPA center on setting and enforcing standards relating to environmental concerns. The EPA has several means of enforcement. Upon finding a violation, it may seek voluntary compliance. If that fails, it can order compliance and take violators to court.

AIR POLLUTION CONTROLS

Most air pollution results from economic activity. Transportation services and industrial processes are mainly responsible for emissions of hydrocarbons, nontoxic organic gases not dangerous by themselves. However, hydrocarbons combine with nitrogen oxides from fuel combustion and vehicular traffic to produce ozone—commonly referred to as smog. Although many other pollutants make up smog, ozone is the substance most closely monitored. The rationale is that ozone produces harmful, albeit transitory, health effects and is a reasonable proxy for the other, unmonitored pollutants.

Table 4.2 shows the substantial amount of pollutants discharged into the air of the United States during a recent year—approximately 99 million tons of

TABLE 4.2 Air Pollutant Emissions in 1999, by Type and Source (In Millions of Short Tons)

Source	Carbon Monoxide	Sulfur Oxides	Particulates	Nitrogen Oxides	Volatile Organic Compounds
Transportation	74.0	1.4	0.8	13.5	7.6
Fuel combustion	6.1	15.3	0.9	10.0	0.3
Industrial processes	9.3	1.5	0.9	1.4	9.8
Miscellaneous	10.0	0.0	20.6*	0.3	1.0
Total	99.4	18.2	23.2	25.2	18.7
Change 1991–2000	−5%	−24%	−47%	−11%	−16%
Change 1981–2000	−18%	−31%	−6%	−14%	−32%

*Mainly fugitive dust, based on 1999 data.

Source: Office of Air Quality Planning and Standards, *National Air Quality Emissions Trends Report, 2000* (Washington, DC: U.S. Environmental Protection Agency, 2001).

carbon monoxide, 18 million tons of sulfur oxides, and 23 million tons of nitrogen oxides.

Another group of major pollutants is sulfur oxides, which combine with water to create sulfuric acid and generate acid rain. A major source of sulfur oxide is electric power plants that burn coal. Carbon monoxide, a colorless and odorless gas that can pose serious health problems in high concentrations, is formed as a result of inefficient combustion of fossil fuels. (The rising concern about the role of carbon dioxide or CO_2 in global climate change is dealt with later in the Appendix to this chapter.)

The Clean Air Act of 1970 (including the substantial amendments enacted in 1990) is the primary legislation dealing with air pollution. Its basic mission is seemingly straightforward: to establish and enforce air-quality standards that protect public health with an adequate margin of safety. The complex regulations issued under the act require four volumes in the *Code of Federal Regulations.* Attorneys specializing in this field have described the Clean Air Act as the environmental equivalent of the Internal Revenue Code—and that is not meant as a compliment.[6]

The EPA has established National Ambient Air Quality Standards for six common air pollutants: carbon monoxide, lead, nitrogen dioxide, ground-level ozone, sulfur dioxide, and particulate matter with a diameter of 10 microns or less. The agency also has set two types of standards: primary and secondary. Primary standards are designed to protect human health. Secondary standards are intended to protect vegetation and physical structures.

Despite significant gains in air quality, many regions of the country had not and would not meet the standards established in the 1970 legislation. Moreover, heightened public concern over issues, such as stratosphere ozone depletion and acid rain, problems not widely recognized when the law was first written, led to increased criticism of then-existing air pollution standards. In 1990, Congress passed one of the most comprehensive environmental laws to date, the Clean Air Act Amendments of 1990.

Among the provisions included in the statute's more than 700 pages is a requirement to phase out ozone-depleting gases such as chlorofluorocarbons and carbon tetrachloride, as well as significant reductions in sulfur dioxide and nitrogen oxide emissions. In addition, oil companies are required to offer new, cleaner-burning fuels to be used in urban areas plagued by ozone and carbon monoxide problems. Innovative approaches such as performance-based standards and emissions trading provide some flexibility in enforcement. However, a new requirement for obtaining five-year operating permits involves smaller firms such as auto-body painting and repair companies, print shops, and gasoline service stations. (See Figure 4.2 for the complexity of business compliance activities.)

The innovation of emissions trading is the major use of the economic approach in the revised Clean Air Act. The basic idea is that, given the opportunity, companies can often devise less costly ways of reducing the amount of pollution they generate than government regulators can. The new Clean Air Act's trading policy for sulfur dioxide emissions is an attempt to take advantage of this fact by creating markets in rights to pollute. The economic benefits of this approach are basic: Trading emissions rights can increase efficiency by concentrating air pollution reduction efforts on those emissions sources that are least costly to control. If one company can reduce emissions more cheaply than another, both can benefit by arranging a trade.

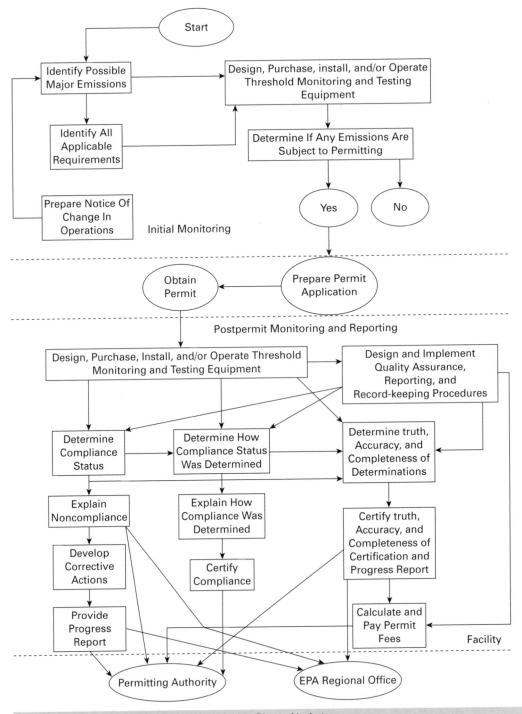

FIGURE 4.2   Company Compliance with the Clean Air Act

Source: Citizens for a Sound Economy Foundation.

Emissions trading has resulted in substantial economic gains, in the form of reduced compliance costs for business, with no harm to the environment.[7] The basic unit of currency for emissions trading is the one-ton emission reduction credit. Credits are created when pollution sources, such as electric utilities, reduce their emissions below the levels allowed by their permits. These reductions can be achieved in a variety of ways: burning cleaner fuel, installing new control equipment, or shutting down a polluting facility altogether. Emissions allowances may be bought, sold, or banked like any other commodity. If a utility holds surplus allowances, it may sell them to units whose emissions levels exceed their allowance supply, or it may save them for use in future years. A brisk market for pollution credits has developed (see box, "Emissions Trading: An Illustrative Example").

WATER POLLUTION CONTROLS

The Clean Water Act is the basis for the nation's water cleanup program. The act sets two specific national goals. The interim goal, commonly referred to as the "swimmable–fishable" goal, is to restore polluted waters, wherever possible, to a quality that allows for

BOX 4-1

EMISSIONS TRADING: AN ILLUSTRATIVE EXAMPLE

Consider a hypothetical example of two neighboring electric power plants that emit sulfur dioxide (SO_2). Suppose that both plants emit 100 tons of SO_2 each year, so total emissions are 200 tons, and the regulatory agency has set an emissions target of 140 tons a year for these two sources. Under the traditional approach, the agency could mandate a known technology (e.g., an SO_2 scrubber) that would reduce both plants' emissions to 70 tons each. Each plant would need to eliminate 30 tons of emissions. Assume that it will cost Utility A $600 to reduce the thirtieth ton of emissions, and $9,000 to reduce all 30 tons of emissions, and that it will cost Utility B $300 to reduce its thirtieth ton, and $4,500 to reduce all 30 tons. The total cost for both utilities of reducing emissions to 40 tons a year is thus $13,500.

However, since the costs of reducing emissions vary significantly between these two plants, a market-based approach can achieve substantial savings. If these two utilities can engage in emissions trading, they will find it economic for Utility B, with lower emissions abatement costs, to reduce its emissions level below 70 tons a year.

Utility B finds that it can reduce its emissions down to 60 tons a year, at which point the fortieth unit of abatement costs $400, and the total cost of reducing all 40 tons is $8,000. Utility A can reduce emissions down to a level of 80 tons a year, at which point the twentieth unit of abatement also costs $400, and the total cost to reduce all 20 tons of emissions is $4,000. Utility A would save money by purchasing tradable permits for 10 tons of emissions at $400 a ton from Utility B, because this is less than it would pay if it had to undertake emissions reductions on its own to achieve the 70 ton emissions level. Utility B would make money by selling 10 tradable permits at $400 a unit, because this is more than what it costs to reduce emissions. With the sale, the total costs for Utility A are $8,000: $4,000 for emissions abatement and $4,000 for purchasing 10 permits. Total costs for Utility B are $4,000: $8,000 for emissions abatement less $4,000 from the permit sale. The compliance cost for both facilities with trading would be $12,000, or 11 percent below the cost with the mandated technology standard ($13,500).

SOURCE: Adapted from *Economic Report of the President*, February 2000, p. 249.

the protection and propagation of fish and wildlife and for recreational use. The final goal—which in practice is more in the nature of a wish—is to eliminate all discharges of pollutants into the nation's navigable waters. Two very different basic control strategies are employed: (1) tough compulsory controls at the point of discharge for municipal and industrial polluters, and (2) largely voluntary efforts for other sources of water pollution, such as runoffs from city streets and farms.[8]

Not too surprisingly, some of the major pollution sources are the nonpoint discharges from streets and rural areas. New storm water regulations are beginning to reduce nonpoint source pollution from urban areas.

Specific provisions of the Clean Water Act have strong teeth. The EPA can enter and inspect any polluting facility to check its records and monitoring equipment and to test its discharges. Failure to report the discharge of oil or other hazardous substances into the water can result in large fines. Dumping hazardous substances from a vessel can be punished with a fine of up to $5 million; also, heavy cleanup costs can be assessed to the polluter. Both the Clean Air and Clean Water laws empower citizens to bring suit against anyone violating these statutes. Citizens can also take court action against the EPA itself if it fails to perform any duty required by the two laws.

HAZARDOUS AND TOXIC SUBSTANCES CONTROLS

Four major environmental statutes cover hazardous and toxic substances; they are usually referred to by their acronyms: TSCA, RCRA, FIFRA, and CERCLA or Superfund.

The Toxic Substances Control Act (TSCA) gives the EPA substantial power over the chemical industry, including the following:

- Authority to require testing of new and existing chemical compounds.
- Mandates for premanufacturing notices 90 days prior to the production of any new chemical or significant new use of an existing chemical.
- Power to control the manufacturing, processing, distribution, use, and disposal of any chemical substance.
- Required reporting, which covers each chemical produced by every chemical manufacturer.

Because of the detailed authority the EPA possesses under other statutes, much of the power granted by the TSCA remains latent (the proverbial "stick in the closet"). Under the Resource Conservation and Recovery Act (RCRA), the EPA regulates the current disposal of hazardous wastes. The law requires generators of wastes to create a record-keeping system to track the material from the point of generation to ultimate disposal. Large producers of hazardous wastes are required to furnish information on the waste to transporters and to designate a permitted disposal or treatment facility to which the residues must be taken. Under the RCRA, the EPA regulates the construction and operation of landfills, encourages the use of recycled products through government procurement programs, and oversees the development of state solid waste management plans.[9]

Under the Federal Insecticide, Fungicide, and Rodenticide Act (FIFRA), products to eliminate agricultural pests and diseases are controlled to keep hazardous chemicals off the market and to prevent "unreasonable" adverse effects on humans or on the environment. Manufacturers of new products must register with the EPA. In 1996,

Congress amended the law to protect consumers against serious, albeit noncancerous, risks in raw and processed fruits and vegetables. In what may become a valuable precedent for other environmental programs, the Congress requires the EPA to publish, "in a format understandable to a lay person," a discussion of risks and benefits posed by chemicals in pesticides.

In 1980, Congress established a "superfund" to finance the cleanup of abandoned or inactive hazardous waste dump sites. The superfund law—the Comprehensive Environmental Response, Compensation, and Liability Act (or CERCLA)—attempts to assign the costs of cleanup to "potentially responsible parties." The statute initially required the collection of a fee levied on the feedstocks for the chemical and oil industries to cover the cleanup costs where those responsible for the problem cannot be found. When it renewed the superfund statute in 1986, Congress increased the funds available for cleanups but permitted the special fee to lapse.

Remedial actions under the CERCLA have been slow and costly. The program also has been controversial, especially since the reach of the law is retroactive to times when dumping was legal. Moreover, major shares of the costs incurred go for legal and court activity rather than actually cleaning up the dump sites.

One part of the 1986 law, known as the Emergency Planning and Community Right-to-Know Act, requires nearly every facility that produces or uses any of 329 designated hazardous substances to make two sets of reports. First, it must file detailed inventories of those hazardous substances with the local fire department. Second, it must report to the EPA and designated state officials on the emissions of designated substances into the air, land, water, and waste treatment facilities—the toxic release inventory or TRI report. Thousands of companies are affected by this reporting requirement, ranging from major chemical manufacturing facilities to local dry-cleaning establishments.

The availability of information concerning the volume of discharges into the environment has had an important feedback effect on business decision makers. One chemical company responded by announcing that it would voluntarily reduce emissions of the listed chemicals by 90 percent. Monsanto achieved that goal by a variety of means, including changing production processes and closing down some high-polluting facilities.[10]

BENEFITS AND COSTS OF A CLEANER ENVIRONMENT

Compliance with pollution standards is neither easy nor cheap. Public and private expenditures for pollution abatement is estimated by the EPA to have risen from $152 billion in 1990 to $225 billion in 2000. The lion's share of these expenditures is made by the private sector, with the petroleum, chemical, primary metals, food, and paper industries making the largest outlays. Ultimately, people, as consumers and taxpayers, pay the costs of cleaning up the environment—and also receive the benefits that ensue.

THE BENEFITS OF ENVIRONMENTAL REGULATION

The benefits achieved by environmental regulation are substantial. Before examining the dry statistics on environmental improvement, it is helpful to recall the ecological condition of the United States when the EPA was first established in 1970. In Cleveland, the

Cuyahoga River exploded into flames. Vast areas of the Atlantic coastline and the Great Lakes shoreline were closed to swimming and fishing. The shores of the Potomac River near Washington, D.C., were marked by signs warning citizens not to touch the water.

Each of those highly publicized environmental situations has been improved. More broadly, as measured by traditional indexes such as the amount of pollutants in surface water and air, the overall quality of the environment in the United States has risen substantially since the EPA became active. The number of days when air quality has not met national standards is declining. Numerous streams and rivers are once more fishable and swimmable. A dramatic instance is the cleanup of the Willamette River in Oregon that has permitted the salmon to run again.

America's air continues to get cleaner. Almost all of the pollutants for which the EPA has set national standards show substantial declines in emissions from 1970 to 2000. Carbon monoxide levels in the air decreased 25 percent; lead levels, 98 percent; particulate matter, 88 percent; and sulfur dioxide, 44 percent. Emissions of nitrogen oxide, the exception, rose 20 percent (see Figure 4.3).

The quality of the nation's water likewise has shown a marked improvement. By 1990, 70 percent of the rivers and 60 percent of the lakes in the United States met the Clean Water Act's interim goal of "fishable and swimmable" water quality.[11] In addition, advances in sewage and industrial waste treatment technology since the mid-1970s have led to significant improvements in water quality, offsetting the adverse effects of population growth and industrial expansion. Agricultural and urban runoffs remain serious problems, especially because environmental legislation and regulation focus on "point" discharges of pollution, legislation that mainly covers specific facilities such as

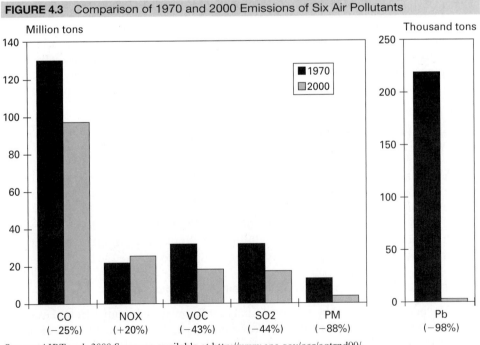

FIGURE 4.3 Comparison of 1970 and 2000 Emissions of Six Air Pollutants

Source: *AIRTrends 2000 Summary* available at http://www.epa.gov/oar/aqtrnd00/.

factories and public treatment works. Clearly, the pollution control measures enacted in recent years have had a very positive effect on the nation's environment. Determining the benefits to human health from this cleaner environment, however, is complex and fraught with uncertainty. One complication centers on the limited reliability of conventional risk assessments. In order to quantify the human benefits from pollution abatement, the health risks posed by a given pollutant must be known. Obtaining such information often requires relying on studies in which human health effects are extrapolated from animal studies. Unfortunately, demonstrating that animals react in a given way when exposed to very high doses of a toxin does not imply that much lower levels of exposure in humans will produce the same result. Moreover, rather than portraying the danger a pollutant poses to the average person, the government's risk assessments tend to be worst-case or upper-bound estimates. Current regulations, based on these exaggerated estimates, therefore tend to overvalue the benefits of pollution abatement. As one FDA official observed, "Linear extrapolation of rodent . . . data embodies the regulator's credo ('It's better to be safe than sorry') far more than it does the scientist's ('It's better to be right than wrong')."[12]

In some instances, it is possible to more fully achieve the public's regulatory desires while avoiding cost increases or even reducing the burden of compliance. As shown in the accompanying box ("The Second Battle of Yorktown"), that will take some statutory changes and those are difficult to achieve.

THE COSTS OF ENVIRONMENTAL REGULATION

The costs of complying with environmental regulations are also substantial. For a great many American companies, a considerable portion of the funds available for modernization and expansion is used instead to meet the EPA standards—or state environmental

BOX 4-2

THE SECOND BATTLE OF YORKTOWN

A landmark undertaking in 1989–1991 by the EPA and a private company—a joint study of Amoco's Yorktown, Virginia, refinery (Amoco is now a part of BP)—showed the benefits of focusing on overall environmental performance rather than following the customary detailed regulatory standards. Approximately 97 percent of the required hydrocarbon emission reductions could be achieved for about 25 percent of the cost that Amoco was incurring.

For example, complying with the controls on sewers required by Clean Air Act regulations cost $31 million and captured less than 10 percent of the benzene emitted from the refinery. Controls on a different source—barge loading operations—would have resulted in capturing 55 percent of the plant's benzene emissions, at a cost of only $6 million. Thus, Amoco could have achieved over five times the emission reductions at one-fifth the cost. Unfortunately, the statute continues to prohibit the company from substituting marine facility controls for the required sewer controls. Despite the successful results, the Yorktown experience has not yet led to modernizing environmental law to generate the benefits shown in the experiment.

Source: Robert W. Hahn, *Reforming the Clean Air Act,* Testimony Before the Subcommittee on Oversight and Investigation, U.S. House of Representatives, June 29, 1995, p. 4.

agency requirements. It has been estimated that for each $1 increase in environmental compliance costs, total factor productivity is reduced by $3 to $4.[13] By increasing investment and operating costs, many environmental regulations work like a tax on capital equipment. This reduces total investment and capacity and thus leads to higher prices at lower levels of production.

Opening new production facilities involves surmounting literally a host of regulatory obstacles. William D. Ruckelshaus, former administer of the EPA, has described the process vividly:

> Think of what it now takes to site a major industrial facility. A firm often must obtain agreement from perhaps dozens of agencies and authorities at each of three levels of government, not to mention the courts. And it doesn't help to satisfy . . . a majority of interests involved; a single "no" anywhere along the line at any time in the process can halt years of planning, effort and investment.[14]

The costs of compliance with environmental laws is quite uneven. A proportionately greater burden is borne by small factories because of the economies of scale involved in regulatory compliance. These expenses also vary substantially among competitors due to differences in production methods, economies of scale, and product mixes. Firms whose compliance costs are below average operate at a competitive advantage, increasing market shares or attaining higher profitability. In contrast, companies whose costs are greater suffer reduced profits, lower sales, or both.

New producers are usually subject to more stringent controls than existing producers, which tend to be "grandfathered," but they may also be able to employ the latest cost-reducing technology. Where new capacity has higher abatement costs than existing capacity, environmental controls can confer a competitive advantage on existing firms. To some extent, therefore, regulation protects the "ins" against the "outs," or potential new competitors. New investment and development of new products are discouraged by treating existing pollution sources more leniently. Simultaneously, strict "new source performance standards" increase the value of existing plants and equipment and discourage their replacement by more economically efficient facilities.[15]

Profit-maximizing firms may choose to risk penalties for noncompliance or to gain waivers or exemptions from regulations rather than comply. These may be desirable lower-cost alternatives for the firm, although they produce lower regulatory benefits to society. On the other hand, companies can go beyond merely adding the required abatement devices to existing production processes. They may shift to advanced production technologies that are less polluting. In such cases, regulation hastens the development and adoption of new technology.

Under the National Environmental Policy Act, environmental impact statements are required by federal agencies on various actions that affect the environment. The coverage of the law is broad. Detailed statements are usually triggered in the case of any private development requiring a federal permit. As shown in Table 4.3, environmental impact statements are very detailed—in part to guard against court challenges. The process also provides for community participation in determining whether the project should be built at a given location. It often takes 18 to 24 months to obtain the permits before beginning a major construction project. In contrast, the construction of the Empire State Building in Manhattan in the 1930s took less than two years from start to finish, including demolishing the earlier building on the site.

TABLE 4.3   Environmental Impact Analysis Required for a Residential Construction Project

Condition to Be Examined	Characteristics Required to Be Analyzed	Example of an Analysis
Land and climate	Soil: general characteristics, load-bearing capacity, existing and potential erosion, permeability Topography: general characteristics, slope grade Subsurface conditions: geological characteristics, geological faults Special conditions: flood plain; potential for mudslide or earthquake	No special climatic, subsurface, or unusual conditions Soil: permeable, clayey Topography: average, 3 percent slope
Vegetation, wildlife, and natural areas	Unusual climatic conditions: subject to flash floods, hurricanes, or tornadoes, extremes of temperature Extent and type of vegetation and wildlife; existence of on-site or proximity to wildlife breeding area, parks	Site 50 percent covered with beech, oak, sassafras, and dogwood trees Adjacent to 20-acre urban park
Surrounding land uses and physical character of area	Type of development: family or high-rise residential, industrial commercial, open space	Mixed: single-family, high-rise, and open-space area Density: about 60 dwelling units per acre in immediate site area
Infrastructure	Water supply, sanitary sewage and solid-waste disposal, storm sewers and drainage, energy and transportation	Site controlled by waste system and sanitary and sewer system; there is ample capacity Site on bus line
Air-pollution levels	Extent of pollution: smog, dust, odors, smoke, hazardous emissions	No obvious dust, odors, or smoke in site area Community has smog alerts in summer
Noise levels	Source: nearby airport, railway, highway	Project is on major arterial road, but noise exposure is minimal
Water-pollution levels	Ground and surface water: source of water supply, water bodies with implications for health and recreation uses	No streams are on project site; there are no bodies of water nearby
Community facilities and services	Description: location; relation to existing demand for schools, parks, recreational and cultural facilities; police, fire, and health facilities	Complete community facilities within walking distance of site (i.e., 200-bed hospital, library, museum, police, and fire station)
Employment centers and commercial facilities	Employment centers and commercial facilities servicing site	Site is 1/4 mile from shopping center, 1–1/2 miles from central business district

Continued

TABLE 4.3 (cont.)		
	Characteristics	
Condition to Be Examined	**Required to Be Analyzed**	**Example of an Analysis**
Character of community	Socioeconomic and racial characteristics	Mainly white, 30 percent African-American, 4 percent Hispanic, and 10 percent elderly
Existing aesthetic community	Aesthetic characteristics; proximity to historic, archaeological, or architectural site	The Historical Society is across the street from the site

On the other hand, creative solutions can at times convert a cost into a benefit. For example, an Allied-Signal Corporation plant in Metropolis, Illinois, created a veritable sea of calcium fluoride sludge as a by-product of its manufacture of fluorine-based chemicals. It was generating the sludge at the rate of 1,000 cubic yards a month. Analysis showed that the sludge could be mixed with another waste stream to produce a reaction. The result: neutralization of the waste and production of synthetic fluorspar that the company uses as a raw material at another location. The $4.3 million facility to accomplish these results saves the company about $1 million a year, an attractive return on an investment that also eliminates the problem of disposal of a growing stream of sludge.

BALANCING BENEFITS AND COSTS

Given the difficulties of estimating benefits and costs of many environmental programs, determining the balance is both difficult and controversial. Nevertheless, the net effect seems to be clear in some, although not all, cases. For example, the American public achieves substantial net benefits from the removal of lead from gasoline and from reducing the concentration of lead in drinking water. The benefits also exceed the costs of reducing the amount of sulfur dioxide and particulate matter in the air and cleaning up the worst of the hazardous waste sites. These environmental efforts share the common characteristics of reducing widespread threats to human health, especially mortality.[16]

Nevertheless, economists report that some environmental efforts generate more costs than benefits. These include much of the regulation of discharges into the nation's waterways (except for several badly polluted lakes and rivers), and many of the regulations, standards, and cleanup decisions taken under the Toxic Substances Control Act, Superfund, and the Safe Drinking Water Act. Imposing more stringent standards on new factories is counterproductive when it encourages companies to continue operating less efficient and more polluting old factories.[17] In these cases, society would presumably be better off by shifting resources from these programs to the ones that generate more benefits than costs.

GLOBAL ENVIRONMENTAL PERSPECTIVES

The United States is by no means the only country in the world to devote considerable resources to addressing environmental issues. Other industrialized nations have also attempted to curb pollution and protect endangered resources. Recent attention to worldwide concerns, such as ozone depletion, global warming, and the loss of biodiversity, has led to a variety of international agreements to deal with these issues. As a result, environmental factors are coming to play a significant role in defining how businesses and governments function on an international scale.

ENVIRONMENTAL POLICIES OF OTHER NATIONS

As was the case in the United States, the amount of environmental legislation enacted in Europe grew at an unprecedented rate during the 1980s and 1990s. Between 1989 and 1991 alone, the European Union (EU) issued more ordinances concerning the environment than in the previous 20 years combined. Businesses must now follow over 450 environmental regulations or directives, with approximately 100 new rules added yearly. By establishing community-wide standards, EU ministers hope to prevent individual national governments from using environmental regulations as obstacles to trade. Without uniform guidelines, nations with more stringent pollution controls would find their goods at a competitive disadvantage. They would face such unpleasant choices as reducing their environmental standards or violating EU agreements by excluding goods manufactured in countries with lower environmental requirements.[18]

For many years, Western Europe lagged behind the United States in environmental protection. The EU did not require catalytic converters on cars until 1992, a move this country made in 1975. Whereas the United States debates how tough wetlands protection should be, the EU has no law to protect wetlands—or to deal with the underground storage of hazardous wastes.[19]

Nevertheless, in recent years the EU has moved ahead. Some European nations have used "green" taxes in novel ways. Sweden taxes batteries, while Belgium has a special levy on disposable razors. Denmark, Finland, the Netherlands, Norway, and Sweden tax emissions of carbon dioxide, a major greenhouse gas—which helps to explain why the EU outpaces the United States in supporting firm targets for reducing carbon dioxide emissions.[20] Hosting the Kyoto Conference on Global Warming in 1997 gave Japan a strong prod to become a world leader in climate change.

The favorable environmental trends in the industrialized nations contrast sharply with the rising pollution in many developing countries. Large cities such as Lagos and Delhi lack the basic pollution controls instituted in the United States and the EU decades ago. In many developing countries, wastewater treatment is unknown and children dying of unsafe drinking water is a frequent phenomenon.[21]

THE UN AS A FOCAL POINT FOR REGULATION

The success of the UN-sponsored Montreal Protocol (1987) and the London Conference (1989) in curtailing global reliance on ozone-depleting gases has led to a number of other international accords. In total, over 200 multilateral agreements have been enacted since 1960, covering almost the entire gamut of environmental issues.

The most ambitious international effort on the environmental front resulted from the 1992 Earth Summit in Rio de Janeiro. The major commitment made was ratifying the UN Framework Convention on Climate Change, designed to return worldwide emissions of greenhouse gases to 1990 levels. In 1997, a UN-sponsored conference in Kyoto, Japan, agreed on binding targets for reducing emissions of greenhouse gases (see Appendix, "Policies to Respond to Global Warming").

Conclusions

Governmental and private efforts to reduce environmental pollution have been expanding in recent decades and, judging from the strong citizen support in most industrialized nations, that upward trend is very likely to continue. Simultaneously, more attention is being given to ways of achieving environmental objectives in the least disruptive manner and with a minimum use of society's resources. In large measure—although not entirely—the heated debates in earlier periods on the necessity for specific types of environmental regulations have been transformed into more positive discussions on how to develop ways of achieving a cleaner environment.

The multiplicity of environmental laws and regulations has tended to obscure underlying changes in the focus of governmental and private efforts to improve the environment. Three waves of change in these regulations have been identified. The first wave, during the 1960s and 1970s, was characterized by new statutes establishing minimum standards. This reflected confidence in government's capacity to influence business decision making via specific rules.

The second wave of environmental regulation, during the 1980s and 1990s, focused on taxes, trading systems, and other ways of providing economic incentives to improve private environmental performance. The third and most recent wave emphasizes the provision of more and better information on environmental impacts to foster improved decision making in both the public and the private sectors.[22]

APPENDIX

—◈◈◈—

POLICIES TO RESPOND TO GLOBAL WARMING

The most far-reaching environmental issue facing the United States today is how to deal with global warming (see box, "What Is Global Warming?"). Proponents of taking substantial action rely on a key passage from a 1995 report of the UN's Intergovernmental Panel on Climate Change (IPCC), an impressive group of scientists and government officials. That widely cited portion of the report's summary states, "The balance of evidence suggests that there is a discernible human influence on global climate." The report goes on to tell about the uncertainties that have been raised by scientists who have analyzed the complex global climate change phenomenon.[23]

Nevertheless, after taking account of all the *caveats*, a large portion of the scientific community concurs with the oft-quoted statement in the IPCC report and believes that the 1°F warming of the globe over the past century is likely to accelerate. On balance, the massive and unprecedented scale of CO_2 emissions into the atmosphere is a source of genuine worry. That the effects of those emissions, however measured, can be augmented by serious natural fluctuations (such as activity related to the Sun) underscores the concern over, as well as the continuing uncertainties involved in, developing global

<hr/>

BOX 4-3

WHAT IS GLOBAL WARMING?

Global warming is a scientific theory or scenario in which increased levels of atmospheric CO_2 are linked to generally rising temperatures around the world. The process is rather complex. Sunlight heats the earth, but the earth would be far cooler if not for the presence of water vapor and greenhouse gases in the atmosphere. These gases let sunlight through to warm the earth but trap some of the heat escaping back into space in the form of infrared radiation. In this manner, the gases act like the glass walls and ceiling of a greenhouse.

Increasing the level of greenhouse gases in the atmosphere is like using thicker glass in the greenhouse: less heat escapes. Many scientists believe that the CO_2 released by human activities is intensifying the greenhouse effect and contributing to an increase in the earth's

overall temperature. This general increase in the earth's temperature is commonly known as global warming and the potential effect on the environment may be substantial. Among the consequences predicted by some scientists are more rainfall, melting polar ice caps, rising ocean levels, and increased flooding. Other analysts emphasize the benefits of expected increases in farm production and milder winters.

The evidence of an acceleration of global warming is not conclusive, but most scientists who study the issue believe that it is occurring to a significant degree. Considerable uncertainty remains about the magnitude of the change, the precise role of CO_2 as a contributing factor, and the environmental and economic consequences.

<hr/>

warming policies. In 1997, 160 nations reached agreement (the Kyoto Protocol) in Kyoto, Japan, on a timetable for reducing emissions of CO_2 and other greenhouse gases (see box, "The Kyoto Protocol").

Many organizations have analyzed the economic impacts of meeting the Kyoto targets. Each analyst comes up with a different set of numbers, depending on the assumptions made and the model used to estimate the effects. One overriding point emerges from examining these impact studies: The costs of meeting the proposed "caps" on CO_2 usage will be substantial—ranging from tens of billions to hundreds of billions of dollars a year. Much would depend on the specific methods chosen to curb the energy usage that generates CO_2 emissions. Alternatives suggested range from a tax on the production of fossil fuel to a tax on the CO_2 emissions generated to stringent direct regulation of energy use.[24]

The major energy-using sectors would be heavily affected, notably petroleum refining, chemicals, paper, cement, steel, and aluminum—plus transportation. The electric utilities—most of which produce energy by burning fossil fuels such as coal and natural gas—would be directly impacted. Because the utilities serve virtually every part of society, the results of a substantial cutback in CO_2 emissions would be pervasive. Even before the Kyoto Protocol comes into force, private companies in four countries have voluntarily agreed to reduce substantially their releases of CO_2 and other greenhouse gases. These seven companies are working in partnership with Environmental Defense, a private organization.

One important aspect of the Kyoto Protocol is limiting the CO_2 "caps" to the industrialized nations. The developing nations will not be subject to limits on their fossil fuel usage for the foreseeable future. Some analysts worry that the reduction in

BOX 4-4

THE KYOTO PROTOCOL

The Kyoto Protocol requires the industrialized nations to reduce their average greenhouse gas emissions over the period 2008–2012 to about 5 percent below 1990 levels. The protocol includes the major greenhouse gases and takes into account changes in forest and land use patterns. It also contains the general elements of a program for international trading of greenhouse gas emissions. Such trading would rely on market incentives to help ensure that the lowest cost methods are used. The Kyoto agreement stops short of adopting a specific plan for trading reductions of CO_2 emissions.

The U.S. target is 7 percent below the 1990 level, slightly less than the EU's target (8 percent), and slightly more than Japan's (6 percent). None of the developing countries is required to set any limits. The United States, in contrast, would have to reduce its emissions by an estimated 25–30 percent below the emissions levels it would expect to experience under current policies.

Although the Clinton Administration signed the Kyoto Protocol in 1997, it did not send it to the Senate for ratification (the Senate by a unanimous vote stated that it would not approve the protocol if the developing nations were not required to participate in the emissions reduction effort). In 2001, President George W. Bush rejected the Kyoto Protocol.

energy use by the industrialized nations will be offset by the expansions of the developing nations who adamantly oppose limiting their economic growth by restricting the use of energy. They believe that it is unfair to expect them to cap their CO_2 emissions when their per-capita levels of energy use and economic output are still so much lower than those of the developed countries.

One suggestion for a global approach to reducing CO_2 emissions is to set up a "trading" mechanism similar to that developed under the 1990 amendments to the Clean Air Act. Under this approach, the industrialized nations could purchase "credits" from the developing nations. In turn, the money would be used to reduce the rapid growth of CO_2 emissions in the developing countries by such benign means as more efficient methods of producing and using fossil fuels and also encouraging them to use energy sources that do not emit CO_2 (such as water and wind power).[25]

The timing of the policy response to global warming is a key to the total costs that would be incurred. Gradually phasing in new policies minimizes the costs. A gradual transition means replacing the existing capital stock as it wears out with more advanced capital equipment that uses less fossil fuel. A crash program would require prematurely retiring much of the nation's capital stock.

Another, not mutually exclusive, alternative is for all nations to embark on a "no regrets" policy to do the sensible things that are desirable for domestic economic reasons and that would simultaneously reduce CO_2 emissions. Examples include eliminating the various tax and budget subsidies that artificially encourage the use of fossil fuels. Meanwhile, greater emphasis could be placed on improving the base of scientific and engineering knowledge to raise the efficiency with which energy is used. This could make it possible to reduce the costs of curbing CO_2 emissions.[26]

Notes

1. Gardner M. Brown and Ralph W. Johnson, "Pollution Control by Effluent Charges: It Works in the Federal Republic of Germany, Why Not in the U.S.?" *Natural Resource Journal,* October 1984, p. 935.
2. Robert W. Hahn, "Economic Prescription for Environmental Problems: How the Patient Followed the Doctor's Orders," *Journal of Economic Perspectives,* Spring 1989, pp. 104–106; David Roodman, *Getting the Signals Right* (Washington, DC: Worldwatch Institute, 1997), pp. 10–11.
3. Allen Kneese et al., eds., *Managing the Environment* (New York: Praeger, 1971), Appendix E.
4. Quoted in Frank P. Grad et al., *Environmental Control* (New York: Columbia University Press, 1971), p. 49.
5. "Environment and White House Policy," *New York Times,* July 31, 1996, p. A12.
6. See Frederick R. Anderson, Daniel R. Mandelker, and A. Dan Tarlock, *Environmental Protection: Law and Policy* (Boston: Little, Brown, 1984), pp. 135–143.
7. Richard Schmalensee et al., "An Interim Evaluation of Sulfur Dioxide Emissions Trading," *Journal of Economic Perspectives,* Summer 1998, pp. 53–68.
8. See James Lis and Kenneth Chilton, *Clean Water—Murky Policy* (St. Louis, MO: Washington University, Center for the Study of American Business, 1992), pp. 40–44.
9. The 1976 RCRA law contains an interesting finding: One of the causes of the rising amount of solid wastes is "sludge and other pollution treatment resolves" generated "as a result of the Clean Air Act . . . and other Federal and State laws respecting public health and the environment."
10. The public focus on pollution by business firms results, at least in part, from a strange omission in the Community Right-to-Know provisions: Government installations are exempt from the reporting requirements, even though some of the biggest polluters are federal agencies, such as the Department of Defense and the Department of Energy.

11. Gregg Easterbrook, "Environmental Doomsday," *Brookings Review,* Spring 2002, p. 3.
12. Robert J. Scheuplein, "Uncertainty and the Flavors of Risk," *AIHC Journal* 1, no. 2, Summer 1993, p. 16.
13. Wayne B. Gray and Ronald J. Shadbegian, *Environmental Regulation and Manufacturing Productivity Growth* (Cambridge, MA: National Bureau of Economic Research, 1993).
14. William D. Ruckelshaus, "'Not in My Backyard!' Institutional Problems in Environmental Protection," speech to the Economic Club of Detroit, April 15, 1984, p. 8.
15. Robert N. Stavins, "What Can We Learn From the Grand Policy Experiment?" *Journal of Economic Perspectives,* Summer 1998, pp. 69–88.
16. A. Myrick Freeman III, "Environmental Policy Since Earth Day I," *Journal of Economic Perspectives* 16, no. 1, Winter 2002, pp. 125–146.
17. Freeman, "Environmental Policy"; Howard K. Gruenpecht and Robert N. Stavins, "New Source Review Under the Clean Air Act," *Resources,* Spring 2002, pp. 19–23; Alan J. Krupnick, "Does the Clean Air Act Measure Up?" *Resources,* Spring 2002, pp. 2–3.
18. See David Vogel, "Environmental Protection and the Creation of a Single European Market," *Business & the Contemporary World,* Winter 1993, pp. 48–66.
19. Linda G. Stuntz, *Debunking the Myth of the Environmentally Ugly American,* a presentation at the M.I.T. Center for Energy and Environmental Policy Research, Cambridge, MA, April 30, 1992, p. 2.
20. "Taxes for a Cleaner Planet," *The Economist,* June 28, 1997, p. 84.
21. Easterbrook, "Environmental Doomsday," pp. 4–5.
22. Mary Graham, "Is Sunshine the Best Disinfectant?" *Brookings Review,* Spring 2002, pp. 18–19.

23. See *Common Questions About Climate Change* (Nairobi, Kenya: United Nations Environment Programme, undated).

24. See Stephen P. A. Brown, "Global Warming Policy: Some Economic Implications," *Federal Reserve Bank of Dallas Economic Review,* Fourth Quarter 1998, pp. 26–34; Robert W. Hahn, *The Economics and Politics of Climate Change* (Washington, DC: American Enterprise Institute, 1998); *A Guide to Global Warming* (Washington, DC: George C. Marshall Institute, 2000).

25. Henry D. Jacoby et al., "Kyoto's Unfinished Business," *Foreign Affairs,* July/August 1998, pp. 54–66; Warwick McKibbin and Peter Wilcoxen, "Climate Change After Kyoto," *Brookings Review,* Spring 2002, pp. 7–10.

26. Thomas C. Schelling, "What Makes Greenhouse Sense?" *Foreign Affairs,* May/June 2002, pp. 2–8.

5

ACHIEVING EQUAL
EMPLOYMENT
OPPORTUNITY

In a great variety of ways, government influences hiring and firing, pay and working conditions, training and retirement plans, relations with unions, and many other human resource practices of the private sector. Equal employment opportunity and related affirmative-action programs are among the most important of these government influences on the workplace. (Chapter 6 covers other government regulation of human resource policies.)

ADMINISTERING EQUAL EMPLOYMENT OPPORTUNITY

Government responsibility for eliminating job discrimination in the United States rests primarily with two federal agencies: the Equal Employment Opportunity Commission (EEOC) and the Office of Federal Contract Compliance (OFCC) in the Department of Labor.

THE AGENCIES AND THEIR MANDATES

Title VII of the Civil Rights Act of 1964 prohibits job discrimination on the basis of race, color, religion, sex, or national origin in all employment practices, including hiring, firing, layoffs, privileges, conditions, or benefits of employment. The law covers firms and labor unions with 15 or more members, joint labor–management committees for apprenticeship and training, employment agencies, educational institutions, and state and local governments.

The EEOC was established by Title VII to help carry out the 1964 law. The commission conducts its enforcement through the following procedure: People who believe they have been discriminated against file charges (see Figure 5.1). After receiving a charge of discrimination, the EEOC investigates to determine if sufficient evidence of discrimination exists. If so, the commission tries to persuade the employer to remedy the situation voluntarily. If the conciliation attempts fail, EEOC files suit in federal court. Court-ordered compliance with Title VII often results in large expenses to the employer, usually exceeding the cost of voluntary affirmative action. Expensive settlements are partly a result of the retroactive liability of the employer. A company can be held liable for an employee's back pay for two years prior to the filing of the charge and, if as much as two additional years are required to settle the case, the employer would be liable for four years' back pay.

The Labor Department's OFCC examines the antidiscrimination programs of companies with federal government contracts or subcontracts of $50,000 or more and

(PLEASE PRINT OR TYPE)

CHARGE OF DISCRIMINATION	EEOC CHARGE NO.	FORM APPROVED OMB. NO. 124-R0001

INSTRUCTIONS

If you have a complaint, fill in this form and mail it to the Equal Employment Opportunity Commission's District Office in your area. In most cases, a charge must be filed with the EEOC within a specified time after the discriminatory act took place. IT IS THEREFORE IMPORTANT TO FILE YOUR CHARGE AS SOON AS POSSIBLE. *(Attach extra sheets of paper if necessary.)*

CAUSE OF DISCRIMINATION

☐ RACE OR COLOR   ☐ SEX
☐ RELIGIOUS CREED
☐ NATIONAL ORIGIN

NAME *(Indicate Mr. or Ms.)*	DATE OF BIRTH
STREET ADDRESS	SOCIAL SECURITY NO.
CITY, STATE, AND ZIP CODE	TELEPHONE NO. *(Include area code)*

THE FOLLOWING PERSON ALWAYS KNOWS WHERE TO CONTACT ME

NAME *(Indicate Mr. or Ms.)*	TELEPHONE NO. *(Include area code)*
STREET ADDRESS	CITY, STATE, AND ZIP CODE

LIST THE EMPLOYER, LABOR ORGANIZATION, EMPLOYMENT AGENCY, APPRENTICESHIP COMMITTEE, STATE OR LOCAL GOVERNMENT WHO DISCRIMINATED AGAINST YOU *(If more than one, list all)*

NAME	TELEPHONE NO. *(Include area code)*
STREET ADDRESS	CITY, STATE, AND ZIP CODE

OTHERS WHO DISCRIMINATED AGAINST YOU *(If any)*	

CHARGE FILED WITH STATE/LOCAL GOV'T. AGENCY ☐ Yes ☐ No	DATE FILED	AGENCY CHARGE FILED WITH *(Name and address)*

APPROXIMATE NO. OF EMPLOYEES/MEMBERS OF COMPANY OR UNION THIS CHARGE IS FILED AGAINST	DATE MOST RECENT OR CONTINUING DISCRIMINATION TOOK PLACE *(Month, day, and year)*

Explain what unfair thing was done to you and how other persons were treated differently. Understanding that this statement is for the use of the United States Equal Opportunity Commission, I hereby certify:

I swear or affirm that I have read the above charge and that it is true to the best of my knowledge, information and belief.	N O T A R Y P U B L I C	SUBSCRIBED AND SWORN TO BEFORE ME THIS DATE *(Day, month, and year)*
DATE CHARGING PARTY *(Signature)*		SIGNATURE *(If it is difficult for you to get a Notary Public to sign this, sign your own name and mail to the District Office. The Commission will notarize the charge for you at a later date.)*
Subscribed and sworn to before this EEOC representative.		
DATE SIGNATURE AND TITLE		

Previous editions of this form may be used.

U.S. GOVERNMENT PRINTING OFFICE: 1973-728-451/1250
G P O 821.188

EEOC   FORM   JUN 72 **5**

FIGURE 5.1   EEOC Form for Filing Discrimination Charges

Source: U.S. Equal Employment Opportunity Commission.

50 or more employees. These companies are required to have affirmative action plans listing the specific goals and timetables for the hiring of women and minorities. If one division of a company has a government contract of $50,000 or more, the entire firm must participate in the required affirmative action program.

The statutes governing antidiscrimination guidelines are numerous and complex. Individual or class action suits can be filed against a firm under any one or a combination of the following laws and directives:

- The Fifth and Fourteenth Amendments to the Constitution.
- The Civil Rights Acts of 1866, 1870, 1871, 1964, and 1991.
- The Equal Pay Act of 1963.
- The Age Discrimination in Employment Act of 1967, as amended by the Older Worker Benefit Protection Act of 1990.
- Executive Order 11246, as amended by Executive Order 11375.
- Executive Order 11478, Equal Employment Opportunity in the Federal Government.
- The Equal Employment Opportunity Act of 1972.
- The Comprehensive Employment and Training Act of 1973.
- 1973 Amendments to the Omnibus Crime Control and Safe Streets Act.
- The Vocational Rehabilitation Act of 1973.
- The Vietnam Era Veterans Readjustment Assistance Act of 1974.
- The Pregnancy Discrimination Act of 1978.
- The Americans With Disabilities Act of 1990.

The regulations issued under these laws and directives cover a majority of the population (although with varying degrees of stringency): women and African-Americans; those of Spanish, Asian, Pacific Island, American Indian, or Eskimo ancestry; Vietnam-era veterans and the handicapped; workers between the ages of 40 and 64 (and most of those 65 and over); and members of religious and ethnic groups, such as Jews, Catholics, Italians, Greeks, and Slavs. These categories overlap significantly. However, the requirement for an affirmative action program covers many, but not all, of the categories.

Government contractors must maintain special efforts to recruit, train, and promote members of the following designated groups: African-Americans, women, Spanish-surnamed Americans, those with disabilities, and Vietnam War veterans. Other companies have been required to set up affirmative action programs when the courts have found them to have discriminated, and still others have established affirmative action programs voluntarily.

Each federal contractor and subcontractor with 100 or more employees and a contract in excess of $100,000 must develop a written affirmative action plan for the increased utilization of women and minorities. The requirements for an acceptable affirmative action plan include the following:

1. An analysis of the major job categories at each facility, with explanations if minority group members are "underutilized."
2. Specific goals, timetables, and affirmative action commitments designed to correct the deficiencies.
3. Compilation and maintenance of support data and analysis.

4. Special attention to six categories that the government has identified as most likely to show underutilization of minorities: officials and managers, professionals, technicians, sales workers, office and clerical workers, and skilled craft workers.

LITIGATION

Practitioners of EEOC litigation report that employers usually try to settle these cases out of court. The potential legal costs involved are a powerful incentive to do so, aside from the unfavorable publicity attached to the very institution of a suit. The interrogatories, motions, depositions, and hearings that precede trial of an EEO case can be expensive. In addition, there is the risk that an individual charge of discrimination will escalate into a costly class action suit. The data show the rising tendency for such expensive settlements to occur. In 1994, 7 percent of antidiscriminatory and sexual harassment suits were settled for over $1 million each. By 2000, 20 percent of the awards were for $1 million or more.[1] (See Table 5.1 for some large recent settlements.)

In 1997, Texaco formed a high-level, independent Task Force on Equality and Fairness to evaluate its progress in hiring and promoting minorities and to examine potential improvements in its human resource programs. The task force was part of a settlement reached with African-American employees who had sued the company on grounds of racial bias. In the case of American Express, the company also agreed to appoint a diversity officer, institute mandatory diversity training for managers, and by 2005 hire women for 32 percent of all new financial adviser positions.

The cost to shareholders in terms of the adverse consequences of news of an EEOC case on the price of a company's stock can exceed the amount that firms spend to settle the case. A study of 241 EEO cases between 1964 and 1985 estimated the average loss of equity value on the day a suit, decision, or settlement was announced at $29 million. The drop in the corporation's share value may arise from many causes, such as the expected costs of changing employment practices and the negative information revealed about the firm's management.[2] An offsetting factor is the concern that an out-of-court settlement may encourage employees to bring groundless suits.

SEEKING VOLUNTARY RESPONSES

The EEOC itself presses business firms to agree to sex and minority hiring goals voluntarily, without resorting to court action or the cancellation of federal contracts. Employers are asked to make what are viewed as good-faith efforts. The commission

TABLE 5.1   High Cost of Discrimination

Company	Settlement or Jury Award (in Millions)
Coca-Cola	$192
Texaco	176
Shoney's	105
Publix	85
Denny's	46
American Express	31

Note: Amounts cover settlements or jury awards against companies for racial or gender bias in hiring, promotions, or layoffs.

BOX 5-1

EEOC AFFIRMATIVE ACTION PROGRAM GUIDELINES

The following is from a directive of the EEOC: The most important measure of an affirmative action program is its results.

Extensive efforts to develop procedures, analyses, data collection systems, report forms and fine written policy statements are meaningless unless the end product will be *measurable, yearly improvement in hiring, training and promotion of minorities and females in all parts of your organization.*

Just as the success of a company program to increase sales is evaluated in terms of actual increases in sales, the only realistic basis for evaluating a program to increase opportunity for minorities and females is its actual impact upon these persons.

The essence of your Affirmative Action Program should be:

- Establish strong company policy and commitment.

- Assign responsibility and authority for program to top company official.

- Analyze present workforce to identify jobs, departments and units where minorities and females are underutilized.

- Set specific, measurable, attainable hiring and promotion goals, with target dates, in each area of underutilization.

- Make every manager and supervisor responsible and accountable for helping to meet these goals.

- Re-evaluate job descriptions and hiring criteria to assure that they reflect job needs.

- Find minorities and females who qualify or can become qualified to fill goals.

- Review and revise all employment procedures to assure that they do not have discriminatory effect and that they help attain goals.

- Focus on getting minorities and females into upward mobility and relevant training pipelines where they have not had previous access.

- Develop systems to monitor and measure progress regularly. If results are not satisfactory to meet goals, find out why, and make necessary changes.

SOURCE: U.S. Equal Employment Opportunity Commission.

does not view minority hiring goals as mandatory quotas, but it expects employers to take the kinds of actions that will enable them to reach the goals. The accompanying box, "EEOC Affirmative Action Program Guidelines," lists specific actions urged by the commission.

The influence of the EEOC has permeated the human resource function in many ways, including the nature of personnel selection via interviews and testing. At the job interview, general questions such as "Do you have a disability?" are considered unlawful. Questions must be limited to those specific disabilities that relate to a particular job to be performed (see Table 5.2). Formal testing has been reduced or abandoned in many instances because of the time and expense of demonstrating the validity and bias-free nature of the tests. The informal oral interview, however, may present other, less measurable opportunities for bias.

TABLE 5.2   Employment Interviews and Antidiscrimination Rules

Subject	What Employers Can Ask	What Employers Cannot Ask
Age	Are you between 18 and 65? If not, state your age	How old are you? What is your date of birth?
Religion	Nothing	Which church do you belong to? What religious holidays do you observe?
Race	Nothing	What is your skin color or complexion?
Sex	Nothing (unless directly job related)	Do you have a picture you can send us?
Disability	Can you perform the job?	Do you have a disability?
Name	Have you ever worked for this company under a different name?	State other names under which you have worked.
Citizenship	Are you a citizen of the United States?	Of what country are you a citizen?
Character	Have you been convicted of a crime?	Have you ever been arrested?
National origin	Nothing	What nationality are you or your parents?
Education	Where did you go to school?	
Experience	What kind of jobs have you held?	
Relatives	Do you have any relatives working for the company?	Are you married? Do you have children?
Organization memberships	Are you a member of any organization? (Exclude those indicating race, creed, color or national origin.)	List all societies to which you belong.

EFFECTIVENESS

A statistical analysis of corporate affirmative action programs by the National Bureau of Economic Research came up with ambivalent conclusions. The researchers reported that the goals were inflated and were not being fulfilled with the rigidity that might be expected of quotas. Moreover, the specific enforcement tools of the compliance review program appeared to be of doubtful utility. Nevertheless, employers that promise to employ more minorities and women actually do so.[3]

Some human resource experts point out that the employee database generated to meet EEOC and affirmative action requirements can also be used for the company's internal management efforts. One electronics company, for example, originally set up such a database, including five-year employment histories and job performance ratings, solely for EEOC work. But company managers found other uses for the information. Some analyze the characteristics of successful production supervisors and use that profile in making assignments. Others examine turnover factors. Compensation specialists study the company's merit pay system to see if it is undercut by automatically rewarding seniority. Some managers try—rules permitting—to target poor performers for layoffs during a business downturn instead of arbitrarily discharging some of their best people.

Despite its imperfections, the EEOC process has alerted company management to the special problems that must be faced in successfully developing and maintaining a diverse workforce containing persons of both sexes and of various races and ethnic backgrounds.

GUIDANCE FROM SUPREME COURT DECISIONS

Heated controversy about the legality and wisdom of affirmative action as social policy characterized much of the 1970s and 1980s. The newness of such efforts meant that a definitive body of law and judicial decisions was not available. The resulting uncertainty about what was constitutionally permitted intensified conflict over specifics. During the 1980s, the U.S. Supreme Court rendered decisions in several key cases. However, each decision came from a divided Court and left many important questions unanswered. In 1991, Congress passed a new Civil Rights Act that modified or superseded many of the later court rulings. The 1991 law provides a sharper emphasis on protection of minority concerns in employment and is the prevailing statute at the present time.

Although both Congress and the courts continue to wrestle with many difficult questions, two fundamental points are clear. First of all, overt discrimination is wrong and illegal. There is no question about that. The continuing controversy deals with what actions or inactions constitute discrimination. Second, there is a continuing role for affirmative action because discrimination and its legacy in the workplace have not been fully eliminated. The specific content of the role for that preferential treatment is still being developed, often on a case-by-case basis.

Justice Sandra O'Connor wrote in a Supreme Court case of "the tension between the Fourteenth Amendment's guarantee of equal treatment to all citizens, and the use of race-based measures to ameliorate the effects of past discrimination. . . ." Under the circumstances, it is useful to review the key cases and statutes that constitute today's policy legacy.

In *Steelworkers* v. *Weber* (1979), a white employee at a Kaiser Aluminum plant in Louisiana filed a complaint that challenged the selection of African-American employees with less job seniority for an apprenticeship training program. A collective bargaining agreement had set aside half the craft openings for African-Americans until the percentage of minority craft workers reflected that of African-Americans in the area's workforce. The white employee charged that this practice constituted a racial preference forbidden by Title VII of the 1964 Civil Rights Act. The Court rejected that reasoning, holding that the Civil Rights Act permitted the private sector voluntarily to apply a compensatory racial preference in employment. African Americans thus were given preference for admission to the company training program. In *Fullilove* v. *Klutznick* (1980), a 10 percent set-aside of federal funds for minority businesses, provided for in the Public Works Employment Act of 1977, was held constitutional.

These cases made clear that the adverse effects of racial preferences under affirmative action programs experienced by the rest of the workforce, sometimes referred to as reverse discrimination, are not by themselves sufficient grounds for invalidating such preferences—as long as the intent of those practices is to make up for past discrimination. But limits to affirmative action were set. In a 1984 decision (*Memphis Firefighters Local Union No. 1784* v. *Stotts*), the Supreme Court ruled that Title VII "protects bona fide seniority systems" even if that means minorities are laid off. The Court also held that it is inappropriate to deny innocent employees the benefits of their seniority in order to provide a remedy in a "pattern of practice" equal employment opportunity suit. Thus, layoffs of workers must follow seniority as specified in a union agreement—unless there are African-American employees who can prove they are victims of race bias.

In *Wygant* v. *Jackson Board of Education* (1986), the Court rejected the Michigan School Board policy of laying off white teachers before minority teachers with less seniority by a vote of five to four. However, the Court held that government might be allowed to give preference in hiring if the plans were narrowly tailored to redress past discrimination. This case, restricting the scope of affirmative action, was soon followed by another that went the other way. In *Local 93* v. *City of Cleveland* (1986), the Supreme Court held that lower courts have broad discretion to approve decrees in which employers settle discrimination suits by agreeing to preferential hiring or promotion.

In *Local 28* v. *EEOC* (1986), the Court again endorsed affirmative action. It approved a lower court order requiring a local of the Sheet Metal Workers Union to meet a goal for minority membership of 29 percent. It also made the union pay for training new minority members. The Court also held that judges may order racial preferences in union membership if necessary to rectify especially "egregious" discrimination.

The Supreme Court also upheld affirmative action in two 1987 cases. In *U.S.* v. *Paradise*, it affirmed a district court order requiring that Alabama promote one African-American state trooper for every white trooper promoted. The justification was to make up for severe past discrimination. Another strengthening of the legal foundations of affirmative action occurred in *Johnson* v. *Transportation Agency*. The Court ruled that public employers may voluntarily implement affirmative action that favors women over men in hiring even if the purpose is merely to change the balance of employment between men and women. No instance of overt discrimination need be involved.

However, in 1989, the Supreme Court demonstrated that the role of affirmative action had not been clearly delineated by the courts. In four cases, the Court reduced the scope of affirmative action. The decisions also triggered a backlash that resulted in the passage of the Civil Rights Act of 1991 (discussed later).

In *City of Richmond* v. *Croson*, the Court disallowed the city's set-aside plans that required that 30 percent of the subcontracts awarded for a public project go to minority-owned firms. The Court noted that the city's plans did not require a clear history of discrimination. *Martin* v. *Wilks* made it easier to challenge labor agreements establishing affirmative action plans. The Court ruled that employees of the Birmingham, Alabama, fire department could challenge a settlement on the grounds that they were not part of the original agreement. Thus, claims of reverse discrimination could be made. (This ruling was reversed by the 1991 law.)

Wards Cove Packing Co. v. *Antonio* was a key case reversed by the 1991 law. This ruling imposed tougher standards on employees trying to prove discrimination via statistics alone. By requiring signs of overt discrimination, the Court reduced the grounds for class action discrimination suits. *Patterson* v. *McLean Credit Union* affirmed an earlier ruling prohibiting discrimination in the private sector, but the Court also held that an 1866 civil rights statute banned racial harassment only in hiring and in promotion, but not in the workplace. (This decision was also reversed by the 1991 law.)

The Civil Rights Act of 1991 overturned the *Wards Cove Packing* case by placing the burden of proof on employers, making them justify practices that are alleged to adversely affect women and minorities. The law describes the circumstances under which employers can impose a requirement on or test employees (and prospective hires) without being accused of discrimination: Once a plaintiff shows that an employment practice has a "disparate impact," the burden of proof shifts to the employer.

Thus, the employer must justify the questioned employment practice as "job-related for the position in question and consistent with business necessity." For example, requiring a college degree for a given position, which may keep out a larger percentage of blacks than whites, must be justified for a specific job. Plaintiffs in discrimination cases must specify the hiring or promotion methods they consider to have a "disparate impact" on the workforce. Because the law avoids defining these terms, the courts have to decide, for example, what constitutes "business necessity."

DEVELOPMENTS IN EQUAL EMPLOYMENT OPPORTUNITY

The scope of equal employment opportunity legislation has been expanding over the years. The Pregnancy Discrimination Act of 1978 makes clear that discrimination in employment based on pregnancy, childbirth, or related medical conditions constitutes unlawful sex discrimination under Title VII of the 1964 Civil Rights Act. Thus, benefits from health insurance plans for sickness or temporary disability must be given to pregnant women.

Also in 1978 and again in 1986, the Age Discrimination in Employment Act was amended to restrict and ultimately ban mandatory retirement (with a few exceptions, such as workers in high-risk jobs and highly paid executives). In the words of one attorney, "It's very hard to convince a jury that a nice, white-haired man who lost his job after 20 years doesn't deserve something against the big, bad corporation."[4] Even casual asides—such as a supervisor referring to an employee as "the old man"—can be evidence of discrimination. Age discrimination cases are often linked with "wrongful discharge" of employees. The traditional "employment at will" (or "fire at will") doctrine has been eroded. It has become much more difficult for a company to fire a worker without demonstrating just cause and proper procedure—especially in the case of an older employee.

Sexual harassment on the job goes back to Old Testament days; Joseph was cast into prison when he would not lie with his master's wife (Genesis 39:6–13). The EEOC has issued guidelines forbidding sexual harassment of employees by their supervisors. (Excerpts from the ruling are contained in the box, "EEOC Rules on Sexual Harassment.")

In 1990, Congress passed landmark legislation to give disabled people increased access to services and jobs. The Americans with Disabilities Act (ADA) bars employment discrimination against people with physical or mental disabilities. It also requires access to public buildings, mass transportation, and government services for people who have disabilities covered by the ADA.

Considerable litigation has resulted from the vague wording of the law: What is a "reasonable accommodation"? What is an "undue burden"? What is an "essential" job function?[5] Many of the regulations issued under the ADA, however, are quite specific. Five percent of the rooms in a hotel and about half of the drinking fountains on each floor of an office building must be fully accessible to disabled people, including

╭─────────────────────────────────╮
                    BOX 5-2
╰─────────────────────────────────╯

EEOC RULES ON SEXUAL HARASSMENT

Here is an excerpt from EEOC instructions: Harassment on the basis of sex is a violation of Section 703 of Title VII of the Civil Rights Act of 1964. The Equal Employment Opportunity Commission (EEOC) has provided specific definitions of what constitutes sexual harassment: unwelcome sexual advances, requests for sexual favors, and other verbal or physical conduct of a sexual nature when (1) submission to such conduct is made, either explicitly or implicitly, a term or condition of an individual's employment, (2) submission to or rejection of such conduct by an individual is used as the basis for employment decisions affecting such individual, or (3) such conduct has the purpose or effect of substantially interfering with an individual's work performance or creating an intimidating, hostile, or offensive working environment.

In determining whether alleged conduct constitutes sexual harassment, the commission looks at the record as a whole and at the totality of the circumstances, such as the nature of the sexual advances and the context in which the alleged incidents occurred. The determination of the legality of a particular action is made from the facts, on a case-by-case basis.

Applying general Title VII principles, EEOC states that an employer, employment agency, joint apprenticeship committee, or labor organization is responsible for its acts and those of its agents and supervisory employees with respect to sexual harassment regardless of whether the specific acts complained of were authorized or even forbidden by the employer and regardless of whether the employer knew or should have known of their occurrence.

SOURCE: Equal Employment Opportunity Commission.

those in wheelchairs. The rules also prescribe how many parking spaces must be reserved for disabled people and specify the maximum slope of ramps and the maximum pile height for carpet—one-half inch. (A steep slope or a plush carpet cannot be navigated easily in a wheelchair.) Violators of the rules may be punished by a fine up to $50,000 for a first offense and $100,000 for any subsequent offense.

Many companies have tried to adopt a compliance mode that avoids generating ADA complaints (see Table 5.3). Since the enactment of the ADA, "hidden" impairments such as mental illness and back injury, as well as more exotic disabilities such as "multiple chemical sensitivity," have become the most cited impairments in charges filed against employers. Those not readily visible disabilities now exceed in frequency of charges the more familiar and apparent disabilities such as those involving sight, hearing, and mobility.[6]

In 2002, the Supreme Court narrowed the coverage of the ADA law. The Court ruled that, to qualify for protection, a person must have substantial limitations in abilities that are "central to daily life," and not only to life in the workplace (*Toyota Motor Manufacturing Inc.* v. *Williams*). The ruling overturned the finding of a federal appeals court that an assembly line worker who suffered from carpel tunnel syndrome was disabled in the "major life activity" of doing manual tasks.

In the aggregate, the employment rate of people who report that their disabilities limit the amount or type of work they can perform declined from 42 percent in 1990 to 34 percent in 1999—despite the strong economic expansion during that

TABLE 5.3   Corporate Efforts to Improve Treatment of Disabled Persons

Company	*Action*
Ford Motor Company	Tests managers' knowledge of ADA
Intermagnetics	Schedules meetings on ground floors
Nike	Adopted hiring policies to highlight contributions by the disabled
Mycogen	Eliminated requirement for lab workers to be able to stand for several hours a day
AT&T	Employs specialists to help disabled employees get necessary equipment
Qwest	Provides special headsets for blind customer service representatives
Pioneer Hi-Bred	Reviews job descriptions to conform with ADA
Sears, Roebuck	Lowers work platforms for wheelchair users

decade.[7] In contrast, the average employment rate for the same group rose when the economy grew in the late 1980s, prior to the ADA law. The reasons for the decline since the advent of the ADA are complex. Some analysts put the onus on the law itself, contending that its costly provisions have reduced the willingness of some employers to hire people with disabilities. Others contend that the simultaneous expansion of the government's disability benefit payments has encouraged some workers to leave the labor force.[8] The likelihood is that a combination of factors is involved.

It is useful to note that the ADA is an antidiscrimination statute, not an affirmative action program. In a 1996 decision, a federal circuit court held that "it prohibits employment discrimination against qualified individuals with disabilities, no more and no less."[9]

The Family and Medical Leave Act of 1993 requires employers with at least 50 workers to provide up to 12 weeks of unpaid leave a year to employees who are dealing with births, adoptions, or family medical problems. During the leave, the employer must continue to provide the health care coverage the employee had been receiving. After the leave, the employee must be taken back with no loss of job responsibility or seniority.

EQUAL PAY FOR COMPARABLE WORK

Women in the labor force in the United States, on average, earn only three-fourths as much as men. A widely held belief is that much of the difference results from discrimination. In partial response, Title VII of the Civil Rights Act of 1964 requires employers to pay equal wages to men and women working in the same jobs. That law was designed to end the practice of a lower wage scale for women for a given job.

The Wage–Gender Gap

The overall wage differences between men and women remain substantial, but the gap has been narrowing. In 1980, working women earned an average of 60 percent of the wages earned by men. By 2000, the U.S. Department of Labor reported that the ratio of women's median weekly earnings to men's had risen to 76 percent (see Figure 5.2). Although that still sounds quite discriminatory, those numbers are just the beginning of any serious analysis. Numerous choices made by men and women outside the work

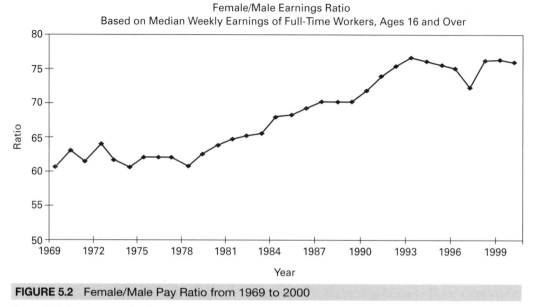

FIGURE 5.2   Female/Male Pay Ratio from 1969 to 2000

Source: U.S. Department of Labor, Bureau of Labor Statistics.

environment—such as those relating to marriage and child rearing—have powerful effects on differences in wages and other elements of compensation.

On the positive side, the greatest gains in relative compensation have been recorded by the youngest female age groups—a good indication of continuing progress. Controlling for education, union status, and other measurable variables, the earnings of women in the group aged 16 to 29 had risen to 92 percent of the male average by 1993. An even smaller adjusted wage gap between men's and women's earnings shows up when data are isolated for people who are childless. For ages 27 to 33, such adjusted women's earnings are reported to be approximately 98 percent of men's.[10]

Women increasingly are making the same kind of schooling and occupational choices as men. In 1999, the National Science Foundation reported that, on average, women engineers earned 13 percent less than the men in their profession. However, when controlling for years of experience (on average, women engineers have five fewer years of work experience), the gap fell to 3 percent.[11] Nevertheless, all of the analyses leave a gap, an unexplained residual that likely includes discrimination—as well as other factors not subject to direct measurement.

One indication that the "unexplained residual" will not quickly disappear is the extent to which women dominate the student body in the types of schools whose graduates take on the relatively low paying jobs. According to a 2002 study by the National Women's Law Center, the female preponderance in studies for child care and cosmetology was 97 percent in Illinois and 94 percent in Missouri. In contrast, men constituted the overwhelming majority of students for higher paying vocations such as automotive repair (94 percent in Illinois and 96 percent in Missouri).[12]

A relatively new response to the continued difference in earnings is the doctrine of *equal pay for comparable work*. The doctrine rests on the observation that certain occupations are filled predominantly by women and others mainly by men. For example, lawyers, physicians, and the building trades have been traditionally male occupations, whereas women have typically obtained jobs as schoolteachers, nurses, and secretaries.

Table 5.4 shows average earnings for occupations with the largest concentration of men and women. On average, the male-dominated occupations pay more than the female-dominated jobs. Yet, variations within and between the categories are substantial. Thus, the highest paid female-dominated occupation (registered nurses) is paid more than any of the five most male-dominated occupations (such as carpenters) and four times the lowest paid female-dominated occupation (child care workers). Clearly, many factors are involved in the determination of pay scales, including the differential pattern of unionization. For example, highly paid, male-dominated, blue-collar categories are heavily unionized, while low-paid, female-dominated occupations tend to be unorganized. The unions, perhaps not surprisingly, are in the forefront of support for comparable worth legislation.

Advocates of equal pay for comparable work believe that wage differences between male- and female-dominant occupations mainly reflect bias against women. Accordingly, they suggest reinterpreting Title VII to prohibit a lower rate of pay for employees of one race or sex for jobs that require an equivalent amount of skill, effort, and responsibility. Opponents of this approach maintain that relative wages result from the interplay of many other forces, especially "supply side" factors. Even in the absence of prejudice and when performed under conditions of equal skill, effort, and responsibility, the real market value of dissimilar work can differ markedly. Studies restricted to white males have yielded such results.[13]

TABLE 5.4   Male- and Female-Dominated Occupations, 1996

Female-Dominated Occupations	Percent Women	Median Income	Male-Dominated Occupations	Percent Men	Median Income
Registered nurse	92	$36,100	Aerospace engineer	96	$57,100
Speech therapist	94	36,000	Mechanical engineer	93	50,400
Licensed practical nurse	95	24,200	Electrical equipment repairer	100	37,100
Secretary	99	21,100	Firefighter	98	34,400
Dental assistant	98	18,700	Plumber	98	30,500
Kindergarten teacher	98	18,700	Crane and tower operator	97	29,000
Receptionist	97	17,300	Driver-sales worker	95	26,800
Preschool teachers' assistant	98	12,000	Truck driver	97	25,200
Maid	93	11,500	Auto mechanic	99	25,000
Child care worker	99	10,300	Carpenter	99	24,700

Source: U.S. Department of Labor, Bureau of Labor Statistics.

Market Effects of Wage Differentials

Economists point out that wage differences play a constructive role: They serve to guide labor into those occupations and locations where it is in short supply and discourage people from entering those in which an excessive supply is already available. Artificially forcing wage increases in occupations now filled mainly by women could increase the number of individuals preparing for careers in these occupations while employers would be reducing their demand for these now more expensive jobs.

The experience of high schools illustrates the problems of the comparable-worth doctrine. Historically, teachers are paid on the basis of years of service and level of education, ignoring the market forces that affect different specialties. The results have been uniform over the years: chronic shortages of math and science instructors and continuing surpluses of gym teachers. If colleges were to adopt the comparable-worth approach—and equalized pay across the various schools and departments—they would go bankrupt if they raised liberal arts faculty to the pay scales of medicine. Conversely, any attempt to bring down the salaries of medical faculty to the university average would cause an exodus of their teaching staffs.

Practical Problems

Washington State was the first government unit to make the concept of *comparable worth* operational. Its experience provided the precedent for other states studying or applying comparable-worth pay adjustments. Many of those states are in earlier stages, such as commissioning studies of their current pay structures. Several county and city governments also have adopted variations of the comparable-pay approach (or pay equity, as it is often called).

The Washington State government hired Willis and Associates, a job-evaluation firm, to examine and identify salary differences that pertained to job classes predominantly filled by men compared to job classes predominantly filled by women, "based on job worth." At that time, pay rates had been based on prevailing market rates.

The firm worked with an evaluation committee, composed primarily of Washington State employees, to rate jobs based on four factors: knowledge and skills, mental demands, accountability, and working conditions. For each job, points were assigned to each of the four factors and were aggregated to determine total job value. The Willis job-evaluation technique differed sharply from the market in its judgment of job "worth" throughout the range of occupations studied.

- A level IV registered nurse was worth 573 points, more than any other job studied, whereas a computer systems analyst received only 426 points. In the market, on the other hand, computer systems analysts are among the most sought-after and highest-paid workers. They earn substantially more than registered nurses.

- A clerical supervisor was assigned points equal to a chemist in knowledge and skills and was granted more points overall—whereas the market would pay the chemist significantly more than the clerical supervisor.

- Truck drivers were placed at the bottom of the new ranking system. They were given fewer points in knowledge and skills, mental demands, and accountability than the lowest-ranked telephone operators or retail clerks. The market—or at least union contracts—judged otherwise, paying the drivers far more than retail clerks.[14]

On average, the Willis job-evaluation system determined that Washington State underpaid women-dominated occupations by 20 percent. However, when Washington State sought the expertise of a second consulting firm, it found that job-evaluation studies varied substantially. The second firm, Jeanneret and Associates, examined the same set of positions and found that no disparity in compensation existed on the basis of "job worth." The second firm criticized the work of the first for:

> ... the failure to use expert job evaluators in the conduct of the study, the limited number of factors used in studying such a large, diverse employer, and the lack of objectivity in the scoring of job worth.[15]

These differences are symptomatic of the problems that arise when comparisons are made across states, even adjacent ones. As shown in Figure 5.3, a secretary is ranked first among the three jobs shown in Washington State and Iowa, but last in Minnesota and Vermont. A data entry operator places first in Minnesota but third in Iowa, whereas Vermont and Washington rank the job second.[16]

Alternative Approaches

Alternatives to "comparable worth" have been suggested for bridging the pay gap between men and women. One approach is to let existing policy work. An indication of the progress being made is the narrower wage gap for younger people than for older workers.

Change appears to be greatest in the professions requiring higher education — and slowest in the occupations with heavy craft union membership. For example, between 1970 and 1995, the percentage of women accountants more than doubled (from 25 percent to 52 percent) and the ratio of women to men lawyers jumped from 5 percent to 26 percent. During the same period, the proportion of women automobile mechanics and plumbers stayed at 1 percent.[17] Women as well as minorities tend to do better in newer and more merit-driven industries (computer software, entertainment, professional athletics) than in the more tradition-bound companies (insurance and utilities).

Nevertheless, there is evidence of the continued existence of the well-publicized "glass ceiling" on the advancement of women. In a study of the ten industries that employed the most women in the period 1995–2000, the General Accounting Office

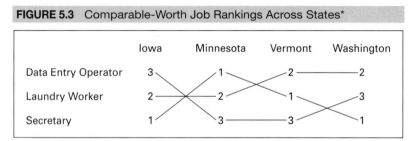

FIGURE 5.3   Comparable-Worth Job Rankings Across States*

	Iowa	Minnesota	Vermont	Washington
Data Entry Operator	3	1	2	2
Laundry Worker	2	2	1	3
Secretary	1	3	3	1

*Rankings are from 1 to 3, with 1 being the highest rated of the three jobs and 3 the job of least value among the three.

Source: Weidenbaum Center on the Economy, Government, and Public Policy, Washington University.

(GAO) reported that the gap between the salaries of men and women had widened further for managers in seven of the ten industries. The largest gain for women managers occurred in educational services, where the ratio rose from 86 percent to 91 percent. Although the GAO report did not adjust for years of employment and other relevant factors, the reported trend in the rates of pay for male and female managers surely is not a sign of progress.

Conclusions

On balance, serious studies of the benefits and costs of equal employment opportunity programs and especially of affirmative action programs come down on the positive side. Critics maintain that such interventions in the marketplace create divisive workplaces and often harm the intended beneficiaries, aside from the general objection to government intervention in the private economy. Nevertheless, the balance of evidence is that these programs produce tangible benefits for women and minorities and thus for the overall economy. One comprehensive analysis concludes that the relative number of women and minority employees has been increased by 10 to 15 percent. Women hired under affirmative action, the studies show, largely match their male counterparts in credentials and performance. Blacks and Hispanics hired under affirmative action generally lag behind in credentials such as education, but they usually perform about as well as other employees.[18]

Notes

1. Reed Abelson, "Surge in Bias Cases," *New York Times,* January 9, 2002, p. C1.

2. Joni Hersch, *EEO Law and Firm Profitability,* Working Paper No. 87/7 (Eugene, OR: University of Oregon, Department of Economics, 1987).

3. Jonathan S. Leonard, *The Impact of Affirmative Action Goals* (Cambridge, MA: National Bureau of Economic Research, 1984).

4. Sydney P. Freedberg, "Forced Exits? Companies Confront Wave of Age-Discrimination Suits," *Wall Street Journal,* October 13, 1987, p. 7.

5. Robin Andrews, "The Americans with Disabilities Act of 1990," *Cumberland Law Review* 21, no. 3, 1991, pp. 629–646.

6. Jack Faris, *The Americans with Disabilities Act* (Washington, DC: National Legal Center for the Public Interest, 1996), pp. 7–9.

7. Richard V. Burkhauser and Mary C. Daly, "U.S. Disability Policy in a Changing Environment," *Journal of Economic Perspectives* 16, no. 1, Winter 2002, pp. 213–224.

8. Daron Acemoglu and Joshua Angrist, "Consequences of Employment Protection? The Case of the Americans with Disabilities Act," *Journal of Political Economy* 109, no. 5, October 2001, pp. 915–957; John Bound and Timothy Waldmann, *Accounting for Recent Declines in Employment Rates Among the Working-Aged Disabled* (Cambridge, MA: National Bureau of Economic Research, 2001).

9. Cited in Faris, *Americans with Disabilities Act,* p. 25.

10. Diana Furchtgott-Roth and Christine Stalba, *Women's Figures: The Economic Progress of Women in America* (Washington, DC: AEI Press, 1999), p. 14.

11. Bhavja Lal, Sam Yoon, and Ken Carlson, "How Large Is the Gap in Salaries of Male and Female Engineers?" *Issue Brief* (Washington, DC: National Science Foundation, July 26, 1996), pp. 1–3.

12. James Collins, "Law Center Says Vocational Schools Steer Women to Low-Paying Careers," *St. Louis Post-Dispatch,* June 8, 2002, p. 29.

13. Jacob Mincer, "The Distribution of Labor Incomes: A Survey with Special Reference to the Human Capital Approach," *Journal of Economic Literature,* March 1970, pp. 1–26.

14. June O'Neill, "The Trend in the Male-Female Wage Gap in the United States," *Journal of Labor Economics* 3, no. 1, 1985.

15. Quoted in U.S. Office of Personnel Management, *Comparable Worth for Federal Jobs* (Washington, DC: U.S. Government Printing Office, 1987), p. 41.

16. Richard E. Burr, *Are Comparable Worth Systems Truly Comparable?* (St. Louis, MO: Washington University, Weidenbaum Center on the Economy, Government, and Public Policy, 1986).

17. Jane Katz, "Occupational Divide," *Federal Reserve Bank of Boston Regional Review,* Spring 1996, p. 17.

18. Harry Holzer and David Neumark, "Assessing Affirmative Action," *Journal of Economic Literature,* September 2000, pp. 483–568.

6

GOVERNMENT AND
THE WORKPLACE

The rising role of government in the workplace is a key example of the public's unwillingness to accept all of the impacts on society that result from the unregulated workings of the free market. Equal employment opportunity regulations and affirmative action programs by no means constitute the entire catalog of the federal government's involvement in human resource matters.

The Occupational Safety and Health Administration in the U.S. Department of Labor also takes important actions affecting the workplace. In addition, many other agencies, ranging from the National Labor Relations Board to the Pension Benefit Guaranty Corporation, play significant roles in setting and enforcing workforce regulations.

JOB SAFETY REGULATION

The Occupational Safety and Health Administration (OSHA) was created in 1970 "to assure so far as possible every working man and woman in the nation safe and healthful working conditions."[1] Congress provides several means—both voluntary and compulsory—for OSHA to use in fulfilling this mandate:

1. Encouraging employers and employees to reduce hazards in the workplace and to institute health and safety programs.
2. Establishing responsibilities and rights for employers and employees (mainly responsibilities for employers and rights for employees).
3. Authorizing OSHA to set mandatory job safety and health standards.
4. Providing an enforcement program.
5. Encouraging the states to take responsibility for administering their own job safety and health programs, which must be at least as effective as the federal program.
6. Setting up reporting procedures for job injuries, illnesses, and fatalities.

Compliance with OSHA regulations is enforced through inspections. These inspections may be triggered by serious accidents or employee complaints. Inspections can be aimed at "target industries" or "target health hazards," or they may be randomly selected workplaces. Target industries—those with injury rates more than double the national average—include longshoring, meat and meat products producers, roofing and sheet metal manufacturers, lumber and wood products mills, and miscellaneous transportation equipment producers. Target health hazards are associated with the five most hazardous and most commonly used toxic substances: asbestos, carbon monoxide, cotton dust, lead, and silica.

If, upon inspection, an employer is found in violation of an OSHA regulation, the violation is placed in one of the following four categories:

- *De minimis.* A very minor condition having no direct or immediate relation to job health and safety (e.g., lack of toilet partitions).

- *Nonserious violations.* A condition directly related to job safety and health but unlikely to cause death or serious physical harm (e.g., a tripping hazard). A penalty of up to $7,000 is optional. Such a penalty may be reduced by as much as 50 percent, depending on the severity of the hazard, the employer's good faith efforts, the history of previous violations, and the size of the business. Another 50 percent reduction occurs if the employer corrects the violation within the prescribed time.

- *Serious violation.* A condition in which substantial probability of death or serious physical harm exists, and in which the employer knew or should have known of the hazard (e.g., absence of guards on punch presses or saws). A penalty of up to $7,000 is mandatory. This penalty also may be reduced up to 50 percent for good faith efforts. The law requires a minimum penalty of $5,000 for willful violations. Maximum fines are $70,000 for willful violations, $7,000 for serious as well as "nonserious" violations, and $7,000 a day for failure to abate violations.

- *Imminent danger.* Where there is reasonable certainty that the hazard can be expected to cause death or serious physical injury immediately or before the hazard can be eliminated through regular procedures. If the employer fails to deal with the violation immediately, OSHA can go directly to a federal district court for legal action.

Although the OSHA regulations are designed primarily to benefit employees, the agency's efforts are aimed at employers. It is the employer's responsibility to assure that safe and healthful conditions exist in the workplace and to purchase equipment necessary to correct unsafe or unhealthy conditions. The employers must make sure that the employees adhere to safety rules and safe practices. For example, if an employee is instructed to wear a particular piece of personal protection equipment, such as safety-toe footwear, but fails to do so and sustains an injury as a result of this failure, the OSHA law requires that any penalty be levied against the employer. Contributory negligence by the employee is not a defense for the employer, nor is the worker cited.

REACTIONS TO OSHA

The Occupational Safety and Health Act was passed by an overwhelming vote in the Congress—83 to 3 in the Senate and 383 to 5 in the House of Representatives—clearly indicating strong support on the part of the public's congressional representatives. But, despite the obvious worthiness of the agency's objectives (who is opposed to safer workplaces?), the agency has been subjected to a constant barrage of criticism from almost every quarter: business, labor, academic researchers, and the media. Corporate and trade association executives claim that the agency's standards are needlessly burdensome and costly. Union representatives complain that OSHA is spread too thin and is not tough enough. Economists criticize the agency for not being cost effective.

Unintentionally, OSHA has been the target of an array of jokes about government incompetence. "Did you hear the one about the OSHA inspector who required separate 'his' and 'hers' employee toilets for a two-person business where the employees were married to each other?" "Did you see the OSHA regulation requiring that spit-toons be cleaned daily?" "Did OSHA really require a company to print its signs in both English and Spanish because it had an employee of Spanish descent (who only spoke English)?" Other continuing criticisms, however, have been far more substantive.

Economists contend that the agency is not effective in achieving its basic objective. The conclusions of a study by Thomas J. Kniesner and John D. Leeth are typical of aca-demic research: Large percentages of workplace accidents result from workers' care-lessness or momentary physical hazards such as wet floors. If every firm in the country were to comply fully with OSHA's standards, total injuries would be reduced by only 10 to 20 percent. The data on workplace fatalities illustrate the remote relationship between OSHA standards and many real-world hazards. Approximately three-fourths of all on-the-job deaths are caused by transportation accidents (notably on the high-ways) or by assaults and violent accidents (primarily homicides).[2] Formal job safety standards are not very helpful in most of these cases.

Labor-union representatives have criticized OSHA for administrative ineptness, extended delays, and in general not being tough enough. Except for a few large and highly publicized cases, the average OSHA fine is only a few hundred dollars. Moreover, inspections are infrequent. The average employer faces a visit from OSHA once in perhaps 66 years.

Many analysts contend that the inspection plus fine approach ignores the extent of market incentives for safer workplaces. In a competitive market economy, the riskier the job, the higher the pay, other things being equal. W. Kip Viscusi estimates that, in one recent year, the "risk premium" paid to workers in the private sector of the United States totaled $69 billion, or $925 a worker. Such large pay premiums provide a strong incentive for employers to make workplaces safer. OSHA fines come to a small fraction of the amount.[3]

Nevertheless, a study at the National Bureau of Economic Research reveals that OSHA inspections do significantly reduce injuries. This effect comes exclusively from inspections that impose penalties. Factories that are inspected—and penalized—in a given year experience an average 22 percent decline in their injuries in the following several years. Inspections that do not impose penalties appear to have no effect on injuries.[4]

A more powerful, albeit indirect, incentive to curb on-the-job accidents comes from the workers' compensation program. Surging medical costs have pushed outlays for workers' compensation to over $50 billion a year. The state laws typically require employers to pay 100 percent of the medical costs resulting from on-the-job injuries.

IMPACTS ON BUSINESS

OSHA has had a significant impact on company capital investments. Business firms in the United States devote more than $5 billion in plant and equipment outlays annually to meet OSHA requirements. Many manufacturing departments have revised their procedures to conform with the agency's regulations pertaining to air, noise, and heat. Although the cost of compliance rises, on the average, with the size of the company, the increases are not proportional. The smaller firms tend to bear a disproportionately large share of the expenses that arise from employee safety and health regulation. Larger employers benefit from the economies of scale involved in complying with

OSHA rules (and many other types of government regulation). They can afford to maintain professional safety departments that have the capability to keep abreast of the government's mandates and to learn the OSHA lingo.

The OSHA approach to safety regulation is based on the notion that employers can best prevent workplace accidents and disease. In a series of cases, the Occupational Safety and Health Review Commission ruled that employers should do more than merely make protective equipment available. Employers must establish an effective policy to ensure that the equipment is used and must continually monitor its enforcement to make certain that their employees are complying with it.

There are limits to a company's responsibility for employees' lack of safety consciousness. In one case (*Secretary of Labor* v. *Standard Glass, Inc.*) where the evidence demonstrated that the employer had done all that could reasonably be required to ensure that employees used their protective equipment, the commission ruled that the isolated failures of employees to use it were not employer violations. The commission held that the employer could not be expected to guarantee that all employees would observe good safety practices at all times.

Successful private industry safety programs place great emphasis on training, education, and awareness. Several consulting firms offer specialized training in jobs where accident data reveal specific hazards. When unsafe conditions or procedures are discovered at specific job sites, some firms issue safety alerts, warning managers of other divisions with similar working conditions. In job safety, as in other areas, information is a widely used tool in voluntary programs. Campbell Soup Company found that over one-third of its workers had developed carpal tunnel syndrome as a result of repetitive cutting and cleaning chicken for soup. The company responded by buying new equipment, developing exercise programs for its employees, and setting up a job rotation system. As a result, lost workdays due to on-the-job physical problems dropped 47 percent.[5]

BENEFITS OF JOB SAFETY REGULATIONS

Although it is useful to be aware of the problems encountered in regulating job safety and health, the benefits from a less-hazardous work environment should also be recognized. The advantages of a safer workplace constitute an incentive to business to minimize job-related hazards, even in the absence of government regulation. Many of the most important results of focusing on occupational safety and health are substantial but not readily quantifiable—at least not without making difficult assumptions about the value of an arm, of hearing loss, or of life itself. Nevertheless, we can identify the various types of benefits that can be expected. The following constitute the major benefits that accrue from enhanced workplace safety:

1. Greater productivity of those who would have sustained a job-related injury or illness in the absence of the effort to improve job safety.
2. Greater enjoyment of life by those who avoided work-related disabilities.
3. Savings of resources that would have had to be used in the treatment and rehabilitation of victims in work-related injuries or illnesses.
4. Savings of resources that would have had to be used to administer workers' compensation and insurance and to train those who would have been needed to replace the sick or disabled.

5. Decrease in damage to buildings and equipment.
6. Savings that result from less disruption of work routines, plus potential improvements in the morale and productivity of the workforce.

OSHA EFFECTIVENESS

How effective is OSHA? We can answer that question indirectly by examining the trend of workplace injuries and illnesses in the United States since the agency was created. Figure 6.1 shows that the total number of reported job-related accidents and illnesses declined substantially, from 11 per 100 workers in 1973 to 6 per 100 in 2000. However, the numbers of serious cases (those where the employees lost at least one day of work) did not show such a dramatic improvement. Lost workday cases actually rose from 3.5 per 100 workers in 1973 to 4.5 per 100 in 1979, before declining to 4 in 1989 and to 3 in 2000. The main point of these statistics is that, despite some progress, the problem of workplace safety has not been solved. Thus, analysis of the underlying question of job hazards is in order.

Researchers who have focused on workplace safety and health regulation almost uniformly conclude that the fundamental flaw in the OSHA approach is the decision by Congress at the outset to rely primarily on government-promulgated standards. In theory, such a decision would be made only after an analysis of the causes of job injuries and illnesses and an evaluation of the alternative methods to reduce them. But Congress did not spend time analyzing the causes and cures of occupational safety and health. In drafting the OSHA statute, no serious consideration was given to any approach other than regulation via the promulgation of government standards.

FIGURE 6.1 Occupational Injury Incidence Rates in the U.S. Private Sector, 1973–2000

Source: U.S. Department of Labor, Bureau of Labor Statistics.

Many safety professionals believe that OSHA's reliance on standards and its resultant emphasis on capital equipment clashes with their knowledge that workers' behavior is the prime determinant of accidents. One study estimated that only about 10 percent of injuries are preventable by enforcement of OSHA standards.[6] According to a report in a highly regarded medical journal, different employees working at almost identical jobs experienced exposures to lead that differed by ratios of up to 4 to 1. This was attributed totally to personal differences in working habits.[7] Hence, the role for training would seem to merit more attention than it receives under the traditional OSHA approach.

Management's responsibility is broader than that, however. An analysis of offshore drilling rigs concludes that the role of management is crucial. "There's no point in taking the companies with good safety records and beating them over the heads with nitpicking regulations. . . . If you're going to change safety offshore, you have to change the attitude of management in the companies where the safety record is poor."[8] (See box "How One Company Responds to Workplace Injuries.")

Two investigators attempted to determine if states with stiffer regulations and tighter enforcement had lower injury rates. Neither was able to show any significant effects. Moreover, other studies show that inexperienced workers have high accident rates. At lower production rates, there is more time for training and repairing equipment. Statistically, the turnover rate among workers is the most important single factor in determining injury rates.[9] During rapid expansions in production, characterized by new hires, there is more pressure on workers to produce and less time for educational efforts and machinery maintenance. Moreover, new employees tend to be less experienced, or their skills are rusty if they have been out of work for some time.

The Scripps Clinic reports that people are especially likely to make errors if they have not slept seven to eight hours within the previous 24 hours. Also, people are most likely to make mistakes between midnight and 6 A.M., even when they have slept seven to eight hours during the day.[10] Under the circumstances, there seems to be an important role in workplace safety for both training and for changes in work procedures.

The way in which a safe and healthful work environment is achieved is a managerial matter. Some companies reduce job hazards by buying new equipment; others initiate new work procedures. Still others do it by better training of workers and supervisors. Yet other employers provide financial incentives to their employees—for example, paying them to wear earmuffs instead of spending much larger sums on so-called engineering noise containment. In this vein, a U.S. district court barred OSHA from preventing a company's use of "personal protection devices" instead of the more expensive engineering controls. The judge noted that the company's current program of earplugs and earmuffs was more effective than OSHA's preferred alternative. The judge's order stated:

> Defendants [OSHA and the Secretary of Labor] must leave plaintiff alone in this issue, unless or until the Secretary can specify and prove the feasibility of some engineering or administrative controls . . . which will do as effective a job of employee protection as the present personal protection devices at comparable cost.[11]

BOX 6-1

HOW ONE COMPANY RESPONDS TO WORKPLACE INJURIES

In the first few years following the establishment of OSHA, Deere & Company, a large manufacturer of agricultural equipment, continued to experience a rise in accident rates. However, in 1974, the company shifted away from what it termed the "OSHA approach" to workplace safety, which focuses on compliance with standards. By 1987, the incidence of injuries and illnesses was reduced by 90 percent and it has since remained very low (see Figure 6.2). Deere's injury and illness rates are now one-fourth the national average. This improvement in employee welfare was accomplished by means of a four-point program:

1. *Create an accurate information base by which to identify and control hazards.* An extensive computerized data-collection program was developed that identified where injuries and illnesses were occurring by job classification, the nature of the injury or illness, the body part affected, the accident type, and the object that caused the accident.

2. *Focus available resources on the most serious and most numerous injuries and illnesses.* Deere emphasized preventing those injuries and illnesses that were contributing most substantially to its safety problem. It discovered that about 85 percent of its job accidents were due to actions, often unintentional, of individual workers—an aspect of the safety problem that it believed must be overcome by motivation and education.

3. *Recognize safety as a joint employee–employer responsibility.* Both supervisory and hourly employees pointed out practices that made jobs safer, and their suggestions were taken seriously.

4. *Recognize that safety is a sensible corporate investment.* Apart from moral or regulatory considerations, the economic rewards to the company resulting from a safer work environment were considered great enough to justify the safety program.

FIGURE 6.2   Deere & Company Injury and Illness Incidence Rate*

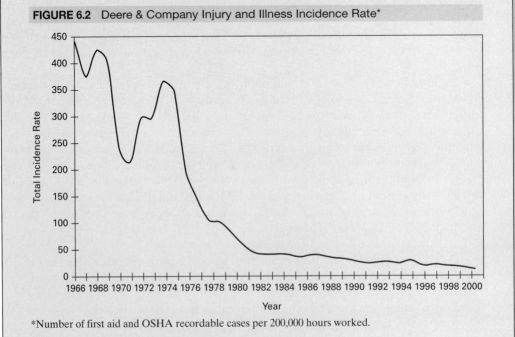

Year

*Number of first aid and OSHA recordable cases per 200,000 hours worked.

THE ATTRACTIONS OF PRIVATE ACTIONS

Tough enforcement of existing liability laws provides great incentive to management. Some state courts have held that companies can be charged with criminal action in connection with industrial hazards. In 1984, California's highest court affirmed a decision on a construction accident that declared for the first time that corporations can be charged with manslaughter.[12] The following year, a Cook County, Illinois, circuit judge found three top officials of Film Recovery Systems, Inc., guilty of murder for willfully working their employees under conditions that were literally deadly.[13] These cases gained the attention of many other companies.

Two sets of statistics help to understand OSHA's role as well as its limited effectiveness. For many industries, the lost time due to illnesses and injuries off the job far exceeds that due to on-the-job hazards. Exxon Mobil Corp., for example, states that nonoccupational diseases and injuries account for about 96 percent of the time lost due to disability. The OSHA-mandated efforts are thus limited only to the remaining 4 percent of the disability-caused absenteeism in that large company. Along the same lines, B. F. Goodrich reported that in one year its employees experienced almost eight times as many injuries off the job as on and missed work more than four times as often from off-the-job injuries as from those that occurred at work. For the nation as a whole, the National Safety Council reports that workers are four times as likely to suffer a fatal accident off the job than at work.

Table 6.1 contains some comparisons along these lines. The data demonstrate that some popular recreational activities are far more hazardous than employment. For example, approximately 40 deaths occur each year for every 100,000 people who go canoeing, while eight deaths are reported for every 100,000 workers in manufacturing industries—even though the duration of exposure is much greater for factory work than for the typical recreational activity.

Thus, attention must be paid to developing more cost-effective job safety and health standards. Consider OSHA's benzene standard. In that instance, the U.S. Court of Appeals set aside major portions of the regulation that would have required employers to assure that no employee is exposed to airborne concentrations of benzene in excess of one part per million over an eight-hour day. The court stated that it took such action because OSHA had not shown that the costs being imposed bore a "reasonable relationship" to the benefits to be obtained. However, the Supreme Court

TABLE 6.1   Variations in Hazards

Activity	Annual Projected Deaths per 100,000 Participants
Motorcycle racing	180
Horse racing	130
Automobile racing	100
Rock climbing	100
Canoeing	40
Power boating	17
Typical manufacturing job	8

Source: American Industrial Health Council.

subsequently ruled that the OSHA statute forbade even this simple form of benefit–cost analysis.[14]

It seems likely that the optimal mix of safety methods varies by industry, location, and over time. Elements of successful safety programs focus on private, rather than governmental, responsibilities. These include getting top management to recognize safety as an important business concern, involving workers as well as management, finding out more about the nature and causes of on-the-job injuries and health hazards, and focusing on the truly serious safety problems. (Recall Deere's favorable experiences.)

REGULATION OF PRIVATE PENSIONS

The regulation of employee pensions is another important area of government influence on workforce practices. There is a close connection between changes in federal law and the nature of company retirement plans. During World War II, many firms set up pension plans as a way to recruit skilled workers without violating wartime wage controls (fringe benefits were not subject to those controls). The extension of the income tax to working people with modest incomes also made non-taxable fringe benefits more desirable. As a result, private pensions grew rapidly during and after the war, with millions of workers enrolled. Table 6.2 shows that approximately nine out of ten professional and technical employees are covered by an employer-sponsored retirement plan and that better than five out of ten other workers have such benefits. The table also illustrates the wide variety of benefit programs provided.

TABLE 6.2   Percentage of Full-Time Employees Participating in Employee Benefit Programs, 1999

Employee Benefit Program	All Employees	Professional and Technical Employees	Sales and Clerical Employees	Service and Blue-Collar Employees
Paid holidays	75	89	77	69
Paid vacations	90	88	80	75
Paid sick leave	53	81	59	38
Long-term disability	25	48	26	15
Life insurance	56	76	54	48
Sickness and accident insurance	36	49	33	32
Survivor income coverage	3	5	2	3
Accidental death/dismemberment	43	61	38	37
Defined benefit pension	21	34	29	21
Defined contribution plan	36	56	34	28
Child care	6	12	5	4
Medical care	53	68	51	48
Dental care	32	49	30	27

Source: U.S. Department of Labor, Bureau of Labor Statistics.

ERISA REQUIREMENTS

After the collapse of a number of private pension plans, in 1974 Congress passed the Employee Retirement Income Security Act (ERISA). The main purpose of that law is to protect the rights of participants in retirement plans so that workers receive the benefits they have been promised.

ERISA is a complicated law with enforcement powers assigned to both the Department of Labor and the Internal Revenue Service. After the law's enactment, over 10 percent of existing pension plans were terminated to avoid the expense of ERISA compliance, and most of the remaining plans were revised to comply with the new requirements. Since then, many other companies have abandoned their traditional pension plans because of the onerous amount of paperwork and reporting requirements. About 10,000 notices of voluntary plan termination are filed each year, mainly by small employers.

The government's power to compel compliance with ERISA is very substantial. A company's contributions to its pension plan are tax deductible only if the Internal Revenue Service has approved the plan. Seven categories of requirements must be met:

1. *Eligibility.* An employee must be eligible to participate in the retirement plan when he or she is 25 years old and has worked for one year.
2. *Vesting.* Explicit regulations are established on the time it takes for an employee to earn the right to a pension. Once vested, the employee has a right to a pension at retirement even if he or she is not working at the company at the time.
3. *Surviving-spouse benefit.* In the event of the retired employee's death, the surviving spouse must receive at least 50 percent of the pension benefit.
4. *Funding.* Employers must fully fund their annual cost of the retirement program. They must also contribute an additional amount to amortize existing unfunded liabilities over a designated period of time.
5. *Fiduciaries.* Those who manage or administer a pension plan or those who give investment advice for a fee are placed under strict rules of conduct. They must act as a "prudent" person would in similar circumstances.
6. *Plan termination insurance.* The U.S. Pension Benefit Guaranty Corporation (PBGC) guarantees the payment of pension benefits should a plan be eliminated with insufficient assets to pay pension liabilities. Firms are liable for up to 30 percent of their assets if they terminate a pension plan that is not fully funded. The assets of PBGC arise from annual assessments on the companies covered by ERISA.
7. *Reporting and disclosure requirements.* Extensive reports on benefits are required of all employers, including a detailed plan description, a summary plan description understandable to the layperson, and an annual report.

The Labor Department is responsible for enforcing the portion of the law with regard to disclosure and fiduciary standards. Civil penalties may apply to disclosure violations. The Internal Revenue Service enforces the provisions regarding vesting, funding, and participation.

The paperwork requirements of ERISA hit small businesses hardest. Plans must be communicated in nontechnical language, but the plan summary has to include many technical items. Some employers solve the problem through duplicate communications. One publication explains the program in simple language and another in technical, legal language that will satisfy the law. Many smaller companies have abandoned defined benefit retirement plans (where the employer is committed to paying out a given level of benefits). From a peak of 90,000 in 1985, the number of such plans with fewer than 100 participants had declined to 20,500 in 2001.[15]

Many employers have shifted to a defined contribution plan, where the employer makes only a stipulated payment to the employee's retirement savings plan. The latter are often called 401(k) plans, referring to the pertinent section of the Internal Revenue Code. More workers and retirees are now participating in 401(k) kinds of retirement savings plans than in defined benefit plans[16] (see Table 6.2).

In addition to avoiding coverage by the PBGC, defined contribution plans shift the risk of loss from investments from the employer to the individual participant—who also receives the benefit of unexpected appreciation of the assets in which the individual's funds are invested. Although employees lose the protection of the employer commitment to pay retirement benefits, they gain the important advantage of enhanced portability (the ability to transfer the retirement account from one employer to another or to an Individual Retirement Account).

UNDERFUNDED PLANS

Since the enactment of ERISA, concern has focused on companies that lack the financial resources to meet their pension-fund liabilities. That problem plagues many labor-intensive companies in declining industries, many of which have gone through bankruptcy and have transferred their pension liabilities to the PBGC. The resultant burdens on PBGC have required large increases in the annual fees imposed on all covered employers.

The enactment of amendments to ERISA in 1987 and 1994 changed the basis of company premium payments from a flat rate to a variable premium that increases with the underfunding of a pension plan. The largest federal takeover of a private pension plan occurred in March 2002 when PBGC assumed control of three underfunded retirement plans covering 82,000 workers and retirees of bankrupt steel company LTV Corporation. The unfunded LTV pension liabilities are estimated at $2.2 billion. PBGC believes that the vast majority of companies are now maintaining well-funded plans. As of December 31, 2001, the agency's assets exceeded its liabilities by $7.7 billion.[17]

PRESSURES FOR CHANGE

For defined benefit plans, ERISA limits investments in employer securities and real property to 10 percent of the fair market value of the assets in the plan. There is no such limitation for defined contribution plans. The dramatic bankruptcy of Enron in early 2002 was devastating for many of its employees, much of whose 401(k) plans were invested in the company stock, which became worthless. Several proposals for change have been presented, including a bill to limit the portion of any 401(k) account that can be invested in a single company to 20 percent. Other proposals would make it easier for employees to sell the company stock held in their retirement accounts (see Chapter 20 for more basic reforms in corporate governance).

MINIMUM WAGE LAWS AND UNEMPLOYMENT

Raising the statutory minimum wage is politically popular because low-income people seem to receive more generous incomes as a result. (See Table 6.3 for data on the historical growth of this government requirement.) However, this conclusion is controversial, especially among economists. Most—but not all—studies of the minimum wage laws conclude that often the increase in labor costs is inflationary and also raises the overall unemployment rate, especially in the case of minority teenagers.

The basic economic problem arises because Congress can legislate what employers must pay if they hire workers, but it cannot legislate worker productivity. Therefore, people who do not produce enough to justify the minimum wage are denied jobs.

TABLE 6.3   Minimum-Wage Rates ($/hour)

By Year End	Non-Farm Workers Covered	Newly Covered	Farm Workers
1938	$0.25	$ —	$ —
1939	0.30	—	—
1945	0.40	—	—
1950	0.75	—	—
1956	1.00	—	—
1961	1.15	1.00[a]	—
1963	1.25	1.00	—
1964	1.25	1.15	—
1965	1.25	1.25	—
1967	1.40	1.40	1.00[b]
1968	1.60	1.60	1.15
1969	1.60	1.60	1.30
1974	2.00	2.00	1.60
1975	2.10	2.10	1.80
1976	2.30	2.30	2.00
1977	2.30	2.30	2.20
1978	2.65	2.65	2.65
1979	2.90	2.90	2.90
1980	3.10	3.10	3.10
1981	3.35	3.35	3.35
1990	3.80	3.80	3.80
1991	4.25	4.25	4.25
1996[c]	4.75	4.75	4.75
1997[c]	5.15	5.15	5.15

[a]Beginning in 1961, coverage extended to large retail and service enterprises as well as local transit, construction, and gasoline service stations.
[b]Beginning in 1967, farm workers (and some other occupational categories) were covered by the federal minimum wage law.
[c]A subminimum wage of $4.25 an hour is established for employees under 20 years of age during their first three months of employment.
Source: U.S. Department of Labor.

A compulsory minimum wage effectively outlaws some job opportunities, leaving a larger number of workers competing for a smaller pool of jobs. A study at the National Bureau of Economic Research estimates that a 10 percent increase in the minimum wage causes a 1- to 2-percent decline in the number of employed teenagers and smaller declines in employment for young adults.[18]

The impacts are compounded over time. By being denied the chance to work at low wages, young people are prevented from acquiring the skills, experience, and work habits that increase their value to employers. More than 65 percent of employees working at the minimum wage move on to higher paid positions within one year or less.[19]

Labor unions whose members are paid far more than the minimum wage provide much of the pressure for increasing the compulsory minimum wage. This may be a variation of the infatuation on the part of many business firms with government regulation as a means of protecting the "ins" from the "outs." In the case of the minimum wage, each raise means that some category of currently working employees will face less competition from unemployed people who are willing to accept a lower wage. Nevertheless, some studies show that raising the statutory minimum wage by modest amounts does not reduce employment. This would be the case if the major effect was to increase the supply of labor via a more attractive entering wage.

LABOR–MANAGEMENT RELATIONS

UNION REPRESENTATION

In most industrialized nations, unions represent large numbers of employees in bargaining with management over wages and working conditions. In the United States, however, before the Clayton Act of 1914, there were numerous, successful prosecutions of labor unions under the Sherman Antitrust Act, and earlier under the common law. Prior to 1914, any combination of workers was generally viewed as a monopoly. Not until the passage of the Norris–LaGuardia Act of 1932 did labor unions gain effective immunity from antitrust prosecution. That act removed the courts' power to intervene in labor disputes unless violence and property damage occurred.

The substantial unionization in the United States that has occurred since the 1930s makes it difficult to think about an economic environment in this country without a large number of powerful labor unions. Nevertheless, only a minority of the workforce is currently unionized (15 percent in 2000, down from over 30 percent in the 1950s). We can theorize, of course, about the economic effects of the union movement that now exists. Large, nationwide labor organizations attempt to limit employer access to other workers, thus reducing competition for labor. This is especially the case for firms operating under union-shop agreements, which restrict hiring to union members.

The elementary economics of unionized labor markets is straightforward: (1) The lessened competition among workers increases wage rates of workers in unionized plants; (2) the higher production costs that result—unless offset by rising productivity—lessen the demand for the products produced by unionized labor; and (3) hence the demand for unionized labor will be lower than in the absence of unionization.

The actual measurement of the gains to the employed union members and the losses suffered by unemployed union members and nonunion workers involves intricate theoretical and empirical questions. Inevitably, business firms make adjustments to the initial effects of unionization. Within the recruiting restraints that may be imposed, firms try to hire higher-quality workers and increase their capital–labor ratio. The lower turnover that results among unionized workers (encouraged by nonportable pension funds, special seniority provisions, and so on) and the resulting incentives for job-specific training increase the productivity of the unionized firm.

However, union work rules and union resistance to technological change reduce productivity gains: limits on the load handled by workers, restrictions of the tasks performed by employees in given occupations, requirements that unnecessary work be done, requirements for unneeded standby crews or crews of excessive size, and enforcement of limits on the pace of work.

The effects in any industry in any given time period may deviate from the general expectation. Labor unions have incentives to develop innovative institutional arrangements that inhibit the operation of the market forces that yield the results described above. For example, unions use an output tax in coal mining that reduces the effect of unionization on employment but intensifies the impact on product prices.

Other impacts of union activity are noticeable, such as the changes in the geographic distribution of production. The desire for more competitive labor markets has been a factor in the shift of industry from highly unionized urban locations to less unionized suburban and rural areas. In a broader sense, the same motivation exists in the shift of low-skilled labor production from high-cost areas such as the United States and Western Europe to much lower-cost locations in East Asia and Latin America.

The National Labor Relations Act and the major agency it established, the National Labor Relations Board (NLRB), govern many aspects of management dealings with employees and their unions. The board conducts representation elections at which employees decide whether they want a union to represent them in dealing with management. In an effort to protect the rights of union members, the law prohibits the following types of "unfair labor practices":

- Management interference with employee rights to join and participate in unions.
- Company domination of unions or interference with their administration.
- Discrimination against employees for union activity.
- Discrimination for filing charges or giving testimony to the NLRB.
- Refusing to bargain collectively with an authorized representative of labor.

Considerable controversy has arisen over many specific provisions of the National Labor Relations Act and the NLRB's interpretations. In order to avoid setting limits on employers' free speech, an amendment to the act declares that "the expressing of any views, arguments, or opinions shall not constitute or be evidence of an unfair labor practice . . . if such expression contains no threat or reprisal or force or promise of benefit."

In addition to collective bargaining with employers, labor unions also have attempted to use the powers of government to achieve their objectives. Some of these relate fairly directly to wages. For example, the Davis–Bacon Act in effect ensures that union wage rates are used on most federal construction projects.[20] As noted earlier, the minimum-wage law helps to insulate higher union wage rates from competition from lower-paid nonunion workers. Other government activities that have been fostered by unions include various income-maintenance transfer payments and benefit programs. Examples range from Social Security and unemployment insurance to workers' compensation and the establishment of OSHA.

As the unionized portion of the nation's workforce has declined, union attempts to influence government policy has risen. Part of the void left by the decline in union representation has been filled by the growing number of laws regulating employment practices. The number of such regulatory statutes grew from approximately 40 in the 1960s to over 150 by the 1990s. An accompanying development has been an increase in litigation before administrative agencies and the courts.[21]

The legislative wish list of the labor unions increasingly supplements the traditional collective bargaining agenda. These legislative desires range from OSHA reform to mandated health benefits to paid family leave. The increasing globalization of business has generated rising union efforts to include labor standards in international trade agreements. The effect of such action—strongly opposed by both domestic business interests and the governments of poor developing nations—would be to narrow the gap between wages in the United States and in nations with lower living standards and thus lower costs of production.

EFFORTS TO EXPAND MANDATED SOCIAL BENEFITS

Since the issue of reducing federal budget deficits became a serious public policy problem, many interest groups, including unions, have favored off-budget devices for achieving social objectives. Specifically, pressures have risen for Congress to require business to finance various employee benefit programs, ranging from child care to universal health insurance. As noted in the previous chapter, Congress has enacted mandated but unpaid family leave for several types of employee needs.

The impacts of social mandates are controversial. Many employers and economists argue that benefits packages are a zero-sum game, that mandating one benefit reduces flexibility in setting up a full array of fringe (nonwage) benefits. For example, a study of retail establishments in New York City found that, in response to a minimum-wage increase, many stores reduced commission payments, eliminated year-end bonuses, and decreased paid vacation and sick leave. A report on the restaurant industry revealed that, for every 1 percent rise in the minimum wage, restaurants reduced shift premiums by 4 percent, severance pay by 7 percent, and sick leave by 3 percent.[22]

Proponents of mandated social benefits believe that they are necessary to help reconcile a competitive market economy with the needs of a democratic society. They also consider such mandates to be comparable to the conservatives' privatization efforts to contract out government activities. In both cases, the performance of social functions would theoretically benefit from the greater efficiency of the private sector. Moreover, many companies that make liberal health and other benefits available to their employees favor the government's imposing comparable costs on their competitors—albeit via additional regulation. Compulsory fringe benefits rose more rapidly than business payrolls during the period 1960–1985. Since then, the portions of employee compensation devoted to fringe benefits has been fairly constant in the range of 10 percent (see Table 6.4).

TABLE 6.4 Compulsory Employer-Financed Benefits and Private Payrolls ($ in billions)

Cost to Business	1960	1970	1980	1990	2000
Social Security	$ 6	$ 17	$ 56	$ 140	$ 236
Medicare	—	2	12	34	67
Unemployment compensation	3	4	18	22	30
Workers' compensation	1	3	14	37	44
Total	$ 10	$ 26	$ 100	$ 233	$ 377
Private wages and salaries	$277	$427	$1,112	$2,229	$4,069
Compulsory fringe benefits as percent of wages and salaries	4%	6%	9%	10%	11%

Source: U.S. Department of Commerce.

IMPACTS ON HUMAN RESOURCE DEPARTMENTS

The growth in government regulation of the workplace has resulted in a comparable expansion in the size and role of human resource departments of businesses and other employers. The change is symbolized by the upgrading of the traditional personnel director to a vice president for human resources. In effect, a constituency for regulation has been created within the business firm.

In many companies, the business response to family issues has resulted in full-time positions to deal with the various problems that arise. The new jobs bear such titles as director of workforce partnering, family issues coordinator, program manager of work–life balancing, and manager of work–family issues. These new executives write rules for employee concerns such as leaves from work, flexible work schedules, child care, and family benefits planning.

Government regulation has forced many companies to focus more attention on how they manage their workforces and specifically on why they fire one person and promote another. Frequently, the success of the expanded staff offices is judged by their ability to learn to live with the rules issued by the EEOC, OSHA, NLRB, and other such government bodies and to keep their employers out of trouble with the regulators and the courts.

Regulatory agencies affect most aspects of company human resource policies and practices: hiring, promoting, and training activities; employee testing; compensation, including fringe benefits; the composition and funding of pension plans; the physical work environment; and basic work relationships, such as discipline, job termination, union negotiation, and communicating with employees. In some cases, a government agency has effective authority to approve or disapprove company actions (e.g., to decide whether company pension contributions qualify as a tax deduction). In numerous other situations involving requirements, which range from equal employment opportunity to the health and safety aspects of the job, federal agencies can and do file charges against employers.

The widening array of government regulatory legislation has required corporate human resource departments to expand their orientation and training programs. Supervisors, for example, need to be highly trained in many aspects of safety and health. Skills that are taught range from the ability to administer first aid to the leadership capability necessary to convince employees to use protective equipment regularly.

In response to regulatory requirements, companies have been hiring people with specialized capabilities: safety directors and engineers, industrial hygienists, doctors and nurses, and materials buyers with knowledge of protective clothing and hazardous equipment. Moreover, required reports and applications, such as hazardous-waste disposal records, necessitate inputs from many disciplines. As a result, companies find that they must either retain an array of experts on their own staffs or obtain technical advice via consulting arrangements. These specialists are involved in such fields as chemistry, ecology, economics, sociology, geology, climate, engineering, mining, forestry, and aquatic life, as well as public communications. Businesses also use specialized consulting services both to provide advice on meeting consumer product and employee safety standards and to provide more health services to employees (e.g., periodic examinations and return-to-work checkups).

FUTURE TRENDS

An important trend in workplace regulation is a rising sense of expectation among workers, professionals, and executives for more participation in decision making and greater protection of individual rights.

Labor unions focus attention on the economic aspects of the workplace, especially pay, fringe benefits, and working conditions. Other organizations are interested in such nontraditional or social matters as the confidentiality of employee records or other aspects of worker civil liberties on the job. Company managements tend to be ambivalent on employee rights issues, supporting the general notion but also concerned about the inherent reduction of loyalty and attachment to the company.[23]

One aspect of human resource management that overlaps both the standard economic concerns and the newer social concerns is the area of company freedom to terminate employees, the so-called "employment at will" doctrine. Most other developed nations require employers to have a "just cause" for firing an employee. However, in recent years, U.S. judges have been reducing the traditional right of employers to fire workers. This has led many companies to introduce, on a voluntary basis, formal systems to review proposed dismissals. The need for such procedures is underscored by the tendency of state courts to allow employees to sue their employers if they were fired for pursuing an action that was in the interest of public policy ("whistleblowers") or if their employer broke an implicit agreement.

Public policy in this area, as in many others, is driven by extreme situations. *Petermann* v. *International Brotherhood of Teamsters*, a 1959 case, set the precedent for the "at will" cases that followed. That landmark suit was initiated by an employee who was fired because he refused to perjure himself for his employer before an investigative body of the state legislature. The California Court of Appeals ruled that it would be contrary to public policy to allow an employer to discharge any employee "on the grounds that the employee declined to commit perjury." In subsequent cases, courts have ruled in favor of employees fired for serving on a jury or for refusing to participate in an illegal price-fixing scheme.

In 1987, Montana became the first state to pass a law requiring "just cause" for firing an employee.[24] In order to maintain the basic authority to fire employees, some companies are explicitly stating their right to terminate at will in the application forms that prospective employees must sign. There is a difficult balance to be struck between a company's right to fire incompetent people and the desire to cultivate a sense of loyalty and fairness in employee relations.

Notes

1. Occupational Safety and Health Act, Public Law 91–596.
2. "National Census of Fatal Occupational Injuries," *U.S. Department of Labor News,* August 7, 1997, p. 1; Thomas J. Kniesner and John D. Leeth, "Improving Workplace Safety," *Regulation,* Fall 1991, pp. 65–66.
3. W. Kip Viscusi, *Risk by Choice: Regulating Health and Safety in the Workplace* (Cambridge, MA: Harvard University Press, 1983); Joseph M. Johnson, Wendy L. Gramm, and W. Kip Viscusi, "Do Workers Want OSHA's Ergonomics Regulations?" *Journal of Labor Research* XXII, no. 1, Winter 2001, pp. 137–143.
4. Wayne B. Gray and John T. Scholz, *Do OSHA Inspections Reduce Injuries?* (Cambridge, MA: National Bureau of Economic Research, 1991).
5. Joseph Guinto, "What Price Workplace Safety?" *Investors Business Daily,* November 30, 1999, p. 1.
6. John Mendeloff, "The Hazards of Rating Workplace Safety," *Wall Street Journal,* February 11, 1988, p. 22.
7. M. K. Williams et al., "An Investigation of Lead Absorption in an Electric Accumulator Factory with the Use of Personal Samples," *British Journal of Industrial Medicine* 26, 1969, pp. 202–216.
8. David Jarmil, "Maintaining Safety on Offshore Drilling Rigs," *National Academy of Sciences News Report,* May 1984, p. 8.
9. Ann P. Bartel and Lacy G. Thomas, "Direct and Indirect Effects of Regulation: A New Look at OSHA's Impact," *Journal of Law and Economics* 28, April 1985, pp. 1–25; Wayne B. Gray and Carol A. Jones, "Are OSHA Health Inspections Effective?" *Review of Economics and Statistics* 23, no. 3, August 1991, pp. 504–508.
10. Merrill M. Mitler, "Punch the Clock, Hit the Hay," *New York Times,* January 11, 1992, p. 13.
11. "Judge Issues OSHA Noise Decision," *Insight,* August–October 1978, p. 10.
12. "Why More Corporations May Be Charged with Manslaughter," *Business Week,* February 27, 1984, p. 62.
13. Barry Siegel, "Murder Case a Corporate Landmark," *Panorama,* Second Quarter, 1986, pp. 55–65.
14. *American Petroleum Institute* v. *OSHA,* no. 78-1253 (5th Cir., 10-5-78).
15. U.S. Pension Benefit Guaranty Corporation, *2001 Annual Report* (Washington, DC: U.S. Pension Guaranty Corporation, 2002), p. 14.
16. Leora Friedberg and Michael Owyang, "Not Your Father's Pension Plan: The Rise of 401K and Other Defined Contribution Plans," *Federal Reserve Bank of St. Louis Review,* January/February 2002, pp. 23–34.
17. U.S. Pension Guaranty Corporation, *2001 Annual Report,* p 1.
18. David Neumark and William Wascher, *Evidence on Employment Effects of Minimum Wages and Subminimum Wage Provisions* (Cambridge, MA: National Bureau of Economic Research, 1992). But see also David Card and Alan B. Krueger, "Minimum Wages and Employment," *American Economic Review* 84, no. 4, September 1994, pp. 772–793.
19. "Rising Above the Minimum Wage," *Employment Policies Institute Edge,* June 2000, p. 1.
20. In one year, 302 of 530 area prevailing wage determinations were simply union rates rather than the result of wage surveys. See Morgan O. Reynolds, *Power and Privilege: Labor Unions in America* (New York: Universe Books, 1984), p. 136.

21. Thomas Kochan, "The American Corporation As an Employer," in Carl Kaysen, ed., *The American Corporation Today* (New York: Oxford University Press, 1996), p. 251.

22. William T. Alpert, *The Minimum Wage in the Restaurant Industry* (New York: Praeger, 1986), p. 101.

23. Archie B. Carroll, *Business and Society: Managing Corporate Social Performance* (Boston: Little, Brown, 1981), pp. 217–218.

24. Alan B. Krueger, "Regulation of the Labor Market," *NBER Reporter,* Summer 1990, p. 7.

7

TRADITIONAL ECONOMIC REGULATION

—⟨✦✦✦⟩—

Economic regulation—traditionally exemplified by that now-defunct industry regulatory body, the Interstate Commerce Commission—was considered virtually the entire field of regulation 30 or 40 years ago. This form of regulation, which still exists, is characterized by the use of independent, politically balanced agencies organized more or less along industry lines. These agencies attempt to regulate the behavior of the companies subject to their jurisdiction through the control of economic variables, such as maximum and minimum prices, the markets that a firm can enter and leave, and the type of service that it is permitted or required to offer. Major changes are occurring in this staid area of government activity. Moreover, as we will see in Chapter 8, this type of regulation is being cut back as the public learns that competition is often a more effective guardian of consumer welfare.

Simultaneously, antitrust enforcement—a mainstay of traditional economic regulation—has been undergoing a major reevaluation on the part of both practitioners and analysts.

INTRODUCTION

The most widespread use of economic regulation is at the state level, where public utility commissions continue to hold jurisdiction over electric, gas, and telephone utility companies. An example of the limited degree of economic regulation at the municipal level is the franchising of local cable television systems. There has been little outright deregulation by state or local governments, although many public utility regulatory commissions are experimenting with loosening the controls over prices and profits, especially in the case of electric utilities and telecommunications companies.

Examples of economic regulation at the federal level include control by the Federal Aviation Administration over interstate air transportation when it involves the use of aircraft above a certain size and passenger capacity; control by the Federal Communications Commission over interstate telephone rates and broadcasting licenses; control by the Federal Reserve System and the Comptroller of the Currency over the establishment and operation of certain types of banks; and the establishment of rules for issuing securities by the Securities and Exchange Commission.

As of the late 1960s, the industries subject to economic regulation by federal and state agencies accounted for about one-tenth of the gross national product. Thus, the great bulk of economic activity remained relatively unregulated, except for general standards of business conduct, such as the antitrust laws and the exercise of "police powers" by state and local governments over public health and similar matters. But that situation began to change fundamentally in the 1960s with the advent of the kind of social regulation described in earlier chapters.

ELECTRIC UTILITY REGULATION

Let us examine the area of state economic regulation that is most widespread and visible to the public: regulation of the electric utility industry. It will be seen that, even in this most traditional area of economic regulation, the combination of technological advance and economic incentives is forcing a modernization aimed at modifying regulation to provide a greater role for marketplace competition.

THE NATURE OF THE INDUSTRY

The electric utility industry in the United States began in the late 1870s as a street lighting and electric railway business, principally provided by private electric companies. Many small electric companies were formed, and an inefficient duplication and concentration of facilities resulted. In 1907, for example, 45 companies were serving Chicago, while in rural areas there was a lack of facilities.

Some municipally owned electric systems were established to provide street lights and to replace arc lighting systems during a depression period, when electric companies were unable to secure funds for expansion. State regulatory bodies began to establish service territories and to grant exclusive rights to sell electricity within these territories, along with the obligation to provide service for all who applied. Through the years, electric utilities have grown to become one of the nation's largest group of business enterprises.

Electricity service is customarily viewed as consisting of three parts: production of power, transmission of the energy over high-voltage lines, and local distribution for short distances over low-voltage lines to final consumers. Until recently, most private firms in the industry were vertically integrated, providing generation, transmission, and distribution services as a single firm or through separate companies controlled by the same holding company. As we will see, significant structural changes are occurring in the generation and transmission segments.

The federal government entered the commercial power industry only incidentally; electric power was produced as a by-product of irrigation and flood-control projects. Power not needed in the operation of the projects was sold commercially, with preference to municipalities. Later the preference was changed to "public bodies and cooperatives."

Numerous federal multipurpose projects, including power, were undertaken in the 1930s. The Tennessee Valley Authority and the Bonneville Power Administration were formed and became major commercial power enterprises. The federal government also provided loans and grants for the formation of new state and district power agencies and municipal electric systems. Rural electric cooperatives were formed with financing provided by the federal government's Rural Electrification Administration.

Currently, private electric companies provide about three-fourths of the electric power generated in the United States. The federal government's share is only one-tenth. The remainder consists of municipalities, state and district agencies, and cooperatives.

THE NATURE OF UTILITY REGULATION

The movement to regulate electric power resulted from two basic factors. First, consolidation in the early 1900s of competing utilities often produced price fixing. Second, most students of the subject assumed that utilities are natural monopolies and that attempts to introduce competition would increase unit costs by forcing duplication of costly transmission and distribution networks. (See Chapter 2 for analysis of natural monopoly.)

The principal solution to these problems, which evolved over a considerable number of years, is to permit franchised monopolies to operate under government rule making. Regulation is designed to serve as a substitute for competition so that the economies resulting from using a single supplier are passed on to the customers.

The primary emphasis of state regulatory commissions has been on regulation of rates, although their activities extend into many phases of company operations: granting the basic franchise, approving financing, establishing uniform accounting systems, auditing, validating costs, reviewing depreciation policies, and overseeing with reference to safety, adequacy of service, and impact on the environment.

On the federal level, the Securities and Exchange Commission has limited regulatory authority over utility holding companies. The Federal Energy Regulatory Commission (FERC) regulates wholesale rates of all companies operating in interstate commerce—typically, a utility in one state selling power to a utility in another; as a practical matter, this includes about 95 percent of the companies. The FERC also approves issuance of securities for some of the companies, prescribes accounting systems, requires extensive and detailed reporting, and reviews applications for development of hydroelectric projects on navigable rivers.

CURRENT RATE REGULATION

An important function of most state regulatory commissions—often the most crucial one—is to determine the proper level of return on investment, or profit, that can be allowed for the companies subject to their jurisdiction. This, in turn, requires that the commission validate the expenses of the utility and arrive at conclusions concerning the "cost of capital." The purpose of this validation process is to provide firms with some incentive to keep costs down. As noted below, many state commissions are experimenting with alternative ways of encouraging utilities to control their costs—and hence to restrain the rates they can charge to their customers.

Added to these tasks is the difficult job of verifying that prices charged to different classes of customers are reasonable and based on an equitable distribution of cost. The end results, the maximum allowable rates to be charged, are fundamentally based on two key objectives:

1. To protect consumers against exorbitant charges that might otherwise result from the monopoly aspect of public utility franchises.
2. To set rates for service at levels that will afford the companies an opportunity to earn a fair and reasonable rate of return.

In carrying out their functions, regulatory commissions are concerned that their current decisions maintain the capability of the regulated companies to fulfill their obligations to serve customers in the future. Thus, regulatory decisions attempt to take into account the long-term needs of the customers to be served and the capital required to provide the facilities to meet these needs. The long lead times that characterize electric utility plant construction mean that new facilities must be planned and financing arranged many years before the facilities enter into service.

The courts have consistently upheld the general principles of a reasonable rate of return on investment for regulated utilities. In the landmark *Hope* case (1944) the U.S. Supreme Court laid down the following guidelines:

> [I]t is important that there be enough revenues not only for operating expenses but also for the capital costs of the business. These include service on the debt and dividends on the stock. . . . By that standard the return to the equity owner should be commensurate with risks on investments in other enterprises having corresponding risks. That return, moreover, should be sufficient to assure confidence in the financial integrity of the enterprise, so as to maintain its credit and to attract capital.[1]

This sounds as though a substantial measure of financial protection is assured by law. However, public utilities are not guaranteed any specific rate of profit or level of earnings. This has been clearly stated by the Supreme Court in the *Natural Gas Pipeline* case (1942), when the Court said:

> [T]he utility gets its return . . . by rates sufficient, having in view the character of the business, to secure a fair return upon the rate base, provided the business is capable of earning it. But regulation does not insure that the business shall produce net revenues, nor does the Constitution require that the losses of the business in one year shall be restored from future earnings . . . the hazard that the property will not earn a profit remains on the company in the case of a regulated, as well as an unregulated business.[2]

Rate-of-return-on-investment regulation continues to be the dominant feature of electric utility regulation. However, quite a few state commissions have been experimenting with more flexible approaches to utility regulation, such as permitting utilities to vary rates within a stated price "cap" or a freeze on rates with profits above a certain level shared between the company and the customers.

Beginning in the early 1980s, state commissions began approving limited variations from traditional cost-of-service regulation. For example, the Alabama Power Company was given an "earnings deadband" under which it was authorized to keep the profits it earned within a designated range or "deadband." In turn, the company agreed to a moratorium on initiating new rate adjustment cases. Subsequently, the Public Service Company of Colorado was required to share its additional earnings with its customers if it agreed to a moratorium on requesting higher rates (thus the utility could keep a portion of the earnings in excess of customary regulatory norms). Similar arrangements were granted to Mid-American Energy of Iowa, the Mississippi Power Company, and Rochester Gas and Electric of New York State.

Electric companies in several states have been granted a combination of a ceiling or "cap" on their rates together with the ability to share earnings growth with their customers. Examples include Bangor Hydro-Electric of Maine, Entergy of Louisiana, the Montana Power Company, and the Narragansett Electric Company of Rhode Island. A number of variations from these new departures have been introduced.

A close variation is a rate freeze combined with profit sharing. Such arrangements were made in the case of AmerenUE of Missouri, New York State Electric and Gas, and Tampa Electric Company of Florida. San Diego Gas and Electric in California was given a revenue cap with profit sharing. The South Dakota Commission granted the

Black Hills Power and Light Company a simple rate freeze, while the Washington State Commission approved a price cap for the Puget Sound Energy Company.

In most cases, these variations from traditional regulation have been viewed as experimental and have been of limited duration. At times, a state commission has tried one form of performance regulation for a time and then shifted to another (see Table 7.1). For example, for the period 1995–1997, the Consolidated Edison Company of New York was given a combination of earnings sharing and a cap on revenue per customer. For the period 1997–2000, the utility operated under earnings sharing combined with a moratorium on initiating new rate cases. For the period 2001–2005, it has been granted earnings sharing with a rate freeze on transmission and distribution services. In the case of Illinois utilities, the combination of a price cap with profit sharing was modified by rate adjustments based on regional comparisons of average retail rates. By 2000, 28 utilities in 16 states were operating under some form of broad-based incentive regulation.[3]

UTILITY PRICING STRATEGIES

Whatever overall pricing strategy is followed, setting rates for specific categories of users presents difficulties to both the companies and the regulatory agencies. Efficiencies are involved in delivering energy to heavy users, such as the savings achieved by using high-voltage lines to deliver electric service to large customers. In contrast, residential customers require expensive and complex distribution networks. One recurring suggestion for change is to replace the present system of declining rates for greater use with a structure that more nearly approximates marginal-cost pricing. In other words, the user is charged according to how much it costs to deliver the last unit of electricity consumed in a given period of time. Such a structure would include peak-load rate differentials for both time of day and season of the year. This practice is defended on the basis of the underlying economics. The total cost per kilowatt-hour tends to decline with volume, as many items of fixed cost are spread over a larger number of units. In this approach, price is related to cost of service.

Another approach to promote the more efficient use of energy resources is to use electricity pricing to even out usage and thus reduce the need to build expensive new power plants. There is precedence in other industries for discouraging usage in peak periods, when production is more costly, and to encourage off-peak use, when the cost of production is very low. Many movie houses, parking lots, and other kinds of businesses set their prices according to the time of day in order to spread the use of their facilities in the most efficient pattern. Telecommunications companies do this by charging higher rates for long-distance calls in the daytime and thereby encouraging nighttime, off-peak use of their facilities. Similarly, many airlines offer lower "night-owl" and Saturday rates. Electric utilities have taken limited steps in this direction, such as charging lower rates for dusk-to-dawn lighting. Also, some companies promote electric heating in winter months by offering bargain rates in an effort to offset the summer air-conditioning peaks. Ironically, summer air-conditioning was originally encouraged by the utilities when their peaks resulted from winter heating demands.

Another suggestion for changing the structure of utility charges is to invert the rates, eliminating the discounts now given to large users and, to foster conservation, increasing a customer's unit charges as demand rises. Such a change would constitute a fundamental departure from the principle that prices should reflect marginal costs.

TABLE 7.1 Variations in Performance-Based Regulation of Electric Utilities

State	Rate Case Moratorium — With Earnings Deadband	Rate Case Moratorium — With Earnings Sharing	Price Cap — With Earnings Sharing	Price Cap — Without Earnings Sharing	Rate Freeze — With Earnings Sharing	Rate Freeze — Without Earnings Sharing	Revenue Cap — With Earnings Sharing	Revenue Cap — Without Earnings Sharing
Alabama	X							
California			X				X	
Colorado		X			X			
Florida					X			
Illinois			X					
Iowa		X						
Louisiana		X						
Maine			X	X	X			X
Massachusetts				X		X		
Mississippi		X						
Missouri					X			
Montana			X					
New York		X	X		X		X	X
North Dakota			X					
Oregon				X			X	
Rhode Island			X		X			
South Dakota						X		
Washington State				X				

Source: Compiled from data in David E. M. Sappington et al., "The State of Performance-Based Regulation in the U.S. Electric Utility Industry," *Electricity Journal,* October 2001, p. 75.

RESTRUCTURING ELECTRIC UTILITIES

The electric utility industry is being restructured by a series of legislative, regulatory, and organizational changes. At the outset, these developments were motivated by the notion that technological progress obviates the need for much of the traditional regulation of this sector of the economy. However, mixed experiences to date have caused some states to rethink their positions on the general subject of reforming utility regulation and to adopt a more cautious attitude.

Improvements in the technology of transmission have made spatial location of power generation less important, allowing producers at different locations to compete effectively in the same markets. The impetus for promoting this form of deregulation also comes from concern about the future adequacy of supplies of electricity. Many utilities have canceled or postponed new construction for a variety of reasons, including uncertainty about demand and operating costs arising from gyrations in fuel prices and adverse rulings by state public service commissions on charges for new capital costs.[4]

Under these circumstances, at times other firms can be in a better position to both build and operate power plants, selling the electricity to traditional utilities. This relieves the regulated firms of the risk of building plants only to find that they cannot recover the full costs from their own customers. The new competitors have the opportunity to earn more on their investments than utilities do because they are not subject to the same state regulations governing prices charged and allowable rates of return.

Moreover, the utilities' monopoly on power generation has been broken by several thousand small power plants that have been built as a result of the Public Utility Regulatory Policies Act of 1978. That law requires regulated utilities to buy the power produced by "alternative" generators of electricity, such as solar energy, even if the costs are higher than the power traditionally available to them.

The Comprehensive National Energy Policy Act of 1992 encouraged the entry of a new class of power producers—so-called exempt wholesale generators—to generate and sell electricity wholesale. That law also requires utilities to share their transmission lines. Thus, a utility in a high-rate state like New Hampshire can buy much cheaper electricity from West Virginia and have it delivered for a fee across regional transmission lines.

The success of the alternative or independent producers of electricity has inspired some utilities to set up subsidiaries to sell power to other utilities and to compete for contracts with large industrial customers. These subsidiaries are usually structured as joint ventures with independent producers of electricity. They tend to operate outside of the utility's jurisdiction and, therefore, are exempt from traditional utility regulation.[5]

Important advances have occurred in the technology of power transmission. Line losses, which increase with distance, have been sharply reduced by more efficient transformers. Major transfers of bulk power now occur over long distances. Utilities in the Southwest obtain power from Oregon and Washington, where low-cost hydroelectricity is available. Local utilities in different states are increasingly interconnected through regional power grids.

In turn, these organizational and technological innovations have spurred a variety of proposals for change (see Box, "Scenario for Deregulation of Electric Utilities—Present and Future"). As shown above, the electric utility industry is in the early stage of a deregulation process.

BOX 7-1

SCENARIO FOR DEREGULATION OF ELECTRIC UTILITIES — PRESENT AND FUTURE

PHASE I

1. Spin off generation from existing electric utilities, which have performed generation, transmission, and distribution.

2. Remove territorial restrictions on sales to distributors and large industrial customers.

3. Eliminate price and entry regulations in the generation of electric power.

PHASE II

1. Separate transmission from existing electric utilities, which continue to operate as franchised monopolies in the distribution of energy to end users.

2. Continue regulation of retail rates at the state level and of interstate power pooling and wheeling agreements at the federal level.

PHASE III

1. Eliminate federal and state price and entry regulation.

2. Encourage mergers among small wholesale power producers to foster more coordination and pooling.

3. Scrutinize under the antitrust laws all major mergers as well as memberships in power pools and joint ventures.

4. Require separation of electric and gas utilities.

THE CALIFORNIA EXPERIENCE

To date, the most extensive effort to restructure the electric utility industry has occurred in California. The negative experiences in that state have caused many other states to adopt more moderate approaches or to rethink departures from traditional regulatory patterns. Although the problems that arose may not have been inherent in deregulation, it is useful to examine the way that California carried out its attempted reforms.

In the late 1990s, California was facing retail electricity prices that were among the highest in the United States. It launched an ambitious program of industry restructuring and reforms designed to create competitive wholesale and retail markets for electricity. The utilities were required to divest most of their generating capacity and to buy power in the wholesale market at unregulated prices. Moreover, they were not permitted to enter into long-term contracts with wholesale power suppliers, thus increasing their dependence on the volatile "spot" market for day-to-day purchases.

Simultaneously, retail prices of electricity were rolled back approximately 10 percent and a four-year price freeze was instituted. For the initial period April 1998 to April 2000, the California experiment seemed to be working well. Prices remained low for consumers and the utilities were able to earn favorable rates of return. Then the "perfect storm" hit in mid-2000.

Drought conditions reduced the availability of hydroelectricity and natural gas prices began to rise nationally. The demand for electricity in the Southwest rose substantially (reducing the retail price of electricity was not exactly a conservation measure). As a result, prices in the spot market for electricity began to rise rapidly. The June 2000 average of $143 per megawatt hour was more than twice as high as in any other month since April 1998. With the freeze on the retail prices they could charge and a rapid rise in their costs, the California utilities faced a financial crisis. For some time, the state utility commission refused to lift its freeze on retail prices. The two largest utilities in the state became insolvent. The state government took over the function of buying electricity at wholesale, spending more than $1 billion a month at prices far above the maximum retail rates that the utilities were allowed to charge. Ultimately, the state commission relented, allowing rate increases and the Federal Energy Regulatory Commission placed temporary limits on wholesale prices of electricity. The crisis ended, although the state was burdened with about $40 billion of long-term wholesale power contracts that it had entered into with unregulated electricity suppliers.

The California experience with restructuring of the electricity industry cannot accurately be labeled "deregulation," although the term was widely used. Both the tight control on retail prices and the prohibition on long-term contracts for power were examples of new and onerous regulation. In many other states that have restructured their electric utility industries, the sale of generating facilities has been accompanied by contracts that required a certain amount of power sales back to the utility at a predetermined price, which helped to avoid the California experience. Economists generally conclude that the problems experienced by California were not inherent in deregulation. Rather, the shortcomings reflected primarily the manner in which government attempted to carry out the policy—plus a large amount of bad luck. All this was exacerbated by the likelihood that the wholesale market was manipulated (possibly illegally) by energy traders such as Enron as well as by the analysts who helped set up the state electricity grid.[6]

Some energy experts have gleaned some lessons for the future from the California experience:

1. Replacing regulation with a well-functioning competitive market is not easy. Some midcourse corrections are likely to be needed.
2. Consumers cannot be insulated from changes in wholesale prices.
3. The real benefits of electricity deregulation come from encouraging new investments in more efficient power plants.[7]

REGULATION VIA THE ANTITRUST LAWS

Competition is fundamental to a market system and to the private enterprise activity that characterizes economies such as that of the United States. Economists' suspicion of efforts by business to restrain trade dates back at least to Adam Smith's often-quoted statement, "People of the same trade seldom meet together, even for merriment and diversion, but the conversation ends in a conspiracy against the public, or in some contrivance to raise prices." Without vigorous competition, the private enterprise system probably would not attract and maintain sufficient public support for its continuance. In order to promote that objective, Congress has enacted three key antitrust statutes that outlaw attempts at monopoly and agreements in restraint of trade on the part of private firms.

THE DEVELOPMENT OF ANTITRUST LAWS

The term *antitrust* derives from a form of business organization (the trust) that was popular in the latter part of the nineteenth century. The trust was a device for pyramiding control over several operating companies. Key examples included the sugar trust, the tobacco trust, and—by far the best known—the oil trust (Standard Oil).

The Sherman Antitrust Act

The grandfather of antitrust law in the United States is the Sherman Act, passed in 1890. Its ringing language is noteworthy. Section 1 declares that "Every contract . . . in restraint of trade or commerce . . . is illegal." Section 2 states, "Every person who shall monopolize or attempt to monopolize any part of . . . trade or commerce . . . shall be . . . guilty."

The Sherman Act is primarily enforced by the Department of Justice, which initiates lawsuits against alleged violators. Such litigation may be either "criminal," aimed at establishing guilt and assessing fines or other penalties, or "civil," designed to secure court decrees requiring cessation of illegal practices or remedial changes in illegal situations. The trigger to government action is a "contract," "combination," or "conspiracy." In the absence of some cooperative conduct or joint action involving at least two separate companies, the act does not apply.

The real contribution of the Sherman Act has been to turn restraint of trade and monopolization into offenses against the federal government and to require enforcement by federal officials. Initially, the act was used mainly as a means to break strikes. In 1897, it was employed to convict a price-fixing ring. In 1904, President Theodore Roosevelt used it to justify trust busting. Since then, the act has been the mainstay of U.S. policy on competition.

A variety of specific business practices—many of which are legal in other western nations—may be found illegal under the Sherman Act:

- Agreements to fix or stabilize the prices or terms at which products or services are sold. In some industries, at times, there has been a widespread understanding that "gentlemen do not chisel on price."

- Group boycotts or concerted refusals by two or more companies to deal with a third company.

- Agreements to divide markets geographically or to limit the total volume of production or sales.

- Tie-in sales, wherein the seller has a dominant position in one product and requires the buyer also to purchase other products as a condition of sale.

- Reciprocal dealing, wherein sellers use their buying power to induce their suppliers to buy from them also. (But it is apparently legal for the federal government to require some of its suppliers to purchase special equipment from government facilities.)

Clayton Act

The second major antitrust law is the Clayton Act, passed in 1914 and amended on various occasions since. Under the Clayton Act, it is illegal to engage in several important types of business policies or conduct that might be conducive to monopolization or the restraint of competition—even though they do not violate the Sherman Act. These prohibited actions include price discrimination, exclusive and tying contracts, and interlocking boards of directors—where the effects of the practices "may be to substantially lessen competition or tend to create a monopoly." The Clayton Act is generally enforced either by the Department of Justice through direct court litigation or by the Federal Trade Commission (FTC) through its investigative and hearing procedures.

Federal Trade Commission Act

In 1913, Congress passed the Federal Trade Commission Act, which has been since amended. This act proscribes unfair methods of competition and, since 1938, unfair or deceptive acts or practices in commerce. The substantive prohibitions of the act against unfair competition are enforced by the commission, a quasi-administrative and quasi-judicial body empowered to make investigations, hold hearings, and issue orders requiring violators to "cease and desist" from their illegal practices.

Many unfair methods of competition or deceptive practices are illegal under the Federal Trade Commission Act. They include deceptive advertising, bait-and-switch selling techniques, harassment and untruths about competitors' products, inherently coercive marketing systems, deceptive guarantees, breach of contract inducement, intimidation, and commercial bribery.

However, several types of monopolies are legal in the United States. The federal government grants inventors patent monopolies for a period of 17 years. State governments, as noted earlier, grant monopoly franchises to regulated public utilities such as telephone, gas, and electricity suppliers. Local governments franchise noncompeting cable television stations.

Moreover, all levels of government operate commercial enterprises while prohibiting private firms from competing with them. The U.S. Postal Service is the largest example. The federal government's Express Mail statutes prohibit private carriers from offering first-class mail delivery service. Several states operate retail liquor stores on a monopoly basis. Quite a few localities own and run their own electric or gas utilities, again with no competition.

It is interesting to note that the original justification for antitrust laws was not to protect consumers but to help weak competitors. During the congressional debate on the Sherman Act, the following argument was made by a leading proponent:

> [T]rusts have made products cheaper, have reduced prices; but if the price of oil were reduced to one cent a barrel, it would not right the wrong done by the trusts which have destroyed legitimate competition and driven honest men from legitimate business enterprises.[8]

GOALS OF ANTITRUST

Two conflicting viewpoints dominate economic theorizing on antitrust. One (often called the *efficiency approach*) claims that the only legitimate goal of antitrust is consumer welfare, which is equivalent to economic efficiency.[9] Because some consumers benefit from the economies stemming from a merger, society as a whole also benefits. Mergers eliminate duplication and generate cost savings difficult to obtain from internal growth. The savings can be passed on in the form of reduced prices, resources saved, and stockholder gains.

Adherents of the efficiency approach believe that antitrust policy should not favor one group of consumers (buyers) over another group (stockholders). Thus, the correct goal is seen as economic efficiency, under which society can maximize the size of the pie without regard to considerations of income distribution or redistribution. Some of the newest thinking along these lines notes the importance of competition policy fostering innovation, rather than focusing exclusively on price.[10]

An alternative view is the *competitive approach*. Its proponents believe that the intent of the Sherman Act is to establish the right for buyers to pay no more than the competitive price. Thus, any merger that raises prices transfers money from buyers to sellers (primarily stockholders).

In general, improved economic efficiency resulting from a merger will result in either (1) lower prices and increased profits or (2) if market power is enhanced in the process, higher prices and small cost savings. In the case of higher prices and cost savings, profits could rise more than the increase in price (expenditure) to the buyers. The efficiency approach would allow such a merger because shareholder gains are greater than buyer losses. In contrast, the competitive approach would oppose such a merger, favoring buyers over stockholders. The counterargument is that such action may benefit buyers, but it lowers aggregate consumer wealth by preventing the economy from operating more efficiently.

MARKET VERSUS STRUCTURAL APPROACHES

Antitrust policy is more than a series of statutes and judicial decisions. It represents a political and social philosophy, and interpretations of the support for that philosophy vary considerably. Practitioners and analysts who adhere to a *market* or competitive view of the antitrust process generally believe that current laws should be enforced to allow the economic system to operate closely to the free market norm.

In this view, antitrust is the antithesis of regulation. Its objective is to maintain markets sufficiently competitive that they will regulate themselves. Proponents of the market approach view laws prohibiting price fixing as merely requiring firms to conform with the model of a competitive market economy. With varying degrees of enthusiasm, they support the laws controlling mergers and attempts to monopolize, although increasingly they question their need and effectiveness. This approach does not regard large enterprises as inherently bad so long as they have evolved as a result of the operation of natural economic forces.

Market Enthusiasts

A small but growing minority holding the market viewpoint has grown totally disenchanted with the notion of antitrust laws. This group notes a part of Adam Smith's *Wealth of Nations* that is rarely quoted: "It is impossible indeed to prevent such meeting [of 'people of the same trade'], by any law which either could be executed, or would be consistent with liberty and justice." Thus, the most adamant holders of the market position believe that the most dangerous sort of market power is that which emerges from government-granted protection. In contrast with the traditional market or competitive view of the antitrust laws, these critics from the right would allow liberal amounts of price discrimination and tying agreements and would not impede conglomerate mergers or vertical integration in most markets. They generally defend internal growth even if it results in a more concentrated market structure.[11]

Most holders of the market or competitive approach believe that corporate expansion is the reward for outperforming competitors and that such growth benefits consumers. Many large enterprises, they contend, benefit from economies of scale and greater innovation through investments in research and development, which raise productivity and keep prices down.

Some studies do tend to show that profits are related more closely to market share than to degree of concentration of the market.[12] Thus, it seems that higher profits associated with a larger market share are correlated with lower costs, rather than with higher prices. Profits of oligopolists may be more likely attributed to efficiency than to collusion. High concentration ratios may be more an indication of virtue than a sign of vice. In this view, using the antitrust laws to break up such companies would destroy the benefits that competition itself has produced.

To summarize the market viewpoint, large companies have gotten big because they are effective at meeting customers' desires, not because they are successful at ripping off consumers. The top 100 corporations in the United States now hold a smaller percentage of business assets than was the case in 1970. So do the top 200.

Structuralists

On the other hand, those who take a *structural* view of the antitrust process believe that these laws should be used to reorganize the economy. Many structuralists believe that if companies grow too large, they are no longer subject to the discipline of competition. Like the proponents of the market or competitive approach, the structuralists have a range of viewpoints. Some believe that bigness by itself is bad and that the power of large corporations should be curtailed drastically. When then FTC Chairman Michael Pertschuk was asked by a congressional committee if he thought "bigness is necessarily bad," he replied, "Actually, I do." Pertschuk defended this view of antitrust by contending that antitrust does not merely deal with the allocation of resources, "but of power."[13]

The structuralists contend that large companies not only produce adverse economic consequences but also exercise excessive social and political power (see Chapter 19 for examples of the campaign contributions of large corporations). Other structuralists advocate reorganization of certain important segments of the economy. They are not necessarily opposed to bigness as such, but only to very large corporations that control a dominant share of a given market. They point, for instance, to several major industries (such as aluminum and automobile production) where the sales of three or fewer companies comprise a major share of the domestic market, ranging from 50 percent upward.

It is claimed that such industry leaders have discretion to set prices and target profit margins where they wish and have the power to drive new competitors out of the market or at least keep them small. However, there is considerable dispute among economists over the patterns of profits, prices, and innovation in concentrated industries. Some of the structuralist economists find that the large firms in concentrated industries earn higher rates of return on investment. More market-oriented economists tend to find no evidence of this relationship and also note the increasingly global nature of the markets in which large U.S. corporations compete.

From the structuralist viewpoint, antitrust enforcement is not controlling the adverse effects of concentrated industries. Those who hold this view condemn the fact that many industry leaders are increasing their market shares through internal growth and through mergers and acquisitions.

ANTITRUST POLICY IN RECENT ADMINISTRATIONS

The Reagan Administration followed the market or competitive approach. In 1982, the Antitrust Division of the Justice Department replaced a simple standard established in 1968 that generally held that a merger was suspect if it resulted in an industry in which four or fewer companies held 60 percent of the market. The revised rules applied a formula (the Herfindahl Index) that measures competition by taking account of both the total number of firms serving a market and the relative power they wield, giving proportionately greater weight to the larger companies (see Table 7.2).[14]

A merger likely would be permitted if it created an industry in which four equally sized competitors controlled 60 percent of the market while an additional 40 firms controlled 1 percent each. If, on the other hand, a merger created one firm with 57 percent of the market, it might be challenged immediately, even though the dominant firm still had 43 competitors. This approach focuses the administration of the antitrust laws on those company actions that directly inhibit price competition.

In 1984, the Justice Department revised its merger guidelines to give greater consideration to various judgmental factors, such as efficiency claims, imports, barriers to new entrants, and the problems of declining industries. Under the revised merger guidelines, the Justice Department is not expected to try to stop or reverse a merger if entry into a market is easy, regardless of the degree of market concentration in the industry or the market shares of the merging partners.

In 1992, the Department of Justice and the FTC jointly issued revised Horizontal Merger Guidelines, which were a modest modification of the 1984 version. The major innovation was to substantially reduce the possibility that either agency would challenge a proposed merger that is unlikely to injure competition. Antitrust enforcement officials were expected to look beyond the raw concentration data and attempt to ascertain the practical impact of the merger on competition. Several very large horizontal combinations were carried out during the Reagan and subsequent presidencies. Such agreements would undoubtedly have met stiffer challenges in previous years.

TABLE 7.2   Alternate Measures of Market Concentration

Company Rank	Traditional Method (Market Share)	Herfindahl Index (Market Share Squared)
1	18%	324
2	16	256
3	10	100
4	9	81
5	7	49
6	6	36
7	5	25
8	4	16
9	4	16
10	4	16
Total	83%	919
	Four-firm concentration ratio = 53%	Herfindahl Index = 919

The approval of a joint venture between two major rivals, General Motors and Toyota, while easily accepted given the current realities of the global marketplace, would have been unthinkable two decades earlier. The two companies agreed to a Toyota-designed automobile from parts supplied by both companies, with Toyota supplying top management and GM furnishing the production site.

The Clinton administration did challenge several mergers that, in the earlier period, likely would have been allowed to proceed without federal intervention. In 1996, the FTC objected to the proposed merger of two large drugstore chains: Rite-Aid and Revco. The following year, the commission rejected the planned merger of two large office supply discounters: Staples, Inc., and Office Depot, Inc. In both cases, the FTC claimed that the combination would lead to higher prices for the consumer even though each of the proposed mergers would have represented a small fraction of national sales in the respective markets. Thus, little consideration was given to the formal measures of market concentration promulgated earlier.

The number and size of mergers hit record highs in the late 1990s (see Figure 7.1). Moreover, many of these combinations involved large companies operating in the same sector of the economy. In energy, Exxon acquired Mobil for $79 billion. In banking, Nationsbank merged with Bank America in a $62 billion deal. In finance, giant Travelers Group paid $73 billion for Citicorp. Several telecommunications giants merged:

MCI Worldcom bought Sprint for $115 billion; SBC and Ameritech linked up in a $63 billion merger; Bell Atlantic acquired GTE for $71 billion; and AT&T merged with TCI in a $70 billion transaction. The largest merger involved the diversified service giants—AOL and TimeWarner—in a $156 billion deal. During the same period, an extended series of mergers occurred among major defense companies (see Chapter 16).

One of the most controversial antitrust suits was launched in 1997 by the Clinton administration when it attacked the alleged monopolization of computer

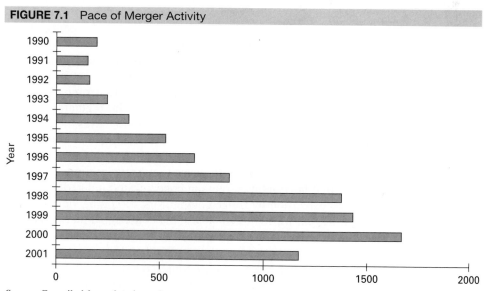

FIGURE 7.1   Pace of Merger Activity

Source: Compiled from data in various sources.

software markets by giant Microsoft. The core of the case involved the company's ownership of its Windows operating system, which has become the *de facto* standard by which much of the nation's information technology is linked. Rather than raising the usual question about the adverse effect of monopolies on prices paid by consumers, the Justice Department charged that Microsoft was stifling innovation by competitors. The district court judge ruled against Microsoft. However, as of mid-2002, the details of the case had not yet been decided, especially ways to remedy the situation.

CONTESTABLE MARKETS

A relatively recent intellectual innovation in the antitrust field is the development of the concept of "contestable markets." This approach relies heavily on the idea that competition is fostered by the knowledge that potential new entrants can contest the positions of entrenched companies. Thus, where entry is unimpeded, measures of market concentration lose their significance as predictors of business behavior.

Conceptually, a contestable market is one into which entry is free and exit is costless. Freedom of entry does not necessarily signify that entry is costless or easy but that an entrant will suffer no disadvantages in terms of production techniques or perceived product quality. In a contestable market, firms need not be small or numerous, nor need they produce homogeneous products. The crucial feature is the market's vulnerability to easy entry and its hospitality to painless exit.[15]

However, large sunk costs can create barriers to entry. Not many new firms are anxious to invest the large sums required to build automobiles or airplanes. On the other hand, many types of assets are mobile. Jet airliners, for example, have been called "capital on wings." In the modern high-tech economy, information is a key asset and readily mobile.

The question naturally arises, "Why should antitrust lawyers challenge mergers in industries with easy entry?" The answer, it turns out, is not as simple as it may appear. William Baumol, the leading figure in the contestable-market literature, warns that no industry in reality is perfectly contestable or is ever likely to be. He also adds that many are not even approximately so.[16] In Baumol's view, where markets are characterized neither by a large number of incumbents nor by ease of entry, public-sector intervention may be required to prevent the exercise of monopoly power. In such cases, there is a strong presumption that the regulatory or antitrust agencies serve the public interest best if their intervention secures the sort of behavior on the part of existing firms that effective market pressures might otherwise enforce.

In any event, there is still a strong consensus that horizontal price fixing is anticompetitive and also that horizontal mergers in concentrated industries, protected by barriers to entry or to expansion by fringe competitors, should be viewed with suspicion. An example of the real-world difficulty with the contestable-market notion is the airline market. Since the advent of deregulation, it would seem that the carriers could readily shift their equipment from one airport to another. However, landing slots are restricted and it is necessary for a newcomer to undergo the difficult process of buying a slot from an existing holder. In practice, this typically means a firm can enter a given air-travel market only by acquiring a company already in that market.

ANTITRUST AND THE GLOBAL MARKETPLACE

Whatever its proclivities, every recent presidential administration finds itself strongly influenced and perhaps inhibited by the pervasive and growing scope of the global marketplace. Competitive reality is that larger U.S. firms are increasingly competing against overseas giants as well as against smaller domestic companies.

In recent years, antitrust authorities have been grappling with the challenge of reshaping a government policy that was developed when the largest markets were primarily national or smaller. Between 1992 and 1997, the proportion of the Justice Department's Antitrust Division work that had an international dimension rose from 2 percent to almost 30 percent.[17] As the pressures of increasing world competition grow, the efficiency of a firm's operations assumes new weight as a reason for mergers and other actions that are likely to result in demonstrated savings in cost. The critical antitrust task of defining the relevant market includes locating the appropriate geographic boundaries in which the competitive battle occurs.[18]

Foreign competition can no longer be factored into the antitrust equation simply by counting imports as the totality of foreign firms' share of the U.S. market. In many domestic industries, which are relatively concentrated according to conventional measures, American firms are competing directly with foreign enterprises that may be much larger. Increasingly, the relevant market may be virtually the entire global marketplace. The reach of government antitrust agencies is being undercut by three key factors: the internationalization of production; the increased cross-border flows of information, money, and technology; and the resultant rise of the transnational enterprise (see Chapter 11).

In the case of key industries such as automobiles, steel, and chemicals, this global view means that what seems to be a very concentrated U.S. industry is really part of a larger group of worldwide competitors. For example, Table 7.3 shows only two U.S. firms on the list of the top 18 global automobile manufacturers. (DaimlerChrysler divides its production between several continents, primarily Europe and North America.)

More striking relationships hold in other large, important sectors of the economy. For example, nine of the world's ten largest electrical and electronics corporations are headquartered overseas, as are seven of the ten largest banking companies, and seven of the ten biggest insurance enterprises.

Under the International Antitrust Enforcement Assistance Act of 1994, the Antitrust Division has stepped up its prosecution of international antitrust cases involving foreign defendants and overseas violations of the antitrust laws. However, foreign governments regard such cases as unjustified extraterritorial enforcement of the domestic laws of the United States. Many new factors are involved in broadening the traditional U.S. antitrust approach. The range of foreign government intervention in international trade must be taken into account, including public-sector subsidies to home industries and restrictions of foreign competitors. As we will see in later chapters, however, American hands are not as clean in this regard as we may think.

Globalization complicates the enforcement of antitrust laws in a fundamental way. Conflicts arise because individual nations have different types of such statutes and also may interpret them in various ways. An important example is the failed merger of two U.S.–based multinational companies, General Electric and Honeywell. In May 2001, the U.S. Department of Justice approved the transaction, subject to the divestiture of Honeywell's helicopter engine division. However, the deal could not be consummated because in July 2001, the European Union rejected it.

Rank	Company	Country	Sales (Billions of Dollars)
1	GM	USA	$177
2	Ford	USA	162
3	DaimlerChrysler	Germany	137
4	Toyota	Japan	121
5	Volkswagen	Germany	79
6	Honda	Japan	59
7	Fiat	Italy	52
8	Nissan	Japan	50
9	Peugeot	France	46
10	BMW	Germany	34
11	Renault	France	33
12	Hyundai	Korea	31
13	Mitsubishi	Japan	26
14	Volvo	Sweden	18
15	Mazda	Japan	17
16	Man	Germany	15
17	Suzuki	Japan	13
18	Isuzu	Japan	13
	Total		$1,083

TABLE 7.3 The Global Automobile Industry, 2001

Source: Compiled from individual company data.

The U.S. antitrust authorities concluded that the merger would have been procompetitive and thus beneficial to consumers. They found that the combined firm could offer better products and service at more attractive prices than either firm could offer individually. However, the European counterpart ruled against the merger on the grounds that it would place competitor firms at a disadvantage. The views of the EU and the United States differed fundamentally: One focused on the effects on consumers, the other on the effects on other companies in the industry.

Although both sets of antitrust authorities based their decisions on high-minded legal and economic principles, a certain amount of self-interest seems evident. The ruling of the U.S. Justice Department would have created a stronger U.S. competitor in Europe and elsewhere. The action by the European Union maintained the competitive strength of the European segment of the industry.[19] It is interesting to note that the United States antitrust authorities did not object to two important cases whereby EU firms acquired large U.S. companies (Daimler-Benz and Chrysler in the automotive industry and British Petroleum and Amoco in the energy industry).

Conclusions

The influence of federal economic regulatory agencies on the transportation, banking, and communications industries has greatly declined in the past decade. The most pervasive example of industry-specific regulation is now state-level regulation of utilities.

However, because of improved technology and updated approaches to the role of government, the standard natural-monopoly justifications for utility regulation are now being questioned. Meanwhile, experiments are being made with innovative approaches to pricing policies and to the structure of regulated utilities.

Antitrust regulation has also changed significantly during recent decades. The criteria for judging harmful levels of industry concentration have been altered. Market proponents who challenge the need for continued strict enforcement of the Sherman Act and Clayton Act are squaring off with the more traditional "structuralists," who are concerned with the power—economic and political—of large firms. Meanwhile, the increasingly important international economy looms ever larger in hitherto domestic decision making.

Notes

1. *F.P.C.* v. *Hope Natural Gas Co.,* 320 U.S. 591, 603 (1944).

2. Cited in Charles Tatham, *Measures of Public Utility Bond Quality* (New York: Bache and Co., 1970), p. 19.

3. David E. M. Sappington et al., "The State of Performance-Based Regulation in the U.S. Electric Utility Industry," *Electricity Journal,* October 2001, pp. 71–79.

4. An example of the latter situation was the inability of the Long Island Lighting Company to operate its $5 billion Shoreham nuclear power plant because the governor of New York State would not approve the preparation of an emergency evacuation plan.

5. Jeannie Mandelker, "The Change in Power," *Infrastructure Finance,* October 1996, pp. 11–16.

6. Severin Borenstein, "The Trouble with Electricity Markets: Understanding California's Restructuring Disaster," *Journal of Economic Perspectives* 16, no. 1, Winter 2002, pp. 191–211; Paul Joskow, *California's Electricity Crisis* (Cambridge, MA.: National Bureau of Economic Research, 2001); "Enron Rigged Power Markets in California, Documents Say," *Wall Street Journal,* May 7, 2002, p. A1 et ff; Richard A. Oppel, Jr., "Perot Systems Shares Drop Over Accusations on California," *New York Times,* June 6, 2002, p. C6.

7. Paul Joskow, "California's Electricity Crisis: A Postmortem," *Milken Institute Review,* Second Quarter 2002, pp. 30–44.

8. Cited in Thomas J. DiLorenzo, "The Origins of Antitrust: An Interest Group Perspective," *International Review of Law and Economics,* 1985, no. 5, pp. 80–81.

9. Robert H. Bork, *The Antitrust Paradox* (New York: Basic Books, 1978). See also John H. Shenefield and Irwin M. Stelzer, *The Antitrust Laws: A Primer,* 4th ed. (Washington, DC: AEI Press, 2001).

10. William Baumol, *The Free-Market Innovation Machine* (Princeton, NJ: Princeton University Press, 2002).

11. Fred L. Smith, Jr., "Why Not Abolish Antitrust?" *Regulation,* January–February 1983, pp. 23–24.

12. See P. Pautler, "A Review of the Economic Basis for a Broad-Based Horizontal-Merger Policy," *Antitrust Bulletin,* Fall 1983, pp. 571–651.

13. Quoted in "New Wave in Antitrust," *Perspectives on National Issues* (Washington, DC: National Association of Manufacturers, 1979), p. 2.

14. James A. Langenfeld, "The Merger Guidelines As Applied," in Malcolm Coate and Andrew Kleit, eds., *The Economics of the Antitrust Process* (Boston: Kluwer Academic Publishers, 1996), pp. 41–47.

15. William J. Baumol, John C. Panzar, and Robert D. Willig, *Contestable Markets and the Theory of Industry Structure* (New York: Harcourt Brace Jovanovich, 1982); William J. Baumol, "Contestable Markets, An Uprising in the Theory of Industry

Structure," *American Economic Review,* March 1982, pp. 1–15.

16. William J. Baumol, "On Contestable Market Analysis," in *Antitrust and New Views of Microeconomics* (New York: Conference Board, 1986), pp. 13–14.

17. Joel I. Klein, "International Antitrust Enforcement," in George C. Landrith III, ed., *A Day with the Department of Justice* (Washington, DC: National Legal Center, 1997), p. 1.

18. John H. Shenefield and Irwin N. Stelzer, *The Antitrust Laws: A Primer* (Lanham, MD: AEI Press, 1993).

19. See *Economic Report of the President, February 2002* (Washington, DC: U.S. Government Printing Office, 2002), pp. 125–126.

8

ECONOMIC
DEREGULATION
—⟨∾∾⟩—

The substantial deregulation of American transportation, telecommunications, energy, and financial markets, underway since the late 1970s, represents a fundamental break from the developments of the previous 90 years. From the establishment of the Interstate Commerce Commission in 1886 to the passage of the Toxic Substances Control Act in 1976, government regulation of economic activity in the United States steadily expanded, creating in its wake powerful constituencies who benefit from the regulation. Despite the many gaps between the ideal and the reality, on balance the deregulation that has occurred in recent years has strengthened the economy and benefited the consumer.

The unprecedented reduction of economic regulation was not caused by a realignment of political forces. The most significant developments were supported by a bipartisan coalition in both the legislative and executive branches of the federal government. Consumer activists such as Ralph Nader offered support at vital points, as did leaders of both political parties, including presidents Ford, Carter, and Reagan. But the most important role was played by a very unusual set of actors in the public policy arena: economists, political scientists, legal scholars, and similar purveyors of ideas.

ORIGINS OF DEREGULATION

Three streams of economic research and policy analysis dealing with different aspects of regulation reached a confluence in the 1970s. The first, and most substantial, focused on the fact that the widely distributed burdens imposed by economic regulation, especially in the field of transportation, were much larger than the far more concentrated benefits. The second stream dealt with the fundamental nature of the regulatory process, especially the relationships between regulators and those regulated. The third focused on the costs of regulation, especially to the consumer.

It is difficult to pinpoint the exact start of the influential research that led to transportation deregulation. *The Economics of Competition in the Transportation Industries*, written by John R. Meyer and his associates in 1959, was a landmark study.[1] Important work followed on each of the major modes of transportation, notably by George W. Douglas and James C. Miller III on airlines and by Thomas Gale Moore on trucking.[2]

The airline industry provided the clearest examples of the heavy cost of regulation, particularly the differential prices charged by regulated and nonregulated airlines. Interstate travel was under the jurisdiction of the Civil Aeronautics Board (CAB); intrastate travel was beyond the CAB's purview. Research found that a traveler could fly 500 miles from San Diego to San Francisco in the unregulated California market and pay less than someone flying 300 miles from Portland, Oregon, to Seattle, Washington, under the CAB's control. During the 1970s, most economists writing in this field also concluded that Interstate Commerce Commission (ICC) regulation was protecting the carriers (railroads and truckers) while increasing costs to shippers by billions of dollars a year.

A consensus gradually emerged. Transportation regulation in the United States did not protect its purported beneficiaries—consumers—but instead was benefiting the employees, executives, and shareholders of the companies being regulated. Government rule making shielded entrenched firms from potential new competitors and kept a high-price umbrella over the regulated industries.

The second, and related, stream of research focused on the political efforts of interest groups that benefited from regulation.[3] In 1955, political scientist Marver Bernstein presented a "capture" theory of regulation. As the only political force in a regulatory agency's environment with any stability, the industry would eventually force an agency to accommodate its needs. Economists George Stigler and Sam Peltzman generalized this theory, contending that regulatory policy reflects the interests and the power of the concerned groups, not necessarily the consumer's.[4] In 1982, Stigler was awarded the Nobel Prize in economics for his seminal research on the theory of regulation and his empirical studies of the effect of regulation on specific industries.

The third line of research—focusing on costs to consumers—saw the topic move from the business pages and academic journals to the front pages and the nightly news. The American Enterprise Institute led the way in the mid-1970s with several widely cited reports on the high cost of regulation, among them my own on government-mandated price increases via regulation, Sam Peltzman's on pharmaceutical regulation, John P. Gould's on the Davis–Bacon Act, and Rita Ricardo-Campbell's on food safety regulation.[5] The issue hit a responsive chord with the media, influential policy groups, and finally Congress.

Deregulation was politically attractive because it presented policy makers with an opportunity to curb inflation in a way that did not involve a trade-off with jobs. Indeed, reduced regulation would cut both costs and barriers to production and employment.

The burdens of regulation were characterized as a hidden tax on the consumer. Carefully researched examples of regulatory silliness also helped bring these concepts to the public's attention. Perhaps the first example was the "dead haul"—regulators required that trucks return empty from delivery even though there was ample opportunity to fill them with cargo. The public needed no great expertise in industrial organization to resent the waste that resulted.

An unusual form of applied research (horror-story telling) concentrated increasingly on the Occupational Safety and Health Administration (OSHA). Jokes about OSHA, based on that research, became a staple of business conversation. Is it true that OSHA made one company build separate his and her toilets even though the only two employees of the firm were married to each other? Did OSHA really issue a bulletin to farmers telling them to be careful around cows and not to step into manure pits? Both of those questions could, quite accurately, be answered in the affirmative.

By the late 1970s, support for regulatory reform had become widespread. It included business executives who found themselves inundated with a flood of rules to follow and reports to file, lawyers and political scientists who thought the regulatory agencies often were captured by the regulated industries, and economists who believed that regulation reduced competition and increased costs. Congressional hearings on the subject yielded support for less regulation from such disparate groups—and surprising allies—as the American Conservative Union and the Consumer Federation of America.

PROGRESS TOWARD DEREGULATION

Progress on deregulation built up slowly but gathered strong momentum in the mid- and late 1970s. In 1968, a Supreme Court decision permitted non–AT&T equipment to be hooked to the Bell telephone system. The following year, the Federal Communications Commission (FCC) allowed a non-Bell company to connect its long-distance network to local phone systems. Although these two actions attracted little attention at the time, they triggered the forces that led ultimately to the breakup of the Bell system.

In the 1970s, interest rates on deposits of $100,000 and over were deregulated. Again, one move toward deregulation ultimately led to another. As securities firms took advantage of this loophole, banks responded. A process was set in motion that has resulted in eliminating interest-rate ceilings altogether, allowing payments of interest on consumer demand deposits, and resulting in greater competition among financial institutions.

Two important regulatory changes took place in 1975. The Securities and Exchange Commission (SEC) ordered an end to fixed brokerage fees for stock market transactions, and the ICC prohibited rate bureaus for either trucking firms or railroads from protesting independent rate filings by members. Clearly, the regulatory ice was breaking.

In 1977, the Civil Aeronautics Board (CAB), led by two economists, Chairman Alfred Kahn and member Elizabeth Bailey, instituted several changes that ultimately led to airline deregulation. The CAB gave airlines greater freedom in pricing and easier access to routes not previously served. The results were spectacular. Coach fares fell sharply, planes filled, and airline profits soared. The CAB experience provided a striking example of how regulation had been hurting the traveling public. In response, a bipartisan coalition in Congress passed legislation in 1978 that phased out the CAB and its authority to control entry and prices.

The year 1980 was an eventful one for deregulation. The FCC eliminated most federal regulation of cable television. Economist Darius Gaskins became chairman of the ICC and economist Marcus Alexis was appointed a member of the commission. That, in turn, encouraged the trucking industry to support congressional leadership of reform in this field, in the expectation that the changes would be less drastic than those pursued by the new leadership of the ICC. Later in the year, a trucking law provided much more pricing freedom to individual carriers, made entry into the market much easier, and eliminated many costly ICC restrictions—but the ICC presence was retained. Also passed in 1980, the Staggers Rail Act gave the railroads new pricing freedom.

In 1981, the FCC eliminated much regulation of the radio industry. President Reagan decontrolled crude oil prices and petroleum allocation and terminated the Council on Wage and Price Stability and its wage–price guidelines. But the pace of deregulation slowed significantly after 1981. A backlash in the environmental area, fueled in part by the controversial personalities of some of the administration's appointees, put the regulatory reform movement on the defensive.

Nevertheless, changes continued to be made. Banking legislation enacted in 1982 allowed savings and loan associations to make more commercial and consumer loans. The interest-rate differentials between banks and thrift institutions also were removed. (As we will see, that incomplete deregulation was as much bane as blessing.) The Bus Regulatory Reform Act of 1982 permitted bus companies to change routes and fares. In 1984, the Shipping Act enabled individual ocean shipping companies to offer lower rates and better service than so-called "shipping conferences" (really cartels). Also in that year, AT&T agreed to divest local operating companies as part of its historic antitrust settlement with the Justice Department.

AIRLINE DEREGULATION

The greatest progress to date toward deregulation has occurred in the transportation area, especially the commercial aviation industry. Until the late 1970s, the Civil Aeronautics Board (CAB) regulated the airline industry extensively. It allocated inter-state routes among the airlines and controlled airline fares on those routes. Through its power over air routes, the CAB restrained entry into the industry. From its inception in 1938 until the late 1970s, the CAB did not allow any new airline to enter the interstate markets that served major population centers.

In 1977, the CAB began to ease restrictions on fares and entry. In 1978, Congress affirmed and extended the agency's actions by passing the Airline Deregulation Act, which provided for the gradual deregulation of the airlines. The CAB's domestic route authority was ended in 1981, and its domestic pricing authority was terminated in 1983. The CAB itself ceased to exist in 1985.

Consequently, any domestically owned airline that the Department of Transportation deems "fit, willing, and able" can fly on any domestic route. The Federal Aviation Administration (FAA) focuses on whether an airline is operating in accord with safety standards and other designated operating procedures.

Let us examine the pluses and the minuses of airline deregulation.

POSITIVE EFFECTS SINCE DEREGULATION

A host of other factors involved makes it difficult to analyze the effects of a funda-mental change such as airline deregulation. Nevertheless, it is clear that air traffic has grown faster and air fares have fallen more rapidly than they did while the industry was regulated. During 1966–1970, Americans flew an average of 110 billion miles a year. During 1996–2000, the annual average rose to 630 billion miles. Simultaneously, employment rose and productivity increased.

Despite several highly publicized crashes, the safety record of U.S. airlines since deregulation is superior to that for the earlier period. During 1966–1970, the United States experienced 1.3 deaths a year per billion miles flown. In 1996–2000, the deaths reported from air crashes declined to 0.14 a year per billion miles. According to the General Accounting Office, "Airline deregulation has led to lower fares and better service for most air travelers. . . ."[6]

On a case-by-case basis, more communities have fared better under deregulation, but some are worse off. For instance, cities located within an hour's drive of major air-ports have tended to lose air service because travelers from those cities now drive to the major hubs where they can get discounts and more flight choices. Those smaller cities lack enough passengers for the airlines to stop there. In contrast, locations with a good population base that were not well served by the major carriers have attracted more regional and commuter airlines.

One clear benefit of airline deregulation has been an increase in service in terms of number of flights and number of routes (or "city-pair" markets) served. Following the relaxation of entry restrictions in airline markets, airlines developed "hub and spoke" networks. These networks have led to increased flights to medium-size and smaller cities because the increased passenger volume makes it profitable to enhance service to these "feeder" destinations.

Hub and spoke systems allow airlines to use their aircraft more efficiently, carrying more passengers per flight and operating aircraft more hours per day. Average load factors on many flights have increased substantially. Moreover, the proportion of trips involving a change in plane has declined. Competition has forced the carriers to pass on these savings to their customers.

Overall, a larger proportion of the American public is flying today than ever before. That welcome development has been fostered by a more competitive fare structure for air travel. The annual benefits to travelers from airline deregulation—in the form of lower fares and increased frequency of flights—has been estimated at over $20 billion a year. Moreover, since deregulation the number of domestic airline passengers in the United States more than doubled, from about 300 million in 1978 to over 600 million in 2000.[7]

Average air fares are substantially lower than they would have been in the absence of deregulation. One estimate is that, as of mid-2001, fares in real terms are almost 40 percent lower.[8] Although that would seem to be a fairly straightforward statement, it is too subtle for the typical passenger to appreciate. After all, who can make a mental adjustment for general inflation or the changing price of fuel? The more usual approach is simply to conclude that fares are higher today than yesterday or, in any event, that fare schedules are far more confusing than they used to be.

Prior to deregulation in 1976, only 15 percent of all airline passengers received discount fares; most paid standard fares. At present, the great majority of airline passengers travel on discount tickets (which are often more complicated in terms of special provisions such as penalties for changing flight plans).

AIRLINE SAFETY

Although the Airline Deregulation Act of 1978 did not change the authority of the FAA to regulate the safety of air travel, public concern about safety has risen since deregulation. The improved safety record noted earlier has occurred at a time of enormous increase in passenger volume. Two decades ago, only one American in 10 had ever flown in an airplane. Today, more than one-third of the population flies each year.

Economists have suggested methods of increasing safety and reducing airway congestion by encouraging the airlines to avoid bunching their takeoffs and landings in the most popular times. As in the case of telephone services, higher prices would be charged during periods of peak usage and lower fees at times when demand is low (e.g., fewer planes are flying).

Also, congestion at major airports arises because landing fees for executive, personal, and other small and noncommercial aircraft are lower than the costs such planes impose on the air transportation system. At present, landing fees are set by weight with no regard to "rush hour" needs. Thus, the light slow-moving aircraft pay less than the heavier, faster aircraft that use less airspace in a given period of time. Raising the fees charged these lighter airplanes for using the larger airports would encourage their operators to shift to less popular times of day or to smaller, less frequently used airports. Most aircraft accidents involve at least one light airplane. When the

Massachusetts Port Authority proposed raising landing fees at Logan Airport in Boston, the pressures from the owners and operators of light planes was so intense that the matter was tabled.

NEGATIVE EFFECTS SINCE DEREGULATION

After the initial burst of new entries following deregulation, a handful of airline companies has gained very large market shares. Overall, the number of major carriers has declined from 11 prior to deregulation to 7 in 2002. This net change came about from an initial expansion of the number of carriers followed by a series of mergers and bankruptcies.

Most proponents of airline deregulation did not expect the market concentration that has occurred. In good measure, that situation has resulted from Congress's giving DOT authority (which lapsed in 1989) to review the antitrust aspect of airline mergers. The DOT approved every prospective airline merger, many over the strenuous objections of the Justice Department's Antitrust Division. Airline mergers, on balance, exert an upward force on the fares for the routes for which competition has been reduced.[9] The three major U.S. airlines hold a 51 percent share of the domestic market, compared to 37 percent in 1981 (see Table 8.1). (The decline in the share of the top three firms in the industry from 57 percent in 1993 results from the rise of Southwest Airlines, a strong low-cost competitor.)

As noted in Chapters 9 and 15, the terrorist attacks of September 11, 2001, and the launching of a comprehensive antiterrorism response have contributed greatly to the financial and operating problems of the airlines. The increased complexity of airport security has encouraged some travelers to switch to other modes of travel—or to substitute sophisticated communication systems for transportation. On balance, the security measures, however necessary, have reduced the demand for air travel while increasing the costs. The greater presence of direct federal regulation of airports, however, has not reversed the essence of airline deregulation—the freedom of the companies to set rates and to serve specific markets.

TABLE 8.1   Share of U.S. Airline Traffic Held by the Three Largest Carriers (Passenger Miles)

Year	Combined Share	Year	Combined Share
1981	37	1991	52
1982	37	1992	56
1983	38	1993	57
1984	37	1994	56
1985	35	1995	55
1986	39	1996	55
1987	41	1997	54
1988	44	1998	54
1989	47	1999	52
1990	46	2000	51

Source: U.S. Department of Transportation.

In general, passengers flying from a hub city with substantial airline competition pay lower fares than those departing from a city with one or two dominant carriers. In one recent year, the General Accounting Office found that fares at "concentrated" airports (where one or two carriers dominate) were 22 percent higher than fares at less concentrated airports, even when differences in the distance flown were accounted for.[10]

The failure of government—which owns most of the airports and manages the air navigation system—to keep pace with rising demand has led to congestion in airports and in the sky and thus to delays and flight cancellations. As a result, some small- and medium-size communities in the East and Upper Midwest have experienced higher fares and worse service since deregulation.[11] Local governments, which run most airports in the United States, usually enter into long-term leases with the airlines for individual gates. At times, this results in one airline's gates at an airport being underutilized while another airline at the same airport battles congestion.

It is tempting to conclude that, since airline deregulation, Americans are flying more but enjoying it less. Because of the enhanced popularity of air travel, planes are more crowded than ever and delays are frequent. As noted earlier, part of the difficulty is that deregulation was limited in its scope. The San Francisco airport authority had to obtain approvals from 31 agencies to reconfigure a runway. It took five years for Orlando to get approval of the environmental impact statement for a new runway—and an additional eight years to get the necessary permits and zoning.[12]

DEREGULATION IN SURFACE TRANSPORTATION

Deregulation in surface transportation has been more piecemeal than in air transportation. The degree of regulation was reduced by the passage of the Railroad Revitalization and Regulatory Reform Act in 1976, the Motor Carrier Act of 1980, the Staggers Rail Act of 1980, and the Bus Regulatory Reform Act of 1982. After the benefit of reduced regulation became apparent, in 1994 Congress passed the Trucking Industry Regulatory Reform Act, eliminating much of the remaining trucking regulation and prohibiting states from regulating rates for in-state transportation of nonhousehold goods. In 1996, the ICC was eliminated and its residual functions shifted to the DOT.

TRUCKING DEREGULATION

Estimates of annual savings from trucking deregulation—including lowered inventory needs—range up to $50 billion a year. Operating costs per mile are down about one-third since 1980.[13] Service to small communities has not deteriorated, as was originally predicted by the opponents of deregulation.

The number of trucking firms has increased substantially, although the short-run adjustments in the industry were substantial. More than 300 truckers went out of business in the first three years following the passage of the 1980 legislation. During the same period and continuing to the present, however, thousands of new, low-cost nonunion truckers entered the business, as the ICC barriers to entry were removed. The number of carriers in operation mushroomed, from about 47,000 in 1982 to more than 500,000 in 2001.

RAILROAD DEREGULATION

The experience since the partial deregulation of railroads in 1980 is similar to that of trucking. Although not everyone has benefited, overall the cost of transportation has been reduced. Railroads have increased their shipments of some commodities, such as fruits and vegetables, that were previously carried almost exclusively by trucks. Over 27,000 miles of their more unprofitable rail lines were abandoned by 1990. Following a difficult period of bankruptcies and liquidations, the remaining firms in the railroad industry are in stronger financial condition, and the future of this troubled industry has brightened. A substantial reduction in operating costs has occurred because, since the Staggers Act of 1980, the railroads can keep as much of their gains from greater efficiency as competition will allow.

Railroad rates dropped substantially following deregulation, on average declining by 62 percent between 1982 and 2000. Managerial innovations, such as intermodal operations and use of double-stack cars helped. During the same period, railroad costs per ton mile of freight hauled dropped about 33 percent. Moreover, the cost cutting that followed lessened regulation enabled the railroads to pay for upgrading equipment and long-deferred maintenance. Accident rates declined by 66 percent between 1980 and 2000.[14]

Responding to the pressures of competition in a deregulated environment, major U.S. railroads are operating with 20 percent fewer locomotives than in 1980, 200,000 fewer employees, and thousands fewer freight cars. The implicit increase in productivity in varying degrees has been passed on to those industries using the railroads, enhancing their market positions at home and abroad.

DEREGULATION OF TELECOMMUNICATIONS

In 1982, the federal government and AT&T announced that they had settled an eight-year-old government antitrust suit with a consent agreement that required AT&T to spin off its local telephone operating companies. Since 1984, consumers no longer have been able to buy their basic local telephone service and long-distance services from the same company.

Splitting up the Bell System was expected to enhance competition and lower prices to the consumer. Competition certainly was enhanced. Prices followed a more complicated route. In comparison to the Bell System monopoly of long-distance telephone service in the United States prior to the breakup, approximately 95 percent of telephones now have access to at least three competitive long-distance companies. More densely populated areas are often served by five or more firms. In addition, the widespread use of cellular telephones has increased substantially the choices available to consumers.

This competition has lowered prices significantly. The decline in long-distance rates, however, has been partially offset by a rise in the rates for local telephone service. In part, this reflected a deliberate attempt by the FCC to reduce the subsidies for local telephone service that traditionally had been received from long-distance service. To fully understand the implications of the AT&T breakup, it is necessary to take into account the historical development of telecommunications regulation.

HISTORICAL REGULATION OF TELEPHONE RATES

For decades, telephone service has been regulated at the federal and state levels by commissions whose concerns have been more with "fairness" than with economic efficiency. Until the 1970s, few users or policy makers objected if long distance subsidized local telephone service—as long as AT&T, its local operating companies, and the independent local telephone companies did not appear to earn excessive rates of return. Local rates were priced on a flat monthly basis. Long-distance calls were priced at a standard rate per mile, even though this approach meant that callers in high-usage urban areas paid substantially above cost, whereas callers in low-usage rural areas paid below cost.

When transmission costs declined in the 1960s and 1970s, state and federal regulators did not allow long-distance rates to fall proportionately. A larger share of local service costs was allocated to long distance. But as long as the overall cost of telephone service kept dropping, few complained. Throughout that period, telephone rates in general fell substantially relative to inflation. Between 1960 and 1980, real telephone rates fell by more than 50 percent. In large part, this decline was caused by rapid technological progress. In addition, rates were suppressed in the inflationary 1970s by a regulatory process that relied on historical cost accounting.

The combination of distortions in telephone rates and changing technology began to invite new entrants in the 1960s. At first, this competition was limited to private lines used by large businesses and to simple devices attached to telephone lines. By the mid-1970s, alternatives were available for most terminal equipment—such as private branch exchanges (PBXs) and telephone handsets—and, more importantly, for long-distance service. Companies such as MCI and Sprint began to compete actively for long-distance customers.

The new marketplace forces in long-distance service began to exert downward pressure on rates during the late 1970s. AT&T responded by reducing its private-line rates and by trying to frustrate the new competitors' efforts to reach customers through AT&T–owned operating companies. These activities induced the Justice Department to file an antitrust suit, which was settled by the 1982 decree that forced AT&T to divest itself of its local operating companies.

TELEPHONE REGULATION SINCE THE AT&T BREAKUP

The structure of telephone rates has been undergoing dramatic changes as a direct result of government policy. Long-distance rates have been falling in real terms while local rates have tended to rise. Telephone receivers and other terminal equipment are now rarely leased from the local phone company; most subscribers own their equipment. Subscribers are much more likely to be charged substantial installation fees because local telephone companies are not able to capitalize these installation costs on their balance sheets. As a consequence, the price of local service is now more nearly based on the number of calls made and the length and duration of these calls.

State regulatory commissions, however, have been moving away from traditional cost-of-service determination of rates for telecommunications service. As in the case of electric utilities, regulated telephone companies have been granted the ability to operate more freely, but subject to a firm limit on the rates that they can charge (price caps). This procedure has given them the incentive to cut their costs and thus directly

TABLE 8.2   Status of Local Telephone Regulation in 2000

Type of Regulation	Number of States
Traditional cost of service	7
Rate freeze	1
Earnings sharing	1
Price cap	39
Other	2
Total	50

Source: David Sappington, "Price Regulation and Incentives," in *Handbook of Telecommunications Economics* (Amsterdam, The Netherlands: North-Holland Publishers, 2001).

enhance their profitability. By 2000, 39 of the 50 state commissions allowed price caps for local telephone service. Only seven states continued to follow traditional cost-of-service regulation (see Table 8.2).

MONOPOLY OR COMPETITION?

In its earliest form, the telephone industry may well have been a "natural" monopoly. Stringing paired copper wires between homes or businesses and telephone switching centers initially was more efficient when conducted by a single monopolist than by a number of competitors. But even during those early years, there was not a compelling case for AT&T also monopolizing the manufacture and distribution of handsets and other terminal equipment. After all, local gas utilities have a natural monopoly in distributing gas, but they do not try to control the sales of water heaters, furnaces, and kitchen ranges. Thus, it was not surprising that a long-running debate occurred over AT&T's right to produce the equipment used in the delivery of its services.

In the 1950s, technological changes occurred that greatly complicated the problem of regulating the telephone monopoly. Users began to demand the right to attach to their telephone lines equipment not provided by the telephone company. At first, these were simple devices. Eventually, however, subscribers began to demand the right to connect their own answering machines, computer modems, and PBXs to the lines. Users even wanted to own their handsets—perhaps even some that were unlike any offered by the local telephone company.

Technological change also altered the nature of telephone signal transmission. Long-distance calls began to be transmitted by microwave radio, a technology with modest economies of scale on dense routes. Large users could opt out of AT&T services altogether by using microwaves.

The FCC gradually responded to the demand for entry into long-distance communications and terminal equipment. In the late 1960s, the commission began to allow competitive entry into private-line (point-to-point) services and installation of terminal equipment on the grounds that these services and products could be supplied most efficiently by a competitive market. AT&T's offering of these services and products, however, continued to be regulated. The commission refused to allow new entrants into the "network" that involve both local and long-distance services because it was not persuaded that competition was a viable and efficient means for delivering these services. Local service, regulated by state public utilities, also remained under monopoly control.

The entire regulatory process came unglued in the mid-1970s when MCI (originally formed as Microwave Communications, Inc.) entered the switched long-distance market without FCC permission. The commission had authorized MCI to provide private-line service, but it had not contemplated that MCI would try to offer ordinary long-distance service. At first, the FCC tried to block MCI's expansion, but it was defeated in court proceedings because it failed to demonstrate that competition in long-distance markets was either infeasible or socially undesirable.

By the late 1970s, the FCC and the courts had transformed the telephone monopoly into a set of competitive long-distance carriers and equipment vendors, each connecting their services or equipment to the lines of franchised local monopolists. AT&T could operate in the long-distance market subject to regulatory restraints, and it did so with such aggressive effect that it became the target of a wave of antitrust suits. But a 1956 decree continued to prohibit AT&T from competing in the new world of mixed communications and computer services.

The FCC and the state commissions had no special guidance on how to set rates efficiently and how to establish fair ground rules for the new world of competitive telecommunications markets. The FCC tried for nearly two decades to separate the various costs of telecommunications services from each other, but the nature of the services and the rapid pace of technological change in the industry made the commission's task difficult if not impossible.

The new competition in terminal equipment and long-distance service had predictable effects. The regulators could no longer attempt to subsidize basic monthly service from excess charges for long-distance service. As long as the FCC and the state commissions combined to keep long-distance rates artificially high, new competitors would eagerly enter this market. As MCI, Sprint, and others began to make inroads into AT&T's erstwhile long-distance monopoly, AT&T tried to fight back through competitive rate reductions and actions designed to frustrate its competitors' access to customers through AT&T's local operating companies.

THE DIVESTITURE

In 1982, AT&T agreed to its own dismemberment in settlement of the government's 1974 antitrust suit. In return, AT&T was given the right to retain Western Electric (now Lucent Technology, which is an independent company). The 1956 consent decree that barred AT&T from entering new computer-related businesses was set aside. The divested operating companies were prohibited from manufacturing equipment and offering long-distance or information services but were required to develop "equal access" technology for all long-distance carriers.

The decree was designed to separate the suppliers of access to local subscribers— the regional AT&T operating companies—from those offering long-distance and other information-age services. As a result, the divested operating companies were not allowed to compete with MCI, AT&T, Sprint, or other companies in the long-distance market. To preserve fair competition, the local operating companies were limited in much the same way that AT&T was under the now-defunct 1956 decree.

AT&T was free to compete for any business except local exchange service. It remains a regulated carrier. At first, the divested telephone operating companies were owned by seven independent regional holding companies (Ameritech, Bell Atlantic, NYNEX, Pacific Telesis, Southwestern Bell, and so on). In the late 1990s, several of these holding companies merged. For example, Southwestern Bell acquired Pacific Telesis and Ameritech to form SBC Communications; Bell Atlantic acquired NYNEX and independent GTE and was renamed Verizon.

TELECOMMUNICATIONS ACT OF 1996

Continued technological advance generated opportunities for a greater degree of competition in telecommunications services—for the possibility of local telephone companies providing long-distance service, for long-distance carriers entering or reentering the local service market, and for telephone and cable companies competing directly with each other. In an effort to rationalize this process, Congress passed the Telecommunications Act of 1996. The ostensible purposes were to end the franchised monopolies that state regulatory commissions have granted local telephone companies, to permit local telephone companies to enter the long-distance market, and to allow telephone companies to offer cable television service.[15]

The results have not been that straightforward. Rather, they are reminiscent of the loaded question on a final examination given by the author—does the federal government deregulate as badly as it regulates? The answer, at least in this case, is "yes." Thus far, the 1996 law, coupled with the way the FCC is administering it, has generated very limited opening of the local exchange market to competition.[16]

To complicate matters, the existing local telephone companies are forced by state regulators to serve small towns and rural areas at prices substantially below their costs. This means having to charge business customers and residences in large cities rates substantially above costs. Economists call this convoluted rate structure "cross subsidies." Compounding the problem, many state regulatory commissions are reluctant to let the below-cost rates rise. They prefer instead to finance these subsidies from a "universal service" tax on all telecommunications carriers. Furthermore, the FCC has added on charges required by the 1996 law to pay for linking libraries, schools, and medical services to the Internet.

PARTIAL DEREGULATION OF FINANCIAL INSTITUTIONS

Although public discourse is filled with allusions to deregulation of financial institutions, a variety of federal agencies continues to influence the operations of banks and other financial enterprises. These regulatory bodies include the Federal Reserve System, the Comptroller of the Currency, the Federal Deposit Insurance Corporation, and the Securities and Exchange Commission. In addition, state banking departments and other state-level agencies are active, notably insurance and securities regulators. As will be covered in a subsequent chapter, many savings and loan associations and some banks have gotten into great financial difficulties and have been closed down or otherwise "bailed out" by the federal government.

ECONOMIC DEREGULATION EFFORTS

The degree of competition among financial institutions is great today. Some of that change results from legislation. The pace of change also results from technological advances and institutional innovation. But the enhanced scope for marketplace competition is occurring in a political and economic climate that is more conducive and encouraging than in the past. That marketplace, moreover, is increasingly global.

In the 1990s, Congress eliminated the two statutes that most severely restricted competition in financial markets. The Interstate Banking and Branching Efficiency Act of 1994 made the McFadden Act, which inhibited interstate banking, virtually irrelevant. Under the 1994 law, a bank holding company can acquire a bank in any state—so long as the holding company does not control 30 percent of the deposits in the state and it is judged to be adequately capitalized and managed. Also, its CRA record (the Community Reinvestment Act is described later) must pass review by the Federal Reserve Board. Acquisition of a failing bank need not meet these requirements.[17]

The second restrictive law, the Glass–Steagall Act (which erected a wall of separation between commercial and investment banking) was repealed in 1999. Many financial institutions had found innovative ways around the restrictions of Glass–Steagall even before it was eliminated. Through purchase and operation of commercial banks in certain states, brokerage houses offered their customers deposit and withdrawal services. In turn, bank holding companies offered their customers a variety of financial services, including purchase and storage of government bonds.

The 1999 statute, known as the Gramm–Leach–Bliley Act, brought sweeping changes to the financial landscape of the United States. It modified banking regulations to permit single bank holding companies to offer banking, securities, and insurance services under one roof. Financial subsidiaries of banks are now allowed to engage in most types of financial activity—except for insurance underwriting and commercial investments made by insurance companies, real estate investment and development, and certain aspects of merchant banking.

The new law authorizes the creation of a new banking entity, the financial holding company. This new type of holding company can own banks as well as other subsidiaries that are "financial in nature" or "incidental to financial activities" or even "complementary to financial activities" (unless the Federal Reserve determines that the nonbanking activities will affect the soundness of the banks). In effect, financial holding companies can market virtually the entire range of financial products.

Under the Gramm–Leach–Bliley law, the Federal Reserve and the Comptroller of the Currency continue to examine banks and affiliated companies. But insurance and securities regulators, state and federal, examine many of the nonbanking subsidiaries of the holding companies.

Even before the 1999 statute was enacted, technological changes were blurring the distinctions between commercial banking, securities activities, and insurance services. The new law codifies the blurring of those distinctions and makes more likely that the trend for their combination will accelerate. The challenge facing regulators is to protect the safety and soundness of the financial system while not deterring the continuing innovations that reduce costs or improve service.[18]

SOCIAL REGULATION IN FINANCE

Despite the reduction of economic regulation, Congress has continued to impose social regulation on financial institutions. The Equal Credit Opportunity Act prohibits financial institutions from discriminating in granting credit on the basis of sex, race, religion, or marital status. The Home Mortgage Disclosure Act requires depository institutions to disclose where their mortgage and home-improvement loans have been made so that depositors and others can judge whether they are meeting the housing-related credit "needs" in the local community.

Other social regulation of banking and finance includes the Truth-in-Lending Act, the Fair Credit Billing Act, the Fair Credit Reporting Act, the Consumer Leasing Act, the Real Estate Settlement Procedures Act, and the Electronic Fund Transfer Act. These regulations extend from home-purchase closing costs to information on the cost of credit.

The Community Reinvestment Act (CRA) encourages banks and other institutions to help meet the credit needs in their respective communities. It is a legislative response to the complaints of low-income housing advocates that many lenders "red line"—draw a figurative line around a low-income neighborhood and stop or restrict lending to its residents and businesses, regardless of the merits of their individual applications for credit.

The law requires the regulatory agencies to rate the performance of individual lenders in meeting the mandate of the CRA and to take this performance into account when reviewing the lender's applications for expansions, acquisitions, or mergers. This provision gives community activists opportunity to negotiate with a bank that wants to avoid the delay that occurs when a proposed acquisition is challenged on CRA grounds.

The Interstate Banking and Branching Efficiency Act requires the CRA reviews to be conducted on a state-by-state basis, even if a bank has branches in several states. That provision effectively eliminates the practice of using out-of-state branches primarily for generating deposits. It also runs counter to the trend toward national banking by perpetuating the notion that depositors want their deposits to stay in their locality.

THE OUTLOOK

Much of the motivation for continuing government involvement in the regulation of financial institutions derives from the government's exposure to the risk of loss resulting from its role in deposit insurance and the Federal Reserve's provision of credit to banks by "discounting" their loans. Simultaneously, however, banks and other financial institutions have responded to technological innovation and intensive competition by expanding the bundle of products and services they deliver. The multiproduct provider of financial services is evolving through a combination of competition, consolidation, and relaxation of regulatory restrictions.

Conclusions

It is evident that a great deal of the traditional economic regulatory apparatus has been cut back. Table 8.3 shows the highlights of the deregulation movement since the late 1960s. In general, reduced regulation—ranging from outright deregulation to simplification and streamlining of rule making—has enabled the competitive process to work

TABLE 8.3   Milestones in Economic Deregulation

1968	Telecommunications: U.S. Supreme Court in Carterfone decision permits non–AT&T equipment to be hooked to AT&T's system.
1969	Telecommunications: FCC allows MCI to connect long-distance network with local phone systems.
1975	Energy: Energy Policy and Conservation Act provides for decontrol of gasoline and petroleum products by 1981.
1978	Financial institutions: Financial Institutions Regulatory and Interest Rate Control Act establishes uniform reporting systems for banks, S&Ls, and credit unions.
1978	Energy: Natural Gas Policy Act provides for partial decontrol of natural gas by 1987.
1978	Transportation: Airline Deregulation Act gives carriers freedom to decide fares and routes and phases out CAB.
1980	Financial institutions: Depository Institutions Deregulation and Monetary Control Act phases out interest rate ceilings and permits S&Ls to offer interest-bearing checking accounts.
1980	Transportation: Staggers Rail Act enables railroads to adjust rates without government approval and to enter into contracts with shippers.
1980	Transportation: Motor Carrier Act removes barriers for new entries and lets operators establish fares and routes with little ICC interference.
1982	Financial institutions: Garn–St. Germain Depository Institutions Act creates federally insured money-market accounts, allows S&Ls to make more commercial and consumer loans, and removes interest rate differential between banks and S&Ls.
1982	Transportation: Bus Regulatory Reform Act allows intercity bus companies to change routes and fares.
1984	Telecommunications: AT&T agrees to divest local operating companies as part of antitrust settlement with Justice Department.
1984	Transportation: Shipping Act permits individual companies to offer lower rates and better service than shipping conferences.
1994	Banking: Interstate Banking and Branching Efficiency Act permits more interstate branching.
1996	Transportation: Interstate Commerce Commission is abolished. Residual functions are transferred to new Surface Transportation Board in DOT.
1996	Communications: Telecommunications Act attempts to increase competition in the industry.
1999	Financial institutions: The Gramm–Leach–Bliley Act repeals the Glass–Steagall Act restricting banks from providing other financial services.

better. More people are traveling by air at lower real costs. Depositors in financial institutions are receiving higher returns on their money, as a greater variety of companies compete for their business. Telephone users are finding that greater competition has resulted in lower long-distance rates, while subsidies to local services have been reduced. Technically, no industry in the United States has been totally deregulated. In the case of aviation, the demise of the Civil Aeronautics Board did not affect the continued government regulation of airports, aircraft safety, and air traffic control systems. The Department of Transportation has inherited the residual functions of the ICC.

Inevitably, the wrenching changes brought about by deregulation have generated problems for specific companies. Managers and workers of many deregulated firms have seen their pay and fringe benefits decline to the competitive norm. Some companies have been unable to survive in the new competitive environment and have gone out of business or have been acquired by stronger firms. All economic change involves transitional costs, which at first may even seem to outweigh the benefits.

Although generalizations are always difficult to make, several types of effects on the competitive structures of the deregulated industries have emerged to date. First of all, the range of variability of performance among the companies in the deregulated industry increases.

Second, the most profitable products come under substantial price pressure. Competition grows most rapidly in those markets. In the brokerage industry, commission rates in the lucrative institutional segment fell 26 percent in the four months following deregulation. In the less profitable area of brokerage sales to individuals, rates decreased only 2 percent.

Third, the resulting industrywide profit squeeze forces personnel reductions and other cost-cutting efforts. These economizing activities occur in both small and large firms, in the latter case primarily to meet competition from new entrants. The pressures on costs tend to be greatest in established firms with higher labor costs than in new entrants into the industry.

Financial institutions have responded to rate deregulation by closing branch offices and reducing payrolls. In contrast, when the government limited the interest they could pay on deposits, banks tended to compete by providing greater convenience and other services.

On the positive side, two types of winners emerge from deregulation. The first category consists of companies that tend to serve national markets with a full line of products and services. For example, the brokerage firm Merrill Lynch took innovative steps prior to the various deregulation steps affecting financial institutions to position itself to expand into segments of the industry that it now was free to enter. Its cash-management account, which combines conventional banking and investment banking features, is an example of the melding of new technology and new markets. Delta Airlines took steps prior to deregulation to position itself for rapid geographic expansion. Heavy capitalization with relatively low debt-to-equity ratios gave it the flexibility to weather the profit squeeze.

The second category of winners under deregulation is low-cost producers that focus on a highly price-sensitive segment of the market. Some of the new entrants turn out to be the successful, low-cost producers—notably, Southwest Airlines—although often the undercapitalized enterprises stay small and unprofitable. Many established old-line firms are burdened with heavy cost structures built up during regulation, and such outlays are difficult to reduce quickly.

The major winners under deregulation are the customers of the previously regulated industries. In the case of freight hauling, company traffic and distribution managers now have a far greater array of carriers to choose from. They have access to an abundance of rate and service package plans not permitted by the ICC. Further, they can enter into long-term agreements with railroads or truckers with few restrictions. Alternatively, the shippers can rely on their own trucking operations via various types of leasing arrangements, even in coordination with other carriers. On balance, it appears that the initial and clearest successes in deregulation occurred in industries that were not natural monopolies, notably trucking and airlines. Thus, eliminating artificial barriers to competition—originally established by government—is most readily justified.

Notes

1. John R. Meyer et al., *The Economics of Competition in the Transportation Industries* (Cambridge, MA: Harvard University Press, 1959).
2. George W. Douglas and James C. Miller III, *Economic Regulation of Domestic Air Transport* (Washington, DC: The Brookings Institution, 1974); Thomas Gale Moore, *Freight Transportation Regulation* (Washington, DC: American Enterprise Institute, 1972).
3. Marver Bernstein, *Regulating Business by Independent Commission* (Princeton, NJ: Princeton University Press, 1955).
4. George J. Stigler, "The Theory of Economic Regulation," *Bell Journal of Economics and Management Science,* Spring 1971, pp. 3–21; Sam Peltzman, "Towards a More General Theory of Regulation," *Journal of Law and Economics,* August 1976, pp. 211–240.
5. Murray L. Weidenbaum, *Government Mandated Price Increases* (Washington, DC: American Enterprise Institute, 1975); Sam Peltzman, *Regulation of Pharmaceutical Innovation* (Washington, DC: American Enterprise Institute, 1974); John P. Gould, *The Davis–Bacon Act* (Washington, DC: American Enterprise Institute, 1971); Rita Ricardo-Campbell, *Food Safety and Regulation* (Washington, DC: American Enterprise Institute, 1974).
6. John H. Anderson, Jr., *Airline Deregulation* (Washington, DC: U.S. General Accounting Office, 1997), p. 1.
7. Steven Morrison and Clifford Winston, "The Government's View of Airline Deregulation," *Milken Institute Review,* Third Quarter 2000, p. 22; Gautam Gowrisankaran, "Competition and Regulation in the Airline Industry," *Federal Reserve Bank of San Francisco Economic Letter,* January 18, 2002, p. 2.
8. Cait Murphy, "Deregulation Isn't the Problem; It's the Answer," *Fortune,* June 25, 2001, pp. 116–123.
9. E. Han Kim and Vijay Singal, "Mergers and Market Power: Evidence from the Airline Industry," *American Economic Review,* June 1993, pp. 549–569.
10. *Airline Competition* (Washington, DC: U.S. General Accounting Office, 1993), p. 2.
11. Clifford Winston and Steven Morrison, *The Evolution of the Airline Industry* (Washington, DC: Brookings Institution, 1996).
12. Murphy, "Deregulation," p. 116.
13. Council on Competitiveness, *Legacy of Regulatory Reform* (Washington, DC: U.S. Government Printing Office, 1992), p. 19; *Economic Report of the President, 1997* (Washington, DC: U.S. Government Printing Office, 1997), p. 190.
14. *New Technologies Improve Safety and Efficiency* (Washington, DC: Association of American Railroads, 2001), p. 1.
15. Robert W. Crandall, "Are We Deregulating Telephone Services?" *Brookings Institution Policy Brief,* March 1997, pp. 1–11.
16. Robert W. Crandall, *Managed Competition in U.S. Telecommunications* (Washington, DC: AEI–Brookings Joint Center for Regulatory Studies, 1999); Thomas W. Hazlett, *Economic and Political Consequences of the 1996 Telecommunications Act* (Washington, DC: AEI–Brookings Joint Center for Regulatory Studies, 1999).
17. "The Nation's New Interstate Banking Law," *Federal Reserve Bank of Philadelphia Business Review,* November/December 1994, p. 21.
18. James Wilcox, *The Repeal of the Glass–Steagall Act and the Advent of Broad Banking in the United States,* Presentation to the National Economists Club, Washington, DC, September 20, 2000, pp. 1–2.

9

TERRORISM
AND BUSINESS

The extensive and multifaceted national responses to the terrorist attacks of September 11, 2001, are altering the balance between the public sector and the private sector in the United States. Threats to the national security are always present. At the end of the Cold War in the late 1980s, defense planners knew that the nature of those threats were changing, particularly those "unconventional" forms of warfare such as terrorism. But the rise of audacious international terrorism networks was not widely appreciated until the virtually simultaneous assaults on the Pentagon and the twin towers of the World Trade Center in lower Manhattan. The attitude both in the United States and in other nations changed abruptly.[1]

At least for a while, the struggle against international terrorism has become the number one priority among federal government programs and activities. Issues closely related to terrorism have been elevated in terms of the attention and financial support given, while many other aspects of government—such as reforming Social Security and dealing with global warming—have been downgraded, at least in relative importance, for the foreseeable future. International terrorism is an enduring phenomenon and the issue is likely to remain an important spur to government activity (see Figure 9.1 for a measure of the long-term trend of terrorist incidents).

The larger role for government is taking many forms: increased military spending, unprecedented emphasis on homeland security, special assistance to companies heavily affected by terrorism, and a rapid expansion in the form and extent of government regulation of private activity, especially business. A useful starting point in analyzing the impacts of these government activities on business is to examine the array of new or expanded government activities that are designed to respond to terrorist threats (see box, "What Is Terrorism?").

GOVERNMENT'S NEW ROLE

The recently created Office of Homeland Security, located in the Executive Office of the President, has overall responsibility for developing governmentwide policies on enhancing the nation's domestic security. Operating responsibilities are assigned to a variety of departments and agencies, which deal with businesses on an individual basis.[2]

DEPARTMENT OF THE TREASURY

The first major antiterrorist step on the part of the federal government in response to the September 11 attacks was an economic action, in the form of a presidential executive order issued on September 24, 2001. It provided for a freeze on the bank accounts and other assets of specific terrorists and terrorist groups. The Department of the Treasury was given the basic assignment to carry out the order.

FIGURE 9.1   International Terrorist Attacks, 1977–2000

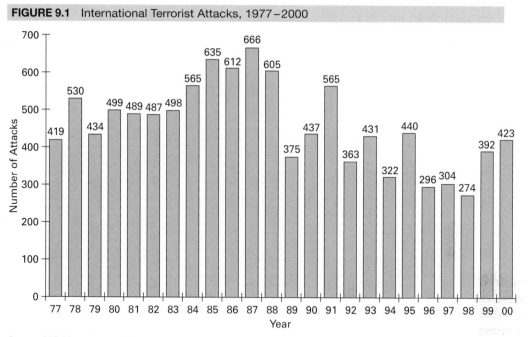

Source: U.S. Department of State, *Patterns of Global Terrorism*, 2002.

BOX 9-1

WHAT IS TERRORISM?

There is no universally accepted definition of terrorism. In fact, many discussions of the subject proceed without any formal terminology. One of the most useful definitions is provided by Christopher C. Harmon, professor of international relations at the Marine Corps University:

Terrorism is the deliberate and systematic murder, maiming, and menacing of the innocent to inspire fear for political ends.[3]

As would be expected, official definitions are more detailed as well as more broad. In the Executive Order of September 24, 2001, blocking terrorist funds, President George W. Bush used the following language:

. . . terrorism means an activity that—

(i) involves a violent act or an act dangerous to human life, property, or infrastructure; and

(ii) appears to be intended—

(A) to intimidate or coerce a civilian population;

(B) to influence the policy of a government by intimidation or coercion; or

(C) to affect the conduct of a government by mass destruction, assassination, kidnapping, or hostage-taking.[4]

President Bush's definition of terrorism is deliberately broad, especially in using the phrase "appears to be intended."

The impacts of the freeze on terrorists' funds were widespread, extending beyond banks to cover brokers, mutual funds, insurance companies, commodity traders, casinos, and money transferors such as American Express and Western Union. The Treasury Department has directed these private companies to do many things (at their own expense):

1. To conduct more "due diligence" investigations of account holders, especially private banking clients, to make sure they are not terrorist groups.
2. To set up anti–money laundering programs — or to expand their existing efforts — in order to prevent the conversion of illegal funds into legitimate financial accounts. Special focus is to be given to private banking accounts, particularly those owned by foreign political figures.
3. To report "suspicious" activities to the Treasury Department (see Figure 9.2 for the required Suspicious Activity Report form).
4. To cease transactions with "shell banks" that have no physical presence in any country.
5. To gain more information about the foreign banks that they do business with.
6. In the case of hedge funds, not to accept money from anonymous sources.

In carrying out these new rules, financial institutions are required to designate special compliance officers, train employees to detect money laundering, and commission independent audits. The companies also establish specific policies and procedures to identify risks and minimize the likelihood of potential terrorists slipping through the various safeguards.

These new functions underscore the role of the Treasury Department as the federal government's second largest law enforcement agency, behind the Department of Justice. The Comptroller of the Currency and the Financial Crimes Enforcement Network in the Office of the Secretary are directly involved in dealing with financial institutions. The increased emphasis on antiterrorism work has expanded the role of the Treasury Department's Bureau of Customs that inspects goods entering the United States from foreign sources. The Internal Revenue Service is also involved in these law enforcement activities, as is the Alcohol, Tobacco, and Firearms Bureau.

DEPARTMENT OF TRANSPORTATION

The largest antiterrorist-induced expansion in civilian agencies has occurred in the Department of Transportation (DOT) with the passage of the Aviation and Transportation Security Act of November 19, 2001. That law established a new Transportation Security Agency in DOT and required the federal government to overhaul its security policies on all modes of transportation. With a target workforce of over 30,000, this new bureau took over from private companies the responsibility for examining baggage and dealing with other security matters at airports and other such terminals. Previously, airport security was not a federal responsibility, but shared between public airport authorities and commercial airlines.

The DOT shares with the Treasury Department and the Federal Reserve System the responsibility for administering the Air Transportation Safety and System Stabilization Act of 2001. That law provided $5 billion to compensate the airline industry for losses resulting from the September 11, 2001, terrorist attacks. It also authorized

Suspicious Activity Report			1

Suspicious Activity Report

ALWAYS COMPLETE ENTIRE REPORT
(SEE INSTRUCTIONS)

FRB:	FR 2230	OMB No. 7100-0212
FDIC:	6710/06	OMB No. 3064-0077
OCC:	8010-9,8010-1	OMB No. 1557-0180
OTS:	1601	OMB No. 1550-0003
NCUA:	2362	OMB No. 3133-0094
TREASURY:	TD F 90-22.47	OMB No. 1506-0001

Revised June 2000 (This revision supersedes all others)

1 Check box below only if correcting a prior report.
  ☐ Corrects Prior Report (see instruction #3 under "How to Make a Report")

Part I   Reporting Financial Institution Information

2 Name of Financial Institution

3 EIN

4 Address of Financial Institution

5 Primary Federal Regulator
  a ☐ Federal Reserve   d ☐ OCC
  b ☐ FDIC   e ☐ OTS
  c ☐ NCUA

6 City   7 State   8 Zip Code | | | | | — | | | |

9 Address of Branch Office(s) where activity occurred   ☐ Multiple Branches (include information in narrative, Part V)

10 City   11 State   12 Zip Code | | | | | — | | | |

13 If institution closed, date closed
  ___/___/___
  MM   DD   YYYY

14 Account number(s) affected, if any   Closed?   Closed?
a _____ ☐ Yes ☐ No   c _____ ☐ Yes ☐ No
b _____ ☐ Yes ☐ No   d _____ ☐ Yes ☐ No

Part II   Suspect Information   ☐ Suspect Information Unavailable

15 Last Name or Name of Entity   16 First Name   17 Middle

18 Address

19 SSN, EIN or TIN

20 City   21 State   22 Zip Code | | | | | — | | | |

23 Country

24 Phone Number – Residence (include area code)
  (   )

25 Phone Number – Work (include area code)
  (   )

26 Occupation/Type of Business

27 Date of Birth
  ___/___/___
  MM   DD   YYYY

28 Admission/Confession?
  a ☐ Yes   b ☐ No

29 Forms of Identification for Suspect:
  a ☐ Driver's License/State ID   b ☐ Passport   c ☐ Alien Registration   d ☐ Other _____
  Number _____   Issuing Authority _____

30 Relationship to Financial Institution:
  a ☐ Accountant   d ☐ Attorney   g ☐ Customer   j ☐ Officer
  b ☐ Agent   e ☐ Borrower   h ☐ Director   k ☐ Shareholder
  c ☐ Appraiser   f ☐ Broker   i ☐ Employee   l ☐ Other _____

31 Is the relationship an insider relationship? a ☐ Yes   b ☐ No
  If Yes specify: c ☐ Still employed at financial institution e ☐ Terminated
             d ☐ Suspended   f ☐ Resigned

32 Date of Suspension, Termination, Resignation
  ___/___/___
  MM   DD   YYYY

Continued

Part III	Suspicious Activity Information		2

33 Date or date range of suspicious activity
From ____/____/_____ To ____/____/_____
MM   DD   YYYY   MM   DD   YYYY

34 Total dollar amount involved in known or suspicious activity
$ | | . | | | . | | | . | | .00

35 Summary characterization of suspicious activity:

a ☐ Bank Secrecy Act/Structuring
Money Laundering
b ☐ Bribery/Gratuity
c ☐ Check Fraud
d ☐ Check Kiting
e ☐ Commercial Loan Fraud

f ☐ Computer intrusion
g ☐ Consumer Loan Fraud
h ☐ Counterfeit Check
i ☐ Counter Credit/Debit Card
j ☐ Counterfeit Instrument (other)
k ☐ Credit Card Fraud

l ☐ Debit Card Fraud
m ☐ Defalcation/Embezzlement
n ☐ False Statement
o ☐ Misuse of Position or Self Dealing
p ☐ Mortgage Loan Fraud
q ☐ Mysterious Disappearance
r ☐ Wire Transfer Fraud

s ☐ Other _____
(type of activity)

36 Amount of loss prior to recovery (if applicable)
$ | | . | | | . | | .00

37 Dollar amount of recovery (if applicable)
$ | | . | | | . | | .00

38 Has the suspicious activity had a material impact on, or otherwise affected, the financial soundness of the institution?
a ☐ Yes   b ☐ No

39 Has the institution's bonding company been notified?
a ☐ Yes   b ☐ No

40 Has any law enforcement agency already been advised by telephone, written communication, or otherwise?
a ☐ DEA   d ☐ Postal Inspection   g ☐ Other Federal
b ☐ FBI   e ☐ Secret Service   h ☐ State
c ☐ IRS   f ☐ U.S. Customs   i ☐ Local
j ☐ Agency Name (for g, h or i) _____

41 Name of person(s) contacted at Law Enforcement Agency

42 Phone Number (include area code)
(   )

43 Name of person(s) contacted at Law Enforcement Agency

44 Phone Number (include area code)
(   )

Part IV	Contact for Assistance

45 Last Name

46 First Name

47 Middle

48 Title/Occupation

49 Phone Number (include area code)
(   )

50 Date Prepared
____/____/_____
MM   DD   YYYY

51 Agency (If not filed by financial institution)

FIGURE 9.2 Suspicious Activity Report Required of Financial Institutions

Source: U.S. Department of the Treasury.

$10 billion in loan guarantees to airlines meeting a variety of federal requirements (see Chapter 14 for details).

Other parts of the Transportation Department are involved in the struggle against terrorism. The Federal Aviation Administration regulates various aspects of aircraft operations, including setting new standards for guarding pilots and their cockpits and for training crews to deal with terrorist incidents. The DOT's Coast Guard has a broad mandate to patrol and protect the nation's long coastlines. That agency is working with commercial fishermen who provide "eyes and ears" to report suspicious vessels or incidents. The fishermen participating in this effort are required to register and to undergo background checks.

DEPARTMENT OF JUSTICE

The USA Patriot Act of October 26, 2001, gave the Justice Department expanded powers of investigation and surveillance, including authority for nationwide search warrants as part of antiterrorism investigations. Under the Patriot Act, the federal government can seize voice mail pursuant to a warrant as well as require consumer credit agencies to furnish information to federal agencies for use in combating international terrorism.

The new far-reaching powers of the Department of Justice include collecting information on alien students from flight schools, language schools, and other vocational institutions. Committing an act of terrorism against a mass transit system also becomes a federal crime. It is now illegal for people or groups to possess substances that can be used as biological or chemical weapons unless their purpose for holding them is "peaceful."

The Department of Justice's Immigration and Naturalization Service (INS) has expanded the scope of its operations, especially to provide more intensive inspection of people trying to enter the United States and to deal with those who overstay their legal entry period. The Justice Department shares with the State and Treasury Departments the expanded authority of the Enhanced Border Security and Visa Entry Reform Act of 2002. That law seeks to make it more difficult for terrorists and their weapons to enter the United States.

THE DEPARTMENT OF HEALTH AND HUMAN SERVICES

A variety of health-related antiterrorist responsibilities has been assigned to the Department of Health and Human Services. Under the Bioterrorism Preparedness Act of 2001, the department's Public Health Service is heavily involved in dealing with biological and chemical terrorist threats. That law expands the National Strategic Pharmaceutical Stockpile and gives a wider role to the Centers for Disease Control and Prevention. Specific actions include better controls on dangerous biological agents, acceleration of the production of smallpox vaccine, and improved training for public-health laboratories in disease surveillance and response.

In 2002, the department's Food and Drug Administration issued voluntary guidelines designed to help prevent terrorist attacks on the nation's food supply. Separate guidelines cover importers and domestic food producers, processors, and retailers. For example, the FDA urges the food industry to check job applicants against a federal list of known criminals. The companies are also requested to establish procedures for checking suspicious liquids or powders found on imported food (see Table 9.1 for details on the FDA guidelines). These FDA issuances are not legally binding, but are a cogent example of the "moral suasion" power of the federal government described in Chapter 1.

OTHER FEDERAL DEPARTMENTS AND AGENCIES

Many other government agencies are involved in the struggle against international terrorism. Enhanced infrastructure protection involves a host of other agencies that deal with private companies. The Nuclear Regulatory Commission focuses on the security of nuclear power plants, while the Federal Energy Regulatory Commission has

TABLE 9.1   FDA Guidelines for Food Supply Security
• Inspect incoming and outgoing vehicles for suspicious activity
• Restrict access to laboratories and to bacteria and toxins
• Beware of employees coming in unusually early or staying late
• Prevent employees from bringing personal items into food-processing areas
• Conduct regular inspections of employees' vehicles, bags, and lockers
• Restrict access to computer control systems
• Inspect ingredients, compressed gas, packaging, and returned products—for signs of tampering
• Watch for unusual behavior by new hires
• Guard against unexpected visitors

Source: U.S. Food and Drug Administration.

a broader charter covering power plants generally, transmission lines, and natural gas pipelines. The Federal Communications Commission has an important responsibility for the integrity of the nation's telecommunications systems.

Following the anthrax episodes of late 2001, the U.S. Postal Service, and especially its corps of postal inspectors, is alert to terrorist threats involving the processing and delivery of the mail. Although not considered to be a federal regulatory agency, the Capitol Police has an important role in restricting traffic and the entry of people into an important part of Washington, D.C. The Secret Service has a similar responsibility in the area surrounding the White House.

State and local governments are also involved in the heightened security arrangements. Virginia's Preparedness and Security Panel has developed a comprehensive program, including construction of an emergency operations headquarters, improved terrorism response training programs for emergency personnel, and increased physical security at bridges and ports. Georgia's Terrorism Task Force includes state agencies for public health, transportation, emergency management, defense, and natural resources. The state's homeland security coordinator works with the Georgia Intelligence Sharing and Tracking Center. Pennsylvania has set up nine regional counterterrorism task forces, composed of police and fire chiefs, medical professionals, and business executives.

Approximately 60 federal, state, and local agencies were involved in providing comprehensive security at the February 2002 Winter Olympics held in Salt Lake City, Utah. The Salt Lake City activities were the first listing in a new federal government category of "National Security Special Events."

THE ROLE OF BUSINESS IN FIGHTING TERRORISM

The private enterprise system plays an important and varied role in the fight against terrorism. At the outset, Secretary of Defense Donald H. Rumsfeld explained these business aspects in vivid terms:

> The uniforms of this conflict will be bankers' pinstripes and programmers' grunge just as assuredly as desert camouflage.[5]

CUTTING OFF THE MONEY FLOW TO TERRORISM

The first role of business in the struggle against terrorism is helping to cut off the money flows to the terrorists. Numerous banks and other financial institutions are involved in a great many other nations. The flow of money is vital to the international terrorist groups, but they use relatively small amounts. The 1993 bombing of the World Trade Center killed six and injured more than 1,000 people. The cost to the conspirators, however, has been estimated at less than $50,000 in bomb materials and other expenses. The cost to the terrorists of the far more deadly September 11, 2001, attacks is estimated at approximately $500,000—compared to over $135 billion of property losses, cleanup costs, and government bailouts that resulted. Thus, the effort to curtail the flow of funds to terrorists and to inhibit their use of the money is akin to the proverbial search for a needle in a haystack. The global financial "haystack" is especially daunting, with over $1 trillion crossing borders each day.[6]

The anti–money laundering and related antiterrorism efforts of financial institutions, although difficult to estimate in terms of additional expenses incurred, surely increase the overhead costs of these businesses. To the extent that they inconvenience their legitimate customers in the process, the new procedures may also reduce the amount of business that they transact.

Banks are not the only companies participating in the effort to stem the flow of money used to promote terrorism. As noted earlier, the antiterrorist regulations extend to many other types of financial "intermediaries," including brokerage firms, mutual funds, casinos, and wire transfer services. From September 2001 to May 2002, $34 million in terrorist assets were frozen in the United States. Another $70 million worth of assets in known terrorist organizations were blocked by 161 other nations that are participating in the overall effort to respond to terrorism.[7]

BUSINESS AND HOMELAND SECURITY

The federal government sets the basic policies on screening transfers at border crossings and airports and determines many other internal security matters. However, on a day-to-day basis, most people interact more frequently with corporate security personnel and, especially in their working lives, they encounter the security policies of businesses (see Table 9.2).[8] Thus, private enterprises such as factories and private building management companies increasingly screen customers, visitors, and their vehicles. Private employers more frequently do background reviews on new hires, while mail and other deliveries to private establishments are more carefully checked than prior to September 11, 2001.

Business also designs and produces the antiterrorist equipment and systems used by both the public and private sectors. This market is hardly stagnant these days. The demand for bomb-sniffing dogs has increased dramatically. A man-and-dog team costs $100 to $250 an hour, with a typical daily minimum charge of $2,000. Sales of gloves and other protective devices for people as well as explosive-detecting gadgets have risen rapidly. Guards and inspectors of all sorts are in demand, as are the metal detectors that they use. The construction of barriers as "checkpoints" for vehicles has become increasingly common, as has the use of identification cards and security keys and readers. The application of new technology is in high demand, notably stepped-up research and development and production of new electronic systems to locate and

TABLE 9.2   Responding to Threats From Terrorism

Color Code/Risk of Terrorist Attack	Recommended Response
GREEN/LOW	• Refine and exercise preplanned protective measures. • Ensure that emergency personnel receive training on protective measures. • Regularly assess facilities for vulnerabilities and take measures to address them.
BLUE/GENERAL	• Check communications with designated emergency response or command locations. • Review and update emergency response procedures.
YELLOW/ SIGNIFICANT	• Increase surveillance of critical locations. • Coordinate emergency plans with nearby jurisdictions. • Assess further refinement of protective measures. • Implement contingency and emergency response plans as appropriate.
ORANGE/HIGH	• Coordinate necessary security efforts with armed forces or law enforcement agencies. • Take additional precautions at public events. • Prepare to work at an alternate site or with a dispersed work force. • Restrict access to essential personnel only.
RED/SEVERE	• Assign emergency response personnel and preposition emergency response teams. • Monitor, redirect or constrain transportation systems. • Increase or redirect personnel to address critical emergency needs.

Source: U.S. Office of Homeland Security.

identify terrorists. Invariably, consultants with various specialties are heavily involved, especially those with experience relevant to terrorism and other forms of unconventional warfare.

In addition, business develops and produces the medicines and the related equipment used to respond to biological and chemical attacks. Unlike nuclear materials (which are almost all controlled by governments), chemical and biological agents are mainly the purview of private industry. Thus, business bears the primary responsibility for devising ways to keep such material out of the hands of potential evildoers. Shortly after September 11, 2001, Air Products and Chemicals Corporation established a high-level director of product safety integrity. This new function combines corporate security with the activities of the company's product safety specialists.

Medicines to alleviate and vaccines to prevent such diseases as anthrax and small-pox have become an important category of health care budgets, and a great variety of new items is being marketed. An example of special equipment is the Bio-Threat Alert Test Set-Up. This small plastic device detects anthrax, botulism, plague, and other toxins. Moreover, business designs and produces the weapon systems used by our armed forces in military operations against terrorist groups and against the nations that harbor and support them. Current outlays and future budgets are rising for procurement of aircraft, bombs, missiles, ships, and related equipment, especially tracking and communication devices.

THE INDIRECT ROLES OF BUSINESS IN RESPONDING TO TERRORISM

Business also contributes in many indirect ways to the fight against terrorism. In its overseas activities, private enterprise helps bolster the economies of the nations that are America's allies in the struggle against terrorism. Many of those countries are poor and developing and so are a fertile ground for recruitment of future terrorists. Their economic health as well as their national stability often depends in good measure on their income from exports. Pakistan, an especially strategically located ally, employs about 60 percent of its industrial workforce in textiles and apparel manufacturing. The continuing openness of the U.S. market is especially important to this vital industry of a key ally.

Thus, international trade policy intersects with antiterrorist policy, although the two are developed by different executive agencies and congressional committees. The interest of the Department of Commerce and the U.S. Trade Representatives in negotiating market-opening policies would seem to support the efforts of the State and Defense Departments in maintaining a global coalition in the struggle against terrorism. Unfortunately, instability in Pakistan—in part a result of its cooperation in fighting terrorism—has diminished the attractiveness of its textile and clothing industries as sources of supply to American retailers.[9]

At home, private enterprise contributes in many ways. Companies provide a variety of assistance to domestic victims of terrorism. Direct corporate financial contributions to the victims and their families have been substantial. Counseling services to employees are also provided, especially in industries either hit by terrorists or that are particularly liable to terrorist attacks. Psychiatrists, psychoanalysts, and terrorism experts are called upon increasingly to help allay fears and to help victims deal with the aftereffects of September 11.

The most indirect role of business may be the most powerful—to maintain the flow of goods and services to consumers and, in the process, to generate the jobs, incomes, and taxes that keep the economy moving ahead and the government adequately financed. Psychologically, maintaining the pace of economic activity in the face of rising costs and disruptions from the struggle against terrorism is an important positive response to the fears that terrorist groups are trying to generate.

The role of economic policy is very different in these circumstances than in conventional wars. In previous conflicts, civilian spending had to be restrained in order to provide adequate resources for a military effort that quickly used up a great amount of resources. Under current circumstances, however, the need is to maintain the strength of the national economy so it can support a long-term struggle against terrorism. There are few shortages of supplies for military operations. Most of the actual operations involve equipment already in the Pentagon's inventory, or items that can easily be ordered from existing production lines. Thus, the main task of business is to continue "minding the store."

Perhaps the most underappreciated role of business is its day-to-day interaction overseas with the residents of other countries. In many foreign countries, more of the local people interact with U.S. businesses than with U.S. government officials— either as employees of U.S. companies or their suppliers or as purchasers and users of U.S.–produced or -designed products and services. The latter cover a wide terrain

ranging from the food and refreshments marketed by well-known American companies such as McDonald's, Coca-Cola, and KFC to movies, music, and videos.
Numerous U.S. companies doing business overseas are employers of local labor, and
these companies often impose standards that are higher than locally prevailing
ones.

However, such a benign relationship is not always the case. Some products identified with the United States may violate prevailing local customs and mores. Overseas
contractors and subcontractors of U.S. companies do not always follow the highest
standards in dealing with their employees. Business needs to be aware of the powerful
albeit indirect impacts of its actions overseas, particularly in the vital worldwide battle
for hearts and minds.

THE NEGATIVE SIDE

From the viewpoint of the individual enterprise, heightened security measures are
basically an expense. A bigger outlay for these overhead items raises the cost of production. For the economy as a whole, this means, as a general proposition, producing
the same output with more input—which results in a decline in productivity and is a
downward force on the national standard of living. These new costs are numerous:
security services, personnel investigations, protective equipment, higher insurance
premiums, more inventory to protect against delays in delivery, and the acquisition of
teleconferencing equipment and services to replace travel.

For example, in making the deliveries of the company's products, Filterfresh's
250 drivers report an average delay of about an hour a day due to increased security
arrangements in the buildings of their customers. Economist David Hale estimates
an increase of 15 percent, or approximately $18 billion, in overall workplace secu-
rity costs in the year following the September 11 attacks. Total additional costs
due to companies responding to the continuing threats of terrorism have been projected at $150 billion a year, with increased costs of logistic and insurance the major
components.[10]

Simultaneously, a slowdown in globalization is occurring, notably a review of
global supply chains with a view toward their curtailment. New antiterrorist measures to check cargoes intended for the United States prior to their leaving the
exporting nation are estimated to extend from eight to ten days or more—the time
it normally takes for shipments to cross the Atlantic Ocean from Western Europe.[11]
There is also greater reluctance to travel by air, especially abroad. Fewer Americans
want to work overseas, especially in countries where terrorism is a major threat.
Thus, the outlook is for reduced investments in developing nations due to higher
perceived risks, and higher costs of exports and imports due to delays resulting from
heightened border security. In effect, terrorism has imposed a new tax on international business.

Surely, many security measures have been very effective. A striking example was
provided by the immediate grounding of all planes within U.S. airspace on September
11, 2001, which prevented a fifth hijacking—and maybe others. More indirectly, the
costly planning efforts for Y2K in late 1999, widely viewed with skepticism in early
2000, were essential in returning many companies to operation quickly after the
September 11 terrorist attacks.

NEW BUSINESS OPPORTUNITIES

The continuing struggle against international terrorism, although it imposes significant costs on society in general and on business in particular, also is a source of new or expanded market opportunities for some companies. The rise of terrorist threats also influences business decision making in other important ways. These latter impacts range from locational decisions and changes in procurement patterns to a far more fundamental shift in emphasis from enhancing productivity via new investments and toward controlling rapidly mounting overhead costs.

PRODUCING ANTITERRORIST EQUIPMENT AND SERVICES

Many companies who have been producing for conventional markets are adapting their products to meet the rapidly rising demand for antiterrorist equipment. Thus, InVision Technologies is retooling medical CAT–scan technologies into machines that scan luggage for explosives. Bismuth Cartridge, which sells duck-hunting bullets that shatter on impact, offers its product to sky marshals in case they must shoot while in the passenger cabin of an airplane (the bismuth prevents the bullets from penetrating the body of the airplane).

Other companies find that their products are directly relevant in the new market-place. Traditional providers of security services, such as Pinkerton and Wackenhut Corporation, have experienced substantial increases in demand for their services, as have suppliers of gloves and other equipment used by mail sorters who fear another anthrax episode.

Traditional suppliers of military equipment have been trying to adopt their products and capabilities to homeland security needs. Northrop Grumman believes that some of its advanced technology can be used in developing difficult-to-counterfeit "smart cards" containing biometric and other personal identification information. Raytheon is experimenting with advanced communications equipment that would help direct police, fire, and medical personnel in responding to terrorist attacks. Boeing is studying whether sensors designed to track missiles could be used to identify hijacked airliners; the company obtained a major order (in excess of $500 million) to install and maintain explosives-detecting machines at U.S. airports. Lockheed Martin has won contracts to train the newly federalized workforce of airport baggage and passenger screeners. The company also received a contract to redesign airport security checkpoints to accommodate new metal detectors and federal screeners. General Dynamics hopes to sell armored personnel vehicles to police departments.[12]

Table 9.3 provides a sample of the variety of companies involved in antiterrorist activity, ranging from bomb-detecting dogs to voice recognition and other personnel recognition systems.

SHIFTING PURCHASING PATTERNS AND OPERATING SYSTEMS

Following the dramatic terrorist attacks of September 11, 2001, many companies have altered the way they do business. Acquiring antiterrorist equipment and services, as described in the previous section, is the most obvious "first order" type of response.

TABLE 9.3 Companies Providing Antiterrorist Equipment and Services	
Company	*Typical Product or Service*
American Science and Engineering	Makes X-ray gear
Annin & Co.	Manufactures flags
Bankers Systems	Offers software to comply with the Patriot Act
Bayer	Produces CIPRO, used to counter anthrax
Bismuth Cartridge	Makes safer bullets and shotgun shells (composed of bismuth)
Blue Lance	Provides computer security products
Boeing	Produces explosives-detection machinery
Choice Point Inc.	Does employee background screening
Control Risks Group	Offers security consultant services
Detection Support Services	Hires out bomb-detecting dogs and handlers
Forensic Investigative Associates	Gives advice on security systems
Hire Right	Checks employee backgrounds
Identix	Sets up security systems using fingerprints for identification
InVision Technologies	Develops machines that scan luggage for explosives
Lockheed-Martin	Redesigns airport security checkpoints
Meridian Medical Technologies	Markets equipment that injects antidotes to nerve gas
Nuance Communications	Supplies voice recognition technology
Pearl Software	Makes tools for Internet monitoring
Tetracore, Inc.	Manufactures devices to detect toxins
Versar Inc.	Tests mailrooms for biological contamination
Wackenhut Corp.	Provides security guards and related services

The "second order" responses may become far more important in the ensuing years. Domestically, some companies are decentralizing their operations to avoid excessive concentration of resources in one highly visible and vulnerable headquarters office. Specifically, several financial institutions that had centered their operations in or near the World Trade Center in Manhattan have been moving portions of their activities to nearby locations in Connecticut and New Jersey. Many individuals, in business and as consumers, are using the railroad with far greater frequency than in the recent past and phone calls and e-mail rather than conventional post office services. Overseas, some U.S. corporations are shifting activities from nations deemed unstable and thus risky locations for business to more stable, albeit more expensive, areas of operation.

Similarly, senior executives of widely known companies, concerned about kidnapping or other hazards, are often changing the pattern of their day-to-day activities. CEOs who only occasionally hired an unarmed bodyguard to accompany them on some overseas trips now prefer armed guards and armed drivers, as well as bullet-proof vehicles.[13] Using private airplanes based at company-controlled locations has become more popular. Such moves are also encouraged by the increased "hassle factor" involved in going through the more burdensome security procedures of major airports and commercial airlines.

Some of these changes may expand domestic employment. Movie producers, who have often used lower-cost overseas locations, are shifting away from some of the "exotic" locales that are now deemed to be relatively dangerous. Thus, more carpenters, hairdressers, lighting technicians, and extras—all of whom tend to be hired in the locality where the movies are made—are finding jobs with film studios in the Los Angeles area.

At all levels of management, telecommuting is increasingly popular, as more people work from an office at home. In some ways, working at home can be a substantial cost saver, especially when combined with various forms of advanced technology. Thus, meetings, which hitherto required the participants to fly to a common location, are often now replaced by conference calls or videoconferencing. Frequently, such activity requires a variety of communication or transportation support services, including sending each participant the material to be covered at the meeting via e-mail, fax, or special messenger service.

The continuing concerns about future terrorist attacks are prompting companies of all sizes to do more disaster planning. For larger companies, this often involves some form of "off-site" computer backup to supplement in-house records should those records be destroyed. Private companies, such as Iron Mountain, Inc., store paper records and computer tapes at numerous locations around the world. Following the September 11, 2001, attacks, nearly 100 Iron Mountain customers ordered more than 1 million tapes from the company's vaults. Its prompt service was critical to the quick recovery experienced by many firms in lower Manhattan's financial district.

Antiterrorism planning often requires developing a closer interaction with the local community. Because of the multiplicity of chemical plants in New Jersey, companies in the chemical industry have taken the lead in setting up Community Advisory Panels (CAPs). The CAP for Woodbridge, N.J., in addition to five chemical companies, consists of representatives of a railroad, a refinery, a natural gas pipeline, and a utility. The CAP briefings are attended by local government officials and interested civic leaders.[14]

Some businesses are developing their own contingency plans to deal with future terrorist attacks, particularly if they operate in a variety of countries. As a result, risk assessment and risk reduction services report expanded demand as their analyses of country risk receive more serious attention. The services desired include risk profiles for senior executives who may face challenging situations, especially overseas.

Conclusions

The struggle against terrorism is being waged on two fronts. The first is the most obvious: Government forces, military and civilian, directly fight the terrorists and their networks. The second front is also vital, especially in a long struggle. It is to maintain—and utilize—the economic power of the United States. The heart of that strength is the private enterprise system (in World War II, it was called the Arsenal of Democracy).

In time, business is likely to develop more effective and less costly ways of responding to the concerns generated by terrorist threats. Nevertheless, the ongoing activities of international terrorist groups will continue, in effect, to levy a hidden tax on American business in the form of added costs of operation.

Notes

1. *To Prevail: An American Strategy for the Campaign Against Terrorism* (Washington, DC: CSIS Press, 2001).
2. In June 2002, President George W. Bush recommended to Congress creating the Department of Homeland Security and transferring to it major security-related agencies in the Departments of Agriculture, Energy, Justice, Transportation, and the Treasury and several other federal organizations.
3. Christopher C. Harmon, "Advancing U.S. National Interests: Effective Counterterrorism," *Vital Speeches of the Day,* December 15, 2001, pp. 135–136.
4. President George W. Bush, *Executive Order Blocking Property and Prohibiting Transactions with Persons Who Commit, Threaten to Commit, or Support Terrorism* (Washington, DC: The White House, September 24, 2001), p. 3.
5. Donald H. Rumsfeld, "A New Kind of War," *New York Times,* September 27, 2001, p. A25.
6. Sidney Weintraub, "Disrupting the Financing of Terrorism," *Washington Quarterly,* Winter 2002, pp. 53–60.
7. Kimberly L. Thachuk, "Terrorism's Financial Lifeline," *Strategic Forum,* May 2002, p. 4.
8. Murray Weidenbaum, "Economic Warriors Against Terrorism," *Washington Quarterly,* Winter 2002, pp. 43–52.
9. Keith Bradsher, "Pakistanis Fume As Clothing Sales to U.S. Tumble," *New York Times,* June 23, 2002, p. 3.
10. Anna Bernasek, "The Friction Economy," *Fortune,* February 18, 2002, pp. 104–112; David D. Hale, *Rethinking Safety and Security in Business and Government,* Presentation to the Davos World Economic Forum, New York City, February 2, 2002.
11. "Ports in a Storm," *The Economist,* July 6, 2002, p. 62.
12. Yochi Dreazen, "Spreading the Wealth," *Wall Street Journal,* March 28, 2002, p. R7; James Dao, "Internal Security Is Attracting a Crowd of Arms Contractors," *New York Times,* March 20, 2002, p. C11; Stephen Power and J. Lynn Lunsford, "Boeing, Lockheed Martin Win U.S. Pacts to Secure Airports," *Wall Street Journal,* June 10, 2002, p. A4.
13. Carol Hymowitz, "Business's New Agenda," *Wall Street Journal,* March 11, 2002, p. R6.
14. Rick Mullin, "Getting a Jump on Hometown Security," *Chemical Weekly,* July 3, 2002, p. 50.

10

REFORMING GOVERNMENT REGULATION

⟞⟝⟞⟝⟞

Over the years, many efforts have been made to improve the process of government regulation of business. Some of the changes have required legislative enactments; they have been slow in coming. Many others could be carried out by executive branch authority; substantial progress has occurred in that way. In the aggregate, most of the proposals for reform share a common approach: Governmental decision makers should examine the many impacts of regulatory programs before they issue new regulations. Requiring various types of benefit–cost analyses before rules can be promulgated is the most frequent and ambitious approach that has been followed, but many other potential improvements have been suggested.

The advent of a professional literature on measuring the impacts of regulation[1] has fueled a concern about improving the effectiveness and reducing the burden of the vast network of rules, prohibitions, and requirements that government imposes on the private sector.

EXECUTIVE BRANCH REFORM INITIATIVES

Growing public awareness of the high costs of regulation has provided the impetus for the executive branch of the federal government to undertake important changes. President Gerald Ford instituted a requirement whereby federal agencies had to prepare "inflation impact" statements prior to issuing new regulations.[2] With modifications to cover more than the cost or inflationary aspect, this requirement for analyzing the impacts of pending regulations continues to the present time.[3]

President Jimmy Carter created a Regulatory Analysis Review Group (RARG), headed by the chairman of the Council of Economic Advisers, to review the economic impact of 10 to 20 proposed major regulations a year. The knowledge that a proposed regulation would be reviewed by the RARG increased the regulatory agencies' awareness of costs and other economic impacts. The Carter administration stressed that its requirements for a regulatory analysis should not be interpreted as subjecting rules to a strict benefit–cost test. It believed that requiring agencies to demonstrate mathematically that benefits outweigh costs would act as a straitjacket to inhibit new regulations.

The Reagan administration took a major step by formally requiring benefit–cost analysis in the regulatory development process, and this approach was continued by President George H. W. Bush. By executive order, President Reagan mandated that regulatory impact analyses be made an integral part of the process in which rules are developed, instead of being mere after-the-fact justifications. The new policy statement also created stronger White House oversight of regulatory activity through the Office of Management and Budget (OMB). Regulatory agencies under the president's jurisdiction were required to make their regulatory decisions according to benefit–cost and cost-effectiveness criteria, to the extent permitted by law.

Under the executive order, all regulations had to be submitted to OMB for review at least 60 days prior to publication in the *Federal Register*. On occasion, OMB asked for further information before a rule was published, but its concurrence was not required. Regulatory agencies determined which of their new regulations were major and submitted regulatory impact analyses to OMB along with their proposals. An economic impact of $100 million a year was the designated threshold for determining whether a regulation was "major," although there were many exceptions.

The Clinton administration rescinded the Reagan executive orders on regulatory review. Nevertheless, by Executive Order 12866, President Clinton reaffirmed OMB as the central agency charged with review of proposed regulations. However, the regulatory agencies only had to find that the benefits of the intended regulation "justified" its costs. OMB could require a demonstration that the benefits generated by a regulation exceeded the costs imposed. Clinton's executive order told the agencies to do many sensible things in the process of drafting rules, including identifying alternative ways of meeting governmental objectives, considering benefits and costs, and using market-based alternatives and performance standards. (See box, "Economic Analysis of Federal Regulations.")

The administration of President George W. Bush has kept in force the Clinton executive order on regulatory review, underscoring the point that OMB review of proposed regulations and the use of benefit–cost analysis had become a bipartisan policy. In addition, it issued supplemental instructions and guidance designed to put more "teeth" into the process. In March 2001, the Bush administration told the regulatory agencies that each risk assessment should be "an objective, realistic and scientifically balanced analysis." It recommended that the agencies subject their regulatory analyses and supporting technical documents to independent peer review. Further, the agencies were warned that proposed regulations submitted for OMB review might be returned on any of the following grounds:

- The analyses are inadequate.
- The proposed regulatory standards are not justified by the analysis.
- The regulation is not consistent with the presidential executive order on regulatory review.

In the Bush administration's first year in office, it returned 17 proposed regulations for further work by the promulgating agencies (the Clinton administration turned back only 16 rules in its entire eight years in office).

SHORTCOMINGS AND ACCOMPLISHMENTS

On balance, all formal systems of review since the Ford presidency have tried to convince the often reluctant officials of the federal regulatory agencies to analyze the implications of their rules before issuing them. That approach has been somewhat successful in getting regulators and their supporting interest groups to think about the costs and the benefits they impose on society.

Nevertheless, shortcomings of the regulatory review process have become apparent, although some of them have existed from the outset. The most serious of these is

BOX 10-1

ECONOMIC ANALYSIS OF FEDERAL REGULATIONS

According to the Office of Management and Budget, an economic analysis of federal regulations should contain the following elements:

1. *The need for the proposed action*
   a. Does the problem to be dealt with constitute a significant market failure?
   b. If not, is there another compelling need for it, such as concerns relating to income distribution or improving governmental processes?
   c. Is the proposal the result of a statutory or judicial directive?

2. *An examination of alternative approaches*
   Show that the government agency has considered alternative approaches to the problem and provides the reasoning for selecting the proposed regulatory change over such alternatives. The agency should consider:
   a. More performance-oriented standards for health, safety, and environmental regulations.
   b. Different requirements for different segments of the regulated population.
   c. Alternative levels of stringency.
   d. Other methods of ensuring compliance and other measures of compliance.
   e. More market-oriented approaches, including relying on better information.

3. *Analysis of benefits and costs*
   a. *General considerations:* Assumptions should be made explicit and the effects of using alternative assumptions should be analyzed. Where benefits and costs occur in different time periods, they should be discounted to present values, the discount rate approximating the opportunity cost of capital (the before-tax rate of return to private investment).
      In choosing among alternatives, benefit–cost ratios should be used with care. Selecting the alternative with the highest benefit–cost ratio may not identify the best alternative, since an alternative with a lower benefit–cost

ratio may have higher net benefits (the absolute difference between the benefits and the costs).
   b. *Benefits:* State the beneficial effects of the proposed regulatory change and its principal alternatives. Include estimates in monetary terms of the present value of incremental benefits to society to the maximum extent possible. Benefits estimated in monetary terms should be expressed in constant dollars. Other favorable effects should be presented and explained.
      There should be an explanation of the mechanism by which the proposed action is expected to yield the anticipated benefits. A schedule of monetized benefits should be included, showing the type of benefit and to whom and when it would accrue. The principle of "willingness-to-pay" captures the notion of opportunity cost by providing an aggregate measure of what individuals are willing to forego to enjoy a particular benefit. In expressing the benefit of reducing fatality risks, the analysis may estimate the value of life years extended by the proposed regulation.
   c. *Costs:* Include estimates in monetary terms of the present value of all incremental costs to society of the proposed regulatory change and its principal alternatives. Other costs should be presented and explained. Estimates of costs should be based on credible changes in technology over time, such as a slowing in the rate of innovation because of delays in the regulatory process.

4. *Choosing the proposed regulatory action*
   When an agency determines that a regulation is the best available method of achieving the regulatory objective, it shall design its regulations in the most cost-effective manner to achieve the regulatory objective.

the inherent limitations of executive branch review of regulatory agency decisions. The most critical part of the regulatory process occurs earlier—when Congress writes and enacts the statutes under which the regulatory agencies operate. That crucial legislative stage is exempt from any requirement to examine the potential impact or effectiveness of the proposed regulatory law.

Compounding the problem, many regulatory statutes, especially in the area of environment and safety, prohibit or severely restrict any use of economic analysis in the executive branch's rule-making process. For example, the Supreme Court, in two related decisions, *Industrial Union Department, AFL–CIO* v. *American Petroleum Institute* (1980) and *American Textile Manufacturers Institute* v. *Donovan* (1981), effectively prohibited the use of cost-effective analysis in the development of regulations under OSHA.

Thus, it is often futile for any president to direct a regulatory agency to choose "the most cost-effective approach." This is certainly the case, and frequently so, when the governing statute closely prescribes the specific actions to be taken, which may be far from the most cost-effective approach.[4]

Another shortcoming of the regulatory review process is the exemption of the various independent regulatory agencies from any presidentially mandated regulatory review process, although they may voluntarily choose to follow some of the procedures. This limitation means that many large agencies of the regulatory establishment are beyond the purview of OMB's reform efforts, namely the Federal Communications Commission, the Federal Energy Regulatory Commission, the Federal Trade Commission, the International Trade Commission, the National Labor Relations Board, the Nuclear Regulatory Commission, the Securities and Exchange Commission, and the Federal Reserve Board.

Concern about controlling the cost of regulation has resulted in the introduction in Congress of hundreds of bills on the subject. These proposed laws cover a wide variety of approaches, ranging from mandating that all executive branch agencies prepare economic impact statements for proposed regulations to requiring scientific justification. Several key alternatives, not necessarily mutually exclusive, have received the bulk of the attention in legislative hearings and public debates.

PROPOSALS FOR REFORM

The proposals to reform government regulation extend from those with the lightest touch, such as suggestions merely to provide more information about the prospective impacts of a regulatory change, to creating firm mathematical tests of benefits and costs that must be passed before a new regulation is issued.

ECONOMIC ANALYSIS

The most frequently encountered suggestion to reform the process of issuing government regulations is to establish by statute a formal requirement for the agency to provide an economic analysis of the proposal. The institution by executive order of economic impact statements for new regulations is an important and useful innovation, but that approach has basic limitations. As noted earlier, the *independent* regulatory commissions, such as the FCC (in contrast to the cabinet departments and operating agencies), are not subject to presidential review on regulatory matters. Moreover, the courts have held that many regulatory agencies (the FDA and OSHA, for example) are prohibited or limited by their legislative charters in weighing economic factors in their decision making. A general law passed by Congress requiring each government agency to perform economic analyses of its regulations before issuing them might overcome such objections. Several variations of this idea have been introduced, but none has been enacted.

Under some legislative proposals, the government agency issuing a proposed rule also would be charged with preparing a statement analyzing many of its impacts, including (1) cost to consumers and business; (2) effects on employment, productivity, and competition; and (3) identification of alternatives, including an explanation of why they were rejected. Such requirements for merely analyzing the impacts of regulation constitute the mildest reform approach.

Specifying the weight given to economic factors in agency decision making presents another opportunity for reform. After all, a reluctant agency can merely go through the motions of studying the effects of its actions on the economy and proceed as it originally intended. To deal with this concern, proposals have been made to codify the formal benefit–cost analysis that has been required through executive order (which can be changed by any successor).

Formal benefit–cost tests with numerical measurements of the advantages and disadvantages represent a logical follow-through. Thus, regulation could be carried to the point where the added costs equaled the benefits, and no further. Overregulation (regulation for which the incremental costs exceed the benefits) would be avoided. But the actual implementation of this approach involves difficult conceptual and measurement questions. There is a natural tendency for a government agency, or any other organization, to be generous in estimating the good that it does (the benefits) and to deprecate the magnitude of the resources required to achieve those results (the costs).

In recent years, Congress has considered, but not enacted, legislation to require regulatory agencies to perform detailed assessments of costs and benefits. In 1995, the proposed Comprehensive Regulatory Reform Act was passed in the House of Representatives but failed in the Senate by one vote. This proposal would have required each regulatory agency to prepare a comprehensive benefit–cost analysis prior to issuing a new rule.

A REGULATORY BUDGET

The appropriations for the regulatory agencies are relatively small portions of the government's budget; the totals for 55 federal regulatory agencies in fiscal year 2003 came to less than 2 percent of all federal outlays. As a result, limited attention is given to regulatory expenses during the budget preparation and review process. One reform approach is to give each regulatory agency a "budget" of private compliance costs that it can impose by its regulations. Not only would an agency be given $X million a year for operating costs, it also would be assigned a ceiling of $Y billion of social costs that it could generate during the same period. Under the regulatory budget concept, Congress would be focusing on the total costs involved in the process of government regulation.

A regulatory budget can be viewed from three different perspectives: as an information mechanism, a policy-management device, or a method of expenditure control.

As an information mechanism, a regulatory budget would require statistical reporting of regulatory outlays and the compilation of a regulatory database that would be similar to the existing national income and product accounts.

Alternatively, a regulatory budget could be a part of the policy-making process. Regulatory budget goals would be established as an important part of determining regulatory policy, but not as absolute ceilings. A third approach would be to establish a regulatory budget process analogous to the existing fiscal budget process. This would involve preparation of the regulatory budget under the supervision of the president, review by Congress, and supervision of the execution by the OMB. Because regulatory budget ceilings would be enforced, the regulatory budget process would become a key control over policy.

Thus far, Congress has only enacted a requirement for OMB submitting annual estimates of regulatory costs and benefits.[5] Such preliminary action is intended to stimulate the development of a database needed for any subsequent move toward regulatory budgeting.

SUNSET LAWS

Many government programs tend to prolong their existence far beyond their initial need and justification. Under the sunset approach, Congress would periodically review each regulatory agency to determine whether its continuation was worthwhile in light of present circumstances. This procedure would provide Congress with a formal opportunity to revise the underlying regulatory statutes or to determine that a given agency is no longer needed and that the "sun" should be allowed to "set" on it. Several states have enacted similar proposals, with uneven results to date. At the federal level, the sunset mechanism might be an effective way of pursuing a deregulation approach in the case of the remaining older, one-industry regulatory agencies.

The sunset device is viewed by its proponents as an action-forcing mechanism because the prospect of termination of an agency's charter (in the absence of positive congressional action) would force needed reviews of existing regulatory programs. However, as some skeptics note, the impact of this reform may be less than intended. The reviews may be perfunctory, and the extension of popular regulatory legislation might even be the occasion for adding irrelevant or undesirable riders to the renewal statute.

STATUTORY REFORM

The most significant legislative action in the regulatory reform area to date has been in the transportation area, notably the Airline Deregulation Act of 1978, which put the Civil Aeronautics Board (CAB) out of business (see Chapter 8). In contrast, none of the procedural reforms described earlier—economic analyses, regulatory budgets, or sunsetting—has been enacted by Congress.

The relative success of the CAB experience has drawn attention to the possibility of fundamentally revamping the statutory basis for individual regulatory agencies. Experience over the years confirms that the fundamental shortcomings of government regulation result more from statutory than from executive deficiencies (see Chapter 7).

Laws that mandate the pursuit of unrealistic goals or unreasonable methods for social regulation are attractive candidates for revision. In the case of the basic statutory approach underlying the regulation of job safety, for example, regulatory reform is not only a matter of achieving greater economic efficiency. To achieve a major improvement, it is necessary to shift to a regulatory regime that is more likely to achieve the intended goal of a safer workplace.

REDUCING REGULATORY INVOLVEMENT

The CAB experience has also generated increased attention to the general notion of using alternatives to regulation for achieving public objectives. In the case of other traditional, one-industry types of regulation of business (such as by the FCC), a greater role could also be given to competition and to market forces. "Unregulated" markets are subject to the antitrust laws, a form of government intervention designed to maintain a workably competitive marketplace. As discussed in Chapter 7, antitrust enforcement is a form of government regulation—but, unlike other regulations, it can be designed to foster the conditions of a competitive market rather than attempting to offset its defects.

IMPROVED INFORMATION

In the area of consumer safety, as we have seen in Chapter 3, a greater provision of information on potential hazards can be more effective than attempting to ban specific products or setting standards requiring expensive alterations in existing products. The information approach takes into account the great variety of consumer desires and capabilities. More widespread dissemination of data on product-associated accidents, for example, might encourage firms to devote more attention to safety in the design of the goods they sell. (See box, "Views on Regulation of Cancer-Causing Chemicals," for an indication of consumer support for relying on better information.) A similar approach might be taken in the case of circulating data on factory accident statistics in an effort to promote safer workplaces.

Although mandatory disclosure is a form of regulation, it may be viewed at times as a preferable alternative mechanism because it neither interferes with the production process nor restricts individual choice. The greater flow of information may also be seen as an effort to achieve a more competitive economy. However, when the government sets the standards for information rather than relying on competitive forces, many inefficiencies can result, such as overloading the consumer with unusable details (such as the hard-to-read fine print frequently encountered on consumer packaging).

USING MARKET INCENTIVES

Through its taxing authority, government can send strong signals to the market. Pollution control taxation can provide a more effective and less costly mechanism than the conventional reliance on standards to achieve desired ecological objectives. As noted in Chapter 4, such taxes, by increasing the prices of highly polluting means of production and consumption, could encourage shifts to more ecologically sound products and processes. The basic approach, then, would be to reduce the incentive to pollute—on the assumption that people and companies alike pollute when it is easier or cheaper to do so. The reliance on price incentives tends to force regulatory agencies to explicitly consider the cost of cleaning up pollution, whereas direct controls make it very easy to adopt extremely expensive and unrealistic goals.

<BOX 10-2>

VIEWS ON REGULATION OF
CANCER-CAUSING CHEMICALS
(EXCERPT FROM A NATIONAL SURVEY)

We are surveying public reaction to four different kinds of chemicals that studies have shown
to cause cancer in some people. Please tell us

which one of the four approaches you think the
federal government should take.

	Percent of Respondents			
Chemical	Ban	Warning Label	Do Not Regulate	No Opinion
Used to preserve food like bacon (nitrites)	33%	57%	5%	5%
Used as an ingredient in some hair dyes	31	60	3	6
Saccharin	16	66	12	7
Used to color food like hot dogs and soft drinks (red dye #2)	47	44	4	5

Source: From a survey sponsored by the Council for Environmental Quality and the Environmental
Protection Agency.

Fees for discharging effluents into bodies of water would encourage the most
extensive efforts to improve pollution abatement by those who can do so at relatively
low cost and who would thereby avoid paying the fees. Less antipollution effort would
be made by those for whom the costs of reducing pollution would be greater than the
required fees. Standards, in contrast, do not make such distinctions. By virtue of their
uniformity, standards result in higher costs to attain the same total environmental
cleanup. Perhaps the greatest virtue of pollution taxation, in lieu of rigid standards, is
the ability to provide incentives for behaving in a socially desirable fashion without
freezing technology or eliminating individual choice. Incentives using the price system
reward additional reductions in pollution. The less the firm discharges, the lower its tax
bill. This continuing incentive to find more effective ways to reduce pollution is absent
once a company meets the detailed standards in conventional regulation. (See box,
"Limits to the Use of Economic Incentives.")

JUDICIAL RESPONSES

Another alternative to detailed regulation is to rely on the courts more heavily for
handling individual claims. In such cases as product hazards, job accidents, and environmental pollution (where risks may not be well known), scholars have suggested
changes in tort law that would encourage the production of safer products or the
greater use of pollution-free processes. The notion behind these proposals is to
increase the risk of liability, and thus the expense, for those firms that can most readily
reduce the risk of accidents or the level of pollution. However, in the case of some
hazards, the costs of using the courts can be high, and the deterrent effect may not be
sufficiently great to obviate the need for standards or other regulatory approaches.

⟨ **BOX 10-3** ⟩

LIMITS TO THE USE OF ECONOMIC INCENTIVES

A town was once plagued by an alarming growth in the number of rats, which ate crops and bit people while they slept and generally made life unpleasant. The town council, in desperation, decided on strong measures to reduce the rat population. The town would pay a bounty of so many dollars for each dead rat brought into the town pound. At first, this measure, though costly, seemed very successful.

There was a gratifying decline in the rat population. After several months, however, the town treasurer noticed a striking increase in the disbursements for dead rats. He quietly started an investigation to determine where they were coming from. To his dismay, he discovered that some of the more enterprising citizens had taken to raising rats—and had found it most profitable.

SOURCE: A mythical tale.

Clearly, there are many ways of responding to the concerns that give rise to government involvement in business decision making. Given the great variety of areas subject to regulation and the multiplicity of regulatory devices that are used, it is unlikely that any single set of reforms will eliminate the shortcomings of the status quo. There does seem to be a useful role for formal analysis of regulatory impacts to provide an ancillary guide to policy makers in this area. The next section presents an introduction to such economic analysis.

BENEFIT–COST ANALYSIS

The motive for incorporating benefit–cost analysis into public decision making is to lead to a more efficient allocation of government resources by subjecting the public sector to the same types of quantitative constraints as those in the private sector. In making an investment decision, for example, business executives compare the total costs to be incurred with the total revenues expected to accrue. If the expected costs exceed the revenues, the investment is usually not considered worthwhile. To be sure, the limits of capital availability require a further sorting to determine the most financially attractive investments.

The government agency decision maker, however, usually does not face such constraints. If the costs to society of an action by an agency exceed the benefits, that situation has no immediate adverse impact on the agency, as would be the case if the private business executive makes a bad investment decision. In fact, such analytical information rarely exists in the public sector, so that, more often than not, government decision makers are not aware that they are approving regulations that are economically inefficient. In requiring agencies to perform benefit–cost analysis, the aim is to make the government's decision-making process more effective, eliminating those regulatory actions for which the net benefits are negative. This result is not ensured merely by performing a benefit–cost analysis. Political and other important but nonquantifiable considerations may dominate, resulting in actions that are not economically efficient but that are desired on grounds of equity or income redistribution. Yet benefit–cost analysis can provide valuable information for government decision makers.

Such a comprehensive analytical approach also helps counterbalance the strong attraction toward regulatory activity on the part of government agencies and their supporters, who can crow about the benefits and ignore the costs—because the costs are transmitted to the consumer, not by the government in the form of higher taxes but by businesses as prices rise to reflect the growing costs of complying with government mandates.

THE ECONOMIC RATIONALE

It may be useful to briefly consider the economic rationale for making benefit–cost analyses of government actions. Such analyses have been used for decades in examining government spending programs. Thus, benefit–cost reviews are neither a revolutionary idea nor an invention of the far right. In fact, measurement of benefits and costs of government activities has been attacked by both ends of the political spectrum—by the far left because not every proposal for government intervention passes a benefit–cost test, and by libertarians, who oppose it because this way of examining new rules can be used to justify government intervention when the likely benefits exceed the expected costs. No analytical approach is totally value-free, but benefit–cost analysis has less ideological baggage than most alternatives.

Economists have long been interested in identifying policies that promote economic welfare, specifically by improving the efficiency with which a society uses its resources. Benefits are measured in terms of the increased production of goods and services. Costs are computed in terms of the foregone benefits that would have been obtained by using those resources in some other activity. The underlying aim of benefit–cost analysis, therefore, is to maximize the real value of the national output (GDP). For almost a century, benefit–cost analysis has been applied by federal spending agencies, such as the Corps of Engineers and the Bureau of Reclamation, to evaluate prospective construction projects.

Despite important operational difficulties, including choosing an appropriate discount rate that corresponds to a realistic estimate of the social cost of capital, over time these analyses have helped improve the allocation of government resources. They have served as a partial screening device to eliminate obviously uneconomical projects—those for which prospective gains are less than estimated costs. The analyses have also provided some basis for ranking and comparing projects and choosing among alternatives. Perhaps the overriding value has been in demonstrating the importance of making relatively objective evaluations of political actions and narrowing the area in which political forces dominate. Thus, if economically inefficient programs are adopted, government decision makers at least know the price that is being paid for those actions.

BENEFIT–COST ANALYSIS OF REGULATION

Figure 10.1 shows the basic relationship between costs and benefits that tends to exist for most regulatory programs. Typically, the initial regulatory effort, such as cleaning up the worst of the pollution in a river, generates a substantial excess of benefits over costs (this process is often called "picking the low-hanging fruit"). But the resources required to achieve additional cleanup become disproportionately high, and at some point the added benefits are substantially less than the added costs. An example of diminishing returns is

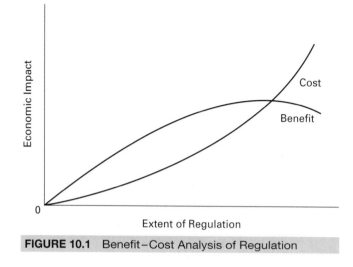

FIGURE 10.1   Benefit–Cost Analysis of Regulation

furnished in a study of the impact of environmental controls on the fruit and vegetable processing industry. The study reveals that it costs less to eliminate the first 85 percent of the pollution created than the next 10 percent.[6] Similarly, in sugar beet processing plants, it costs less than $1 a pound to reduce BOD (biochemical oxygen demand—a measure of the oxygen required to decompose organic wastes) up to 30 percent. But it costs an additional $20 for a one-pound reduction at the 65 percent control level and an added $60 for a one-pound reduction when more than 95 percent control is achieved.[7]

A more aggregate comparison is equally telling. The pulp and paper industry spent $3 billion complying with federal clean-water standards to achieve a 95 percent reduction in pollution. But to reach 98 percent would have cost a further $4.8 billion, a 160 percent increase in costs to achieve a 3 percent improvement in water quality. Thus, it is useful to look beyond the relationship of the total costs and the total benefits of a proposed undertaking to the additional (marginal) benefits and costs that would result from each extension or addition to the activities in a given field.

Ultimately, if regulatory power goes unchecked, the result could tend to be an excess of total costs over total benefits. Thus, performing benefit–cost analysis can be helpful in identifying the optimal amount of regulation, rather than merely being a tool for debating the general pros and cons.

When there is more than one alternative for attaining a regulatory goal, benefit–cost analysis can also be used to compare the various methods and to help choose the most attractive one. Consider the following hypothetical example. Suppose a government agency wishes to control the amount of pollutants a factory is spilling into a river. Assume present technology allows for two possible means of reducing the pollution, system A and system B, of which system B is costlier (see Table 10.1).

System B, in this example, has greater benefits per dollar spent than system A. Despite the fact that system B has a larger total annual cost than system A, we see that system B will yield the larger annual net benefit to society (a larger benefit-to-cost ratio). Thus, the widespread impression that economic analysis always seeks the least expensive alternative is inaccurate. Rather, the purpose of these evaluations is to identify the most efficient ways of meeting regulatory goals.

System	Total Annual Cost	Total Annual Benefit	Benefit– Cost Ratio
A	$14,000	$17,000	1.21
B	26,000	35,000	1.35

TABLE 10.1   Applying Benefit–Cost Analysis

If a business decision in the private sector places an external burden, such as pollution, on its neighbors, the individual firm does not include such a cost in its accounting because it does not bear the burden. Public-sector decision makers, however, ought to consider the effects of their decisions on the entire society. Unlike their private-sector counterparts, regulators should attempt to include all costs and benefits, including those external to the government itself.

The agencies should do so because any regulatory action will have indirect effects on the economy. Requiring safety belts in automobiles has direct impacts on the cost of automobiles and on the safety-belt industry. But it also influences the number of accidents and also produces a ripple effect on the suppliers of the safety-belt industry and on their suppliers. At some point in the benefit–cost analysis, good judgment must be relied upon in deciding which indirect effects are important and which are not.

QUANTIFICATION

In general terms, the benefits and costs attributable to a regulation are measured by identifying the benefits and costs that would not occur in the absence of the regulation. Although the basic idea may seem quite straightforward, its application can be complex. Determining what would occur in the absence of regulation—which establishes a benchmark or reference point for the calculations—may involve a considerable amount of judgment. Table 10.2 shows how the incremental costs (the expenses that would not have been made in the absence of regulation) were computed in one study of water pollution control. It is interesting to note that the bulk of the costs in this case would have been incurred voluntarily.

TABLE 10.2   Calculation of Incremental Cost of Regulation

Steps	Example
Company identifies an action taken to comply with a specific regulation	Installation of wastewater pretreatment system to remove 99 percent of pollution in compliance with the Clean Water Act
Would action have been taken otherwise?	Pretreatment system (without regulation) would have removed only 95 percent of pollutants
What was the cost of the installation?	$1.2 million
How much would the action that would have been taken in the absence of regulation have cost?	$800,000 (the cost of installing a 95 percent system)
What was the incremental cost?	$1,200,000 − $800,000 = $400,000
Recapitulation: Cost of environmental cleanup	$1,200,000
Cost of environmental regulation	$ 400,000

It is useful to examine an actual benefit–cost analysis of regulatory activity. Table 10.3 presents the highlights of such an analysis of the Coast Guard's enforcement of its oil-spill-prevention program. A few points stand out. The bulk of the costs are "off budget," in the form of business compliance with government regulation. The benefits are, in effect, costs avoided. The benefit–cost ratio is clearly positive: It cost society $5.1 million a year in regulatory actions designed to prevent oil spills; the benefits (the cleanup costs averted) are $6.0 million, approximately 20 percent higher.

Sometimes the indirect effects of regulation are as important as the direct. Consider, for example, the question of mandatory standards to ensure the production of less hazardous consumer products. Suggestions have been made from time to time to require more protection in helmets and other equipment used in playing football. Those players using the safer helmets would receive the benefits of fewer or less severe injuries. However, such a safety standard could impose substantial costs on lower-income young people. Perhaps of greater concern, the standards might even contribute to more injuries if the price increases resulted in more youngsters playing football without the protective equipment. This example illustrates another basic thrust of benefit–cost analysis: to view the proposed government action not from the viewpoint of the initial impact on the business firm but from the vantage point of the ultimate effects on the consumer.

COST-EFFECTIVENESS ANALYSIS

When it is not appropriate or practical to put a dollar sign on the benefits, the analyst can use a cost-effectiveness approach rather than a cost–benefit analysis. This methodology estimates the dollar cost of a variety of alternative ways of accomplishing a given objective. Cost-effectiveness analyses permit policy makers to identify least-cost solutions. In this approach, the analyst takes the objective as something worth accomplishing in the first place. In the regulatory field, this approach may be useful in dealing with programs to reduce personal hazards. Rather than dealing with such imponderables as

TABLE 10.3	Benefit–Cost Analysis of Coast Guard Regulation of Oil Spills
Benefits	
Cleanup costs avoided	$1,510,000
Market price of oil saved	985,400
Reduced environmental damages	3,478,000
Total benefits	$5,973,400
Costs	
Coast Guard enforcement	$1,750,000
Industry prevention measures	2,558,000
Industry time spent on inspections	776,000
Total costs	$5,084,000
Ratio of benefits to costs	1.2

Source: Adapted from Mark A. Cohen, "The Costs and Benefits of Oil Spill Prevention and Enforcement," *Journal of Environmental Economics and Management,* June 1986, pp. 167–188.

the value of a human life, the emphasis shifts to identifying those regulatory approaches that will maximize the lives saved or pain avoided from a given dollar outlay. Rather than a "green eyeshade" approach, such attempts at objective analysis, it is contended, show true compassion for our fellow human beings by making the most effective use of the limited resources available to society. (Table 10.4 shows the great variation in cost-effectiveness of a range of EPA regulations.)[8]

BENEFIT–RISK ANALYSIS

In many cases, dollars are an inadequate or inappropriate measure of the impacts of government regulation. That does not necessarily mean there is no opportunity for analysis in the decision-making process. For example, the drug that cures Rocky Mountain spotted fever also causes fatal anemia in one out of every 10,000 people who use it. A simple-minded approach would prohibit the use of this "dangerous" drug. Yet the fever itself kills about eight out of every ten people who contract the disease. Thus, the benefits of the drug tend to greatly outweigh the risks.

A more forceful way of stating the matter is the plaintive statement by a prospective user of beta blockers developed for heart patients (at a time when they had not been approved for general use in the United States because tests on rodents revealed carcinogenicity): "I am over 50. I have had two coronary bypass operations. I have severe angina. I don't give a damn about what happens to the rats."[9]

A comparison of benefits and costs in these cases is not a matter of dollars and cents, but rather involves weighing the advantages of the cure versus the additional risk from the drug's side effects. In practice, this is an instance where the decision making is decentralized. No regulator in Washington rules on the matter. Rather, the individual patient and physician decide. (See box, "The Courts on Benefit–Risk Analysis," for a judicial opinion along these lines.)

TABLE 10.4   Cost-Effectiveness of Selected EPA Regulations*

Regulation	Cost per Premature Death Averted (Millions of 1997 Dollars)
Trihalomethane Drinking Water Standards	$ 0.2
Ethylene Dibromide Drinking Water Standard	6.8
Arsenic Emission Standards for Glass Plants	16.2
Arsenic/Copper Standard	27.6
Hazardous Waste Listing for Petroleum Refining Sludge	33.1
Cover/Move Uranium Mill Tailings (Inactive Sites)	38.0
Cover/Move Uranium Mill Tailings (Active Sites)	54.0
Ban on Asbestos	132.8
1,2-Dichloropropane Drinking Water Standard	784.0
Ban on Disposal of Hazardous Wastes on Land	5,028.5
Atrazine/Alachlor Drinking Water Standard	110,483.6
Hazardous Waste Listing for Wood Preserving Chemicals	6,800,000.0

* 70-year lifetime exposure assumed.

Source: U.S. Office of Management and Budget.

<BOX 10-4>

THE COURTS ON BENEFIT–RISK ANALYSIS

In a decision on pharmaceutical products, the Appellate Division of the Superior Court of New Jersey upheld the notion of "unavoidably unsafe products." The pertinent language follows:

There are some products which, in the present state of human knowledge, are quite incapable of being made safe for their intended and ordinary use. These are especially common in the field of drugs. An outstanding example is the vaccine for the Pasteur treatment of rabies, which not uncommonly leads to very serious and damaging consequences when it is injected. Since the disease itself invariably leads to a dreadful death, both the marketing and the use of the vaccine are fully justified, notwithstanding the avoidable high degree of risk which they involve. Such a product, properly prepared, and accompanied by proper directions and warning, is not defective, nor is it unreasonably dangerous. The same is true of many other drugs, vaccines, and the like, many of which for this very reason cannot legally be sold except to physicians, or under the prescriptions of a physician.

SOURCE: *Carol Ann Feldman et al.* v. *Lederle Laboratories and American Cyanamid Company,* Superior Court of New Jersey, Appellate Division, A-4428–79T1, May 10, 1983.

Risk itself is not a uniform concept. As noted by the Harvard University Center for Risk Analysis, "There is no quantitative level of risk that is universally acceptable or unacceptable."[10] People differ in their perception of risk and in their willingness to assume different types of risk. Many drivers and passengers do not put on their seat belts because they consider the bother to be greater than the risk of injury or death by accident that they voluntarily are willing to take. Some people place a higher personal value on avoiding risks than do others. Thus, some consumers buy used cars or used lawn mowers because they are cheaper. Other consumers would rather do without the product or do without some other product in order to buy a new and safer version. Consciously or subconsciously, each of us makes a benefit–risk decision each time we cross a busy intersection. To cite the words of a federal court ruling on the Consumer Product Safety Act, "A sharp knife might pose a reasonable risk of injury, because dulling the blade to make it safe would also make it useless. A sharp knife in a child's silverware set, however, might be unreasonable."

To avoid the problems inherent in placing monetary values on human lives, benefit–cost analysis can be structured in terms of lives themselves. Sodium nitrite, which is used to preserve food, is a mild carcinogen. Its use creates the possibility that a limited number of people will incur cancer. On the other hand, a large number of people would die of botulism if nitrites were not used as a preservative in meat. A comparison of the costs and benefits of restricting the use of nitrites in meats indicates that more lives are saved by its continued use. This type of comparison was the basis for the federal government's decision not to ban nitrites in meat and, instead, merely to urge a lessening of their use.

A similar situation exists with asbestos, which can cause cancer in employees who work with it in the production of certain foods but is also an important component in brake pads. If the standards for protecting workers were severe enough to stop asbestos production altogether, a large increase in deaths would occur due to inadequate brakes in automobiles. Therefore, the benefits from asbestos regulation in terms of workers' lives prolonged are weighed against the number of individuals expected to die because of poor brakes. Public policy in both cases—nitrites and asbestos—leads to attempts to reduce exposures to carcinogenic hazards, but within some rule of reason.

Moreover, we can compare the cost of saving lives through different mechanisms. It has been estimated that dialysis treatment costs $270,000 per life saved, whereas OSHA's coke-oven emissions standards cost about $5 million per life saved. It is institutional barriers that prevent an obvious reallocation of resources to the more cost-effective activity.[11] It is much easier to assess the coke-oven costs on business than to finance the dialysis treatment out of taxpayers' contributions to the Treasury. (See box, "What Is an Acceptable Risk?")

USES AND LIMITATIONS OF ECONOMIC ANALYSIS

Reliable measures of costs or benefits are not easily specified. Quantification is not always possible. Should the loss of a forest be measured by the value of the timber eliminated? What of the beauty destroyed? What of the area's value as a wildlife habitat? Given such questions, agency decision makers are not faced with simple choices.

The quantification problem is further complicated by a lack of information. The adverse impact of some products on health is often uncertain. Dioxin, for instance, has only recently been found to be a cancer-causing agent, and—despite a great deal of

---

BOX 10-5

WHAT IS AN ACCEPTABLE RISK?

According to Milton Russell, former assistant administrator of the EPA, there are more toxins—natural, and synthetic—than we can ever hope to eliminate. He offers the following explanation:

In a world of limited resources, removing every toxic substance would lead to chasing ever smaller quantities of a pollutant at exponentially rising expenditures of labor, dollars, and scientific and engineering talent. A brute fact should be engraved on our consciousness: given finite resources, when we choose to reduce one toxin, we also choose to tolerate another. Even where we concentrate on one toxin—whether it be PCB or dioxin or whatever—we cannot expect to achieve perfection.

We need a stopping point, at which we will agree that we have cleaned up far enough in a given case, and it is time to turn to another. What is the basis for stopping? It has little to do with the specific toxin or its concentration and much to do with the risk it poses to people and the environment.

If our goal is not purity, or even neatness for its own sake, we must identify risk and reduce it to the point at which it becomes acceptable to our society—thus, the concept of *acceptable risk*. The difficulty of this question for a public policy maker is that it is not scientific, technical, or administrative in nature. To answer it, we must ask ourselves what kind of society we really want.

The American people want a safe and healthy environment, but they also want a strong national defense, first-rate transportation, better and cheaper medical care, good homes, labor-saving appliances, a varied diet, and entertainment. Those who uphold the environment as a primary value compete daily with the advocates of these other worthy objectives.

So what is acceptable risk? That question cannot be answered in any absolute sense. It is a relative thing. It is a function of private ethics and public choice. If that seems little enough to go on, it nevertheless seems to be the best we have.

SOURCE: Adapted from a speech by Milton Russell, then assistant administrator of the EPA, to the Texas Water Pollution Control Association, February 14, 1986.

TABLE 10.5   Benefit–Cost Estimates for Selected Regulations (In Million of Dollars)

Agency	Regulation	Benefits	Costs	Net
FDA	Food labeling	$2,000	$180	+$1,820
CPSC	Childproof lighters	520	50	+470
DOE	Energy standards for air conditioners	740	290	+450
EPA	Disposal of PCBs	150	14	+136
FDA	Mammography standards	140	24	+116
OSHA	Exposure to methylene chloride	130	100	+30
DOT	Roadway worker protection	240	229	+11
OSHA	Exposure to benzene	16	32	−16
EPA	Clean water regulation	160	1,100	−940

Source: U.S. Office of Management and Budget, *Report to Congress on the Costs and Benefits of Federal Regulation,* 1998; Robert W. Hahn, Randall W. Lutter, and W. Kip Viscusi, *Do Federal Regulations Reduce Mortality?* (Washington, DC: AEI–Brookings Joint Center for Regulatory Studies, 2000).

publicity and public concern—the extent of the damage actually caused by the use of this material is at this time not fully discernible. It is often the case that both total costs and total benefits will contain some nonquantifiable variables, leaving much opportunity for political value judgments.

However, the difficulties involved in estimating the benefits or the costs of regulatory actions need not necessarily serve as a deterrent to pursuing the analysis. Merely identifying some of the important and often overlooked impacts can be useful. Examples on the cost side include the beneficial drugs that are not available because of regulatory obstacles, the investments in new factories that are not made owing to stringent environmental requirements for new sources, and the radio and television stations that are not broadcasting because they could not be licensed. On the benefit side, examples range from the more productive workforce that results from a lower rate of accidents on the job to savings in medical care as a result of the safer products and healthier environment achieved from compliance with regulatory efforts.

At times the imperfections of benefit–cost analysis seem substantial. Nevertheless, this type of analysis can add some objectivity to the government's decision-making process. Although benefit–cost analysis deals only with efficiency considerations, the subsequent decisions of elected officials and their appointees might be envisioned as representing society's evaluations of the equity effects of regulatory actions. Economists can provide these decision makers with information via benefit–cost studies and analysis of the distributional impact of regulations (who gets the benefits and who pays the costs), leaving the final decision to society's representatives. With such information, these individuals are better able to make objective decisions on the impacts of the actions they contemplate.

Despite its shortcomings, benefit–cost analysis is essentially a neutral concept, giving equal weight to a dollar of benefits and a dollar of costs (see Table 10.5). After all, showing that a regulatory activity generates an excess of benefits is a strong justification for embarking upon it. For example, the benefits of OSHA's indoor air quality rule ($186 billion) were estimated to be almost double the costs ($94 billion) due to the anticipated gains in productivity.[12] But the painful knowledge that resources available to safeguard human lives are limited causes economists concern when they see wasteful use of those resources because of inefficient regulation.

Conclusions

Given the variety of regulatory statutes and rulings, it is likely that an array of regulatory reforms may be needed. In view of the many serious and difficult questions that regulatory agencies have been set up to deal with, no simple solution is likely to emerge. Nevertheless, a greater availability of reliable information and professional analysis should be useful to decision makers in both the public and private sectors.

At the heart of benefit–cost, cost-effectiveness, and benefit–risk analyses is the proposition that the existence of finite resources requires society to set priorities and to make choices. Ultimately, the type and degree of regulation that the business community and society will face depend more on perceptual and political concerns than on economic reasoning. Statistics are rarely compelling in terms of public awareness and reaction. Nevertheless, it is important to continue to attempt to evaluate the factual basis for public discourse on such controversial areas as government regulation of business.

Notes

1. See Paul MacAvoy, *Industry Regulation and the Performance of the American Economy* (New York: W.W. Norton & Co., 1992); Thomas Hopkins, *Regulatory Costs in Profile* (St. Louis, MO: Washington University, Center for the Study of American Business, 1996); Kenneth J. Arrow et al., *Benefit–Cost Analysis in Environmental, Health, and Safety Regulation* (Washington, DC: American Enterprise Institute, 1996; J. Luis Guasch and Robert W. Hahn, *The Costs and Benefits of Regulation* (Washington, DC: World Bank, 1997); *Making Sense of Regulation: 2001 Report to Congress on the Costs and Benefits of Regulations* (Washington, DC: U.S. Office of Management and Budget, 2001).

2. Executive Order 11821, November 27, 1974.

3. Executive Order 12044, March 24, 1978 (President Carter); Executive Order 12291, February 17, 1981 (President Reagan); and Executive Order 12866, September 30, 1993 (President Clinton).

4. Murray Weidenbaum, "Regulatory Process Reform: From Ford to Clinton," *Regulation,* Winter 1997, pp. 20–26.

5. See, for example, *Making Sense of Regulation* and reports for 1998–2000.

6. U.S. Congress, Joint Economic Committee, *The Economic Impact of Environmental Regulations* (Washington, DC: U.S. Government Printing Office, 1974), p. 203.

7. *Environmental Quality, Second Annual Report of the Council on Environmental Quality* (Washington, DC: U.S. Government Printing Office, 1971), p. 118.

8. EPA is constrained by numerous restrictive legislative requirements and may at times not be free to adopt the most cost-effective manner of regulating a given hazard. See W. Kip Viscusi, *Pricing Environmental Risks* (St. Louis, MO: Washington University, Weidenbaum Center on the Economy, Government, and Public Policy, 1992).

9. Quoted in Murray L. Weidenbaum, *The Future of Business Regulation* (New York: Amacon, 1980), p. 137.

10. See John D. Graham and Jonathan B. Wiener, eds., *Risk Versus Risk* (Cambridge, MA: Harvard University Press, 1995).

11. Thomas G. Marx, "Life, Liberty, and Cost–Benefit Analysis," *Policy Review,* Summer 1983, p. 53.

12. Robert W. Hahn, "Regulatory Reform," in Robert W. Hahn et al., *Risks, Costs, and Lives Saved* (New York: Oxford University Press, 1996), p. 243.

PART III

THE GLOBAL MARKETPLACE

To state that the modern business operates in a global marketplace is merely to acknowledge a phenomenon that is increasingly obvious. Of course, the international economy has been a fact of life since ancient times. What is new and different is the scale and scope of cross-border business activity and especially the impact of technology. It took Marco Polo years to go to China and back. Today's business executive or tourist can fly the round trip in a matter of days. Information can flow across the globe in a fraction of a second.

In this light, Part III presents a global perspective on the external environment facing the business firm. The numerous government policies that influence the flow of international trade and investment are examined, as are the variety of business responses.

11

BUSINESS, GOVERNMENT, AND GLOBALIZATION

Business and government are closely linked in one of the great—and controversial—developments of our time: globalization, the rising tendency for national borders to be crossed by people, goods, services, money, information, and ideas. Many factors are involved in the shifts that are occurring in the world economy. A vital force at play is technological advance, which is a key to the pace of globalization as well as a source of public concern.

Transportation and communication barriers between nations have fallen as new technology has dramatically reduced the expense and time required to move people, goods, and information across borders. The cost of an average international telephone call fell from $2.23 a minute in 1975 to 45 cents in 2000, while transportation costs during the same period declined substantially. As a result, international trade has expanded much faster than domestic production. Between 1948 and 2000, world exports grew at an annual rate of 9.4 percent a year, while world output increased only 4.9 percent annually.

Yet the key changes in international relations have not been economic, although the economic ramifications are powerful. The world has witnessed not only the breakup of the Soviet Union, but also the reunification of Germany, the expansion of the European Union, the emergence of East Asia as an important center of production and trade, and a widespread embrace of liberal political and economic ideals that transcends boundaries of geography and culture. Not all of the changes have been positive. The Middle East and portions of Africa and South Asia have witnessed violent responses by people who, in large measure, do not participate in the modern economy or who believe that they do not benefit from globalization. It is useful, therefore, to look at the various sides of the debate on globalization.

THE PROS AND CONS OF GLOBALIZATION

Most economists and business leaders focus on the benefits of globalization, and they are substantial.[1] A greater flow of international trade and investment stimulates economic growth. World Bank studies show that developing countries that were globalizing in the 1990s grew twice as fast as the developed economies and also reduced their poverty rates at the same time. Increasing output requires more employment and income payments and thus generates higher living standards for consumers. Rising living standards in turn increase the willingness of the society to devote resources to the environment and other important social goals. The litany on the part of the proponents of globalization goes on.

Global competition also keeps domestic businesses on their toes, forcing them to innovate and improve product quality and industrial productivity. According to this line of thinking, competition is good and spreading it out internationally must therefore be even better. More fundamentally, rapidly developing economies tend to generate a new middle class, and that is the bulwark of support for personal liberty as well as economic freedom. The most powerful benefit of the global economy may not be economic at all. It is the ability of people to exchange the most strategic of all factors of production—new ideas. That process empowers individuals in ways never before possible.

Historical experience demonstrates that economic isolationism does not work. The most striking example was sixteenth-century China, where one misguided emperor abruptly cut off trade and commercial intercourse with other nations. China had been the wealthiest, most technologically advanced, and arguably the most powerful nation on the face of the globe. Yet it promptly went into a decline from which it has yet to fully emerge.

The real shortcoming of this line of thinking is not that the facts or analysis are wrong, but that it does not respond to the genuine concerns of the critics of globalization.

Those other voices in the globalization debate emphasize the dark side. Workers feel threatened by unfair competition from low-cost "sweatshops" overseas. Other citizens worry about the conditions in those factories, especially the presence of children in the workplace. People who care about the environment see the pollution caused by the long-distance movement of goods as well as the shift of production to overseas localities with low or no environmental standards. Simultaneously, financial crises arise in many parts of the globe, while mass starvation occurs amidst the collapse of whole societies in Africa.

Meanwhile, concerns abound about the supposed growing inequality of income around the world. Apparently, the poor are getting poorer while the rich are getting richer. Globalization may be good for the compiler of economic statistics but, according to this viewpoint, it is the antithesis of justice and fairness. At the same time, some government officials fear the loss of sovereignty and many individuals see an erosion of liberty with the rise of large multinational corporations and international agencies such as the World Bank, the International Monetary Fund, and the World Trade Organization.

Moreover, global networks of transportation and communication also result in faster transmission of bad news as well as good. Wall Street's woes are quickly shared by such diverse entities as Swiss insurance companies and Arab princes. The financial problems of Japanese banks translate directly into unemployment in South Korea and Thailand. The economy of Finland becomes tied to the fortunes of the U.S. technology sector, in bad times as well as good.

All citizens face the rising power of international crime syndicates, spreading epidemics of AIDS and other threatening diseases, and the rise of global terrorist groups that take advantage of the availability of low-cost international transportation and communication. As a convenient summary, Table 11.1 presents the highlights of the globalization debate.[2]

It is useful to note that economic historians tell us that, measured by trade and investment flows, the world economy may have been more integrated in the nineteenth century than it is today. For example, before passports were generally required for crossing borders, people were freer to travel and to migrate than they are now.[3]

The extent of globalization—economic interdependence across national boundaries—did not decline in the early twentieth century because of mass protests or a bad

TABLE 11.1 The Debate Over Globalization

Pros	Cons
Accelerates economic growth, increasing living standards	Generates widespread poverty in the pursuance of corporate greed
Offers consumers greater variety of products and at lower prices	Results in greater income inequality
Increases jobs and wages and improves working conditions	Moves jobs to low-wage factories that abuse workers' rights
Encourages a greater exchange of information and use of technology	Provides opportunity for criminal and terrorist groups to operate on a global scale
Provides wealth for environmental cleanup	Pollutes local environments that lack ecological standards
Helps developing nations and lifts millions out of poverty	Traps developing countries in high debt loads
Extends economic and political freedoms	Threatens national sovereignty
Raises life expectancy, health standards, and literacy rates	Worsens public health and harms social fabrics of agricultural-based societies

press. The precipitating factors were far more fundamental—World War I, the world-wide depression of the 1930s, and the subsequent separation of the major nations into democratic and totalitarian camps that culminated in World War II. That long period was a time of rising isolationism, both political and economic.

Without responding in detail to the critics, we might conclude that, on balance, globalization is neither the bright sun nor the dark side of the moon. Most economic analyses show that multinational corporations (MNCs) are effective sources of economic development in the poorer countries, providing new technology as well as the investment capital to apply it. U.S. companies, as well as other MNCs, are usually the leaders in offering higher wages (about double the average in low-income nations) and in setting more enlightened business standards.[4] The countries that have not kept up with the progress of the world economy are primarily those that have been bypassed by globalization (rather than having been exploited by the "greedy" MNCs).

It seems to be clear that the substantial internationalization of business activity that has occurred in recent decades is a continuing phenomenon. However, the costs of globalization, even if they are much less than the public believes, are far more visible than the benefits. The companies and workers hurt by imports know who they are, while the beneficiaries of international commerce are widely distributed all through society. The modern global economy, in all likelihood, will be characterized by a combination of substantial involvement of governmental agencies as well as large discretion on the part of the managers of individual business firms.

As in the domestic economy, the involvement of government in business is not a static situation but an evolving phenomenon. Moreover, as in domestic regulation, the way that business responds to the various issues that arise will strongly influence the government's decisions on whether and how to intervene in economic matters in the future. To the extent that public policy pays more attention to those who do not fully share the benefits, the likelihood of a serious backlash against globalization will be reduced.

A TRI-POLAR WORLD

THE RISE OF REGIONAL ECONOMIC BLOCS

The debates over globalization obscure important limitations to the development of a truly global marketplace. For example, most industrial research and development is still performed in the company's home country. Limited amounts are performed in other nations, usually to take advantage of very specialized skills. Even more fundamentally, most cross-border trade is still regional.

A very large share of U.S. trade—33 percent in 2000—is conducted with Canada and Mexico. The regionalization of trade is a widespread phenomenon. Japan is the major exporter to East Asia. The United States is the primary source of imported goods and services for Latin America. Western Europe is the major supplier of goods and services to Eastern Europe. Within the European Union (EU), approximately three-fourths of all trade is with other member nations (the elimination of most barriers to trade inside the EU makes it a special case).

Let us examine the development of the three major trading regions: North America, Western Europe, and the Asian Rim.

NORTH AMERICA AND THE WESTERN HEMISPHERE

In 1994, the United States, Canada, and Mexico entered into the North American Free Trade Agreement (NAFTA), which reduced barriers to commerce and business among the three nations. In the process, considerable potential has been generated for shifting people and other resources within the continent. From the viewpoint of the United States, the neighbor to the north, Canada, has long been our number one trading partner. Since the mid-1990s, Mexico, the neighbor to the south, has become the second-largest market for American-produced goods and services (edging out Japan, the second-largest economy in the world). The trend to greater regionalization of trade is clear in the Western Hemisphere.

The creation of a North American free trade area, after an extended period of adjustment, could generate considerable benefit for the economies of all three nations. In the short run, some painful adjustments have become apparent. During the initial three-year period February 1994–February 1997, 118,000 unemployed U.S. workers qualified to receive special NAFTA Transition Adjustment Assistance. To put the matter into perspective, that came to less than one-tenth of 1 percent of the nation's total labor force (or equal to the number of new jobs usually created in the United States every two weeks). With considerable fanfare, some low-skilled, low-cost work has been moving to Mexico while, more quietly, some higher-tech business activity in Mexico no longer protected by trade barriers has begun to move northward. Overall, the changes resulting from more open trade are turning out to be much less than forecast by either NAFTA's supporters or opponents. NAFTA has led to greater trade and investment among the three member nations, but major displacements have not occurred in U.S. industries.[5]

The partial integration of the North American market has generated specific benefits for American business. The sales in Mexico by U.S.–owned affiliates operating south of the border doubled between 1996 and 1999, while their exports to the United

States rose by a modest 16 percent. Moreover, 47 percent of U.S. investment in Mexico during 1994–2000 was in retailing and other nonmanufacturing sectors of the economy. The real story here is the rise of a consumer class in Mexico following the passage of NAFTA.[6]

Contrary to the expectations of many analysts, the most rapidly growing component of sales of U.S. subsidiaries in Mexico has been to other nations, rather than exports to the United States or to the local Mexican market. Between 1993 and 1999, U.S.–affiliate exports from Mexico to third countries rose nearly sixfold, to a total of $7 billion.[7]

Not all recent changes in public policy make for more open borders between the United States and its neighbors. As noted in Chapter 9, a major expansion has occurred since September 2001 in customs and immigration controls. The cross-border movement of people and goods is subject to more intensive inspection and review than ever before. Nevertheless, the severe bottlenecks that developed at border crossings since September 2001 have been reduced with the adoption of improved inspection methods and better personnel training.

THE EUROPEAN UNION

Across the Atlantic, the European Union (EU) expanded from 12 member nations to 15 when it included Austria, Finland, and Sweden in 1995 (see Figure 11.1). With the elimination of most internal barriers to trade and investment, the European Union has become the world's largest marketplace. From the viewpoint of the United States, Western Europe now presents a high-income market for a wide range of advanced products and services. In 2000, U.S. MNCs received 50.5 percent of their profits from Europe, while the United States is the most important market outside of Europe for most European MNCs. A few examples illustrate the potential for business cooperation across the Atlantic:

- Some models of Boeing commercial jet transports use engines made by the United Kingdom's Rolls-Royce, especially for European airlines.
- Otis Elevator's Elevonic 411 uses electronics designed by its German subsidiary, door systems made by its French branch, and small-geared components made by its Spanish division.
- Unisys is simultaneously a customer of and a supplier to Switzerland's BASF, the Netherlands' Philips, and Germany's Siemens—and also competes with each of these European electronics leaders.
- SBC, the giant regional telephone company, is a 26 percent participant in a joint venture led by Mannesmann to provide mobile telephone service in Germany.

There is also a substantial negative associated with the EU from the viewpoint of other nations. The trade wall around the EU is not coming down. Actually, its external barriers to commerce have become more prominent. In 1960, slightly more than one-half (51 percent) of the foreign trade of the countries that are now members of the Union was outside of the EU. By 2000, only 38 percent of their trade was outside, and a dominant 62 percent of their foreign commerce consisted of exports to or imports from other EU countries.

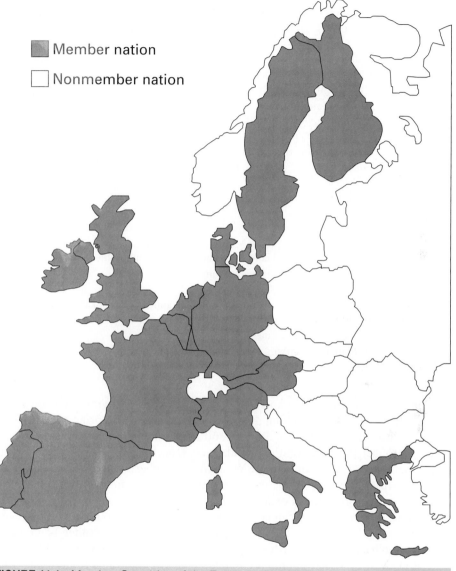

FIGURE 11.1 Member Countries of the European Union

The membership of the EU has not been static (see Table 11.2). It started off with only six countries: West Germany, France, Italy, Belgium, the Netherlands, and Luxembourg. Over the years, the size has more than doubled, with the gradual addition of the United Kingdom, Denmark, Ireland, Spain, Portugal, Greece, Austria, Finland, Sweden, and the former East Germany. Several countries in Eastern Europe—notably, Hungary, Poland, and the Czech Republic—are active candidates for membership in the EU.

The impact of the single market on business is uneven, producing winners and losers on both sides of the Atlantic. The winners include the stronger European

TABLE 11.2	Milestones in the Economic Integration of Western Europe
1951	European Coal and Steel Community (ECSC) established. Members are Belgium, France, Italy, Luxembourg, the Netherlands, and West Germany.
1957	European Economic Community (EEC) created with same members as ECSC.
1959	EEC member tariff reductions.
1962	EEC members adopt Common Agricultural Policy.
1967	EEC renamed the European Community (EC), reflecting cooperation beyond the economic sphere.
1968	EC eliminates internal tariffs and imposes common external tariff.
1973	Denmark, Ireland, and the United Kingdom join EC.
1979	First direct election of the European Parliament.
1981	Greece joins EC.
1986	Portugal and Spain join EC.
1987	Single European Act passed, providing qualified majority member approval of 282 measures needed to achieve a single market.
1993	With signing of Treaty of Maastricht, EC becomes the European Union (EU), with closer focus on economic and monetary union and political unification.
1995	Austria, Finland, and Sweden join EU.
1998	European Central Bank is established.
1999	Euro is adopted as currency for all EU countries except Denmark, Greece, United Kingdom, and Sweden.
2000	Greece adopts the euro.
2002	Euro coins and notes enter circulation.

companies with high-skill and high-tech capabilities, enjoying the economies of scale and the benefits of expanding domestic markets. They also bring a special understanding of European needs, capabilities, and cultures. Many of them are emerging larger and stronger than ever on the global scene. Hoechst, the giant German chemical firm, now employs more people in the Western Hemisphere than in Europe.

A final category of beneficiaries of the single market are the strong North American firms with an established presence in Western Europe. High-tech, well-capitalized North American companies are accustomed to competing on a continent-wide basis. They use one EU country as a base to sell to the other 14. General Motors and Ford have more strength across all of Europe than such well-established European automakers as Volkswagen, Fiat, Peugeot, and Renault. The same holds true for U.S. computer manufacturers such as IBM and Hewlett-Packard.

Losers from the single market include the high-cost European companies that have been sheltered within their national markets. Some of these more tradition-bound firms are being hurt by continentwide competition. Not all barriers are down, however. Each member nation continues to possess individual values, needs, cultures, language — and tax systems. No matter what changes the EU makes, the French are not going to stampede for German wine, for instance, and the British will continue to want autos equipped to drive on the left side of the road.

Some North American firms are also losers as a result of the European economic unification. They find it more difficult to export to Europe. In addition, they face tougher competition in their domestic markets from the stronger EU businesses.

THE ASIAN RIM

The Asian Rim represents a far more complicated political and economic area than either Western Europe or North America. Formally, there is no counterpart to either the EU or NAFTA. The Asian governments have not embarked on a comprehensive effort to link their economies or to eliminate barriers to trade and investment. The Association of Southeast Asian Nations (ASEAN), which includes Malaysia, Indonesia, Philippines, Thailand, Singapore, Brunei, Vietnam, Laos, and Myanmar, is an embryonic effort to develop greater cooperation among the nations in that part of the world.

The commercial and investment relationships across this region are substantial. For example, like the EU nations, major shares of the international trade and investment of the Asian Rim countries stay in the area. The greater part of the capital flowing into China and Southeast Asia comes from Japan, South Korea, and other East Asian nations. The result is a more inward-looking region than many people located outside of the Asian Rim realize.

The stagnation of the Japanese economy has focused more attention on the rapidly growing China market. China contains an array of potential consumers that far exceeds the markets in Europe or the Western Hemisphere. Yet, not all of the vast Chinese mainland can be viewed realistically as a candidate for early modernization. The major economic development is occurring along China's east coast—in the coastal provinces of Guangdong and Fujian, the special economic zones in Shenzhen and Xiamen, and the cities of Shanghai and Beijing. Although these areas are a modest fraction of the entire country, in the aggregate they constitute a very substantial economy.[8]

Viewed from afar, China is becoming a major world center for the low-cost production of consumer goods. Its advantages are many—in addition to wage rates much lower than in most Western and many Asian countries. China's investments in education and training are attracting research as well as production facilities on the part of major U.S. firms such as IBM, Motorola, and Microsoft. China is rapidly developing a critical mass of factories and specialized suppliers, one that is competitive with the more industrialized nations. This industrial expansion, in turn, is generating a rapidly growing consumer base. China's middle class—defined as people with incomes of at least $3,000 a year—numbers about 100 million and is growing around 20 percent a year. Because of state-subsidized housing, little of that money is spent on shelter, the biggest household expense in the West. McKinsey & Company estimates that over 5 million Chinese have assets of $100,000 or more.[9]

BUSINESS RESPONSES TO GOVERNMENT POLICY

Pressures for a more global orientation of business activities offset in part the trend toward regionalization. Among these forces are a partial homogenization of tastes worldwide. Higher incomes in many parts of the world have given rise to international markets for national specialty products, such as Italian shoes, Swiss watches, and Japanese consumer electronics. In addition, the general reduction in trade barriers that began in the 1980s has continued into the present day. Still, governments are under pressure to restrict selective imports and overseas investments to "protect" domestic jobs in politically powerful sectors.

The spark that ignites global competition is the need to find new markets for mass-produced goods when existing markets became relatively saturated in the face of rising industrial productivity. In response, firms extend the scope of operations globally and take advantage of economies of scale.

Governmental barriers to international business take many forms, ranging from tariffs to quotas on trade to restrictions on foreign ownership of domestic business—but the global enterprise often finds ways of overcoming those barriers, albeit at a cost (see Table 11.3).[10]

For example, while Congress was considering costly environmental statutes, U.S. mining firms expanded in South America. National policy keeps drilling rigs out of the Arctic National Wildlife Refuge, while at the same time Chevron has invested billions of dollars in far-away Kazakhstan. In total, U.S.-based oil and gas companies now invest more overseas than in domestic locations.

Likewise, U.S.-based pharmaceutical firms have introduced new drugs in Europe, while awaiting the completion of the intricate domestic regulatory procedures that hold up circulation in the United States. Similarly frustrated by FDA hurdles, makers of innovative medical equipment have been moving their developmental work to the Netherlands and other Western European locations where standards are high but regulatory requirements are less burdensome. Several important U.S.–headquartered companies have located a majority of their assets overseas. In 2001, examples included Manpower, Inc. (75 percent of assets overseas), Gillette (66 percent), Pharmacia and Upjohn (65 percent), and Colgate-Palmolive (58 percent).

In the case of import quotas, exporting companies can shift to higher-priced items on which unit profits are also greater. In the early 1980s, American purchasers of Japanese-made automobiles found they were required to buy all sorts of high-priced

TABLE 11.3   Business Responses to Governmental Barriers

Barrier	Business Response
Trade Barriers	Establish manufacturing operations in target country
Tariffs and quotas	Acquire local firm
Domestic content restrictions	Subcontract or purchase locally
Reciprocity rules	Develop products jointly
Government procurement restrictions	Shift to higher-priced exports (for quotas)
Investment Barriers	Enter into joint ventures with local firms
Limits on foreign ownership of local enterprises	Give away nominal majority ownership
	Franchise local firms
	Enter into licensing agreements
	Set up R&D cooperation or technology swaps
Restrictions on repatriation of earnings	Set up affiliate or correspondent relationships with local firms
Fear of expropriation	
Regulatory and Tax Barriers	Reinvest overseas
In home country	Shift high value-added activities to low-tax,
In foreign nations	low-regulation nations
Informal foreign barriers	Market through local distributors

extras for which they were paying as much as $2,000 above the base price for the reduced supply of Toyotas, Nissans, and other Japanese automobiles. The Japanese producers actually benefited from the restrictions on their exports to the United States, increasing their profits substantially in the face of quantitative limits on their exports. While the Japanese producers sold about 30 percent of their auto production in the United States during that period, they earned approximately one-half of their profits from sales in the United States.[11]

When faced with onerous obstacles to international trade, businesses draw on a variety of alternatives to direct exporting. One approach is to set up new manufacturing facilities (so-called "greenfield operations") in the host nation. When Monsanto's low-calorie sweetener, NutraSweet, was hit with a high duty in response to a charge of dumping in the European Union, the company built a plant in France to produce for the European market.

Many Japanese manufacturers moved the production of textiles, watches, televisions, cameras, and calculators to facilities in Malaysia, Indonesia, Thailand, and the Philippines in response to the restrictions against Japanese imports encountered in some of their major overseas markets (the lower costs of production were an augmenting factor).

Japanese automakers are also producing cars in other nations, especially the United States. This approach provides the Japanese firms with direct access to the markets of the local economies in which they produce and minimizes their exposure to adverse policies by the host government. It also permits the Japanese companies to export to markets in other nations that maintain barriers against products made in their home territory. For instance, Honda sells cars to Taiwan and South Korea from its manufacturing plant in Ohio. Those two countries have traditionally prohibited the importation of automobiles directly from Japan.

Firms also respond by acquiring existing local companies. This has been a popular strategy for foreign businesses responding to the integration of the European market. Many American and Japanese companies fear that the removal of internal regulatory and economic barriers to producers located in the EU reduces the competitiveness of their exports to that region. Thus, acquisitions have been increasing steadily since the 1980s as firms from these two countries seek to gain a foothold in Western Europe. Examples include Emerson Electric's purchase of the French firm Leroy-Somer, General Electric's acquisition of the United Kingdom's Burton Group Financial Services, American Brands' buyout of Scotland's Whyte & Mackay Distillers Ltd., and Scott Paper's purchase of Tungram Company of Germany.

Other alternatives that business firms frequently rely upon to develop positions in foreign markets include subcontracting production, purchasing locally, and developing products jointly with local firms. To overcome political objections to goods produced by workers in other countries, some multinational corporations set up so-called "screwdriver" operations: assembly plants using key components manufactured in the home country and performing no research and development locally. Thus, the economic contribution in the host country is minimized.

Joint ventures, particularly those involving the operation of manufacturing facilities, are often necessary to overcome trade restrictions, especially in the case of the formation of protectionist trade blocs. This trend is evident in the aerospace and automobile industries, where every major company has formed alliances with foreign competitors. For instance, Ford Motor Company has formed a joint venture with a local producer in Taiwan to assemble cars for sale in that market.

In some circumstances, firms are able to export duty-free to countries possessing broad tariff policies in exchange for capital investments, or for using local contractors or raw materials in the production process. A joint venture between General Motors and a state-owned automaker in Poland to manufacture cars domestically provides a significant inflow of capital, technology, and expertise to the beleaguered Polish manufacturer. In return, General Motors is allowed to import into Poland a portion of its automobiles duty-free.

On other occasions, firms face sharp limits to foreign ownership of local enterprises. This type of governmentally imposed barrier becomes more popular when formal trade barriers are reduced. Investment barriers include direct restrictions on investment, or less formal but often equally powerful tax and regulatory advantages limited to local companies. Mergers and acquisitions are the dominant modes of penetrating Western European markets. In some Asian nations as well as in Eastern Europe, however, such foreign direct investment is greatly restricted. As a result, international enterprises, especially in high-technology industries, most often enter into joint ventures with local firms.

Many countries with their own high-tech engineering and advanced manufacturing abilities are reluctant to import weapon systems produced elsewhere. Under these circumstances, U.S. aerospace companies, albeit reluctantly, have licensed their designs to local firms. Thus, Boeing has received royalties for the version of its F-15 fighter aircraft produced in Japan by Mitsubishi Industries working with Kawasaki Heavy Industries. Korean firms, under license, have manufactured Northrop Grumman's F-5 aircraft.

In some circumstances, a host government may be willing to accept the construction, expansion, or acquisition of a local branch by an American company on the condition that the firm meets a specified performance requirement or provides another concession. Before IBM was allowed to increase its operations in Mexico in the pre–NAFTA period, the company agreed to set up a development center for semiconductors, to purchase high-technology components from Mexican companies, and to produce software for Latin America in Mexico. In the case of services, franchising to a domestic enterprise serves a similar purpose to licensing in getting around barriers to direct investment.

In less-developed nations, public-sector deterrents to business take different forms. Governments on occasion restrict repatriation of earnings, or threaten to expropriate assets of foreign companies. Governments may also require local sourcing of raw materials.

Some of the barriers to business enterprise are domestic, and the global economy provides opportunity to overcome them. Companies that have difficulty introducing products in their home country due to delayed approval or stricter governmental requirements can produce them in other countries in an effort to introduce them to markets more quickly. As noted earlier, this practice is followed by some U.S. pharmaceutical firms.

Companies headquartered in developed nations often face high business taxes and onerous regulatory costs. In response, the enterprise can expand overseas or even move existing business operations to another country whose policies provide a more favorable business environment. It is helpful under changing political circumstances to do business in several countries. In that event, when faced with rising government burdens in one nation, a firm can shift its high value-added activities to other nations in which it operates, specifically those with lower taxes and less burdensome regulation. As noted earlier in this chapter, the domestic political repercussions may be substantial.

Traditional business reasons are also involved in the choice among the available methods of penetrating foreign markets. Indeed, those business concerns—such as cost and transportation advantages—may often be the dominating influence. However, in the move toward globalization, individual firms may experience "rough sledding" and reverse some of their foreign commitments. The alliance between General Motors and Daewoo of South Korea went sour when Daewoo's desire to expand in local markets conflicted with GM's global objectives.

Metallgesellschaft AG, the large German metallurgy firm, pulled out of its 60 percent stake in a steel plant in Hungary. The German company said that the Hungarian government partners wanted it to foot a larger portion of the operating costs than its contract provided for. According to an official of Metallgesellschaft, "We learned that contracts which were made at the time were not enforceable at another time."[12]

THE FEEDBACK ON GOVERNMENT POLICY

The tension between business and government is nothing new. It has traditionally existed between large private enterprises and the rulers of developing countries (see Table 11.4). This tension between governments in general (both those with developing and those with more advanced economies) and the business firm is being exacerbated by the rapid rate of economic, social, and technological change.

TABLE 11.4   Tensions Between Goals and Business Activities in Developing Countries

Developing Countries	International Private Enterprises
Promote local ownership	Maintain global standards and efficiency
Increase local control	Minimize cost and complexity of delivering technology and capital
Change payment characteristics and reduce duration of contracts	Receive just returns for risks
Minimize source firm's control over use of technology and capital in user nation	Gain assurance regarding property rights over use of private resources
Separate technology from normal private investments	Provide technology as part of long-term production and market development
Remove restrictive business clauses in investment and technology agreements	Maintain ability to affect the use of capital, technology, and associated products
Minimize proprietary rights of suppliers	Protect right to profit from private investments
Reduce contract security	Use contracts to create an environment of stability and trust
Encourage transfer of R&D to host country	Maintain control of R&D paid for by company
Develop products suitable for domestic markets	Gain global economies of scale to lower cost of products to consumers

Political scientists and economists have long understood that people vote with their feet. They leave localities, regions, and nations with limited opportunity in favor of those that offer a more attractive future. In the contemporary era of computers, telephones, and fax machines, enterprises are far more mobile than that. Information, that key resource, can be transferred in seconds.

The mobility of enterprises—of their people, capital, and information—is reducing the effective power of government. Public-sector decision makers increasingly understand that they have to become internationally competitive in the economic policies they devise. Governmental activities that impose costs without compensating benefits or that reduce wealth substantially in the process of redistributing income undermine the competitive positions of domestic enterprises. The result is either the loss of business to firms located in other nations or the movement of the domestic company's resources and operations to more hospitable locations. Governments are learning that they, too, compete in the global marketplace.

Not all governmental involvement in international business is negative. On many occasions, public-sector policies actively encourage foreign companies to invest, to build new facilities, or otherwise to participate in the local economy. Such supportive actions include tax abatements, tariff waivers, liberal credit terms, and reduction in burdensome regulation.

Even as many public-sector barriers remain, increasingly the private sector is learning how to overcome them or even just to live with them. The most striking examples of that mobility are the experiences of Chinese entrepreneurs. Even in the face of official hostility between Beijing and Taipei, thousands of Taiwanese firms have established their business presence in mainland China. The formal power of government is not to be discounted—and its destructive ability has been vividly demonstrated in innumerable wars. Nevertheless, the continuing ability of entrepreneurs to respond to the power of economic incentives and technological advance is substantial.

THE EMERGING TRANSNATIONAL ENTERPRISE

In the process of adjusting to government obstacles to international commerce, the traditional domestically oriented corporation often becomes transformed into an organization we can call the transnational enterprise (see Table 11.5). The internationalization of management is the clearest example of the transformation of the modern business enterprise. The top 400 people in the banking sector of the Citicorp Group come from 42 countries; only 165 of them are natives of the United States. Of the bank's top 20 executives, only 11 are from the United States. The CEOs of approximately 100 U.S. companies were born in other countries. Examples include Alcoa, Eli Lilly, NCR, Coca-Cola, Goodyear, and Kellogg.[13]

The emerging transnational enterprise is not a monolithic organization that makes or even designs every aspect of the items it produces and markets.[14] Rather, the largest, pace-setting firms are often taking on many of the characteristics of an open and interactive network, selectively sharing control, technology, and markets with different kinds of organizations in many parts of the world. As a result of rapid changes in technology and markets, the customary boundaries between formal enterprises and more informal business relationships are gradually blurring.

TABLE 11.5 Levels of Globalization

Domestic Company	Regional Exporter	Exporting Company	International Company	International to Global (Transition)	Global Enterprise
Operates exclusively within a single country.	Operates within a geographically defined region that crosses national boundaries. Markets served are economically and culturally homogeneous.	Runs operations from a central office in the home region, exporting finished goods to a variety of countries. Some marketing outside the home region.	Regional operations are somewhat autonomous, but key decisions are coordinated from a central office in the home region. Manufacturing, assembly, marketing, and sales are decentralized beyond the home region.	Runs independent and mainly self-sufficient subsidiaries in a range of countries. Some functions (R&D, sourcing, financing) are decentralized. The home region is still the primary base for many functions.	Highly decentralized organization operates across a broad range of countries. No geographic area is assumed to be the primary base for any functional area. Each function is performed in the most suitable location.

Source: Booz-Allen & Hamilton.

The traditional factory, such as Ford's Willow Run operation in Michigan, was fully integrated, with headquarters, design offices, production workers, and factories all located close to each other. In recent years, many of the production functions of large corporations have been farmed out to smaller, more specialized firms. Richard Rosecrance of UCLA refers to the "virtual corporation" as an entity with research, development, design, marketing, financial, and legal functions in its headquarters, but few or no manufacturing facilities—in his words, a company with a head and no body.[15]

Head corporations can design new products for a wide range of production facilities, often in different countries. Some analysts note that even the design of major components can be performed by suppliers who have special skills in that niche of the marketplace. Thus, the leading figures in the computer industry are no longer the integrated producers, but Intel, Microsoft, Oracle, and Hewlett-Packard—those that specialize in one key stage of the process or one vital component.[16]

For an increasing number of transnational companies, including Shell Oil, Exxon Mobil, Ford, Nestlé, and Procter & Gamble, profits and sales from abroad or on occasion from a single foreign country surpass that of the country of origin. In that sense, these businesses are losing their national identities. United Kingdom chemical giant ICI sells 40 percent of its products in the United States and only 10 percent in its "home" country. Quite a few well-known, European-based companies make a majority of their sales to North America, mainly the United States. Examples include media firms such as Pearson and Reed Elseveer and such manufacturing companies as DaimlerChrysler and SmithKline Beecham.

An external observer of these enterprises sees large flows of resources, people, and information among relatively interdependent or autonomous units; the large subsidiaries of Shell and Nestlé in the United States afford cogent examples. This type of arrangement means heavy reliance on a changing process of coordination, cooperation, and shared decision making (see box, "The Global Corporation").

INTERNAL ORGANIZATION

The traditional pyramidal organization facilitated the efficient division of labor in producing large quantities of standardized products. With a more rapid rate of technological change, the life spans of individual products shrink. Simultaneously, consumer incomes in many parts of the world are rising rapidly, permitting great variation in customer tastes and in business responses.

Many firms are attempting to adjust to this new environment by shifting to a more nearly horizontal, decentralized organization. Various innovative forms have been suggested. In one intriguing concept, the dominant business firm of the future consists of a central coordination center and several semi-independent internal organizations. Business activity, in this view, operates on the basis of fluid ties with the internal organizations of other companies and with informal enterprises. The concept of *networking* is traditional in nonmanufacturing industries, notably construction and contract research, where so many of the key decisions on a product or structure are made by firms other than the prime or lead contractor.

Just as there are transaction costs in transfers between firms, there are internalization costs in intrafirm relationships, especially when they occur across national borders. The multinational enterprise relies more heavily on its own intellectual resources than did the old-fashioned exporter. The newer form of enterprise has to gain knowledge of

BOX 11-1

THE GLOBAL CORPORATION

The global enterprise has become an important economic and business phenomenon. Approximately 63,000 multinational corporations (MNCs) are active in the global economy. Their 800,000 foreign affiliates account for roughly 25 percent of global output, only one-third of it in the host countries.

In the United States, MNCs account for over 60 percent of the export of goods and 40 percent of the imports of goods. Over 40 percent of these transactions involve trade between U.S. parent operations and their foreign subsidiaries. Although their foreign affiliates trade with them actively, most of the sales of those affiliates are local, occurring within the host countries (about 60 percent of their sales of goods and 80 percent of their sales of services).

The U.S.-based MNCs employ about 20 million workers in the United States, while U.S. affiliates of foreign companies employ about 5 million workers in the United States. Worldwide, global sales of foreign affiliates in 2000 reached over $14 trillion, twice the total of world exports of goods.

SOURCES: *Economic Report of the President January 2001* (Washington, DC: U.S. Government Printing Office, 2001), pp. 207–208; Thomas Harris, "Current and Future Changes in Corporate Attitudes to National Identity," *Thunderbird International Business Review,* March–April 2002, p. 168.

foreign markets—including production possibilities, cost differences, relations with local suppliers—and deal with several levels of foreign governments. In contrast, a local firm may already have such information or can acquire it more cheaply. The establishment of a new subsidiary may also entail technical training costs similar to, or even higher than, those encountered in interfirm transactions.

Two very different strategies, which the multinational enterprise may follow, are emerging. In some industries, there is a trend toward globalization. With converging buyer preferences and uniform worldwide technical standards, it is possible to produce a narrow range of standardized products from globally oriented factories. In such an environment, there is a premium on efficiency and a preference for internal control unhampered by the divergent preferences of corporate partners.

In other industries, numerous factors—strong local customer preferences, varying technical standards in different countries, transportation and trade barriers, economic nationalism, and high technological risks—point to a more diverse strategy, including alliances with enterprises located in a variety of regions. Clearly, the emerging form of business organization encourages greater ease of entry—and exit.

Some of the larger and more sophisticated multinational companies with strong headquarters staff and substantial numbers of subsidiaries are becoming transnational organizations with activities and responsibilities spread more evenly around the world. In the newer formulation, production for local markets is often regrouped into a few world supply centers. In the words of Wisse Dekker, then chairman of the supervisory board of Philips (the large Dutch electrical and electronics producer), they are becoming "global citizens."[17] Nevertheless, in part as a reaction to serious terrorist threats, many internationally oriented companies are reminded of the benefits—and protection—that flow from their home countries. Thus, some companies that had come to view themselves as global citizens with a national parentage are now once again thinking of their organizations as citizens of a specific nation, albeit with global activities.

Notwithstanding the myriad of individual variations, it is helpful to try to generalize the nature of the corporate transitions. Christopher Bartlett of Harvard Business School sees corporations undergoing four distinct stages in responding to the rising pressures for globalization. The first and traditional step views overseas operations as mere appendages of a centrally directed domestic corporation. Although many assets and decisions are decentralized, the headquarters organization exercises strong financial and planning control.[18]

In a second stage, the enterprise adopts a multinational form of organization. Management comes to view overseas operations as a portfolio of relatively independently operated businesses. Many responsibilities are decentralized, with financial controls continuing to provide the key coordinating link.

In a third, more advanced stage, the company uses a global organizational structure. Overseas operations are treated as delivery pipelines to a unified global marketplace. Central control is maintained over decisions, resources, and information. But it is extremely difficult for such a worldwide operation run from Detroit, Tokyo, or Stockholm to maintain an adequate understanding of consumer expectations in distant markets—no matter how good its research or how many flight hours its executives log each month. Thus, companies increasingly are led to the fourth and most futuristic organizational model: the truly transnational organization. Resources, people, and information flow among interdependent units. In the absence of traditional centralized controls, this structure relies on the goodwill of the many participants. It requires a complex process of coordination, cooperation, and shared decision making.

To an outsider, the performance of the transnational enterprise will likely be recognizable by two key characteristics: The first is the ability to attract employees, capital, and suppliers from global sources; the second is the appeal to customers all over the world—fostered by product designs that are constantly being revised.

Conclusions

The tension between business and government is exacerbated by the rapid rate of social, economic, and technological changes around the globe. In the words of Daniel Yergin, coauthor of *The Commanding Heights: The Battle for the World Economy:* "We still live in a world of nation-states and a global marketplace."[19] However, there is a third force that ultimately may carry the day: the citizen as consumer. Consumers vote every day of the week—in dollars, yen, pounds, and euros. The same protectionist-oriented voters, as customers, purchase products made everywhere in the world. In spending their own money, most consumers give far greater weight to price and quality than country of origin.

To the extent that human capital is increasingly seen as a key resource in business and economic competition, the nations and companies that perform well will be those that can generate, attract, and keep educated, skilled, and experienced workers, managers, and entrepreneurs. The rapidly changing global marketplace of the early twenty-first century provides both threat and opportunity for business firms, governments, and consumers. Invariably, the changes will generate both winners and losers. The outcomes for specific individuals, business organizations, and nations will depend in large part on their ability to understand and to respond promptly to new economic and technological trends (see Table 11.6).

TABLE 11.6 Alternative Business Responses to the Changing Global Marketplace

Alternatives	Characteristics	Advantages	Disadvantages
Direct strategies for marketing abroad	Exporting Turnkey operations	Expands markets Maintains control Maintains domestic production	Faces foreign barriers Sensitive to exchange rate fluctuations
Cooperative contractual agreements	Licensing Franchising Subcontracting	Requires small investments Concentrates on core activities	Minimizes control
Wholly owned affiliates	Greenfield operations Mergers and acquisitions	Maintains full control Localizes production	Requires large investment May be unpopular politically
Strategic nonequity alliances	R&D cooperatives Alliances Joint production/marketing agreements Informal alliances	Accesses markets Provides global presence Flexible Co-opts potential competitors Reduces risk	Exhibits uncertain control Slows down decision making Potentially unstable May lose technology to competitors
Strategic equity alliances	Joint ventures Joint equity swaps Affiliates Other investment alliances	Accesses new markets/fields Minimizes risks Results in lower costs than direct investment	Requires complex, detailed contracts Often difficult to manage

Notes

1. For a representative sample of the debates on globalization, see U.S. Trade Deficit Review Commission, *The Trade Deficit* (Washington, DC: U.S. Government Printing Office, 2000), and accompanying CD-ROM. See also Dani Rodrik, *Has Globalization Gone Too Far?* (Washington, DC: Institute for International Economics, 1997); and Murray Weidenbaum, "Globalization: Wonder Land or Waste Land?" *Society,* July–August 2002, pp. 36–40.

2. John Gray, "A Conservative Critique of Globalization," *AEI Newsletter,* June 2002, p. 3.

3. Michael D. Bordo, "Globalization in Historical Perspective," *Business Economics,* January 2002, pp. 20–29.

4. "Globalization and Its Critics," *The Economist,* September 29, 2001, p. S13.

5. John Mutti, *NAFTA: The Economic Consequences for Mexico and the United States* (Washington, DC: Economic Strategy Institute, 2001), pp. 93–97.

6. Sven W. Arndt and Alex Huemer, "North American Trade After NAFTA," *Claremont Policy Briefs,* March 2002, pp. 1–4; Joseph P. Quinlan and Rebecca McCaughrin, "Mexico—More Than a Low-Wage Production Base," *Morgan Stanley Dean Witter Global Insights,* May 16, 2002, pp. 1–4.

7. Joseph P. Quinlan and Andrea L. Prochniak, "Let's Do Away with NAFTA Trade Statistics," *Morgan Stanley Dean Witter Global Insights,* November 21, 2000, p. 1; Joseph P. Quinlan and Rebecca McCaughrin, "U.S. Trade Follies," *Morgan Stanley Dean Witter Global Insights,* April 25, 2002, p. 2.

8. Murray Weidenbaum and Samuel Hughes, *The Bamboo Network* (New York: Free Press, 1996).

9. Jeffrey E. Garten, "When Everything Is Made in China," *Business Week,* June 17, 2002, p. 20; Joseph P. Quinlan, "Ties That Bind," *Foreign Affairs,* July/August 2002, pp. 116–126; Craig Smith, "China Juggles the Conflicting Pressures of a Society in Transition," *New York Times,* July 15, 2002, p. A5.

10. Harvey S. James, Jr., and Murray Weidenbaum, *When Businesses Cross International Borders* (Westport, CT: Praeger, 1993).

11. Robert W. Crandall, "Import Quotas and the Automobile Industry," *Brookings Review,* Summer 1984, pp. 8–16.

12. Ken Kasriel, "Hungary's Troubled Business Ties," *Christian Science Monitor,* July 7, 1992, p. 2.

13. David Lipchultz, "Bosses from Abroad," *Chief Executive,* January 2002, p. 18; John S. Reed, *Oh, the Modern World!,* CEO Series Issue no. 7 (St. Louis, Mo: Washington University, Weidenbaum Center on the Economy, Government, and Public Policy, 1996), p. 4.

14. Joseph Nemec, Jr., and Barbara A. Faller, *A Special Report on Globalization* (New York: Booz-Allen & Hamilton, 1991).

15. Richard Rosecrance, "The Rise of the Virtual State," *Foreign Affairs* 75, no. 4, July–August 1996, pp. 45–61.

16. Everett M. Ehrlich, "Notes on a Borderless World," *Business Economics,* July 1997, pp. 32–36.

17. Wisse Dekker, "The Rise of the Stateless CEO," *CEO/International Strategies,* March–April 1991, p. 17.

18. Christopher Bartlett, "Managing Across Borders," *World Link,* July–August 1991, pp. 110–111. See also *Organizing for Global Competitiveness* (New York: Conference Board, 2001).

19. Quoted in "Interview with Daniel Yergin," *IMF Survey,* June 24, 2002, p. 206.

12

GOVERNMENT AND INTERNATIONAL COMMERCE

Many discussions of international economic issues ignore the vital role of private enterprises and the effects of public policies on business. Thus, it is commonplace to say that Japan exports automobiles to the United States and that the United States exports jet airliners to Japan. But nations and governments rarely do more than regulate and tax those cross-border transactions. Typically, it is business firms that engage in international commerce.

When we examine foreign trade from that viewpoint, we gain new insights. For example, more than one-third of what governments call foreign trade actually involves cross-border transactions between different parts of the same company. A major share of foreign trade consists of domestic firms shipping goods to or receiving items from their overseas subsidiaries—or foreign firms engaged in similar transactions with their divisions in other countries. In a geopolitical sense, all of this is foreign commerce. But, from a business viewpoint, these international flows of goods and services are internal transfers within the same firm.

At the other end of the spectrum of global activity, an extreme case of transnational business was cited by former U.S. Secretary of State George Shultz. He tells of a shipping label on integrated circuits made by an American firm, which reads: "Made in one or more of the following countries: Korea, Hong Kong, Malaysia, Singapore, Taiwan, Mauritius, Thailand, Indonesia, Mexico, Philippines. The exact country of origin is unknown."

Although many Americans view this nation as the epitome of free trade, in practice the U.S. government has established a variety of restrictions over imports and exports and over the flow of foreign investment into the United States. All nations regulate, at least to some degree, the flow of goods, services, and capital across their borders.

Each year, the United States imports and exports vast arrays of goods and services in the world marketplace. Table 12.1 shows the rising importance of international trade to the U.S. economy. The total volume of foreign commerce (imports plus exports) grew more than twice as rapidly as the GDP between 1970 and 2000. The individual items involved range from automobiles, jet aircraft, textiles, and computer software to clothespins, baseball bats, and works of art.

THE CHALLENGE OF PROTECTIONISM

Domestic producers in nearly all of the industries involved with imports or exports feel the pressures of lower-priced competition from producers in other nations. Foreign penetration of U.S. markets ranges from the overwhelming domination of color television

TABLE 12.1   International Trade in the U.S. Economy, 1970–2000
(Billions of 1996 Dollars)

Category of Trade	1970		1980		1990		2000	
	Amount	Percent of GDP	Amount	Percent of GDP	Amount	Percent of GDP	Amount	Percent of GDP
Exports of goods and services	$159.3	4.5	$334.8	6.8	$575.7	8.6	$1133.2	12.3
Imports of goods and services	223.1	6.2	324.8	6.6	632.2	9.4	1532.3	16.6
Balance of trade	−$63.8	−1.8	+$10.0	+0.2	−$56.5	−0.8	−$399.1	−4.3

Note: Data are on a national income and product accounts basis.

Source: U.S. Department of Commerce.

sets and VCRs to less than 1 percent for folding paperboard boxes. Potentially, any sector of the American economy can be affected by foreign competition—whether autos or clothespins are at stake. As a result, there are almost always calls for protection from imports. The rationale for government intervention varies. It can range from offsetting "unfair" dumping (foreigners selling in U.S. markets at prices below market prices abroad), to combating foreign barriers against our exports (*their* protectionism), to promoting our own perceived national security interests.

Numerous industries—notably automobiles, steel, textiles, shoes, and machine tools—have at times exerted pressure on the federal government to restrain the free flow of trade between the United States and the rest of the world. On occasion, the restrictionist impetus comes from the government itself, often as an adjunct to foreign policy—and these restraints usually aim at limiting exports rather than imports. To further complicate matters, some of the strongest defenders of protectionism wind up importing products or components. In the words of retired Chrysler Chairman Lee Iacocca, "If you don't go to the lowest-cost source, you're an idiot."

KEY INDUSTRY ACTIONS

In the 1980s, some of the most powerful calls for restraint of international trade and investment came from the American automotive industry and the United Auto Workers union, which earlier had been bastions of free trade. This shift in sentiment was rooted in the fact that sales of imported cars, especially those made in Japan, had captured large shares of the domestic market. Beginning in 1981, Japan was cajoled to impose "voluntary" restraints on its exports of passenger motor vehicles to the United States. (See box, "How 'Voluntary' Export Restraints Worked.")

Goaded by foreign competition, domestic automobile producers streamlined their operations, substantially improving productivity and quality. Although Japanese imports continue to win a large but still minority share of the U.S. market, U.S.–headquartered companies have regained the initiative and have stabilized their market shares. Some of the imports have been replaced by production from subsidiaries of Japanese (and also German) firms that have been established in the United States.

BOX 12-1

HOW "VOLUNTARY" EXPORT RESTRAINTS WORKED: THE U.S.–JAPANESE AUTO AGREEMENT

The Japanese imposed restraints on automobile exports to the United States in 1981 to preempt more restrictive measures advocated by many, especially company and labor groups, within the United States. Earlier that year, several senior senators had introduced a bill to limit automobile imports from Japan to 1.6 million units annually during the period 1981–1983. This figure was very close to the Japanese self-imposed "voluntary" export restraint of 1.68 million. Protectionist pressures had been increasing since the late 1970s, as automobile sales by U.S. producers declined and foreign producers captured larger shares of the American market. Thus, the action by the Japanese government headed off the Congressional action.

With the restraints, the prices paid by U.S. consumers for Japanese automobiles rose. This reduced the competitive pressures on U.S. producers and non-Japanese exporters to the United States, increasing prices for these automobiles—but not as much as the rise in prices of Japanese cars.

The restraints on numbers of cars that could be imported induced quality changes as Japanese producers responded by shifting their mix of exports toward larger and more luxurious models (which also generated more profits per unit). In addition, more "optional" equipment was installed in each vehicle. Consequently, the average sales price of Japanese automobiles increased because of the price effect as well as the quality effects associated with the restraints.

For all new cars sold in 1984, prices rose an average of $1,649 (17 percent), which consisted of a pure price effect of $617 per car and a quality effect of $1,032 per car. The higher price led to an estimated reduction in 1984 purchases of approximately 1.5 million.[1]

The price increase of 12 percent for domestically produced automobiles was less than the increase of 22 percent for imports from Japan. This relative price change allowed the U.S. producers to increase their market share by almost 7 percentage points. The number of domestically produced cars was unchanged from the previous year, even though Americans bought fewer new cars in total. Thus, the reduction in U.S. car purchases was borne entirely by foreign producers. These production changes were estimated to generate increased domestic automotive employment in the range of 40,000 to 75,000 jobs.

The higher automobile prices—aggregating over $6 billion for the year—represented one facet of the losses for consumers. In addition, U.S. consumers were worse off to the extent that quotas limited their range of automotive choices. The losses to consumers were in effect transfers to domestic and foreign producers. Of the foreign producers' gain from higher prices, Japanese producers received approximately $5 billion. This figure provides an obvious reason why the Japanese government continued the restraints beyond 1985 when the Reagan administration decided not to request an extension of the agreement. The formal restraints lapsed in 1988. Much of the Japanese imports have been subsequently replaced by domestic production by subsidiaries of Japanese-owned automobile firms (so-called "transplants").

Some of these "transplants" use substantial proportions of U.S. labor and domestically produced parts. The "domestic content" provisions of the North American Free Trade Agreement have encouraged this trend.

The concern of the American steel industry over steel imports, primarily from the European Union (EU) and the Asian rim, predates Detroit's auto import concerns. The net steel trade balance of the United States shifted from positive to negative during a prolonged strike in 1959, and imports have been substantial since then.

This penetration of imports has, from time to time, prompted domestic steel producers to level charges that importers were *dumping,* or selling steel at lower prices than the producers charge in their home markets. United States law provides for antidumping duties to be levied on imports if the sale of dumped goods causes "material harm" to a domestic industry. Also, countervailing duties can be imposed to offset subsidies by foreign governments if subsidized imports cause harm to American producers. Over the years, a variety of specific trade restrictions to protect the domestic steel industry has been adopted.[2] Nevertheless, the financial condition of the domestic steel industry continues to deteriorate. By early 2002, 30 companies had declared bankruptcy.

In March 2002, the International Trade Commission (ITC) ruled that steel imports were a "substantial cause of serious injury" to the domestic steel industry. Under Section 201 of the Trade Act of 1974, such a conclusion does not require the finding of an unfair trade practice, such as dumping. On the basis of the ITC action, President George W. Bush imposed temporary quotas and taxes (tariffs) on steel imports to provide a respite during which the domestic steel companies could restructure themselves and better meet foreign competition. He raised tariffs on a wide array of steel products in a range of 8 percent to 30 percent, to be phased out over a three-year period. In the case of steel slab, the president set a quota of 5.4 million tons, after which a tariff of 30 percent would apply. A variety of exceptions were made, especially to allies in the fight against terrorism. Thus, the main steel imports from Turkey were largely exempted, as were the imports from Canada, Mexico, and many developing nations.

The EU and individual steel-producing nations strongly objected to the protectionist actions in behalf of the American steel industry. On the basis of past experience, it is unlikely that the tariffs and quotas will solve the basic problems facing a high-cost industry that invests relatively little in modernization and devotes large sums to generous health and retirement benefits.

"Voluntary" export quotas, also known as orderly marketing agreements (OMAs), were imposed on footwear imports to the United States in the 1970s. They were terminated in 1981 and the experience was similar to the automobile industry's a decade later. As shown in Figure 12.1, restricting imports of footwear meant that U.S. purchasers of shoes paid more. The OMAs hit low-priced shoes disproportionately hard, as foreign producers attempted to maximize their profits within the confines of the trade restraints. Indirectly, the quotas induced an increase in the supply of higher-quality footwear (which is higher in price), thereby resulting in smaller price increases for those shoes that are generally purchased by higher-income groups.

The implicit tax imposed by footwear quotas on the lowest-income group (individuals then earning less than $7,000 annually) was more than three times that imposed on higher-income groups (those with incomes greater than $25,000 a year).[3] Imports of shoes rose rapidly with the termination of the trade restrictions, and pressures for new quotas mounted in 1984. However, the ITC ruled that the domestic industry was not sufficiently injured to warrant action to restrict imports.

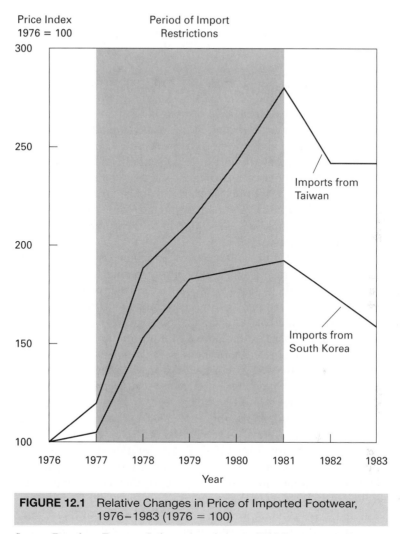

FIGURE 12.1 Relative Changes in Price of Imported Footwear, 1976–1983 (1976 = 100)

Source: Data from Footwear Industry Association and U.S. Department of Commerce.

THE CASE FOR FREE TRADE

Given the widespread use of protectionist devices to inhibit the flow of trade among nations, it is useful to examine the conceptual and historical justifications for an open trading system. The case for free trade is rooted in a basic economic law: the principle of comparative advantage, which holds that total economic welfare is enhanced if each nation specializes in the production of items that it can produce relatively most efficiently. This is an important case of Adam Smith's more general point concerning the advantages of the specialization of labor. To cite Smith's immortal words:

It is the maxim of every prudent . . . family, never to attempt to make at home what it will cost . . . more to make than to buy. The tailor does not attempt to make his own shoes, but buys them of the shoemaker . . . What is prudence in the conduct of every private family can scarcely be folly in that of a great kingdom.

HISTORICAL EXPERIENCE

The argument in favor of freer trade is supported by historical evidence. Through most of the twentieth century, the United States played a leadership role in developing the world trading system. During the 1930s, however, the United States and many other countries followed "beggar-thy-neighbor" trade policies—restricting imports that generated retaliation by other countries in a cycle that contributed to the worldwide economic depression. The Smoot–Hawley protectionist tariff epitomized this approach in the United States. The results for many companies were extremely negative. Firms that had relied on foreign business were limited to the domestic market, which for some was inadequate for survival.

After World War II, the United States embarked on a program of reciprocal trade agreements. Initially arranged bilaterally, they evolved into the further improved multilateral trading system of the postwar years. This approach broke down many of the historical barriers to world trade. In the 1960s, the acceleration in world trade and economic growth followed a sharp and mutual reduction in tariff barriers.

The economic history of the United States provides earlier examples of the benefits of an open economy. If the concept of gross domestic product (GDP) had existed in the eighteenth and nineteenth centuries, people would have pointed to the United States as one of the more open economies, as measured by the share of GDP involved in foreign trade. The United States was then among the more trade-oriented economies in the world, exporting a wide variety of agricultural products and raw materials. In addition, America's service exports, such as shipping, were an important economic activity. In turn, this nation was a major importer of manufactured goods and a recipient of large amounts of foreign capital. These factors continued to play a critical role in the development of the U.S. economy during the nineteenth century.

Around the beginning of the twentieth century, the dynamics of the American economy shifted. Exports and imports became smaller shares of GDP. United States investment abroad increased, transforming an international debtor into a world creditor. Increasingly, we became a self-sufficient economy. Only in the last 30 years has the international sector once again begun to increase its relative importance to the economy.

Generalizing from historical experience, the advantages of freer trade are numerous:

- Open trade contributes to lowering inflationary pressures by increasing the supply of goods and services competing for the consumer's dollar.
- Open trade minimizes the role of government in influencing private-sector decisions in the international marketplace.
- Open trade improves the efficiency with which resources are allocated by permitting the operation of the principle of comparative advantage. Thereby, the society can achieve more growth, higher levels of employment, and an improved living standard.

Current data tend to reinforce these points. In 2002, the tariffs of the wealthy industrialized nations averaged only 3 percent, while those of the poorer, developing countries averaged 13 percent. (Ironically, the trade barriers of the developing countries are more significant restraints on their development than are the trade barriers of the developed countries.)[4] Aside from the direct and measurable aspects, trade stimulates competition, increases national productivity, and speeds the exchange of new ideas.

THE POLITICAL POWER OF PROTECTIONISM

Protectionism is popular because it enables relatively small, well-organized groups to use the political process to their advantage. The benefits are received by the protected industries, while some costs are shifted to other companies that buy from those industries. Ultimately, most of the costs are borne by consumers in the form of higher prices. Thus, protectionism can be viewed as a hidden tax on the consumer. (See Table 12.2 for some examples.) That "tax" was estimated in 1990 at $70 billion in the United States.[5] In the case of the EU, each "protected" job was estimated to cost the economy about $200,000 a year, or ten times the average wage in the protected industries.[6]

In battles over protectionist policies, the balance of political power is extremely uneven. Those who are harmed by the reduced supply of goods and services are generally not even aware of the process by which they are hurt. Although the total costs of protectionism far exceed the benefits, the higher prices to consumers are widely diffused among the 50 states and 250 million residents. Any single consumer's stake in the outcome is small. The individual almost surely is not aware of why the price of a given item is going up. Consequently, resistance at the grassroots level to protectionist measures is often considerably less than pressure for their adoption.

The nineteenth-century reformer Henry George may be best known as the proponent of a single tax (on land), but he provided one of the most telling criticisms of protectionism:

> Protective tariffs are as much applications of force as are blockading squadrons. . . . The difference between the two is that blockading squadrons are a means whereby nations seek to prevent their enemies from trading; protective tariffs are a means whereby nations attempt to prevent their own people from trading. What protection teaches us is to do to ourselves in time of peace what enemies seek to do to us in time of war.

TABLE 12.2   Cost to U.S. Consumers of Protection, 1988

Item	Free Market Price	Price with Trade Restrictions	Cost of Protection per Item	Percentage of Free Market Price
Automobile	$7,500	$10,000	$2,500	33%
Blue jeans	14	18	4	29
Box of candy	2	3	1	50
Clock radio	30	32	2	7
Leather handbag	40	44	4	10
Man's sweater	20	25	5	25
Rubber boots	10	12	2	20
Teddy bear	8	10	2	25
Vinyl handbag	10	12	2	20
Woman's leather gloves	33	40	7	21

Source: Data from Institute for International Economics and U.S. Department of Commerce.

> ◁ BOX 12-2 ▷
>
> ## A TOKYO HOUSEWIFE CRITICIZES JAPANESE PROTECTIONISM
>
> To the Editor:
>
> Many of us city wives are now fed up with having to pay as much as 500 yen to 700 yen for 100 grams of beef because the government keeps restrictions on its import. Husbands are asked to buy beef for omiyage (souvenirs) at American or Australian airports on their way home to bring back to their families because beef is much cheaper in those countries. Oranges and grapefruit can also be much cheaper if only our government liberalizes their imports.
>
> The government says it cannot lift the restrictions because the Japanese farmers should be protected. But the Japanese farmers are now the most privileged people. They are paying much less tax than salaried people in the cities. Some of them are even paid for not growing rice in their paddy fields. The farmers are much better off in politics because rural senkyo-ku (constituencies) elect more Diet members than city senkyo-ku per population. Sometimes a city Diet member represents four times as many electors as a rural MP.
>
> I cannot but suspect that politicians and officials are not so patriotic as they claim, and they seek their own good by spoiling our farmers. Politicians can retain their seats in the parliament and get political funds from the farmers' organizations. Bureaucrats can keep key posts in corporations and other bodies which control the import regulations for their own postretirement jobs. Why should we city people support these farmers (and politicians and bureaucrats) by paying much more for beef and oranges (and rice too) than in other countries?
>
> Etsuko Kinoshita
>
> ──────
> SOURCE: *Mainichi Daily News*, January 20, 1983.

Efforts to "protect" consumers against low prices are not limited to the United States. A letter to the editor of a Tokyo newspaper written by a Japanese housewife furnishes a classic example. (See box, "A Tokyo Housewife Criticizes Japanese Protectionism.")

Protectionism also hits hard the domestic industries that use protected items in their own production. The 1984 voluntary export restraints (VERs) on steel "saved" about 14,000 jobs in American firms producing steel. However, the higher prices for domestic steel that resulted from restricting imports made domestic automobiles and other durable goods less competitive. Consequently, the VERs resulted in 50,000 fewer manufacturing jobs in steel-using industries than would have been the case without the restraints.[7]

FOREIGN OBSTACLES TO U.S. EXPORTS

A perennial source of protectionist sentiment is the numerous barriers that domestic producers of products and services must face in trying to penetrate overseas markets. These obstacles to trade range from direct quotas to complicated licensing requirements.

QUOTAS ON IMPORTS

Many nations maintain *quotas* (numerical restrictions on imports of specific products). Japan maintains a long list of quotas on the products of agriculture and fisheries.

Quotas on foreign films and television programs are common, as are numerical restrictions on service imports.

TARIFFS ON IMPORTS

Tariffs also hamper international trade. Nominal tariffs in China range from 3 percent on goods whose import is being encouraged to 250 percent on automobiles. In practice, however, most transactions involve substantial reductions from these "listed prices," depending on very special circumstances (which provide opportunities for favoritism and bribery).

Tariffs have advantages over quotas for both consumers and exporters. Provided the tariff rates applied are not prohibitively high, foreign producers can remain competitive by cutting costs or improving quality. Quotas do not provide incentives for better meeting consumer needs, since market shares are fixed regardless of the improved efficiency of the potential exporter.

BUY-DOMESTIC RESTRICTIONS

Many foreign countries maintain buy-domestic practices. The criteria for award of a public works contract in Brazil may include "percentage of national ownership" of competing firms. United States international trading partners frequently use their own airlines, place insurance for government projects exclusively with domestic firms, and use only domestic computer capacity for data processing needs, whether by law or "understanding."

OTHER REGULATORY BARRIERS TO IMPORTS

Most nations have adopted internal regulations that, inadvertently or not, serve as obstacles to international trade. India operates a licensing system that bans the majority of foreign-made consumer goods. Laws protecting foreign franchises, patents, and copyrights are often indifferently enforced. Such irregularity makes international use of a patented process or product line both very complicated and vulnerable to pirating. This is a serious problem in the protection of copyrights on telecommunications and computer software, products that are expensive for a U.S. firm to develop and very difficult to protect in another country.

Many governments maintain regulatory restrictions on franchising of foreign firms, whether it be technical, professional services, banking, or consumer services such as restaurants or retail stores. The fact that these regulations are vague and are often subject to interpretation by local bureaucracy makes entry by foreign firms both expensive and time-consuming. China often requires testing and certification of foreign products to ensure compliance with internal specifications and standards not even made available to exporters.

BARRIERS TO FINANCIAL SERVICES

Banking and other financial services are heavily restricted. Discriminatory tax treatment and reserve requirements, outright prohibition of retail banking, and restrictions on foreign ownership often make it difficult for U.S. banks to compete with local financial institutions. In Indonesia, any new foreign bank must be a joint venture between an Indonesian bank and a foreign bank from a country that offers reciprocity. Pakistan does not license new foreign insurance companies.

INVISIBLE BARRIERS

Another aspect of overseas trade barriers is found in internal marketing systems. In Southeast Asia, ethnic Chinese, family-oriented firms are accustomed to conducting informal business dealings with fellow members of the "bamboo network" whom they trust and who have a similar linguistic and cultural background. Such practices make it difficult for other companies to penetrate those markets.[8]

Japan's *keiretsu* distribution system gives preference to local products. American marketers find it difficult to bypass this highly traditional way of doing business. Informal vertical integration, in the form of long-term business "relationships" (often several generations old), tend to deny U.S. firms access to many retail markets. As far as Japan's government is concerned, however, no trade barrier exists.

Many nations inhibit imports by means of administrative procedures that can be more difficult to deal with than formal trade barriers such as tariffs and quotas. China maintains a complex import approval process. Depending on the locality, as many as 15 "chops" (clearances) from various ministries or bureaus may be necessary. Permission to import is often required from both local and central government authorities. Vagueness and uncertainty in enforcement of rules also complicate foreign trade.[9]

THE ROLE OF INTERNATIONAL AGENCIES

The role of intergovernmental agencies in trade policy is complex. Most attention is focused on the World Trade Organization (WTO), which is dedicated to opening markets for international commerce. However, an often overlooked category of impediments to international trade is the array of codes and restrictions enacted by international agencies such as the European Union (EU) and the United Nations (UN) and its many specialized agencies. Some of these efforts—especially those dealing with consumer products—are in the form of advisory resolutions or voluntary guidelines. Other UN actions are legally binding treaties, such as rules for international maritime operations.

THE WTO AND SOCIAL STANDARDS

The WTO is an international institution in which the United States negotiates agreements with 143 other members to reduce barriers to trade. The organization also maintains a forum for dispute settlement that enables its members to resolve trade disagreements. In 2001, the member nations agreed to launch further negotiations on trade liberalization covering a wide agenda—agriculture, services, access to industrial markets, antidumping and subsidies, dispute settlement rules, and a limited set of environmental issues.

Criticism of WTO and its procedures is widespread. Some activists see the presence of large international agencies as threats to individual citizens and simply want to close them down. Other critics support the rule of law on a global basis but wish to reform the operations of the WTO. They contend that it has become too closed and bureaucratic, ignoring the views of interest groups other than trade professionals. Numerous suggestions have been made to open the workings of the WTO, especially the dispute settlement process.

The most serious substantive complaint about the WTO and about agreements on international trade generally is that they do not take adequate account of the impacts on labor standards and the environment. Many union and environmental groups want to make any further trade agreements contingent on adopting the international standards that they advocate in these two areas.[10] At first blush, it might seem that the process of negotiating agreements to open international trade provides a fine opportunity to improve the social conditions in the developing nations.

However, developing countries generally oppose the imposition on their national sovereignty of what they see as unaffordable Western standards for paying workers and spending scarce resources on environmental matters. The developing economies see the imposition of these costly standards as a disguised way of keeping their low-cost products out of the markets of the developed nations. This cynical attitude was conveyed by Youssef Boutros-Ghali, Egypt's trade minister, "Why, all of a sudden, when Third World labor has proved to be competitive, do industrial countries start feeling concerned about our workers?"[11]

Those suspicions were strengthened by the strong union opposition in 2000 to giving even limited duty-free access to U.S. apparel markets to the products of the poorest African countries. The position of the unions was maintained *despite* the linkage of higher worker standards in the African trade bill. The measure was enacted over the protestations of the unions.

Business generally has opposed the linkage of trade and social standards as a costly interference with open markets. That may sound hard hearted and motivated by self-interest, which undoubtedly is the case. However, the results of imposing arbitrary standards on very poor developing countries can be very different from what is anticipated by the human rights and other groups supporting such standards. For example, soon after a bill was proposed in Congress in 1993 to ban imports from countries where children work in factories, garment makers in Bangladesh fired an estimated 36,000 employees. UNICEF, following up, found that few of the fired child workers ended up in school. Apparently, many took even more dangerous jobs or became prostitutes.[12]

Nevertheless, the effort to link social standards with trade agreements has developed strong support in the United States. Labor standards are recognized as a relevant issue in several major trade laws—but precise linkage is not required:

- The 1984 amendments to the Trade Act of 1974 provide that trade preferences for developing countries contain a provision to deny those benefits to any country that "has not taken or is not taking steps to afford internationally recognized worker rights to workers in the country." However, the president can waive this provision "in the international economic interests of the United States."

- The Omnibus Trade and Competitiveness Act of 1988 includes "workers rights" as one of 16 principal trade negotiation objectives, but the law does not require that the trade agreement necessarily has to incorporate specific standards.

- The 1994 trade law calls upon the president to "seek the establishment in . . . the WTO of a working party to examine the relationship of internationally recognized worker rights to the existing international trade regime." (That issue was one of the items that contributed to the deadlock in trade discussions at the Seattle WTO meeting in December 1999.)

- The legislation establishing NAFTA set up commissions on labor cooperation and on environmental cooperation.

- Article XX of the General Agreement on Tariffs and Trade (the forerunner of the WTO) allows countries to ban imports of goods produced using prison labor so long as the bans are not a form of disguised protectionism.

- The U.S.–Jordan Free Trade Agreement states: "The parties shall strive to ensure that such labor principles [referring to the ILO Declaration on Fundamental Principles and Rights at Work] . . . are recognized and protected by domestic laws." The agreement also provides for monetary fines, rather than trade sanctions, as punishment for violating these provisions.

Many proponents of open trade believe that the International Labor Organization (ILO) is better suited to deal with labor standards than the WTO. The ILO is the oldest UN agency. More than 5,000 government ratifications of over 300 ILO policy declarations have been recorded, covering standards dealing with employment, training, working conditions, and industrial relations.

The ILO is unique among international organizations in having equal representation from business, labor, and government. The ILO would seem to be the proper place to take up the issue of international labor standards. In 1998, the ILO adopted four "core" labor standards, which have been referenced in a variety of American and foreign trade discussions: freedom of association and the effective recognition of the right to collective bargaining; freedom from forced labor; the effective abolition of child labor; and nondiscrimination in employment.

Over the years, however, the ILO has earned a reputation for setting high-minded goals but not following up with adequate action. This is especially true with regard to promoting labor standards in developing nations. Part of the problem is that Congress has ratified few of the ILO's "conventions" (13 out of 183) and only two out of four core standards (on the abolition of forced labor and the prohibition of the worst forms of child labor).[13] The United States is limited, at the present time, in its use of the ILO as an enforcement mechanism for workplace standards because it can only initiate complaints with respect to agreements it has ratified. Ironically, the United States has adopted and enforces internal labor standards that equal and often exceed the ILO's (see Chapters 5 and 6).

In the absence of a counterpart to the ILO in the area of the environment, not many positive alternatives to direct linkage with trade agreements have surfaced. One of the few such suggestions is that the range of exceptions to WTO standards be expanded to provide "safe harbors" for trade actions consistent with provisions of specific multilateral environmental agreements. Thus, the United States and other nations could be allowed to protect endangered species by policies that restrict trade, but not to do so on a unilateral basis.

In 1996, the WTO Committee on Trade and the Environment seemed to indicate that WTO rules would permit member nations to exclude imports made in ways that violated an environmental agreement, provided that the agreement allows for such actions and that both the offending nation and the responding nation are parties to the agreement. In the same year, a WTO appeals panel indicated that WTO members could exclude imports under a multilateral environmental agreement.[14]

OTHER UN REGULATORY ACTIVITIES

Companies involved in international trade face a variety of regulatory measures by other UN agencies. The best known of these is the Infant Formula Code, adopted by the UN's World Health Organization. This code calls for a wide variety of restrictions on the distribution of breast-milk substitutes, applying not only to advertising, distribution of samples, and labeling, but to the activities and compensation of marketing personnel. The Infant Formula Code is not legally binding, but major makers of infant formula such as Nestlé have responded to public pressure and are abiding by it.[15]

In other areas, the UN's General Assembly has adopted a consumer protection code, which creates voluntary guidelines on product safety. The Food and Agricultural Organization has approved an International Code of Conduct on the Distribution and Use of Pesticides. The Code provides guidelines for marketing and using pesticides, especially in developing countries. Specific industries are subject to the ruling and guidelines of the International Maritime Organization, the International Telecommunications Union, and the World Intellectual Property Organization.

THE EUROPEAN UNION

Firms operating within the EU have become aware of the costs of complying with a host of international regulations. For example, standards are mandated on the preparation of annual financial reports—covering accounting categories, asset valuation rules, capitalization of companies, inflation accounting, and auditing procedures. Corporations operating in the EU are also required to make public financial reports on the operations of their EU subsidiaries. The reporting requirements depend on the level of parent company ownership and can apply whether or not the headquarters of the controlling company is within the EU.

The EU also requires each multinational with 1,000 or more employees in Western Europe and with at least 150 workers in two different member states to set up a European Works Council. The Council is a formal forum for management to inform and consult with employees. The employer pays the costs involved, including employee time, travel expenses, and interpreters. Depending on the labor relations policies of the individual nations, employers can set a council up on their own or negotiate with unions to do so. French law, for example, specifies that the unions will choose the representatives to the Works Council, while in Ireland the entire workforce participates in that decision. The United Kingdom, in contrast, has opted out of the whole process.[16]

The EU's environmental regulations are often a source of difficulty for U.S. firms doing business in Western Europe. To qualify for the EU's eco-labels (which encourage consumers to buy items with those labels), firms have to agree to cut chlorine and sulfur emissions and curtail energy consumption during the production process. In addition, paper products companies have to demonstrate that the pulp they use comes from environmentally sound forestry practices that maintain biodiverse forests and reduce water effluent levels.

There are liberating as well as the restrictive features to the European Union. Controls on the physical movement of goods across internal national borders within the EU have been removed. Customs checks have largely disappeared and customs forms are no longer required at internal border crossings.

Many of the internal barriers to the movement of people have been eliminated. Citizens of one member nation can reside in any other member nation, although in practice workers are not as mobile as in the United States. The flow of money and credit has been enhanced by the decision that one country will supervise each banking or insurance institution—the country where the organization's head office is located. In addition, mutual recognition of licenses issued in the country of origin is provided. Thus, the authorization of only one member country is required to operate throughout the EU. As a general proposition, all enterprises established inside the EU have equal rights irrespective of the location of their headquarters or source of capital.[17]

U.S. OBSTACLES TO INTERNATIONAL COMMERCE

The United States is hardly an island of free trade in a world of protectionism. The federal government imposes numerous obstacles to imports, restricts various types of exports, and also discourages or prevents certain types of foreign investment.

Five major types of trade obstacles inhibit imports into the United States:

1. Buy-American statutes, which give preference in government procurement to domestic producers.
2. The Jones Act, which prohibits foreign ships from engaging in waterborne commerce between U.S. ports.
3. Statutes that limit the import of specific agricultural and manufactured products.
4. Selective high tariffs on specific items.
5. Regulatory barriers aimed at protecting domestic producers.

"BUY-AMERICAN" AND MERCHANT MARINE STATUTES

Buy-American provisions have been enacted by many government units. The Buy American Act requires federal agencies that purchase commodities for use within the United States to pay up to a 6 percent differential for domestically produced goods. As much as a 50 percent differential is paid for military goods produced at home. In addition, the Surface Transportation Assistance Act requires that, for most purchases over $500,000, American materials and products be used. Also, American flag vessels must be used to transport at least 50 percent of the gross tonnage of all commodities financed with U.S. foreign-aid funds.

The buy-American laws of the states are varied (see Table 12.3). New York requires state agencies to buy American steel. Arizona stipulates that all construction materials must be purchased in the state. The Missouri law also requires cities to adopt procurement guidelines that reflect the buy-American philosophy. In addition, numerous states and municipal authorities require use of American materials in privately owned as well as government-owned utilities.

The Merchant Marine Act (the Jones Act) requires that all oceangoing shipments from one point in the United States to another be transported in U.S. flag vessels. This law effectively bars foreign competition in U.S. domestic marine transport. The per-

TABLE 12.3   Buy-American Practices, by State

State	Buy-American Preference	In-State Preference
Alabama	Construction	
Alaska		All purchasing
Arizona		Construction materials
Arkansas		Commodities, printing, construction
California	Food	Vendors in distressed areas, enterprise zones
Florida	Meats	
Georgia	Beef, lumber	Forestry products
Hawaii		Commodities, printing
Idaho		Printing
Illinois	Steel	Coal
Indiana	Steel	Coal
Iowa	Motor vehicles	Coal
Kansas	General[a]	
Louisiana	Motor vehicles	Products
Maryland	Steel	
Massachusetts		Commodities
Michigan		Printing
Minnesota	General[b]	
Missouri	Products, commodities	
Montana		Commodities
New Jersey	Public works material	
New Mexico	General[c]	Commodities, services, construction
New York	Steel	Food
Ohio	General[b]	Commodities, services
Oklahoma	Beef	Commodities
Oregon		Printing
Pennsylvania	Steel, motor vehicles	
Rhode Island	Steel	
South Carolina	General[d]	Commodities
South Dakota	Beef	Grade A milk processors
Virginia		Coal
West Virginia	Aluminum, glass, steel	Construction, repair, public improvements
Wyoming	Beef	Construction, printing

[a]The purchasing director may reject a bid because a product is manufactured or assembled outside the United States.
[b]The Department of Administration may set a preference for American-made products.
[c]Requires only that goods must be assembled in North America, above the equator.
[d]Requires that first choice be for products made or grown in South Carolina, provided price is no more than 5 percent higher.
Source: National Institute of Governmental Purchasing.

verse effects are great. Tourists from the lower 48 states taking a voyage by sea from the mainland to Alaska typically board ship in Vancouver, Canada (a port not subject to the Jones Act), rather than Seattle. The more convenient port of Seattle suffers the loss of business, with no gain to the American merchant marine. The benefits of trying to restrict commerce are received by foreigners.

IMPORT RESTRICTIONS

Numerous federal statutes and regulations restrict the import of specific products. Section 22 of the Agricultural Adjustment Act of 1938 permits the president to regulate the imports of agricultural products if such imports "materially interfere" with agricultural price-support programs. Section 22 quotas currently limit imports of wheat, peanuts, cotton, and sugar. U.S. companies that believe they have been hurt by "unfair" trade policies or practices overseas have a variety of opportunities to seek federal help (see Table 12.4). For example, the escape clause of the Trade Act of 1974 provides for temporary "relief" from low U.S. tariffs in the case of industries that show threat of serious injury from imports (see box, "How the Escape Clause Works").

Also, the federal government can impose tariff increases in the form of antidumping and countervailing duties on what it considers to be unfair practices in international trade. In the period 1999–2001, action was taken against product categories ranging from pasta to pineapples (see Table 12.5).

Two actions are required before antidumping duties can be imposed: (1) a finding by the Department of Commerce of sales at less than fair value and (2) a finding by the International Trade Commission of "material" injury to domestic producers (ignoring any benefits to American consumers). The official definition of dumping is so broad that it covers many actions that are standard and entirely legal when performed in the United States, notably post-Christmas clearance sales, varying pricing over the life of a product, or even adjusting prices for the fluctuations in the business cycle. Countervailing duties are levied when it is shown that a foreign country is subsidizing an export to the United States. A finding of material injury is also required.[19]

TABLE 12.4   U.S. Laws Dealing with Complaints about Imports

Nature of the Law	Agency's Responses	Action Complained About	Nature of Relief Granted
Section 201 of the Trade Act of 1974	ITC determines injury and recommends relief; president determines relief	Increased imports that cause or threaten serious injury to a U.S. industry	Almost any form of protection and/or adjustment assistance
Antidumping Law	DOC determines dumping; ITC determines injury	Selling foreign goods in U.S. below cost; injuring or threatening to injure a U.S. industry	Antidumping duties equal to the amount by which the goods are sold below cost
Countervailing Duty Law	DOC determines foreign subsidy; ITC determines injury	Foreign subsidies on imports; injuring or threatening to injure a U.S. industry	Countervailing duties equal to the computed subsidy
Section 301 of the Trade Act of 1974	USTR investigates and recommends to president retaliatory measures	Violations of a trade agreement or special foreign market barrier	Negotiations to stop foreign practice, with threat of retaliation

Note: DOC = Department of Commerce; ITC = International Trade Commission; and USTR = U.S. Trade Representative.

BOX 12-3

HOW THE "ESCAPE CLAUSE" WORKS

Although the WTO's primary goal is to establish a more open international trade environment, it recognizes the right of a government to part from free and open trade in certain circumstances. In particular, the WTO allows a country to "escape" from negotiated tariff reductions, if the increased imports can be shown to "cause or threaten serious injury to domestic producers" of competitive products. In those cases, the country can unilaterally elect to reinstate the trade barrier that was in effect before the concession. The provision was meant to give industries time to adjust to increased competition.

In the United States, requests for protection are made to the International Trade Commission (ITC), which has the responsibility for determining whether the industry has been seriously injured or threatened with serious injury by imports. If so, it recommends to the president the type of trade relief needed to alleviate the injury. The following remedies are available:

1. *Tariff increases.* Limited to 50 percentage points above the existing rate. A 20 percent tariff could be raised to a maximum of 70 percent.

2. *Tariff-rate quotas.* A tariff on honey, for example, could allow the first 1,000 tons to enter at a 10 percent rate and imports above that would be taxed at 20 percent.

3. *Quotas.* Must at least equal the amount or value of the product imported during the most recent period.

4. *Other actions.* Some trade privilege currently extended to the exporting nation may be suspended.[18]

The authority to adjust tariffs or impose quotas is reserved for the president. In addition, the ITC can recommend that employees and firms be given trade-adjustment assistance.

In determining appropriate relief, the president is required to consider its effectiveness in facilitating adjustment, as well as its costs on consumers and the economy. Often, the president does not impose relief in cases where the ITC has recommended it. The president may also decide to seek import relief even though the ITC has found that imports were not the major factor behind the industry's injury. There have also been several instances where trade protection has been awarded without a formal escape-clause proceeding.

Section 201 of the Trade Act of 1974 relaxed the requirements to qualify for escape-clause relief. It severed the connection between trade liberalization and import protection, making the term *escape clause* somewhat of a misnomer. In addition, the importance of imports in causing the injury was reduced. Previously, it had to be shown that imports were a more important cause of injury than all other causes taken together. Under the revised standard, imports merely had to be the most important cause. The tariff increases on steel imports in 2002 were made in response to an "escape-clause" proceeding at the International Trade Commission. The "relief" granted to the steel industry was limited to three years because that is the maximum period that the WTO allows prior to authorizing other countries to retaliate or otherwise seek compensation.

SELECTIVE HIGH TARIFFS

Despite low average duties (less than 5 percent), some individual U.S. tariffs are quite high. Customs duties on certain kinds of fabrics range up to 38 percent—three times the rate in Western Europe. The rate on clothing starts at 20 percent (see Table 12.6). However, approximately one-half of the imports entering the United States are duty-free. Thus, when it aggregates all U.S. imports (dutiable and duty free), the ITC estimates that the average tariff collected in the United States comes to about 2.5 percent.

TABLE 12.5   U.S. Charges of "Dumping," Selected Cases 1999–2001

Nation	Product
Canada	Tomatoes
Chile	Raspberries
China	Automotive replacement glass windshields
China	Creatine monohydrate (dietary supplement)
Italy, Turkey	Pasta
Japan	Pipes
South Korea	Steel beams
Russia	Ammonium nitrate
Thailand	Pineapples

Source: U.S. International Trade Commission.

INTERNAL RESTRICTIONS

Domestic regulation often acts to limit imports, whether that is the intent or not. In the United States, more than 2,700 state and local governments require particular safety certifications for products sold or installed within their jurisdictions. These requirements are rarely uniform across the nation. As a result, acquiring the necessary information and satisfying the established procedures can be a major undertaking for a foreign enterprise trying to sell across the United States.

The federal government restricts, and at times prohibits, foreign companies and citizens of other countries from investing in specific sectors of the economy. Foreign corporations are effectively barred from defense contracts and atomic energy facilities; they cannot hold more than 25 percent of the stock of domestic airlines or more than 20 percent in the case of TV and radio stations. The chief executives of fishing companies and dredging firms must be U.S. citizens.

BARRIERS TO U.S. EXPORTS

The United States has adopted more restrictions on its own exports than any other capitalist nation. These barriers range from direct export controls to indirect regulatory barriers. Despite the desire to promote exports, two types of U.S. statutes and regulations prevent or restrict the export of specific commodities, the first relating to

TABLE 12.6   Selected U.S. High Tariffs

Product	Tariff (percent)
Glassware	33–38
Apparel	33
Woolen fabrics	31–33
Porcelain and china	30
Steel	8–30
Trucks (5–20 tons)	25

Source: Data from Commission of European Union, 2000–2001; steel estimate from U.S. Treasury Department, 2002.

national security and foreign policy matters and the second to domestic concerns. Different laws and bureaucracies administer the formal controls, ranging from limiting exports of specific weapons to enforcing embargoes on such nations as Cuba. In addition, a rider to an appropriation act for the Interior Department bans timber exports from federal lands west of the 100th meridian. This supply restriction was adopted in a period of temporary shortage, but the barrier is embedded in permanent legislation.

Three federal departments administer the export control laws: State handles the Arms Export Control Act, Commerce the Export Administration Act, and Treasury and Commerce jointly the Trading with the Enemy Act and the International Emergency Economic Powers Act. The result has been overlapping and confusing regulatory systems and duplicative licensing forms and review staffs.

Numerous inconsistencies arise from the profusion of export restraints. United States commercial jet aircraft are routinely approved for export with all technology intact, where as communications satellites with less technology content are excluded from export. Moreover, the satellites are launched into orbit and are not "delivered" to any foreign customer or country. Most economic sanctions are ineffective because other nations are usually willing and able to serve as alternative suppliers. One international defense systems supplier directed its design engineers to exclude American parts from its products wherever possible "because of the unpredictability and shortcomings of the U.S. export control system."[20] In 2001, China's Semiconductor Manufacturing International cancelled a multimillion-dollar order with a California company after waiting months for the United States to issue an export license. A Swedish company quickly stepped in to supply the sophisticated equipment.[21] Export controls are politically attractive because the costs they impose are "off budget," being borne by the employees and shareholders of the affected companies.

A variety of domestic regulatory activities raise the prices of goods produced in the United States. Foreign producers often are not subject to similar burdens in their home country. Violators of the Foreign Corrupt Practices Act face severe penalties. A company may be fined up to $1 million, and its officers who participate in violations or "had reason to know" of them face up to five years in prison and $10,000 in fines.

Many business executives contend that the language of the law is so sweeping and ambiguous that American firms turn down foreign business when they merely suspect they might be charged with bribery. Businesses are forced into marketing approaches that are unnaturally conservative. That view is supported by the fact that very few cases are prosecuted under the Corrupt Practices Act. One of the major criticisms of the statute is that it has cost American firms export opportunities without reducing the level of foreign corruption. By precluding American firms from taking part in questionable transactions, which may be perfectly legal and acceptable practices in many other nations, the law simply reduces the ability of U.S. firms to compete overseas. A study by the National Bureau of Economic Research supported the conclusion that, by acting unilaterally, the United States weakens the competitive position of American firms without significantly reducing the importance of bribery to foreign business transactions.[22]

Several environmental programs impose special requirements on exports. Under the Federal Insecticide, Fungicide, and Rodenticide Act, exporters of products deemed hazardous in the United States must notify the importing country 30 days in advance of shipment—even if the item is not viewed as hazardous under the laws of the importing country. The importing nation must notify the exporter that the notice was received. No other country has such a restriction.

U.S. BARRIERS TO FOREIGN INVESTMENT

Most countries restrict or prohibit foreign investment to some degree. The United States is no exception. The most significant barrier is the Exon–Florio provisions of the Trade Act of 1988. Under this law, mergers and acquisitions by foreign companies deemed to affect national security are reviewed by an interagency committee chaired by the Treasury Department. If the committee finds that the merger or acquisition will harm the national security, the president may order the foreign parties to divest themselves of those U.S. assets.

The president is required to report to the Congress on the results of each review by the interagency committee. Moreover, that review must cover the potential effect on the international technological leadership of the United States "in areas affecting the national security." Although very few foreign investments have been formally vetoed through the Exon–Florio process, the prospect of going through an intensive public review has discouraged foreign acquisitions of high-tech American firms.[23]

INTERNATIONAL POLITICAL RISK ASSESSMENT

Because of the possibility of sudden and massive changes in the public-policy environment facing multinational enterprises in their various overseas markets, political risk assessments often accompany, if not precede, conventional evaluations of financial and economic risk. The risk of doing business abroad extends to more than customary market uncertainties or even to traditional monetary and fiscal policy shifts. The possibility of fundamental changes in a nation's government policies and institutions cannot be safely ignored nor can the threats of international terrorist groups (see Chapter 9).

Major multinational corporations systematically monitor political risk and the possibility of policy changes in countries where they have or are contemplating foreign direct investments. Other companies usually undertake detailed risk analysis prior to a specific investment decision.

The term *political risk* refers to the legal and social environment in which a firm has to operate. Some analysts rely mainly on written materials, such as newspapers and reference works. Many establish and interview a panel of experts, including those with specialized knowledge of individual countries. Analysis groups also commission outside experts to write reports on specific topics. Early practitioners were influenced by think-tank and military research, relying heavily on quantitative analysis to evaluate the relative risk of investments in different countries. This approach has been broadened as more subjective factors, such as traditions and culture, have been incorporated into the analysis.

The evaluation of the overall degree of turmoil or even uncertainty expected in any nation in a five- or ten-year time span is extremely subjective. Nevertheless, most analyses of political risk classify in the low-risk category the advanced industrialized and democratic countries, such as the member nations of the EU, each of which has a strong legal system. In contrast, most of the nations labeled *high risk* are the relatively undeveloped nations, especially in Africa, with limited economic or political infrastructure, or are subject to severe terrorist threats. Most of the emerging economies in East Asia,

TABLE 12.7   Composite Analysis of Political Risk

Low-Risk Nations	Moderate-Risk Nations	High-Risk Nations	Very High-Risk Nations
Austria	Argentina	China	Afghanistan
Australia	Brazil	Egypt	Columbia
Belgium	Chile	India	Indonesia
Canada	Czech Republic	Israel	Nigeria
Denmark	Greece	Jordan	Somalia
Finland	Hungary	Morocco	Sudan
France	Malaysia	Pakistan	Yemen
Germany	Mexico	Peru	Zimbabwe
Ireland	Poland	Philippines	
Italy	Portugal	Russia	
Japan	Singapore	Sri Lanka	
the Netherlands	South Korea	Turkey	
New Zealand	Spain	Vietnam	
Norway	Taiwan		
Sweden	Thailand		
Switzerland	Venezuela		
United Kingdom			

Note: The entries and categories are a composite of numerous individual analyses of political risk. Borderline cases exist in each category.

South America, and Eastern Europe usually hold intermediate positions (see Table 12.7). There is, in general, a high and inverse correlation between the anticipated level of turmoil and the attractiveness of exports and direct investment in that region.

Conclusions

Perhaps the most striking indicators of continuing American influence, if not power, in the world economy are quite unconventional. Elites everywhere want to send their children to American universities; few want to go for an MBA to Tokyo University or Moscow University. People risk death on the high seas to get into this country; farm laborers and Nobel Prize winners alike want to move to the United States. All the movie studios of Europe and Asia combined cannot break Hollywood's grip on world audiences. Businesses want access to the American market.

Notes

1. Robert W. Crandall, "Import Quotas and the Automobile Industry," *Brookings Review,* Summer 1984, pp. 8–16.
2. William H. Barringer and Kenneth J. Pierce, *Paying the Price for Big Steel* (Washington, DC: American Institute for International Steel, 2000), pp. xxv–xxvii; Dan Ikenson,

Steel Trap: How Subsidies and Protectionism Weaken the U.S. Steel Industry (Washington, DC: Cato Institute, 2002).

3. Joon H. Suh, *"Voluntary" Export Restraints and Their Effects on Exporters and Consumers: The Case of Footwear Quotas* (St. Louis, MO: Washington University,

Center for the Study of American Business, 1981).

4. Jagdish Bhagwati, "The Poor's Best Hope," *The Economist*, June 22, 2002, p. 24.

5. Gary C. Hufbauer and Kimberly Elliott, *Measuring the Costs of Protection in the United States* (Washington, DC: Institute for International Economics, 1994).

6. Patrick A. Messerlin, *Measuring the Costs of Protection in Europe* (Washington, DC: Institute for International Economics, 2001).

7. Arthur T. Denzau, *How Import Restraints Reduce Employment* (St. Louis, MO: Washington University, Center for the Study of American Business, 1987).

8. Murray Weidenbaum and Samuel Hughes, *The Bamboo Network* (New York: Free Press, 1996), pp. 121–151.

9. Office of the U.S. Trade Representative, *Foreign Trade Barriers* (Washington, DC: Government Printing Office, 1993).

10. Murray Weidenbaum, *Looking for Common Ground on U.S. Trade Policy* (Washington, DC: Center for Strategic and International Studies, 2001).

11. Quoted in David E. Sanger, "A Grand Trade Bargain," *Foreign Affairs*, January/February 2001, pp. 66–67.

12. Pete Engardo, "Global Capitalism," *Business Week*, November 6, 2000, p. 76.

13. Douglas Irwin, "Free Trade Under Fire," *Milken Institute Review*, Second Quarter 2002, p. 81.

14. Peter Morici, *Labor Standards in the Global Trading System* (Washington, DC: Economic Strategy Institute, 2001), pp. 17–18.

15. S. Prakash Sethi, "A New Perspective on the International Social Regulation of Business," *Journal of Socio-Economics* 22, no. 2, pp. 141–158.

16. *European Works Council* (New York: Conference Board, 1997), pp. 1–23.

17. Michael Calingaert, "A Perspective for U.S. Business in an Integrated Europe," *Business Economics*, July 1995, pp. 39–43.

18. William H. Lash III, *U.S. International Trade Regulation* (Washington, DC: American Enterprise Institute, 1998), pp. 66–67.

19. The calculation of "fair" price must include an 8 percent profit, compared to the average of 5 percent prevailing in U.S. manufacturing and trade industries in recent years.

20. Cited in David R. Oliver, Jr., "Current Export Policies," *Defense Horizons*, December 2001, p. 2.

21. Craig S. Smith, "China Finds Way to Beat Chip Limits," *New York Times*, May 6, 2002, p. C4.

22. James Hines, *Forbidden Payment: Foreign Bribery and American Business After 1977* (Cambridge, MA: National Bureau of Economic Research, 1996).

23. *Foreign Investment: Implementation of Exon–Florio and Related Amendments* (Washington, DC: U.S. General Accounting Office, 1995), pp. 3–4.

13

GLOBAL GEOPOLITICS
OF ENERGY

$$\text{——}\ \text{◌◌◌}\ \text{——}$$

Energy policy is an amalgam of economic, political, military, and foreign policy concerns. The resulting impacts on business are pervasive and are best considered in a global context.[1] Energy has become a strategic factor in global geopolitics. It is a key to national power as well as a major requirement for economic growth and business prosperity. According to some energy experts, energy wealth and poverty have joined industrialization as a defining factor in a nation's position in the world.

THE ROLE OF ENERGY AND ENERGY MARKETS

A modern economy is characterized by a pattern of large per-capita energy consumption. The demand for energy does not only result from the possession of wealth; the use of energy is an important ingredient in promoting and generating wealth. Thus, relatively low oil prices and abundant energy have been key factors in the establishment of the United States as the world's prime geopolitical power. The average American consumes approximately 70 percent more energy than do people in other developed nations. Because taxes on energy are much lower in the United States, however, the price of energy typically is lower than in Western Europe or Japan. Nevertheless, within the U.S. economy, energy intensity (energy usage per dollar of real GDP) has declined substantially in recent years, by about 40 percent between 1977 and 2000.

The underlying world energy situation is neither benign nor inherently stable. In geographic terms, there is a fundamental mismatch between the location of energy supplies (especially in terms of the areas where oil and natural gas are produced) and the location of energy demand, in terms of where major consumers reside. (Tables 13.1 and 13.2 show that, except for Russia, no nation is both a major oil exporter and a major oil user.) The gap is especially apparent in the case of Japan—which imports most of the energy it uses—and the Arabian peninsula, which exports most of the energy it produces.

In peacetime, especially when governments follow a policy of minimizing public-sector involvement in the economy, the marketplace tends to equilibrate variations in world energy supply and demand, regardless of the uneven geographical distribution. Changes in energy prices fundamentally determine the allocation of available energy supply among the various users. These price changes signal the need for marketplace adjustments in both production and consumption (see box, "Economics of Energy").

A substantial rise in the cost of producing energy from conventional sources creates an opportunity to develop new energy sources and simultaneously emphasizes the need to enhance the efficiency of production from existing sources (e.g., secondary and tertiary recovery of oil). Increases in energy prices also make more attractive the use of less energy-intensive forms of production and consumption. Examples include building structures with fewer glass windows, making use of more subdued outdoor lighting, and wearing sweaters and jackets rather than using more heat in homes and office buildings.

TABLE 13.1   Major Oil Exporting Nations (Millions of Barrels a Day)

Country	1990	2000	Percent Change
Saudi Arabia	6.1	7.8	+28%
Russia	3.2	4.0	+25%
Iran	2.2	2.6	+18%
United Arab Emirates	2.2	2.2	—
Venezuela	2.0	2.7	+35%
Iraq	1.7	2.6	+53%
Norway	1.5	3.2	+113%
Libya	1.3	1.5	+15%
Mexico	1.3	1.7	+31%
Nigeria	1.2	2.0	+67%
Kuwait	1.2	2.0	+67%
Algeria	1.0	1.4	+40%

Source: U.S. Central Intelligence Agency, *Handbook of Economic Statistics; BP Statistical Review of World Energy 2001.*

Similarly, changes in desired energy characteristics affect the mix of fuels used to produce energy. Thus, the growing concern with environmental impacts is making natural gas a more attractive alternative to coal and oil.[2] (See Figure 13.1, forecasting the shift in fuel mix over a 20-year period.)

In the economist's famous "long run," the availability of energy appears to be assured, especially so long as lower-grade production resources exist and labor and capital substitutions for energy consumption can take place. For example, Robert L. Bradley, Jr., of the Institute for Energy Research, estimated in 1998 that "proven" reserves of oil would last 45 years at then current rates of consumption, that natural gas would cover 43 years of current consumption, and that coal would extend to 230 years. He noted that "probable" resources of oil, gas, and coal would last 114,200, and 1,884 years, respectively, at present rates of usage.[3]

TABLE 13.2   Major Oil Consuming Nations (Millions of Barrels a Day)

Country	1990	2000	Percent Change
United States	16.9	18.7	+11%
Japan	5.3	5.5	+4%
Russia	5.0	2.5	−50%
Germany	2.4	2.8	+17%
China	2.3	4.8	+109%
France	1.8	2.0	+11%
United Kingdom	1.8	1.7	−6%
Canada	1.7	1.8	+4%
India	1.2	2.1	+75%
South Korea	1.0	2.2	+120%

Source: U.S. Central Intelligence Agency, *Handbook of Economic Statistics; BP Statistical Review of World Energy 2001.*

BOX 13-1

ECONOMICS OF ENERGY

The basic economics of energy are straightforward. People will tend to use more energy when it is cheaper and less when it is expensive. Conversely, those who produce energy will generally have greater incentive to produce more at higher prices than they will at lower prices. Changing prices thus provide useful signals to both producers and consumers of energy. The reaction to all these signals may vary in speed and extent, but so long as they exist at all, they provide a basis for automatic market adjustment and permit individual consumers and producers some freedom of choice in the process.

On occasion, this adjustment process may not be as rapid as we would like. On the demand side, consumers may own heavy, gas-guzzling automobiles and live in houses with little insulation and large glass windows. Thus, the demand for energy may be relatively inelastic to price changes in the short run. Over the longer run, however, when equipment and energy-consuming habits can be modified more substantially, demand is more responsive to price.

On the supply side, the reactions to price movements are also relatively slow at first. Long lead times are needed in developing new energy sources that become commercially attractive even at higher prices. But those adjustments do occur and work to equilibrate the demand for and supply of energy. Certainly historical evidence shows that price increases provide incentives for the development of energy supply. For example, the number of wells drilled in the United States tends to decline when real prices of crude oil are down and drilling activity tends to expand when the real price level rises.

These specific numbers, albeit precise, are really only rough indicators. Cumulative production of these three fuels has perennially exceeded earlier estimates of reserves. The multinational energy company BP estimates that proven world oil reserves have risen from 660 billion barrels at the end of 1980 to 1,034 billion barrels at the beginning of the year 2000—despite the substantial consumption of oil in those two decades.[4]

FIGURE 13.1   Predicted Changes in World Consumption of Energy, 2000–2020

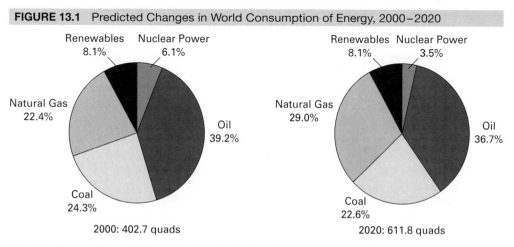

2000: 402.7 quads   2020: 611.8 quads

Note: Quad = quadrillion (1015) British thermal units (Btus)

Source: Reprinted with permission. Sam Nunn et al., *The Geopolitics of Energy into the 21st Century,* vol. 1, *An Overview and Policy Considerations* (Washington, DC: CSIS, 2000).

BOX 13-2

HISTORY OF ENERGY SHIFTS

It is useful to draw upon earlier experiences in American history, when this nation faced substantial shifts in energy production and consumption. Those adjustments proceeded quite satisfactorily in the past. Successive shifts occurred from one energy source to another, as the underlying economics—relative prices—changed.

The first major American switch from exhaustible resource to synthetic fuels and back to exhaustible resources occurred in the nineteenth century. In 1800, illumination in America was provided mainly by candles and oil lamps, with whale oil providing the fuel for the lamps. Whales did not become extinct as the demand for lighting expanded as the population grew. Rather, as the price of whale oil rose from 23 cents a gallon in 1832 to $1.45 in 1865, consumers switched to substitutes such as coal gas, camphene distilled from vegetable oils, and lard oil. In the 1850s, coal oil or kerosene derived from coal distillation dominated the residential market for illumination. In turn, its success was followed by an equally meteoric decline in favor of a new fuel that had appeared in the market, petroleum, which had been discovered in 1859. As crude oil production swelled, its price fell, from a range of $18 to $20 a barrel in early 1860 to 10 cents a barrel in late 1861. By 1863, virtually all coal refiners had switched to crude oil refining, and many new refineries appeared.[5]

Thus, the shifts from whale oil to kerosene to gasoline resulted not from an act of Congress or a subsidy from the Treasury but from successive movements in the price of energy and in the availability of alternative sources of supply.

Global oil reserves in 2000 were more than 15 times greater than when record keeping began in 1948. Similarly, gas reserves were almost four times greater in 2000 than three decades earlier, while estimated coal reserves had risen 75 percent in the previous two decades. Estimates of reserves are invariably sensitive to advances in technology and to changes in the level of prices in the marketplace.

Although they come with a variety of costs, the necessary market adjustments will usually work effectively—so long as governments do not act to prevent those changes. However, time is an important factor in this process. Patterns of energy usage tend to adjust most effectively in the relatively long periods of time required for the orderly replacement of capital equipment, such as the construction of a new generation of factories and homes—which use more or less energy, depending on fundamental changes in energy availability and real prices (see box, "History of Energy Shifts").

In contrast, the adjustments to rapid changes in energy supply are much more painful in the short run. Unexpected price shocks caused by wars, boycotts, disruption of energy production, and other sharp curtailments in energy supply are far more difficult to deal with. Moreover, the centrality of energy to national power—economic, political, and military—increases the effectiveness of threats to interfere with the orderly process of producing, distributing, and using energy in its various forms.

This is so especially because the major industrialized nations import energy from rather unstable regions of the globe and that dependence is estimated to increase in the years ahead. A few examples from recent history underscore the strategic power accompanying the ability to disrupt the normal energy flows in the global economy. The repercussions of the OPEC oil embargo in the 1970s and of the Iran–Iraq war of the 1980s were immense in terms of increasing inflation, reducing industrial production, and causing substantial downturns in the output and employment of leading world economies.

The Gulf War in the early 1990s illustrated the many geopolitical dimensions of the energy supply–demand relationship. Iraq invaded Kuwait presumably to obtain the wealth and power accompanying that nation's abundant oil supply. The United States and its allies responded with great force because of the ramifications that would flow from such an addition of large oil reserves to Iraq's own substantial supply—and the possibility of Iraq subsequently acquiring by force Saudi Arabia's even more abundant energy resources.

Such a series of developments would have altered fundamentally the balance of political and economic power in the region, if not in the globe generally. Iraq might have become the master of the Persian Gulf, virtually determining the amount and the distribution of the oil produced there. In 2000, over one-third of the oil imported by Western Europe came from the Middle East, as did four-fifths of the oil exported to Japan.

In a less dramatic but perhaps more strategic way, low world oil prices in the 1980s were an important influence in the demise of the Soviet Union. Oil had been a vital source of foreign exchange for that financially pressed nation. The decline in the price of its key export made it financially and economically more difficult to cope with the internal stresses facing the regime.[6]

GLOBAL ENERGY TRENDS

A variety of expert analyses and projections point in the same direction over the long term—rising U.S. dependence on foreign oil and natural gas occurring simultaneously with the increased likelihood of recurring worldwide energy supply problems. Although the trade in natural gas is limited by pipeline availability, the United States is the largest importer of gas as well as of oil. A future cutoff of natural gas supply could rival the historic disruptions in oil supply in terms of severity of economic impacts (see Table 13.3 for the geographic distribution of natural gas reserves).

In terms of fundamental movements, the future energy supply–demand balance will be driven by factors already present in the world economy. The most direct are the energy requirements resulting from continued growth in global population and in living standards as more of the population of developing countries clamors for more and more energy. In many nations, developed as well as developing, any prospective imbalances are likely to be exacerbated by the heightened concerns over environmental considerations that often restrict the availability of energy supplies.

In the United States, environmental and related social concerns have led to abandoning new nuclear power generation facilities, declaring many parts of the country off-limits to prospecting for new energy sources (especially in Alaska and key coastal areas), and pressuring to reduce the role of coal and other fossil fuels in response to the growing concerns about global climate change.

A panel of energy experts assembled by the Center for Strategic and International Studies (CSIS) reported in 2001 the results of three years of research and deliberation:

TABLE 13.3   Natural Gas Proven Reserves, Year End 2000 (Trillion Cubic Feet)

Country	Amount	Percent of Total
Russia	1,700	32.1
Iran	812	15.3
Qatar	394	7.4
Saudi Arabia	214	4.0
United Arab Emirates	212	4.0
United States	167	3.2
Algeria	160	3.0
Venezuela	147	2.8
Nigeria	124	2.3
Iraq	110	2.1
Turkmenistan	101	1.9
Malaysia	82	1.5
All others	1,081	20.4
Total	5,304	100.0

Source: BP Statistical Review of World Energy, June 2001.

Global energy demand will grow by 50 percent over the following two decades, with continued reliance on Persian Gulf producers and an increased risk of supply disruptions.[7]

The CSIS report noted that developing countries (such as China, India, Brazil, and Mexico) will increasingly compete with the United States and other industrial nations for the available supply of energy. In the aggregate, developing nations will come to consume more energy than the more developed societies. The recent shift in China's energy position is already dramatic. As recently as 1989, that nation's oil production exceeded its consumption by 500,000 barrels a day. By 2000, the surplus had shifted to a deficit of 1.3 million barrels daily. Because China's per-capita energy consumption is still less than one-half of the world's average, it is reasonable to assume that its continued industrialization will reduce that gap and thus exert further pressure on global energy supplies.[8]

Simultaneously, as noted in Chapter 9, threats of terrorist attacks on oil and gas pipelines are likely to continue. To add to future uncertainty, Iran and Iraq—two nations that have been involved in a variety of military hostilities and diplomatic incidents—are expected to play an increasingly important role in meeting global energy needs. Approximately 50 percent of all proven natural gas reserves is located in Russia, Iran, and Iraq. By 2020, more than half of all the petroleum demand in the world is expected to be met from countries that pose a high risk of internal instability.

A related development is the tendency for the Middle East nations, especially those that were America's allies during the Gulf War, to find themselves at odds with the strategic considerations of the United States. They have become less inclined to lower oil prices in exchange for market security. Also, investments may not be occurring in the energy industries of that region at a rate sufficient to increase future production capacity in line with global needs—which have been expanding at about 2 percent a year over the past decade. Looking to the future when natural gas increasingly becomes the fuel of choice, it is not difficult to contemplate a crisis occurring in one or more of the key energy-producing countries.

A study by an independent task force sponsored by the Council on Foreign Relations (CFR) and the Baker Institute for Public Policy at Rice University came up with findings generally consistent with the CSIS report. The panel concluded that the world is now precariously close to using all of its available oil production capacity. If a major accident or other serious disruption in production occurred—whether in the Alaskan oil pipeline or in the Middle East—the world might experience a serious international oil crisis. Altogether, these are not comforting thoughts for the stability of future global energy supplies.

If economic growth merely continues at recent rates, sporadic price spikes and periodic supply shortages could become recurring events. The CFR–Baker Institute task force concluded that there are no quick solutions to the energy supply and infrastructure bottlenecks facing the United States specifically, and the global marketplace generally. According to the task force, the world appears to have entered a new energy era in which the primary focus is on marshaling capital to develop adequate resources and infrastructure—and to do so subject to a variety of policy restraints, especially environmental.[9]

Those restraints are especially visible in the case of coal, a very abundant and relatively inexpensive—but highly polluting—energy resource. Despite an average economic growth rate of about 8 percent a year and substantial domestic resources of coal, China has been able to reduce its coal consumption by 30 percent from 1996 to 2000. In contrast, use of coal in the United States and in India has continued to increase, albeit at rates much below the pace of economic growth.[10]

SECURING ENERGY SECURITY

As a general proposition, a nation's energy security should be viewed in dynamic terms. Focusing exclusively on the current mix of energy sources or on today's energy balance of trade (either net exports or net imports) is misleading and ignores underlying issues of potential concern. Energy security is truly achieved through actions that enhance an economy's ability to respond to supply shocks and the volatile price changes associated with such shocks. Numerous actions can reduce a nation's vulnerability to aggressive energy geopolitical pressures. Examples include the following:

1. Expansion of emergency stockpiles such as a strategic petroleum reserve.
2. Reliance on a greater variety of standard as well as nonconventional energy sources in order to reduce vulnerability to supply disruptions in any individual region or production category.
3. Developing the flexibility to switch quickly to alternative fuels.
4. Maintaining an effective economic stabilization mechanism, comprising rapid adjustments in monetary and fiscal policies that can help to cope with large and disruptive shifts in energy prices.[11]

Identifying sensible policy options is far easier than translating them into proposals that generate public support. Useful insights into restraints facing energy policy makers were provided in a comprehensive public opinion poll sponsored by the *New York Times* and CBS News in 2001. To the question, "Should increasing the production of petroleum, coal and natural gas be a priority or should conservation?" 68 percent registered in favor of conservation. Only 21 percent favored the production of fossil fuels, while 11 percent expressed no opinion.

The answers to another question indirectly provided some understanding of under-lying public attitudes. When asked, "Should we protect the environment even if it means paying higher prices for electricity and gasoline?" 57 percent gave an affirmative response. Only 36 percent took a negative position; 6 percent had no opinion.[12] Nevertheless, in the same period of time, many consumers and political leaders were vehement in their opposition to rising gasoline prices and, especially on the West Coast, to sharp increases in energy prices generally.

Thus, despite its expressed preference for conservation over production, the American public has demonstrated little support for taking the specific painful actions—such as raising the cost of using energy—that would curtail energy con-sumption. The continued popularity of SUVs and other vehicles that use large amounts of gasoline provides a jarring counterpoint to the stated public preference for conser-vation over production.[13]

The inconsistencies in the various public attitudes and policies that affect energy increase the vulnerability of the United States to future geopolitical pressures from the major energy-supplying nations (see Table 13.4 for details). This is likely to be the case

---

TABLE 13.4   Geopolitical Energy Vulnerabilities

1. The six countries possessing oil reserves in excess of 75 billion barrels are all located in the Persian Gulf. Together, they account for 70 percent of world oil reserves (and 30 percent of proven gas reserves).

2. An average of 14 million barrels of oil moves each day through the Strait of Hormuz, which connects the Persian Gulf with the Gulf of Oman and the Arabian Sea. By 2020, over one-third of oil moving in international trade will likely transit this single choke point.

3. More than 8 million barrels of oil move each day through the Strait of Malaca, connecting the Indian Ocean to the South China Sea and the Pacific Ocean.

4. The Bosporus, the key exit route for Russian and Caspian oil, is only one-half-mile wide at its narrowest point and could be closed by one tanker accident.

5. Disrupting the oil shipped from Saudi Arabia, the top exporting nation, could provoke price increases and production shutdowns substantial enough to trigger a widespread recession. By 2020, one-half of estimated global energy demand will be met from countries that pose a high risk of internal instability.

6. Increasing reliance on natural gas—and thus gas pipelines—will expand the vulnerability of energy infrastructure to various forms of terrorist attack, including cyberterrorism. The construction of new pipelines is also subject to continuous challenge from environmental and local groups.

7. The competing territorial claims of Southeast Asian countries in the South China Sea could become more intense as their continued industrialization requires more energy. These nations also lack strategic energy reserves.

8. Global warming policies designed to reduce emissions of CO_2 will likely focus on reducing the use of coal, the major fuel of the largest developing countries—and the dominant source of electricity in the United States.

9. The lack of reserve capacity in the U.S. oil-refining industry makes gasoline production very sensitive to equipment breakdowns, fires, and other unplanned outages. Dependence on imports will grow because few if any new refineries are likely to be built in the United States due to costly environmental compliance and volatility of revenues.

10. The Balkanization of the U.S. energy market is stretching the U.S. refining and distribution system to its limits. That market now uses more than 50 different types of gasoline to meet regional and local environmental requirements, octane levels, and seasonal fuel needs. Spot shortages in one region can no longer be readily met by shipments from another region.

with reference to the oil- and gas-producing Arab states where energy revenues constitute both a dominant share of national income and their major leverage in international relations.

As the geographic disparities in energy supply and demand are increasingly
matched by political and cultural differences, the outlook is likely to be uncertain, as
well as unstable. The vivid differences in viewpoints and outlook between the energy-
supplying areas and the energy-consuming areas are not immutable but, at least in the
short run, they are expanding. Policies and actions can be taken to reduce the resulting
tension, but that will require greater public understanding and support than has been
the case in recent years.

A MENU OF ENERGY POLICY PROPOSALS

A variety of suggestions has been offered to foster the development of a comprehensive energy policy. The following is a representative sampling:

1. *Rely more heavily on the information approach to conserving energy.* In that spirit,
extend the existing energy labeling program to additional products, appliances, and
services. The National Energy Policy Development Group chaired by Vice President
Richard Cheney recommended setting higher energy standards for products where
technologically feasible and economically justified.[14] A practical problem is that few
such standards meet that double criterion of being both economical and technologically
attractive.

2. *Provide temporary tax subsidies for the purchase of new hybrid fuel cell vehicles.*[15]
A short-term subsidy is likely to provide limited incentive to manufacturers to undertake
expensive long-term development, production, and marketing efforts. Making the
subsidy permanent, on the other hand, would penalize the development of other
approaches to fuel efficiency, which may prove to be more effective.

3. *Spend more government money on improved highway infrastructure to reduce the
amount of gasoline that motorists use.* The federal government could encourage the
private sector to invest in Intelligent Transportation Systems that would reduce road
congestion, such as traveler information and navigation systems, electronic toll
collection, and better management of freeway traffic (including improved signs). This
approach involves significant amounts of additional government spending.

4. *Explore for and extract petroleum from a portion of the Alaska National Wildlife
Reserve (ANWR).* The National Energy Policy Development Group advocates this
approach with the proviso that these energy activities not result in any "significant
adverse impact" to the surrounding environment. However, this position is opposed
strongly by environmental organizations that urge that ANWR should continue to be
off-limits to energy exploration or drilling.

5. *Eliminate or reform Corporate Average Fuel Efficiency (CAFE) standards that
stipulate required minimum motor vehicle mileage in fuel usage* (see Chapter 3). Some
economists contend that mileage standards are inefficient, and advocate other
approaches such as a tax on the use of gasoline or energy. As a practical matter,
Americans have been encouraged to buy large gas-guzzling minivans and SUVs

because of a loophole in federal CAFE regulations—albeit that result was unintended by either the regulators or Congress. The standards on automobiles are tougher than on trucks; in the regulations, minivans and SUVs qualify as light trucks. Thus, CAFE standards unintentionally shift American consumers away from fuel-efficient vehicles defined as automobiles.[16]

6. *Government regulators should adopt "one stop" shopping when it comes to approving energy installations.* Here the United States might learn a lesson from the Japanese experience. It is not easy in that country to get approval for a new power plant (nuclear or conventional) or for a new airport or other major facility. Much time, effort, and analysis go into dealing with all the facets and interest groups involved. But, unlike the approach followed in the United States, once a decision is made, it tends to be final.

In contrast, in this country, at various stages in the planning and construction process, approval must be attained from a variety of regulators with different requirements. Little effort at coordination is in evidence. The resultant approach may remind the reader of a ping pong match: The project proposer is bounced around from agency to agency, often giving up during the tedious and uncertain process.

The most dramatic example of the shortcomings of the existing approach to energy regulation was the experience with the Shoreham nuclear power plant in New York State. After getting all of the required approvals to design and build the facility, construction was completed. However, the entire project was abandoned—and the multibillion-dollar power plant demolished—because, at the very end of the process, New York State refused to issue an emergency evacuation plan (for reasons that seemed to be evident before the project got underway).

7. *Eliminate one of the most serious objections to nuclear power—where to store spent fuel.* Of course, nobody wants a nuclear storage facility in his backyard any more than a smelly factory. In both cases, however, recent advances in technology have made those facilities far safer than in the past. Surely, the lax safety practices of the former Soviet Union would not seem to be relevant to the United States in the twenty-first century. Nevertheless, no community is going to volunteer to accept a major nuclear waste facility because there are no special benefits for doing so.

One reason is to offer a strong economic incentive to the locality that agrees to host the spent fuel: require each power station shipping spent fuel to provide a financial payment to the area where the waste facility is located. That locality thus would receive tangible benefits to offset the intangible costs that it perceives. It is questionable whether the financial incentive would attract sufficient local support.

8. *Promote market forces in the consumption of energy.* One place to start is by eliminating the various government programs that artificially encourage the consumption of energy by subsidizing the companies that produce conventional fuels. The Internal Revenue Code is riddled with special provisions that reduce the cost of producing fossil fuels. The repeal of these archaic provisions is strongly opposed by the industries directly benefiting from them.[17]

Another possibility is to eliminate the "caps" and other regulatory restrictions on rates charged for the use of energy, especially electricity. This change would require a more sympathetic attitude toward increases in the price of energy on the part of environmental and consumer groups who urge energy conservation, yet are reluctant to support using the price system to achieve the desired result.

9. *Promote the construction of natural gas pipelines from the Arctic to the lower 48 states.* Canada is the United States' most secure external source of supply for natural gas, which is increasingly becoming the fuel of choice.[18] Such enhancement of the energy available to U.S. users will require working with the governments of Canada and the state of Alaska to resolve a host of detailed regulatory issues.

10. *Recognize the domestic weaknesses and fragility of some of the major energy exporting nations.* Some experts estimate that, by 2020, one-half of total global energy demand will be met from countries that pose a high risk of internal instability.[19]

Conclusion

Developments elsewhere on the globe have the potential to strongly influence U.S. energy conditions. For example, continuing globalization will increase the demand for importing oil and natural gas over long distances. This will be so especially in the case of the industrializing countries of Asia, such as China, which are poor in indigenous energy resources. In turn, the need to maintain open sea lanes will become even more apparent than is now the case. Thus, future energy concerns are related to U.S. naval capabilities, another example of the interrelationships among geopolitical factors.

The seriousness of the potential impacts of changes in energy availability on our society may encourage governmental leaders to develop foreign policies that improve American relationships with the major energy exporting nations and that enhance their long-term stability.

These relationships may work in two directions. To the extent that U.S. domestic energy policies drift, more power will be lodged in the leaders of the major energy exporting nations. In contrast, reducing dependence on foreign energy—and enhancing the ability to deal with sudden supply shocks—will lead to strengthening the position of the United States in world energy affairs.

Notes

1. This chapter draws heavily from Murray Weidenbaum, "World Energy Geopolitics," in R. E. Oligney, M. J. Economides; and N. Dunn, *Energy—The New Value Chain* (Houston, TX: Round Oak Publishing, 2003).

2. M. J. Economides, R. E. Oligney, A. S. Demarchos, and P. E. Lewis, *Natural Gas: Beyond All Expectations,* a paper presented at the 2001 Society of Petroleum Engineers Annual Technical Conference, New Orleans, LA, September 30, 2001.

3. Robert Bradley, Jr., "Sustainable Energy for the 21st Century: A Market Perspective," *Proceedings of the 17th Congress of the*

World Energy Council, vol. 3 (London: World Energy Council, 1998), p. 609.

4. *BP Statistical Review of World Energy,* June 2001, p. 4.

5. Harold F. Williamson and Arnold R. Daum, *The American Petroleum Industry: The Age of Illumination, 1859–1899* (Chicago: Northwestern University Press, 1959), p. 13.

6. Michael Economides and Ronald Oligney, *The Color of Oil* (Katy, TX: Round Oak Publishing Co., 2000), p. 77.

7. Sam Nunn et al., *The Geopolitics of Energy into the 21st Century,* vol. 1 (Washington,

DC: Center for Strategic and International Studies, 2000), pp. xv–xvi.

8. Joseph P. Quinlan and Andrea L. Prochniack, "China, Oil and Global Supply–Demand Equation," *Morgan Stanley Dean Witter Global Insights,* December 6, 2000, pp. 1–2.

9. *Strategic Energy Policy,* Baker Institute Study No. 15 (Houston, TX: Rice University, 2001), p. 2.

10. Peter Davies, *Testing Time in World Energy Markets* (New York: BP, 2001), p. 8. See also *National Energy Policy,* Report of the National Energy Policy Development Group (Washington, DC: U.S. Government Printing Office, 2001).

11. Michael A. Toman, "International Oil Security," *Brookings Review,* Spring 2002, pp. 20–27.

12. "Public Approval of Bush Policies," *New York Times,* June 21, 2001, p. A16.

13. Paul L. Joskow, "Energy Policy During the 1990s," in Jeffrey A. Frankel and Peter R. Orszag, eds., *American Economic Policy in the 1990s* (Cambridge, MA: M.I.T. Press, 2002), pp. 509–562.

14. *National Energy Policy,* p. 4–11.

15. Ibid., p. 4–11.

16. Paul R. Portney, "New Car Mileage Standards in the United States," *Resources,* Spring 2002, pp. 11–15.

17. Murray Weidenbaum, Christopher Douglass, and Michael Orlando, "How to Achieve a Healthier Environment and a Stronger Economy," *Business Horizons,* January–February 1997, pp. 9–16.

18. M. J. Economides, R. E. Oligney, and A. S. Demarchos, "Natural Gas: The Revolution Is Coming," *Journal of Petroleum Technology,* May 2001, pp. 64–71.

19. Nunn et al., *The Geopolitics of Energy,* p. xvii.

GOVERNMENT PROMOTION OF BUSINESS

"I'm from the government and I'm here to help you," is a staple tongue-in-cheek wisecrack at business meetings. Yet, many government actions—tax incentives, credit programs, and massive procurements—are designed to assist or at least influence some aspect of business operations.

Part IV takes on the task of analyzing the various ways in which government helps—and hinders—business performance.

14

GOVERNMENT CREDITS
AND BAILOUTS
ᴏᴏᴏ

One of the least understood components of the government's arsenal of power over the private sector is its ability to provide credit to various individuals, business firms, and other organizations. Over the years, many programs to extend credit have been established by the federal government, most at terms far more generous than are available in private, competitive markets. Because few of these government credit activities appear in the federal budget, they seem to be a painless way of achieving national objectives. In reality, these credit programs are a form of hidden subsidy and represent a key mechanism whereby government can influence the fortunes of individual companies. At times, substantial direct cost can be incurred by the federal Treasury.

THE NATURE OF CREDIT SUBSIDIES

The federal government subsidizes private economic activity in a great many ways and, as we will see, the typical credit program generates a specific benefit or subsidy to the recipients. The common characteristic of all subsidies—credit programs and other aids—is that they constitute a wedge between the cost to the seller of a product or service and the price paid by the buyer. A subsidy may go to producers or to consumers, or it may be shared. The general intent of a subsidy is to encourage some activity, usually to cause more to be produced or consumed than would result from the unaided operations of the competitive marketplace. A subsidy is not a purchase per se, because the government does not directly acquire the good or service, nor is it a transfer payment, where there is no quid pro quo: The recipient of the subsidy *does* have to engage in a particular undertaking in order to receive it.

Some government subsidies are direct and visible. The public and Congress are readily aware of the magnitude of the federal aid being extended and the identities of the recipients. Examples include farm price supports and shipping industry operating subsidies. In the first case, the U.S. Department of Agriculture pays farmers more than the competitive marketplace. In the second, the DOT offsets a portion of the difference between the high cost of U.S. flag operations and the lower cost of foreign competitors.

Indirect subsidies are more numerous, in part because they are far less visible. For example, at least half of all waterborne shipments by U.S. government agencies must be carried in U.S. flag vessels. Eliminating foreign competition keeps the price up. In the mining industry, restrictions against selling surplus items in the stockpile of strategic materials also keep prices high, benefiting producers at the expense of the users.

In some cases, the creation of winners and losers is quite clear. As noted in Chapter 8, airport landing rights are provided below cost to general aviation (private planes other than scheduled airlines). Airline passengers do not realize that their fares include the cost of higher landing fees to make up the difference. This is an example of cross-subsidization, a process whereby one group is required to pay more for a good or service in order to subsidize its use by others.

Federal credit programs constitute a large part of government subsidies. The benefits to the recipients are usually in the form of lower interest rates than would normally be paid, longer maturities, and less collateral. Thus, the borrower is receiving a benefit from the involvement of the government in the credit market. By the nature of the operation, credit subsidies are indirect or hidden, which adds to their political attractiveness.

Mainly, the federal government merely guarantees private borrowing or sponsors ostensibly private lending institutions, albeit with federal ties. Examples range from the Export-Import Bank to the Small Business Administration to the Federal National Mortgage Association (Fannie Mae).

Is the use of the federal government's credit power a variation of the proverbial free lunch? Many of the recipients benefit from such hidden subsidies as lower interest rates and, at least initially, no federal money seems to be required. But, as will be demonstrated, upon closer inspection we find that the government's extension of credit results in substantial costs to the private sector—to business and consumers—as well as to taxpayers. Furthermore, it generates opportunities for the application of federal controls over private economic activity, credit serving as the sweetener for the acceptance by the recipient of the added regulation. Simultaneously, substantial social benefits accrue from these programs in terms of achieving various national priorities. More housing can be built and more farms and businesses can continue operating that otherwise would go bankrupt or at least would have to reduce their scope of operations. In authorizing credit programs, the legislature rarely considers the costs of attaining these benefits.

The advantages of using the government's credit power arise from its effectiveness in channeling more funds—and ultimately additional real resources—to specific groups in society. In each case, Congress has passed a law stating, in effect, that it believes the national welfare requires that the designated groups receive larger shares of the available supply of credit than would result from the operation of market forces alone.

What are not apparent are the costs and other adverse side effects that result from this expanded use of government credit. If the borrower defaults, the government is left holding the bag. In terms of their overall economic impact, these lending programs do nothing to increase the total pool of capital available to the economy. They result in a game of musical chairs. That is, by preempting a major portion of the annual flow of saving, the government-sponsored credit agencies reduce the amount of credit available to unprotected borrowers; who are mainly consumers, state and local governments, and new and small business firms.[1]

During periods of general credit stringency ("tight money"), it is difficult for some unassisted borrowers to attract the financing they require. They are forced to compete against the government-aided borrowers. It is an uneven contest. Federal loan guarantees reduce the riskiness of lending money to the insured borrowers. The result of that unequal competition is still higher interest rates, especially for unsubsidized borrowers.

Over the years, substantial numbers of credit programs have been created through the legislative process of the federal government. These programs emerged on an ad hoc basis, with each directed toward providing assistance in overcoming a specific problem at hand. As a result of this gradual but substantial accretion, federal credit subsidies are now provided to many sectors of the American economy—housing, agriculture, financial institutions, energy, transportation, health, education, state and local government, small business—and foreigners. Congress has authorized more than 200 separate direct loan programs. In addition, approximately 150 different types of loans can be made by private lending institutions, with interest costs and repayment of the principal guaranteed by a federal department or agency.

Table 14.1 shows the relative importance of the major uses of the federal government's credit power. In fiscal year 2002, the federal government held outstanding direct loans of $193 billion, had guaranteed outstanding private loans of $1,750 billion, and sponsored "quasi-government" enterprises that had extended another $3,798 billion in credit to private borrowers. The great majority of the credit benefits the housing sector of the economy.

TABLE 14.1   Major Federal Credit Programs, Fiscal Year 2002 (Outstanding Amounts, Billions of Dollars)

Agency	Direct Loans	Guaranteed Loans	Government-Sponsored Enterprises	Total
Agency for International Development	$ 9	$ 11	$ —	$ 20
Agriculture	62	22	—	84
Defense	3	4	—	7
Education	86	169	—	255
Health and Human Services	—	2	—	2
Housing and Urban Development	10	1,213	—	1,223
Veteran Affairs	2	245	—	247
Export-Import Bank	13	31	—	44
Farm Credit System	—	—	81	81
Federal Home Loan Banks	—	—	489	489
Federal Home Loan Mortgage Corporation	—	—	1,217	1,217
Fannie Mae			1,783	1,783
Freddie Mac	—	—	187	187
Overseas Private Investment Corporation	—	4	—	4
Small Business Administration	4	39	—	43
Sallie Mae	—	—	41	41
Transportation	2	5	—	7
Treasury	1	4	—	5
All other	1	1	—	2
Total	$193	$1,750	$3,798	$5,741

Source: Budget of the United States Government, Fiscal Year 2003.

TYPES OF GOVERNMENT CREDIT PROGRAMS

DIRECT LOANS BY FEDERAL DEPARTMENTS AND AGENCIES

Direct loans, such as the credit supplied by the Department of Agriculture, involve significant subsidies, because the funds usually are loaned at rates much below those available in the private sector. Also, the maturities are longer and the collateral requirements are lower. In many cases, the federal government also absorbs the administrative expenses and losses arising from loan defaults, further increasing the amount of the subsidy. In recent years, direct loans have become a less important form of federal credit aid, in part because they require unequivocal use of federal money in contrast to other forms of federal credit assistance.

Although not formally considered a federal credit program, the generous progress payments made by the Department of Defense (usually 80 percent of costs incurred) represent interest-free provision of working capital to government contractors on a very large scale. Moreover, the terms are much more generous than usually extended on their commercial business.[2]

LOANS GUARANTEED BY FEDERAL DEPARTMENTS AND AGENCIES

Loan guarantees account for a major share of the current array of federal credit subsidies, far exceeding the volume of direct loans by federal agencies. The primary attraction of loan guarantees to federal policy makers is that the loans are made by private lenders and thus are excluded from the federal budget. Technically, all the government does is assume a contingent liability to pay the private lender if the private borrower defaults. However, when there is little collateral in connection with the guarantee, the government may be assuming high risks. This was the case when the Treasury guaranteed a portion of New York City's debt. If New York City had defaulted, how could the federal government have taken over its "collateral"? Could it have sold Central Park? Given the public outrage that would have precipitated, it is hard to think of a private individual or organization willing to bid on that property.

Loan guarantees, depending on the specific terms, transfer some of the risk of default from the lender to the government. The limiting case would be where the government guarantees the timely payment of 100 percent of the loan principal and interest. Such action would come close to transforming a private loan into a government security. However, the private debt does not have all of the attributes of a government issue. For example, it is likely to be less liquid and not as readily transferable to other investors. Thus, guaranteed loans bear interest rates above the yields on otherwise comparable Treasury securities.

LOANS BY GOVERNMENT-SPONSORED ENTERPRISES (GSES)

Credit extended by enterprises sponsored by the federal government includes a variety of off-budget entities whose outlays are not included in the reported budget totals. These privately owned agencies operate under federal charters that grant them special privileges of great value. They have various tax advantages and are able to borrow funds in financial markets at relatively low interest rates because of the implicit government backing of their debentures and their potential to borrow directly from the Treasury when necessary.

One expert contends that these enterprises function in a *terra incognita,* somewhere between the public and private sectors.[3] Another analyst describes the GSEs as "hybrid" institutions that combine characteristics of public and private organizations.[4]

As a result of the perception of implicit government backing, GSEs operate with higher financial leverage and less capital than other firms in similar lines of business. Thus, these special enterprises have a significant competitive advantage in the marketplace. Loans made by these sponsored agencies have increased sharply over the years. They now comprise the dominant form of federal credit assistance to the private sector. Federally sponsored, privately owned credit enterprises comprise four major groups:

1. The Federal National Mortgage Association (Fannie Mae) and the Federal Home Loan Mortgage Corporation (Freddie Mac) promote access to mortgage credit by purchasing and/or guaranteeing residential mortgages. Fannie Mae and Freddie Mac have become the two largest financial institutions in the United States.
2. The Student Loan Marketing Association (Sallie Mae) purchases guaranteed student loans to create a secondary market. (Sallie Mae is being privatized and is scheduled to be liquidated in 2008.)
3. The Farm Credit System consists of several hundred financial intermediaries providing credit for farmers, ranchers, agricultural firms, and agricultural cooperatives. The Farm Credit System also includes the Federal Agricultural Mortgage Corporation (Farmer Mac), which maintains a secondary market for farm loans, comparable to the role of Fannie Mae and Freddie Mac in the housing area.
4. The Federal Home Loan Banks provide secured loans to financial institutions specializing in residential mortgage lending.

Congress established Sallie Mae to provide funds to college students, the Farm Credit System to aid agriculture, and the other two groups to broaden the flow of credit to the housing market. Although the securities that the government-sponsored enterprises issue are not guaranteed by the federal government, they are afforded many privileges not available to other financial institutions:

- They are exempted from having to register debt issues with the Securities and Exchange Commission.
- Their interest income is exempted from state and local taxes (except for Fannie Mae).
- Their debt issues may be used as collateral when commercial banks borrow from the Federal Reserve.
- The Federal Reserve can buy their bonds in its open-market transactions.
- Their bonds can be used by banks as collateral for public deposits.
- National banks may invest and deal in their securities without limit.

As a result of these benefits, the federally sponsored credit agencies issue their securities at lower yields than the highest-rated corporate bonds of similar maturities (but at higher interest rates than Treasury issues).

During the 1980s, the farm credit banks and the home loan banks encountered substantial financial difficulties due to the widespread distress among farmers and savings and loan associations. In both cases, Congress enacted large programs of direct financial assistance from the U.S. Treasury. Thus, although the legal connection between these enterprises and the federal government may be technically remote, in practice the relationship can be quite close (see Table 14.2).

TABLE 14.2 Government Ties of Federally Sponsored Credit Agencies

Agency	Stockholders	Influence of Executive Branch	Line of Credit with Treasury	Federal Tax on Income*	State and Local Tax on Interest Income of Investors
Federal Home Loan Banks	Member thrifts	These banks are regulated by the Federal Housing Finance Board	$4.0 billion	No	No
Federal National Mortgage Association	Owned by private stockholders	President selects 5 of 18 board members; subject to general supervision by HUD	$2.25 billion	Yes	No
Farm Credit Banks	Owned by farm cooperatives and credit associations	President selects 12 board members	$257 million	No	No
Student Loan Marketing Association	Lenders under the Guaranteed Student Loan Program (individual investors hold nonvoting stock)	President selects 7 of 21 board members including the chairman	$1.0 billion	Yes	Yes

*Interest on all debt of the sponsored agencies is subject to federal taxation.

In the case of the farm credit banks, Congress established three specialized government-sponsored enterprises in 1988 to shore up the federal farm credit system. It created the Farm Credit System Financial Assistance Corporation to help the federal farm banks raise needed capital. Unlike those of the farm banks, the bonds issued by the new corporation are guaranteed by the federal government. The Federal Agriculture Mortgage Corporation (Farmer Mac) provides a secondary market for farm mortgages and rural housing loans. Its initial capital comes from sales of its stock to banks, insurance companies, and other financial institutions. The Mortgage Corporation can borrow up to $1.5 billion from the Treasury. Finally, the Farm Credit System Insurance Corporation insures the bonds issued by the federal farm banks. This insurance corporation is financed by fees collected from the member banks who benefit from the insurance.

As part of the massive bailout of savings and loan institutions (described later), Congress set up the Office of Thrift Supervision in the Department of the Treasury to replace the Federal Home Loan Bank Board as the regulator of the thrift industry. The Federal Home Loan Banks are now regulated by the Federal Housing Finance Board.

IMPACTS ON TOTAL SAVING AND INVESTMENT

The impacts of federal credit programs on the flow of saving and investment in the economy are clear. These programs do nothing to increase that total flow. They mainly change the share of investment funds going to a given industry or sector of the economy.

THE INITIAL IMPACTS

Because these governmental borrowers have few worries about creditworthiness or meeting interest payments, they can preempt large portions of the nation's credit markets. As a result, federal credit programs have become a source of upward pressure on interest rates. (Overall levels of interest rates may not necessarily rise because of offsetting action by the Federal Reserve System.)

This phenomenon requires some explanation. The total supply of credit is broadly determined by household and business saving and the ability of banks to increase the money supply. In an open economy, the available credit also includes funds supplied by overseas investors. The normal response of financial markets to an increase in the demand for funds by a major borrower, such as a federal credit program, is upward pressure on interest rates. The resultant rise in rates helps to balance out the demand for funds with the supply of savings by discouraging some from borrowing while encouraging others to save more.

But the federal government's demand for funds is *interest inelastic.* That is, the Treasury will raise the money it requires regardless of the interest rate it has to pay. Also, the interest elasticity of saving is relatively modest; higher interest rates will not attract a great amount of additional saving. Thus, the rise in federally subsidized borrowing is not likely to be offset fully by added saving. Weak and marginal borrowers will be "rationed" out of financial markets in the process, while the Treasury as well as other borrowers pay higher rates of interest than they otherwise would.

Since federal credit activities primarily involve guarantees and implied guarantees by sponsored credit enterprises, the direct outlays included in the budget are modest. The federal government appears to be able to deliver something for nothing, or almost nothing. But as with all such sleight-of-hand feats, the truth is different. Even when these programs seem to be working well, there are extra costs associated with the operations of government credit agencies in capital markets. These costs include selling issues that are smaller than the minimally efficient size and selling securities that only in varying degrees approximate the characteristics of direct Treasury debt in terms of perfection of guarantee, flexibility of timing and maturities, and "cleanness" of instrument. As a result of such considerations, the market charges a premium over the interest cost on direct government debt of comparable maturity. That premium has ranged from one-quarter of 1 percent on the financially strong Fannie Mae to more than 1 percent on the federal farm credit banks when they were viewed by investors as "troubled."

Reduced efficiency occurs in the economy when a federal "umbrella" is provided over many credit activities without distinguishing among their differing credit risks. A basic function that financial institutions are supposed to perform is assigning appropriate risk premiums to borrowers of different financial strengths. This is the essence of the resource-allocation function of credit markets. As a very large proportion of all issues coming to the credit markets bears the guarantee of the federal government, the scope for the market to differentiate credit risks inevitably diminishes. Theoretically, the federal agencies issuing or guaranteeing debt could perform this role by charging programs varying insurance premiums for the federal guarantee. In practice, these agencies avoid the hard decisions involved in differential pricing of risks.

MORE BASIC IMPACTS

The degree to which federal credit programs, such as loan guarantees, affect the reallocation of resources depends in good measure on the degree of subsidy. At one extreme, the transaction being financed may be considered so risky that no financing would be available without federal participation. In this case, the subsidy will be large and will have a dramatic effect on the allocation of credit.

At the other extreme, the federal credit program may result in only a small subsidy and may not change the allocation of credit to any significant degree. Some beneficiaries of loan guarantees for new home mortgages, for example, would have been able to obtain funds without government support, albeit at a moderately higher interest rate or servicing cost. Table 14.3 shows the subsidy component of a variety of federal credit programs.[5] This information demonstrates the very large subsidies provided in some federal programs (such as one-half of the face value of the loan in the case of rural development) and the much smaller subsidies in other credit activities (such as 11 percent for Export-Import Bank loans and 2 percent for veterans housing loans).[6]

Federal credit programs contain other forms of subsidies, such as deferral of interest, allowance of grace periods, and waiver or reduction of loan fees. Also, default clauses in government loans often offer the borrower greater protection from foreclosure actions by the government than would similar clauses in loans available from private lenders.

TABLE 14.3   Subsidy Portion of Selected Federal
                          Lending Programs

Program	Subsidy As Percent of Loan Disbursement
State Department repatriation loans	80%
Emergency boll weevil loans	60
Farm labor loans	53
Rural development loans	51
Community development financial institutions fund	42
Military family housing improvement fund	38
Bureau of Reclamation loans	33
Small business disaster loans	17
Export-Import Bank loans	11
Small business regular loans	9
Overseas Private Investment Corporation	7
Veterans housing benefit program	2
Rural telephone bank	1

Source: Budget of the United States Government, Fiscal Year 2003.

IMPACTS ON SECTORS OF THE ECONOMY

The very nature of federal credit assistance is to create advantages for some groups of borrowers and thus disadvantages for others. The proponents of credit assistance in Congress as well as in the private sector rarely ask who will tend to be rationed out in the process. It is unlikely to be the large, well-known corporations or the U.S. government. On the basis of past experience, it is more often state and local governments, small and medium-size businesses, home buyers not protected by the federal umbrella, consumers—and marginal borrowers generally.

The competition for funds by federal credit programs also increases the cost to taxpayers by raising the interest rates at which the Treasury borrows its own funds. The size and relative importance of federal government credit demands have been expanding. In the 1960s, the federal portion of funds raised in private capital markets (including Treasury borrowing and guaranteed and sponsored enterprise debt) averaged 17 percent. By the 1990s, the government's share had risen to an average of 60 percent, an all-time high. This trend was described by one analyst as the largest and quietest takeover of the U.S. credit market in the country's financial history.[7]

RELATION TO GOVERNMENT CONTROLS

Federal credit assistance is often accompanied by government controls or influence over the recipients of the credit. For example, federal guarantees for shipbuilders are part of a broader program whereby the federal government requires the builders to incorporate "national defense" features into the vessels.

The largest federal program for guaranteeing private credit, that administered by the Federal Housing Administration (FHA), contains numerous controls that accompany the credit assistance. The FHA conducts an inspection of each residence to determine whether the builder has abided by all of the agency's rules and regulations governing the construction of the homes that it insures. There are four separate "veto" points facing a builder applying for FHA insurance of mortgages for a new project: (1) affirmative marketing to minority groups, (2) environmental impact, (3) architectural review, and (4) underwriting.

Because responsibilities are divided among the various federal housing offices, considerable delay can arise. For example, after the underwriting has been approved, and assuming it yields an appraised value high enough to cover the builder's costs, additional requirements may be imposed by the environmental impact or architectural review offices. These actions can raise the cost of the project significantly. If this occurs, the builder must return to the first office and attempt to obtain a revised underwriting. In these cases, a portion of the implicit credit subsidy being extended by the FHA is, in effect, being absorbed by the federal government's own social objectives.

SUMMARY OF ECONOMIC EFFECTS

Contrary to popular opinion, government credit programs are not costless, either to the Treasury or to citizens in general. Three distinct costs can be identified:

1. *The economic cost.* Since they do little to increase the total supply of investment funds in the economy, government credit programs take credit away from potential private borrowers. These unsubsidized borrowers might have produced more for society than the recipients of government-supported credit.
2. *The initial fiscal cost.* To the extent that government credit programs increase the total size of government-related credit, they cause an increase in the interest rates that are paid in order to channel these funds away from the private sector. Some increase, therefore, results in the interest rates paid on the public debt, which is a direct cost to the taxpayer.
3. *The ultimate fiscal cost.* When defaults occur on the part of the borrowers whose credit is guaranteed by the federal government, the Treasury winds up bearing the ultimate cost of the credit. In 2001, the federal government wrote off $6.1 billion of defaulted direct loans and $1.1 billion of loans that it received as the result of the default of guaranteed loans. At the end of fiscal year 2002, the federal government held $32 billion of defaulted loans that it acquired over the years because it had guaranteed the credit of the private borrowers.

Boiled down to the essence, federal guarantees of bonds issued by business and other institutions do not create new investment funds for the economy. Rather, they move capital to the designated sectors of the economy by taking those funds away from other sectors, and often they lead to similar requests for aid by those unsubsidized sectors. Government guarantees also tend to raise the level of interest rates in the economy, both for private as well as for government borrowers. They thus increase an important element of business costs.

The rise in interest rates leads to pressure on the Federal Reserve System to increase the reserves on the banking system in order to supply adequate financing to the private sector. If the Federal Reserve accommodates these pressures, this action may contribute to the general inflationary condition of the economy. Federal credit programs therefore raise the private cost of production in two ways: (1) by causing an increase in interest rates and/or (2) by resulting in a higher general rate of inflation than would otherwise be the case.

Congress has taken some important—but only partial—steps in an effort to control the expansion of federal credit programs. Since the enactment of the Federal Credit Reform Act of 1990, it must appropriate annually the subsidy component of the new federal loans and loan guarantees to be provided during the fiscal year. It also sets annual ceilings on key loan guarantee programs. By incorporating federal loans and loan guarantees directly into the federal budget, the new law has made governmental decision makers more aware of the cost of this use of the federal credit power. As part of a determined effort to reduce federal budget deficits, the total volume of direct loans has stabilized since 1990. However, as shown in Figure 14.1, a sharply upward trend is still visible in total federal loan guarantees ($374 of new loan guarantees extended in 2002 compared with $43 billion of new direct loans). The volume of both of these types of federal credit is exceeded by the net lending of the government-sponsored enterprises ($466 billion during the same period). This last category of federally related credit is not directly controlled by Congress.

Most fundamentally, an economic climate more conducive to private saving and investment would reduce the need for private borrowers to seek federal credit assistance in the first place. Such a climate would be fostered by a tax system that tilts in favor of saving rather than consumption and a fiscal policy that avoids the Treasury

FIGURE 14.1   Trend of Federal Loans and Guarantees

Source: U.S. Office of Management and Budget.

deficits whose financing competes with private borrowers. Until these fundamental changes are achieved, pressures for continued expansion of federal credit programs can be anticipated.

BUSINESS BAILOUTS: FEDERAL CREDIT ON A LARGE SCALE

When federal credit programs work as intended, they involve little cash drain on the Treasury. Fees paid by users typically cover administrative costs and modest amounts of defaults. In several dramatic cases, however, the federal government has provided credit to selected business firms on a massive scale, and at times the losses to the Treasury have been severe.

THE CHRYSLER BAILOUT

Chrysler has become the favorite example of proponents of federal financial assistance to enterprises in "temporary" difficulties. On the surface, the government's bailout of the company was successful. Not only did Chrysler survive, it repaid the loans guaranteed by the government ahead of schedule. A variety of arguments had been presented in support of Chrysler's request for federal loan guarantees. They boiled down to the claim that it was cheaper for society to provide the assistance than to have permitted the company to go bankrupt. This policy conclusion was based on six key points:

1. The impact on the federal budget of a Chrysler failure would have been greater than the cost of assistance. Projected increases in unemployment benefits, trade adjustment assistance payments, and other social programs, as well as reduced tax revenues, would have exceeded the total amount of assistance provided to Chrysler. Also, the federal aid was only a guarantee and not a direct loan by the federal government.
2. The social upheaval attendant on a Chrysler failure would have imposed substantial, albeit unquantifiable, costs on society. (This is an argument raised for propping up every failing enterprise.)
3. Production and employment at Chrysler were more heavily concentrated in the Detroit metropolitan area than were the other U.S. auto manufacturers. Consequently, the geographic impact of a Chrysler failure would have been felt disproportionately in a major city, one that already had substantial economic problems. (This approach argues against economic change.)
4. A Chrysler failure would have led to further concentration of the domestic automobile industry and greater monopoly power in the hands of the surviving corporations, which would, in turn, have led to higher prices. (This argument ignores the very substantial rise of foreign competition.)
5. The U.S. balance of payments, already severely in deficit, would have been pushed further into the red as foreign producers captured a share of Chrysler's domestic market. (What happened to the Chrysler arguments that the bailout was needed to prevent GM and Ford from assuming "greater monopoly power"?)
6. While Chrysler's ability to produce small cars in model years 1979 and 1980 was restricted to approximately 300,000 units, the company was building up to

a yearly output of almost 1 million small-car units, which promised to sell strongly in the marketplace. (This is an odd argument for a government bailout. It sounds like the standard case for a bank loan.)

A careful analysis of the Chrysler experience concluded that the decision to approve the loan program was made on an ad hoc basis, rather than in response to broad principles. In hindsight, significant shortcomings are visible.[8]

The events that occurred after the congressional approval of the loan guarantee did not follow a simple pattern. The Chrysler Corporation avoided declaring bankruptcy, but it experienced many of the benefits of such action. Specifically, the Chrysler Corporation Loan Guarantee Act of 1979 required creditors to make "concessions" to the company. As a result, Chrysler was able to pay off more than $600 million in debts at 30 cents on the dollar.[9] It also laid off about 40 percent of its workers. More fundamentally, the bailout of Chrysler ignored the negative impacts that Ford and General Motors felt from federal subsidy of their competitor. Ironically, Chrysler is now a component of a German-based company, DaimlerChrysler, and all three companies are experiencing great financial difficulties in the global market competition for motor vehicle sales.

We can only speculate about what would have been the economic health of Ford and General Motors today if in 1979 Congress had rejected the requested financial assistance to Chrysler. We can recall the conclusion of economist Paul Samuelson:

> One of the small virtues of a market laissez-faire system is that when it makes a terrible mistake and produces mousetraps that people don't want or which don't work, somebody runs out of money and gets rapped on the knuckles. That's why the Lord created bankruptcy.[10]

In retrospect, the Chrysler case may not provide a stellar precedent for a generalized program of government financial aid to industrial companies that are in difficulty.

OTHER RESCUE EFFORTS OF INDIVIDUAL ENTERPRISES

The arguments offered for the Chrysler bailout are not unique, in the sense that they can be expressed in more general terms and made in connection with virtually any large corporate failure. Nevertheless, the federal government has not invariably bailed out every loser in the marketplace. Consider the many large firms that went bankrupt during the 1980s and 1990s and reorganized to become leaner and lower-cost competitors. Examples of successful postbankrupt firms range from giant retailer Federated Department Stores to Continental Airlines. Of course, the stockholders suffered during the process, but that is a characteristic—painful but necessary—of a well-functioning, private-enterprise system.

Prior to the 1980s, the federal government provided special assistance to many corporations. The Reconstruction Finance Corporation (RFC) operated in the depression and wartime period of the 1930s and 1940s to shore up companies that could not obtain adequate private financing. The activities of the RFC during the Great Depression and in wartime were generally applauded. However, a great show of favoritism during the post–World War II period led to widely publicized congressional investigations and to the agency's termination in 1952.[11]

Lockheed (now Lockheed-Martin) benefited from $250 million in federal loan guarantees from 1970 to 1977. Conrail, the rail freight system of the Northeast, was extended more than $3 billion in aid to help it maintain its operation. Special tax relief was granted to American Motors, now a part of the DaimlerChrysler Corporation. All of these firms were similar in that they were highly leveraged and had high wage costs. Supporters of aid claimed in each case that it was cheaper to provide government assistance than to bear the costs of their collapse. And supporters of each bailout were able to marshal the political clout necessary to win the required votes.

In addition, the Federal Deposit Insurance Corporation (FDIC) has rescued numerous banks from going under. In each of these cases, the FDIC maintained that it was cheaper to provide the financial assistance to keep the bank in operation than it would have been to pay off the depositors whose accounts were insured up to $100,000 each. Frequently, the FDIC has attempted to merge an ailing bank with a stronger financial institution, often providing some capital infusion to cover a portion of the bad loans assumed by the acquiring bank. The FDIC has responded to hundreds of bank failures since 1980.

In 1984, the FDIC rescued the Continental-Illinois Bank of Chicago in one of the largest bailouts of a private company in American history. To prevent the failure of the bank, whose assets totaled approximately $40 billion in 1983, the FDIC bought its loan portfolio for $3.5 billion and agreed to provide an additional $1.5 billion in direct funding. In this case, the FDIC acted from a combination of motivations. It avoided having to pay off the depositors whose savings it had insured, but it also was concerned over the repercussions throughout the banking industry had one of the nation's largest financial institutions been allowed to fail.[12]

THE S&L BAILOUT

The largest and most expensive bailout in American history occurred in the savings and loan (S&L) industry in the late 1980s and early 1990s. A major portion of the entire industry was liquidated and the federal government wound up selling the remaining assets of the bankrupt thrift institutions, often under "fire sale" conditions. This case dramatically illustrated the potential cost of the federal government "merely" guaranteeing or insuring private credit and related financial transactions.

During the extended S&L bailout (1980–1995), the federal government closed down over 300 S&Ls at a cost of over $30 billion. In addition, over 800 thrift institutions were sold to new owners, typically with the federal government picking up the accumulated losses (over $100 billion). In many cases, the S&Ls, greatly reduced in size from their previous operation, were merged into healthier and often larger financial institutions. The aggregate cost of the S&L bailout was over $180 billion.[13]

Ironically, one of the ways of financing the S&L bailout increased the likelihood of more thrift institutions going under. In order to minimize the already heavy load on the general taxpayer, Congress required that a substantial part of the cost of rescuing the sick S&Ls be paid for by a levy on the healthy S&Ls. Aside from the questionable fairness of well-run financial institutions having to subsidize their poorly run competitors, the added cost may have pushed some of the marginally healthy S&Ls over the brink. In any event, raising the operating costs of thrift institutions made it more difficult for them to compete against commercial banks for the business of individual depositors and consumer borrowers.

Hindsight also reveals that the delays in the 1980s in closing down the failed thrifts increased the size of the bailout substantially. Many managers of insolvent S&Ls

proceeded to make extremely risky investments in the hope that they could turn around the situation—knowing that the government was eventually going to pick up the tab if the deals went sour. The Congressional Budget Office estimated that the delay in closing failed institutions, often as much as two to four years, roughly doubled the ultimate cost of resolving them.[14] In addition, three new agencies replaced older federal instrumentalities:

1. The Office of Thrift Supervision replaced the Federal Home Loan Bank Board in chartering and supervising individual S&Ls.
2. The Savings Association Insurance Fund (SAIF) replaced the Federal Savings and Loan Insurance Corporation (FSLIC) in insuring deposits at S&Ls.
3. The Federal Housing Finance Board replaced the Federal Home Loan Bank Board in regulating the quasi-governmental Federal Home Loan Banks.

OUTLOOK

The provision of credit continues to be a popular way for the federal government to provide assistance to business. However, the strings attached to the aid can be substantial. In 2001, following the terrorist attacks of September 11, Congress established the Air Transportation Stabilization Board (ATSB). The new agency is authorized to extend up to $10 billion in loan guarantees to the airlines.

America West was the first company to qualify for a loan guarantee by the ATSB. The airline had to line up a variety of concessions from its creditors, including the more than 20 companies from which it leased aircraft as well as the aircraft manufacturers. America West also had to set up controls over labor costs and to show how it would repay the loan in seven years or less. Moreover, the airline was required to give the federal government warrants that, if fully exercised over a 10-year period, would represent 33 percent of the firm's common stock (but without voting rights). U.S. Airways also qualified for a large loan guarantee from the ATSB. It, too, had to agree to give the federal government a potential stake in the company and to obtain significant concessions from employees and creditors.

Congress is continuing to receive requests to provide federal financial assistance to other industries hard hit by terrorist threats and attacks, notably insurance companies.

Notes

1. James L. Bothwell, *Government Sponsored Enterprises (GSEs)* (Washington, DC: U.S. General Accounting Office, 1997); W. Scott Frame and Larry D. Wall, "Financing Housing Through Government-Sponsored Enterprises," *Federal Reserve Bank of Atlanta Economic Review,* First Quarter 2002, pp. 29–43.
2. Murray Weidenbaum, *Small Wars, Big Defense* (New York: Oxford University Press, 1992), pp. 143–144.
3. Harold Seidman, "The Quasi World of the Federal Government," *Brookings Review,* Summer 1988, p. 25.
4. Thomas H. Stanton, *Government-Sponsored Enterprises* (Washington, DC: AEI Press, 2002), p. xi.
5. The subsidy is calculated as the difference between the present value of the government's cash outflow for the loan and the present value of the expected payments of principal and interest. The discount rate used

to estimate present value is the interest rate on marketable Treasury securities of like maturity at the time the loan was disbursed.

6. *The Budget of the United States Government, Fiscal Year 2003,* Analytical Perspectives (Washington, DC: U.S. Government Printing Office, 2002).

7. Francis X. Cavanaugh, *The Truth About the National Debt* (Boston, MA: Harvard Business School Press, 1997).

8. Brian M. Freeman and Allan I. Mendelowitz, "Program in Search of a Policy: The Chrysler Loan Guarantee," *Journal of Policy Analysis and Management* 11, no. 4, 1982, pp. 448–482.

9. James K. Hickel, *The Chrysler Bail-Out Bust* (Washington, DC: Heritage Foundation, 1983), p. 2.

10. Paul A. Samuelson, "Some Dilemmas of Economic Policy," *Challenge,* March–April 1977, p. 35.

11. Arthur T. Denzau and Clifford M. Hardin, *A National Development Bank: Ghost of the RFC Past* (St. Louis, MO: Washington University, Weidenbaum Center on the Economy, Government, and Public Policy, 1984); U.S. Senate, Committee on Banking and Currency, *Study of Reconstruction Finance Corporation and Proposed Amendment of RFC Act* (Washington, DC: U.S. Government Printing Office, 1951).

12. Eric N. Compton, *The New World of Commercial Banking* (Lexington, MA: Lexington Books, 1987), p. 14.

13. Congressional Budget Office, *Resolving the Thrift Crisis* (Washington, DC: Government Printing Office, 1993), p. 6.

14. *Resolving the Thrift Crisis,* p. 17.

15

GOVERNMENT AS
A MARKET

⟨⟨⟨⟨⟩⟩⟩⟩

Governments in the United States—federal, state, and local—constitute large and often very special customers for a wide variety of private businesses. As shown in Table 15.1, the aggregate purchases by government agencies are substantial—$864 billion in 2000. These procurements are divided between federal buyers (43 percent) and state and local agencies (57 percent).

But it is far more than a mere matter of size. The composition of government purchases differs greatly among the levels of government and from the typical private-sector buyer, and so does the manner in which these purchases are made. A large share of federal procurement is heavily high tech and devoted to the military establishment. In contrast, states and localities buy variations of more traditional supplies and equipment also available to the rest of the economy.

FEDERAL CIVILIAN PROCUREMENT

Federal civilian procurement typically relies on the selection of the offerer of the lowest price based on sealed bids submitted by "responsible bidders" (those meeting the government's stated standards). Except for purchases of high-tech civilian space equipment by NASA, which uses an acquisition system similar to that of the Department of Defense (DOD), the composition of most federal civilian purchases is comparable, if not identical, to standard commercial items.

The Federal Supply Service in the U.S. General Services Administration is the agency in charge of buying most of the civilian procurements of the federal government. Given the wide variety of missions assigned to the numerous departments and agencies established by Congress, it is not surprising that this market is very broad. As can be seen in Table 15.2, the civilian purchases made by the federal government range from alarm systems to storage tanks, from cattle guards to lawn and garden equipment, and from tires to trophies.

A relatively new and rapidly expanding area of federal civilian procurement results from the increased emphasis that has been placed on homeland security. This new purchasing pattern includes medicines to treat 20 million people for anthrax and other bacterial infections, equipment to find and destroy biological agents of terror in U.S. mail facilities, and explosives detection systems for more careful inspection of airline baggage and passengers (see Chapter 9 for details).[1]

For companies that conduct substantial amounts of business with the federal government (civilian as well as military agencies), the very act of signing a procurement contract forces them to agree to perform a wide variety of socially responsible actions. These vary from favoring disadvantaged groups to showing concern for the quality of life and the environment.

TABLE 15.1   Composition of the Government Market, 2000

Level of Government Purchases	Amount (Billions of Dollars)	Percent
Federal	$375	43
State and local	489	57
Total	$864	100

Source: Compiled from U.S. Department of Commerce data.

The federal government requires that firms doing business with it maintain fair employment practices, provide safe and healthful working conditions, pay "prevailing" wages, refrain from polluting the air and water, give preference to American products in their purchases, and promote the rehabilitation of prisoners. Table 15.3 contains a sample listing of such ancillary duties required of government contractors. The requirements of these social mandates can be extensive. For example, a variety of efforts has been launched since the Resource Conservation and Recovery Act (RCRA) was passed in 1976.

The RCRA requires each federal agency buying more than $10,000 of an item that the EPA has designated as available with recycled content to establish an affirmative procurement program to encourage the purchases of these items. The recycled

TABLE 15.2   Categories of Federal Civilian Procurements

Alarm systems	Office furniture and decorations
Cattle guards	Office machines and supplies
Chemicals and chemical products	Paint
Cleaning supplies	Photography equipment and supplies
Clothing and footwear	Prefab storage buildings
Construction and building materials	Publications
Conveyors and forklifts	Record equipment
Data processing equipment	Recreational equipment
Dental equipment and supplies	Recycling equipment and containers
Drugs and pharmaceutical products	Relocation services
Fire-fighting and rescue equipment	Road maintenance
Food services	Shipping packaging and supplies
Hand and power tools	Signs
Industry machinery	Storage tanks
Internet products	Subsistence foods
Laboratory instruments and equipment	Telecommunication and media supplies
Law enforcement equipment	Tires
Lawn and garden equipment	Training aids and devices
Maintenance and repair shop equipment	Transportation services
Marine equipment	Trophies and awards
Medical supplies and equipment	Water purification and sewer equipment
Musical instruments	Wheel and track vehicles

Source: U.S. Federal Supply Service.

TABLE 15.3　Social and Economic Restrictions on Federal Government Contractors

Program	*Purpose*
Improve working conditions	
Walsh–Healey Act	Prescribes minimum wages, hours, and working conditions for supply contracts
Davis–Bacon Act	Prescribes minimum wages, benefits, and working conditions on construction contracts over $2,000
Service Contract Act	Extends the Walsh–Healey and Davis–Bacon acts to persons imprisoned at hard labor
Favor disadvantaged groups	
Equal Employment Opportunity	Requires affirmative action programs for government contractors
Employment openings	Requires contractors to list suitable employment openings with state employment systems
Prisoner-made supplies	Mandates purchase of specific supplies from Federal Prison Industries
Blind-made products	Mandates purchase of products made by blind and other handicapped persons
Small Business Act	Requires "fair" portion of subcontracts to be placed with small businesses
Labor-surplus area concerns	Requires preference to subcontracts in areas of concentrated unemployment or underemployment
Favor American companies	
Buy American Act	Provides preference for domestic materials over foreign materials
Preference to U.S. vessels	Requires shipping at least half of government goods in U.S. vessels
Protect the environment and quality of life	
Clean Air Act	Prohibits contracts to a company convicted of criminal violation of air-pollution standards
Resource Conservation and Recovery Act	Requires federal agencies to establish programs to encourage procurement of recycled products
Care of laboratory animals	Requires humane treatment by contractors in use of experimental or laboratory animals
Humane Slaughter Act	Limits government purchases of meat to suppliers that conform to humane slaughter standards

products for which the EPA has issued "Comprehensive Procurement Guidelines" include building insulation, carpet, cement, and concrete. Since the 1970s, Democratic and Republican presidents alike have issued executive orders designed to use federal purchasing power to promote environmental goals.[2]

Although aimed at important social objectives, those special provisions are not without expense to the government procurement process. They increase overhead of both private contractors and federal procurement offices. Some of the provisions also exert an upward pressure on the direct costs incurred by the government. Special provisions such as the Davis–Bacon Act increase the cost of public construction projects through government promulgation of wage rates higher than those that would result if the market were allowed to operate without impediment.

In June 2002, Home Depot, Inc., announced that its 1,400 stores would no longer sell its products to the federal government. It cited statutes that require specified affirmative action efforts by anyone doing $50,000 or more in business with the federal government. A company representative stated, "The Home Depot is not and does not plan to become a federal contractor or subcontractor."[3] However, later that month — after receiving considerable criticism — the company reversed its earlier decision and continued to sell products to federal agencies.[4]

One of the social objectives favored by the federal government in its procurement — encouraging purchases of prisoner-made supplies — has generated considerable criticism as well as support. Advocates of the Federal Prison Industries program contend that teaching inmates productive skills generates many favorable results. The prisoners are more cooperative while they are incarcerated and the likelihood is increased that they will make a successful transition to productive activity when their prison terms are over.

However, many small businesses object to the low prices charged for the 150 categories of products and services produced by prison labor. They note that federal agencies and their contractors are required to purchase those products in competition with taxpaying private enterprises.[5]

THE STATE AND LOCAL GOVERNMENT MARKET

Purchases by state and local agencies generally follow a pattern basically similar to that of federal civilian agencies. However, because of the great variety of state, county, and municipal governments, the specific procurement procedures followed are far from uniform. Each governmental unit tends to adopt its own practices, especially as they relate to the nature of competition and the discretion to buy items without a formal bidding process. Schools and highway departments represent the biggest buyers in this portion of the public sector. The importance of construction (structures) compared to other categories of procurement can be seen in Table 15.4, showing the character of state and local purchases.

PRIVATIZATION

In recent years, privatization — shifting functions and responsibilities from the government to the private sector — has become increasingly common. This trend is affecting the size and composition of the government market. Depending on the form

TABLE 15.4   The State and Local Government Market in 2000*

Category of Procurement	Amount (Billions of Dollars)
Durable goods	$74
Nondurable goods	111
Structures	165
Services	139
Total	$489

*Compiled from U.S. Department of Commerce data.

it takes, privatization can expand or contract the amount of goods and services that government purchases from the private sector. Contracting out the performance of an activity that previously had been conducted in-house (for example, in a printing plant operated by civil servants) is the most common form of privatization. However, it is by no means the only way in which government can engage the private sector in its business activities.

There is indeed a range of privatization actions that governments take, and the effects on the private enterprise vary substantially. At one end of the policy spectrum—*service shedding*—the entire function is shifted to the private sector, its financing as well as its performance. A typical example is a government-owned and operated electric utility that policy makers decide should no longer be a public-sector activity. The entire operation is sold to private investors. Under these circumstances, the aggregate size of private markets is likely to expand, while the total amount of government spending contracts. The decision as to how much, if any, of the service to produce is then made in the marketplace by private producers and consumers.

A closely related type of privatization is asset sales, where government sells the ownership of some asset, frequently property that has been declared surplus by a government agency. At the federal level, it may also be a financial asset (a government-guaranteed loan that it holds and is servicing). In this case, government continues to exert substantial influence on the activity because the government guarantee is still in force.

As noted earlier, *contracting out* (or outsourcing) is the most popular form of privatization. Here, government hires private firms, typically to provide a service that the government had been providing to citizens directly. Municipal collection of garbage is a popular example. Unlike service shedding, government continues to finance and sponsor the activity.

The most modest form of privatization is *managed* competition. Under this alternative, the government opens a market—an example might be cleaning government buildings—and private firms are invited to bid against government agencies. The government continues to determine the extent to which businesses can enter these government markets. The extent of privatization depends on a number of factors, including the cost and efficiency of the private enterprise conducting the activity and the political power of the government employees who could lose their jobs in the public sector. Frequently, the former government workers obtain employment with the private company now conducting the activity, but often with a more modest compensation package.

Bringing in competition from the private sector can generate important impacts on existing government operations. For example, in response to government employee concerns that they would lose the work to a low-bid private firm, the city of Indianapolis laid off most of the supervisors in its road maintenance crews. The result was to save some of the municipal employees' jobs as well as to reduce government spending.[6]

At times, states and localities have taken back activities that had been privatized. This is done most easily in contracted out situations. In 1997, Missouri brought back prisoners it had housed in proprietary jails in Texas, after learning of the brutal treatment those prisoners had received there. The various types of privatization efforts are

TABLE 15.5   Examples of Privatization in the United States

Activity	Type of Privatization	Preliminary Results
Maintenance of state autos	Outsourcing	Savings estimated at $300,000 a year (Georgia)
Operations of veterans home	Outsourcing	Cleaner facility and better food (Georgia)
Maintenance of highways	Managed competition	Reduced overtime costs (Massachusetts)
Provision of security at government installations	Outsourcing	Savings estimated at $1.2 million a year (Michigan)
Armories	Asset sale	Michigan gained $400,000 from sale of surplus facilities
Vista Hotel in New York City	Asset sale	New York received $141 million
Wastewater treatment	Outsourcing	Indianapolis saved $16 million a year
Airport management enplaned	Outsourcing	16 percent reduction in cost per passenger (Indianapolis)
Collection of delinquent taxes	Outsourcing	Improved collection of previously uncollectable accounts (Virginia)

Source: Privatization: Lessons Learned by State and Local Governments (Washington, DC: U.S. General Accounting Office, 1997).

generally too newly instituted, so their value is not yet proven. Nevertheless, several researchers claim that the initial results are impressive in terms of savings to taxpayers. Specific examples are shown in Table 15.5.

In many foreign nations, the most popular form of privatization is to sell off large commercial-style activities previously owned and conducted by government agencies, notably the enterprises that provide telephone and other telecommunication services. Unlike the United States, where the arsenal approach is very limited, a great variety of other countries—developed as well as developing—have traditionally conducted a large portion of economic activity in the public sector. In view of the poor performance on the part of these nationalized industries, outright privatization in the form of sales of ownership to private enterprise has often enhanced the efficiency of the national economy, while yielding one-time revenues for the national treasury.[7] Germany and Japan each raised more than $60 billion from the sales of stock in their previously government-owned public utility.

Quite a few countries have sold off all or a major part of what had been a government-owned and operated national telecommunications system. In several cases, the privatized firm quickly joined the ranks of the top 100 global corporations. Examples include Japan's Nippon Telegraph and Telephone, Germany's Deutsche Telekom, the United Kingdom's British Telecommunications, France's Telecom, Italy's Telecom Italia, and Spain's Telefonia. Other recently privatized global giants include British Petroleum, France's Elf Acquitaine, Germany's Volkswagen, Russia's Gazprom, and Brazil's Telebras.

In striking contrast with earlier periods, when the pace of nationalization of private enterprises was substantial, few if any new instances of government ownership of previously private companies have taken place since 1980.

THE SPECIALIZED MILITARY MARKET

The military market is the largest component of public-sector procurement in the United States. As has been demonstrated on many occasions, U.S. citizens continue to live in a dangerous world and that justifies high levels of defense spending. The end of the Cold War with the former Soviet Union did not usher in a millennium of peace. The Middle East and the Balkans are constant reminders of the dangers of armed hostilities. The continued operation of international terrorist groups conjures up other serious threats to the national security.

It can be expected that, for the foreseeable future, the United States will maintain a substantial military establishment and, in a world of advancing technology, a strong defense industry with new or improved weapon systems. Figure 15.1 shows that aerospace programs—aircraft and missiles systems—dominate the purchases of weapon systems, accounting for almost two-thirds of the military procurement dollars in 2002. From the viewpoint of business–government relations, perhaps the most significant aspect of the military market is that the companies producing weapon systems and other equipment for the military establishment constitute the most heavily regulated sector of the American economy.

Private production of government orders generates some of the closest day-to-day interactions between federal agencies and individual companies. The Pentagon was once described as the place where Franz Kafka meets Alice in Wonderland.[8] In practice, military and civilian procurement differ so substantially that they are almost worlds apart. Defense agencies make their procurements through very detailed rules and procedures established by the Armed Services Procurement Act and federal procurement regulations.

Although the defense sector is not called a regulated industry, it is very much controlled by government, far more than is the case in utilities, railroads, and other traditionally regulated companies. In the words of two former senior military procurement officers, "The defense buyer is in fact a regulator."[9] The government's influence and control over defense contractors occur through the detailed process by which the military establishment awards contracts to private firms and monitors the performance on those contracts. Moreover, the military establishment purchases products that are not

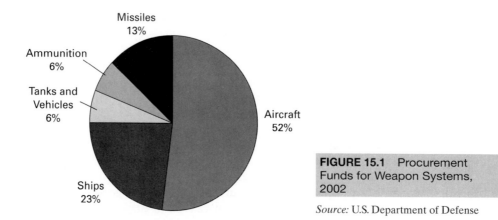

FIGURE 15.1   Procurement Funds for Weapon Systems, 2002

Source: U.S. Department of Defense

yet designed or for which production experience is lacking and at prices for which there is little precedent. As a consequence of these special factors, defense work has developed several distinguishing, if not unique, characteristics.

THE MILITARY MARKET IS MONOPSONISTIC

The DOD is the one customer for aircraft carriers, supersonic bombers, ICBMs, and nuclear submarines. Because the market is so *monopsonistic*—completely subject to the changing needs of this one purchaser—relationships between buyer and seller differ fundamentally from those in civilian sectors of the economy. By its selection of contractors, the government customer controls entry into and exit from this market. Thus, the government also determines the growth of the firms manufacturing military equipment and imposes its ways of doing business on them. The regulations governing military procurement cover more than 2,000 pages, including numerous standard clauses that must be inserted into defense contracts and a host of standard forms that must be used. It is difficult to come up with a civilian counterpart.[10]

This single-customer market makes for an extremely keen and novel type of either/or competition. For a specific product, a company generally is not competing for a share of the market but rather for all of it. Both Boeing and General Dynamics were rivals for the F-111 aircraft contract; General Dynamics won and produced all of this product. Similarly, McDonnell Douglas (now a part of Boeing) produces all of the F-15 aircraft as a result of a design competition it won against two other bidding companies.

The less efficient, commercially oriented firm may lose its market position, but for a period of time, it can count on making some sales of its product line, although at reduced prices. Rarely does it encounter the extreme peak-and-valley nature of military procurement characterized by intense initial government demand followed by the virtual disappearance of the market for the items as one generation of aircraft or missile is followed by the next.

Defense contractors commit their key scientists and engineers (who are their most strategic resource) to programs subject to unpredictable change or even cancellation—and to products where the ultimate profitability will not be known for a decade or more. This aspect of the business, coupled with its research-intensive nature, is much more analogous to the risks of pharmaceutical companies, which are subject to substantial regulation, than to the larger and more traditional category of durable goods manufacturers with which the defense industry is often compared. Under these conditions of uncertainty, it is rarely feasible to predict the cost, schedule, performance, or quantity of the final product with enough precision to permit the buyer and seller to write a firm contract covering the entire process. Instead, the two parties establish what can be called an "uneasy alliance," sharing risks and management responsibilities, under the aegis of a contract that at times is little more than a baseline for negotiations over numerous changes over the course of the program.

Thus, it is not surprising that the government as buyer assumes many of the risks that in more normal business activities are borne by the seller. Along with the assumption of risk, however, there is a corresponding involvement by the customer in the internal operations of its suppliers. The officials of the Department of Defense make many decisions that are normally part of the responsibility of business management.

PRICE IS OFTEN NOT THE DETERMINANT OF SALES

Because of the nature of military requirements, the offer price frequently is a far less important factor than it is in commercial markets. In the case of major weapon systems, price is only one of several key factors considered by the customer. The major products purchased in this market provide examples par excellence of extreme product differentiation. Essentially, the military buyer is concerned with obtaining the product of superior quality—the second fastest fighter aircraft may be no bargain. Since the significant competition occurs before the final product is completely designed, initial estimates of both total cost and final performance are tentative and of limited reliability and utility. The seller's previous cost experiences and demonstrated managerial capabilities are often given greater weight than the price estimates it offers.

TECHNICAL CAPABILITY IS THE MAJOR ASSET

Because of the inherent uncertainty imbedded in a process of purchasing products that do not yet exist, the potential contractor's past record of technical achievement and the attractiveness of its design proposal are often the dominant factors in awarding a contract for a new weapon system. Successful suppliers are principally product quality maximizers rather than cost minimizers. Their basic competence is invention and organization of huge teams of scientists and engineers. Cost overruns may arise from the great uncertainty that abounds in estimating the cost of designing and manufacturing items that have never before been made—and from the numerous changes in specifications that the military customer makes as technology advances.

Whether a particular program will reach the production stage depends in large part on the technical capability displayed during the research and development stage—as well as the budgetary pressures facing the military service sponsoring the weapon system. Competition among the prospective suppliers is keen, but it relates primarily to their technological capability. Nevertheless, elaborate procedures are used in determining price, including a variety of contract types designed to provide some of the incentives of a normal competitive market that otherwise would be absent.

PRODUCTION OCCURS AFTER THE SALE

The market for weapon systems is characterized by production undertaken after an order is received; production for inventory is rare. This differs from most areas of the private economy. Production of major military products—such as aircraft, missiles, space vehicles, ships, and tanks—normally begins after the receipt of the government order. Moreover, the government buyer frequently takes the initiative in developing new products by financing most of the research and development costs.

THE CHANNELS OF DISTRIBUTION ARE SIMPLE

The military market has deceptively simple channels of distribution. Basically, the manufacturer sells and delivers directly to the consumer. This results from the fact that the military establishment itself maintains an extensive internal distribution system. The flow of material—from private-sector producers to central military warehouses to bases and to the military unit actually using the equipment—is analogous to the flow in the private sector from manufacturer to wholesaler to retailer and to the final customer.

However, because the government customer handles most of the distribution, defense contractors have developed very limited and specialized marketing capabilities, which is a barrier to their attempts to market their technological capabilities in civilian areas.

THE INDUSTRIAL DISTRIBUTION OF DEFENSE WORK

Strictly speaking, there is no specific "defense" industry. A great many companies serve as prime contractors or subcontractors to the military services, yet most of them devote the greater portion of their resources to civilian markets. The composition of the major firms and industries supplying goods and services to the Department of Defense varies over time, it being largely a function of current defense needs. For example, during the Korean War, when military requirements were dominated by army ordnance equipment, General Motors (as a major producer of tanks and trucks) was the number-one military contractor. The shift to aircraft and missiles since then has brought aerospace companies into the forefront of military contractors, firms such as Boeing and Lockheed Martin (see Table 15.6).

A relatively few hard-goods-producing industries account for the great bulk of the dollar volume of military contracts: aircraft, electronics, motor vehicles, petroleum refining, chemicals, rubber, and construction. Most American industries, such as lumber, food, textiles, machinery, metal fabricators, services, and trade, do not loom large as prime defense contractors. Some firms in those industries, however, may participate in the military market as suppliers or subcontractors to the major producers.

TABLE 15.6   Major Defense Contractors, Fiscal Year 2001

Rank	Company	Military Awards (Billions of Dollars)	Key Products
1	Lockheed Martin	$14.7	Submarine missile systems; cargo and fighter aircraft
2	Boeing	13.3	SRAM and Minuteman missiles, ADP and telecommunications services; helicopters; cargo and tanker aircraft
3	Newport News	5.9	Aircraft carriers; submarines
4	Raytheon	5.6	Patriot, AMRAAM, Trident, Hawk, and Sea Sparrow missiles; fire control equipment
5	Northrop Grumman	5.2	Fighter and bomber aircraft; radar and navigational equipment
6	General Dynamics	4.9	F-16 fighters; Abrams tanks, Stinger, Tomahawk, Trident and Atlas missiles; nuclear submarines
7	United Technologies	3.4	Aircraft engines; helicopters; advanced tactical fighter aircraft
8	TRW	1.9	Laser systems; training simulators; ICBMs; missile defense systems
9	Science Applications	1.7	Computer systems
10	General Electric	1.7	Aircraft engines; Aegis and Trident missile system components

Source: U.S. Department of Defense.

PRICE FORMATION AND COMPETITION

The typical weapon system contract is awarded to a company chosen as the result of a lengthy series of negotiations. This firm then enters into an extended contractual relationship with the military. This procedure differs fundamentally from the typical civilian agency procurement, where a purchase order is awarded at a fixed price to the company that has offered the lowest sealed bid.

When the military establishment enters into an arrangement with a firm to secure the production of a good or service, the final cost is dependent on the type of contract that the government negotiates. The DOD uses two basic types of contracts: cost reimbursement and fixed price.

The general category of cost-reimbursement contracts, at first blush, appears to be a simple concept, with the government paying the costs and the producer having little incentive to cut expenses. The actual amount that the government pays, however, is dependent on which costs are allowed. Many customary business expenses are not reimbursed by the DOD: technical displays, unapproved overtime, business conferences, bid and proposal expense, employee moving costs, operation of executive airplanes, property tax on equipment, interest payments, patents expense, and public relations. When the government disallows these items, that action arbitrarily reduces the company's profit.

Moreover, the government uses a variety of reimbursable contracts: cost-with-no-fee contract (typically, for dealing with nonprofit organizations), cost-plus-fixed-fee (generally used on developmental contracts), and cost-reimbursable contracts (with an incentive provision to share the reduction in cost below the initial estimate).

COMPETITIVE AND NEGOTIATED PROCUREMENT

In the Competition in Contracting Act, Congress decreed that whenever possible the Pentagon should seek out at least two bidders on a project. In 2000, 80 percent of the military contracts awarded were done so by means of competitive bidding (see Figure 15.2). Another 2 percent of the total consists of contracts to extend production of items already under contract ("follow on" production). However, only a minor share of that category is the result of sealed bids responding to formal advertising. Most "competitive"

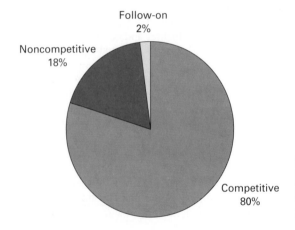

FIGURE 15.2   Distribution of Competitive and Noncompetitive Procurements, Fiscal Year 2000

Source: U.S. Department of Defense

awards rely on negotiation between the government and its suppliers. The DOD maintains that procurement through negotiation does not signify lack of competition. The simple presentation of statistics tends to present a black-and-white contrast in procurement procedures that does not always reflect actual operations. On occasion, procedures under formal advertising and negotiation have tended to blend together. Often, there may be as many or more companies competing for a negotiated award as respond with sealed bids under formal advertising. The remaining 18 percent of the contracts are awarded to firms selected without competitors.

LONG-TERM IMPACTS OF MILITARY PROCUREMENT

In its long-term dealings with those companies or divisions of companies that cater primarily to the military market, the federal government has directly or indirectly assumed many of the decision-making functions that are normally the prerogatives of business management. To a substantial degree, similar relationships develop on the part of the contractors providing specialized equipment and services to the Department of Energy and the National Aeronautics and Space Administration (NASA).

This government assumption of, and active participation in, private business decision making takes three major forms: virtually determining the choice of products the defense firms produce; strongly influencing the source of capital funds that they use; and closely supervising much of their internal operations. The government involvement in private industry arises almost exclusively in the case of the unique and large-scale weapon systems. It does not characterize the procurement of desks, chairs, and other conventional items by government agencies (military or civilian) through fixed-price contracts resulting from sealed-bid competitions.

By awarding billions of dollars of contracts for research and development (R&D) each year, the DOD influences strongly which new products its contractors design and produce. The government customer directly finances much of the supplier's R&D and thus assumes much of the risk of failure of new product development. In the commercial economy, in contrast, costs of scientific and technological advances are not borne by the buyer, but by the seller, who only recovers its investment if it results in the sale of profitable products.

Defense contractors do sponsor and fund much of their own R&D. However, the bulk of their military-oriented scientific and technical effort is performed under government contract or charged as overhead on their government contracts. The DOD also uses its vast financial resources to supply much of the plants and equipment used by its major contractors for defense work. In addition, and as noted in Chapter 14, military contractors receive billions of dollars of "progress" payments (government payments made prior to competition and while the work is still underway).

Military procurement regulations provide specific disincentives for using private working capital. Progress payments equal to as much as 80 percent of the costs incurred on government contracts are provided without interest charge to the contractors. However, should these companies decide to rely on private sources for working capital, their interest payments cannot be charged to government contracts. The interest must come out of their profits. The result is to increase the extent to which public rather than private capital finances the operations of defense contractors.

The most pervasive way in which the military establishment assumes the management decision-making functions of its contractors is through procurement legislation and rules governing the awarding of contracts. Military procurement regulations require private suppliers to accept on a "take-it-or-leave-it" basis many standard clauses in their contracts, which give the government contracting and surveillance officers numerous powers over the internal operations of these companies.

The authority assumed by the government customer includes power to review and veto a host of company decisions: which activities to perform in-house and which to subcontract, which firms to use as subcontractors, which products to buy domestically rather than to import, what internal financial system to use, what minimum as well as average wage rates to pay, and how much overtime work to authorize.

Viewed as a totality, these restrictions represent substantial government regulation of industry. This regulation is not accomplished through the traditional independent regulatory agencies (such as the Federal Communications Commission or the Securities and Exchange Commission) but rather through the unilateral exercise of the government's dominant market position.

Very few of the large aerospace companies—Lockheed Martin is the major exception—are truly government-oriented enterprises, relying on the DOD for most of their income (see Table 15.7). Several others, such as General Dynamics, Northrop Grumman, and Raytheon, obtain over 30 percent of their sales from the military market. In contrast, most major defense contractors—Boeing, General Electric, and

TABLE 15.7   Sales to U.S. Military As a Percentage of Total Sales for Major Contractors, 2001

Rank	Company	Percentage
	40–100% of sales to military	
1	Lockheed Martin	59.2
6	General Dynamics	40.3
	20–40% of sales to military	
5	Northrop Grumman	38.0
4	Raytheon	33.1
9	Science Applications International	28.4
2	Boeing	22.9
	0–19% of sales to military	
18	ITT Industries	17.3
7	United Technologies	12.1
8	TRW	11.6
12	Health Net	9.3
17	Computer Sciences Corp	7.8
22	Textron	4.6
14	Honeywell International	3.8
72	Texas Instruments	2.6
10	General Electric	1.4

Source: Computed from data in U.S. Department of Defense and corporate annual reports.

United Technologies, for example—look primarily to commercial markets for the great bulk of their revenue. General Motors sold its defense electronics activity to Raytheon. Ford, IBM, and Unisys each sold defense systems operations to Loral (which was subsequently acquired by Lockheed Martin). At the same time, several large defense contractors merged—Boeing and McDonnell Douglas, Lockheed and Martin, and Northrop and Grumman. Northrop Grumman subsequently bought the defense division of Westinghouse and acquired Litton Industries, Newport News Shipbuilding, and TRW.

This trend has raised serious concerns about the adequacy of competition for key segments of the military market. For example, the number of U.S. makers of military aircraft has declined from eight in 1985 to three or four. The reality is that, for the foreseeable future, the military customer will be buying a relatively small number of expensive weapon systems from a smaller group of companies than it was accustomed to during the Cold War era. Competition is likely to remain intense whether there are four, three, or two hungry competitors for each new program.[11] The prevalence of adequate competition is made more likely by the upturn in military budgets that has been occurring in the early years of the twenty-first century. The military market once again seems to be an attractive place for defense-oriented companies that have mastered the intricacies of the Pentagon's complicated acquisition system.

The differences between military contractors and typical industrial firms are striking. Compared with commercial operations, the major defense divisions have little commercial marketing capabilities and limited experience in producing at high volume and low unit cost. Moreover, their administrative structure is geared to the unique reporting and control requirements of the governmental customer. Most of the firms that operate in both civilian and military markets maintain separate, insulated divisions that have little contact with each other, merely reporting to the same top management.

In a survey conducted by the Center for Strategic and International Studies (CSIS), 71 percent of the defense contractors stated that the Pentagon's procurement policies make it difficult for them to enter or flourish in civilian markets. Bolstered by in-depth interviews, CSIS concluded that the DOD acquisition system is a major obstacle to civilian diversification and that military production has evolved into a business culture quite distinct and closed off from normal commercial culture. The view of one defense industry representative was typical: "With this high overhead, together with the facilities, manpower, and systems oriented toward that type of work, it is extremely difficult to find civilian markets where we can be cost-competitive."[12]

The lack of commercial marketing experience is another familiar refrain in defense industry circles. Northrop Grumman developed and tried to sell a minivan years before Chrysler (now DaimlerChrysler) popularized the vehicle. The project failed because of the lack of a distribution system. It is not hard to understand why defense company managements have become so reluctant to move from fields they have mastered into lines of business alien to them.

Their lack of knowledge of nondefense business is pervasive. It includes ignorance of products, production methods, advertising and distribution, financial arrangements, funding research and development, contracting forms, and the very nature of the private customer's demands. These differentiating characteristics help to explain why the primary response of the specialized defense contractors to the large cutbacks in military procurement following the end of the Cold War was to downsize, consolidate, and merge.

To a much lesser degree, some of them have diversified into closely related high-tech markets, involving sales to civilian government agencies (including homeland defense).

Clearly, the type of company that can successfully design and build a multibillion-dollar ICBM network or a series of nuclear submarines has a very different capability from that of the soap, steel, toy, or other typical cost-conscious but low-technology company operating in the commercial economy. The point made here was underscored when a former chief executive of Lockheed Martin, a large and successful defense contractor, was asked by the Russians how to convert a tank-producing facility into one producing refrigerators. His response was to tear down the tank plant and build a new refrigerator factory.[13]

Conclusions

Just as commercial markets are far from uniform, the government market consists of a complex array of changing requirements. Much of this complexity, however, reflects a very special factor not present in other markets, at least not to the same degree: the important role of political decision making. Government purchasing is rarely motivated primarily by economic considerations. There is no ultimate consumer that selects in the marketplace the items that are commercially successful. Rather, governmental decision makers—responding to a variety of domestic and foreign policy concerns—decide the size and composition of the goods and services to be provided to the public.

Moreover, the manner of production and distribution is not immune from political pressures. At least on occasion, major contracts are awarded to specific companies because they are located in the district or state of a powerful legislator. The employment generated by a government construction project likewise can be an important consideration in determining the amount of funds it will be provided—or whether the project is approved at all. In addition, public procurement activities, because they draw on taxpayer dollars, are subject to widespread scrutiny unparalleled in the private sector.

On the other hand, the activities of government agencies do not usually generate the economic incentives for good performance to which private enterprises routinely respond. Thus, the rewards and risks of the government market are quite different from those in normal commercial business.

Following the end of the Cold War, a substantial shift occurred in the composition of government purchases—away from the traditional dominance of federal procurement in favor of outlays by states and localities. For over a decade, the volume of defense acquisitions declined, although they still represented a large absolute amount of government purchasing. In contrast, civilian buying at the state and local levels has come to represent a dominant and rising share of the government market (see Figure 15.3).

Since 2000, government procurements from private industry—especially products destined for the armed services—have been expanding once again. State and local government buying reflects the continued importance of the large, public-sector educational activities extending from kindergarten through graduate school. In contrast, the renewed increase in federal purchasing has been primarily a response to the increased recognition of the threats from international terrorist networks.

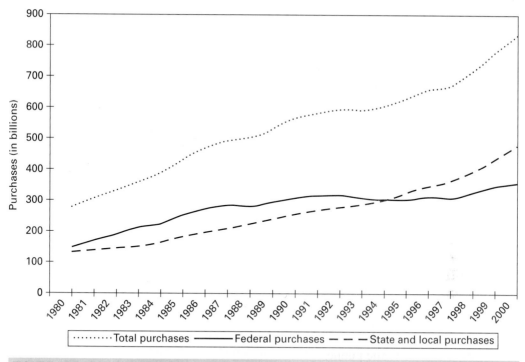

FIGURE 15.3   The Changing Government Market

Source: Computed from U.S. Department of Commerce national income and product account data.

Notes

1. *Budget of the U.S. Government, Fiscal Year 2003* (Washington, DC: U.S. Government Printing Office, 2002), pp. 15–23.

2. Lynn E. Bergeson, "Green Buy Programs: An Important Procurement Factor," *Pollution Engineering*, May 2002, pp. 30–32.

3. Andrew Schneider, "Home Depot Stops Doing Business with Federal Government," *St. Louis Post-Dispatch*, June 16, 2002, p. E11.

4. "Home Depot Reverses Course," *St. Louis Post-Dispatch*, June 29, 2002, p. B8.

5. "Competition from Prison Industries Forces a Company to Close," *New York Times*, August 16, 1998, p. 21.

6. Elaine R. Davis, *Private Solutions for Public Service* (Seattle: Washington Institute Foundation, 1997), p. 14.

7. "Surge in Privatization Boon to Equity Markets," *OECD Letter*, May 1997, p. 5. See also *Bureaucrats in Business* (Washington, DC: The World Bank, 1995).

8. Philip Gold, "Tank Production and a Catch-22," *Insights*, May 14, 1990, p. 22.

9. George Sammet, Jr., and David Green, *Defense Acquisition Management* (Boca Raton, FL: Florida Atlantic University Press, 1990), p. 87.

10. The paperwork required in producing a comparable commercial product, such as a jet airliner, is insignificant by comparison (400 pages).

11. Murray Weidenbaum, "The U.S. Defense Industry After the Cold War," *Orbis*, Fall 1997, pp. 591–601.

12. Leo Reddy, *How U.S. Defense Industries View Diversification* (Washington, DC: Center for Strategic and International Studies, 1991), p. 27.

13. Norman R. Augustine, "The Real Dividend Is Peace," *World Link*, May–June 1990, p. 22.

16

BUSINESS AND
TAX POLICY

‹‹‹⦿⦿⦿›››

Business acts as the major tax collector for government, directly paying the taxes on business sales and earnings and withholding and transmitting the great bulk of the income and employment taxes on individuals. In the process, business also generates much of the data flow needed for the operation of social insurance systems such as Social Security and unemployment compensation.

In turn, taxation influences business decision making in many ways. To a substantial degree, governments act as "partners" in sharing a significant fraction of corporate profits in the form of taxes. The indirect effects of the government's revenue collection are less measurable but are extensive, insofar as companies change their methods of operation so as to minimize their tax burdens or to take advantage of incentives in the Internal Revenue Code.

Federal tax policy encourages employers in powerful ways to provide pensions and health insurance to their employees. If they do so pursuant to law and regulation, their expenditures are tax deductible. Should the employees finance similar benefits on their own, however, they must do so in the main out of their after-tax incomes. Moreover, employer payments of health insurance in behalf of their workers are not considered taxable income to the beneficiaries. As a result, in large measure, of these incentives (positive and negative) generated by the income tax system, employers have become the major suppliers of medical and retirement insurance and benefits. This relationship is taken for granted as customary procedure in the United States, but it is not followed in most other advanced industrialized nations.

In recent years, federal tax and accompanying regulatory policies, unintentionally or otherwise, have encouraged companies to change the fundamental nature of the pension plans they provide their employees. As noted in Chapter 6, the paperwork and regulatory burdens have encouraged many employers to abandon traditional "defined benefit" plans in favor of the 401(k) defined contribution approach. Moreover, in order to subsidize underfunded pension plans, the Pension Benefit Guaranty Corporation—established under the Employee Retirement Income Security Act (ERISA)—has been raising the special tax it levies on covered pension plans. Thus, the financially healthy companies that fully fund their pension programs wind up either subsidizing those in poor financial shape or shifting to the relatively unregulated defined contribution plans.[1]

The collection of revenues by government generates a great variety of impacts on business and reactions by business firms. The cash flow between the public and private sectors is substantial. In the fiscal year ending September 30, 2001, corporations paid into the U.S. Treasury $151 billion in income taxes. In addition, business firms paid $330 billion as the employer contribution to Social Security and related government-sponsored retirement programs, and $28 billion to finance unemployment compensation benefits. As agents of the Internal Revenue Service, business firms also paid

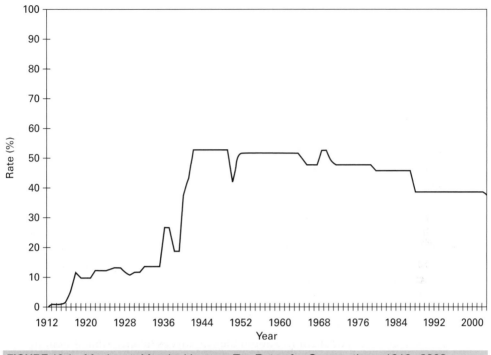

FIGURE 16.1   Maximum Marginal Income Tax Rates for Corporations, 1912–2002

Source: U.S. Internal Revenue Service.

$85 billion in selective sales taxes (excises on such items as beer, cigarettes, and gasoline) and customs duties.

But it is not just a matter of financing a steadily rising stream of business payments to government. Tax rates are changed frequently (see Figure 16.1), and business has to adjust to each of those shifts as well as the frequent changes in the structure of the revenue system. Based on recent experiences, a cynic might conclude that the natural tendency of the Congress is to change the tax system frequently. In the years when the two tax-writing committees of Congress (the Senate Finance Committee and the House Ways and Means Committee) consider major tax reforms, the members of the committees receive substantial campaign contributions from a variety of political action committees. It would be naive to expect such large-scale financial assistance to continue if the Finance and Ways and Means Committees stopped reporting out new tax legislation.

BUSINESS RESPONSES TO TAXATION

The revenue paid to government does not measure the full impacts of the tax system on business. Although official data are not available on the various indirect costs of business compliance with the tax system, there is good reason to believe they are substantial. The cost of complying with the federal corporate income tax can be viewed as the equivalent of a large surtax. Economist Arthur P. Hall of the Tax Foundation estimates that the average annual compliance cost rises from $7,400 for a corporation with assets of $1 million to $500,000 for a $500 million firm to $3 million for a company with the asset size of $10 billion. In relative terms, the proportional burden falls hardest on the smaller companies and eases as the size of the corporation increases. As is the case with regulation, there are economies of scale in complying with governmental directives.[2]

From a somewhat positive viewpoint, compliance with governmental tax systems has generated the market for a specialized industry. Hundreds of thousands of tax lawyers, accountants, and other professionals assist over 7 million individual and self-employed taxpayers in complying with federal tax law. A few measures of compliance indicate the magnitude of the tax reporting effort. Businesses and financial institutions send the Internal Revenue Service (IRS) annually over 1 billion informational returns to report wages, interest, dividends, and other income payments. Each year employers also transmit to the IRS over 30 million employment tax returns. In the process, business taxpayers and their advisers deal with over 2,800 pages of federal tax law and about 9,000 pages of tax regulations—plus many thousands of IRS letter rulings and technical advice memoranda.[3]

CHANGES IN BUSINESS PRACTICES

Companies often shift their ways of doing business in order to respond to various provisions of the Internal Revenue Code. As noted earlier, employer contributions to employee pension plans are tax deductible, providing they meet the requirements of the ERISA. Many firms devote considerable resources, including performing costly actuarial studies, to ensure their conformance with the variety of rules and regulations.

In order to receive special tax credits for the costs of hiring people with low-level skills, companies must employ members of designated "disadvantaged groups." To assure the tax deductibility of entertainment and other business deductions, many companies have had to change their accounting systems in order to provide adequate documentation to meet the standards of the IRS.

To maximize their use of the tax credit for research and development (R&D) equipment, some firms have taken a new look at their existing classification systems for distinguishing between equipment used for R&D and that devoted to manufacturing. As a result, there has been considerable debate as to whether the tax credit has resulted in real growth in business R&D outlays. In the aggregate, the data indicate that company outlays for science and technology are somewhat higher than they would have been in the absence of the credit, but only modestly. Part of the problem has been the unwillingness of Congress to extend the credit for more than a few years at a time. A permanent tax credit for R&D would be more cost-effective, with firms able to make long-term plans on the basis of availability of the credit. The response to a temporary change in the tax credit is estimated to be only about one-half of the reaction to a permanent change.[4]

The sums involved in tax-incentive provisions often warrant substantial business expense and change in order to qualify. Table 16.1 shows the tax savings arising from a variety of special federal tax provisions used by U.S. corporations. In the fiscal year

TABLE 16.1   Federal Tax Incentives for Business, Fiscal Year 2003 (Cost to the Treasury, Billions of Dollars)

Type of Benefit	Amount (Billions)
Overseas operations	
Deferral of overseas income	$7.4
Exclusion of foreign sales income	4.8
Special treatment of inventories	1.4
Subtotal	$13.6
Science and technology	
Expensing of research and experimentation	2.0
Credit for increasing research	2.9
Subtotal	$4.9
Energy—various incentive provisions	$0.9
Natural resources and environment	
Special treatment of mining and timber	0.6
Special treatment of other natural resources	0.3
Subtotal	$0.9
Commerce and housing	
Benefits to financial and insurance institutions	3.0
Housing investment incentives	3.9
Machinery and equipment investment incentives	2.8
Lower tax rate on smaller companies	6.5
Credit for low-skill-level jobs	0.2
Special ESOP rules	1.0
Tax credit for business conducted in U.S. possessions	2.5
Miscellaneous investment incentives	0.8
Subtotal	$20.7
Exclusion of interest	
On industrial development bonds	7.2
On bonds for education	0.3
On bonds for hospitals	0.3
Subtotal	$7.8
Total	$48.8

Source: U.S. Office of Management and Budget.

2003, those tax benefits are estimated to cost the Treasury $48.8 billion. To some extent, however, that is an overstatement of their real cost to the government.

Some of the special tax provisions, notably the investment incentives, encourage economic growth and result in a larger overall tax base, thus creating a positive feedback effect on Treasury receipts. In other cases, such as the tax benefits for scientific activities, the federal government's role is incremental—most of the costs are borne by the private companies doing the research and development. In the absence of the tax provisions, pressure would mount for Congress to enact larger appropriations to fund such scientific activities directly.

POLITICAL RESPONSES

Yet another type of business response to taxation is more political than economic. Because of the large amounts of money involved in governmental revenue matters, many companies find it advisable to participate in the political arena in which tax legislation is developed. As will be shown in Chapter 17, larger companies tend to establish their own offices in Washington, D.C., to represent their interests. Other firms, large and small, work through their trade associations or hire law firms or other lobbying groups as the need arises. Because direct corporate support of federal candidates is illegal, many companies have developed other channels, such as establishing political action committees (PACs) to raise funds from their executives to support individual candidates. These PACs provide political contributions to candidates who may be sympathetic to the firm's positions on public-policy issues (see Chapter 19 for details on these activities).

As a general proposition, business is more effective in obtaining a special tax break for a firm or industry than in influencing the general course of federal fiscal policy.[5] There is no shortage in the federal tax code of "goodies" for individual companies and industries—and for nonprofit institutions as well. Listed below is a sampler of the beneficiaries of special provisions. In accord with customary congressional etiquette, the names of the recipients are disguised in the statute by euphemisms:

- "A paint and glass project which was approved by the management committee of a company on September 11, 1985."
- "Rental property which was assigned FHA number 023-36602."
- A project that was "the subject of law suits filed on June 22, 1984 and November 21, 1985."
- "Any taxpayer incorporated in September 7, 1978, which is engaged in the trade or business of manufacturing dolls and accessories."
- "A corporation which was incorporated on December 29, 1969 in the State of Delaware. . . ."
- ". . . 10 warehouse buildings built between 1906 and 1910 and purchased under a contract dated February 17, 1926."
- A company that entered into a binding contract "on October 3, 1984, for the purchase of 6 semi-submersible units at a cost of $425,000,000."[6]

Business hardly presents a monolithic position on the typical revenue bill. In the case of the 1986 Tax Reform Act, a powerful coalition of firms initially lined up in opposition, including Alcoa, AT&T, Caterpillar, Dow Chemical, DuPont, Exxon, Ford, Rockwell International, Texas Instruments, and Weyerhaeuser. Simultaneously, an equally prestigious group of corporations favored the tax reform bill: Allied-Signal, Dart & Kraft, General Mills, General Motors, IBM, Levi Strauss, 3M, PepsiCo, Philip Morris, Procter & Gamble, R. J. Reynolds, and Sara Lee.

However, by the time Congress was getting ready to enact the final version, most vocal business groups jumped on the tax-reform bandwagon. Their motives varied from not wanting to be seen as sore losers to trying to insert specific provisions in the bill to help their company or industry. The debate on tax increases in 1993 revealed a similar split in the business community. The wood products company Champion International favored the House of Representatives version because it would provide some relief to companies subject to the alternative minimum tax. Yet Weyerhaeuser, another wood products company, supported the Senate bill because it dropped the broad-based energy tax contained in the House version.[7]

FUTURE CHANGES IN THE U.S. TAX SYSTEM

The prospects for reform of the federal tax system ebb and flow. Specific proposals become hot issues, only to cool, at least for a while. Looming on the horizon are proposed taxes on carbon emissions (users of fossil fuels) or on energy in general to deal with the issue of global climate change (see Chapter 4). Another emerging issue in tax policy is how to tax business transactions conducted on the Internet (see box, "Taxing E-Commerce").

SHIFTING TO CONSUMPTION AS A TAX BASE

The most basic change in the nation's revenue structure would be to introduce a new form of federal tax, one levied on consumption instead of income. For years, economists have debated the respective merits of income and consumption as the basis for

---

BOX 16-1

TAXING E-COMMERCE

A congressional moratorium on taxing sales on the Internet has postponed but not eliminated the debate on how to gear the U.S. tax structure to changing technology. The ban on new Internet taxation does not prohibit state governments from enacting and trying to collect sales taxes (called *use taxes*) on out-of-state Internet purchases by their residents—providing the rates are the same as in-state "brick-and-mortar" purchases and in-state purchases on the Internet.

Opponents of taxing e-commerce contend that subjecting business on the Internet to taxation during its formative period could reduce the prospects for its ultimate widespread use. In view of the cross-border nature of e-commerce, it is also feared that a race by state governments to maximize their revenues from this new economic activity would be both disruptive and generate further complexity in the already complicated process of tax collection.

On the other side of the controversy, conventional brick-and-mortar retailers believe that it is unfair to base the decision to tax a purchase solely on whether or not it is made through a conventional sales outlet. From their point of view, exempting e-commerce purchases and sales from taxation would give these newcomers an unfair competitive advantage.

This controversy also illustrates the difficulty of reconciling policy and practice. In theory, if a state has a sales tax on consumer purchases of furniture, citizens of the state should pay the tax on new purchases whether those purchases were from a furniture store down the block or from an out-of-state supplier selling on the Internet. In practice, it is much easier for the state revenue department to collect the tax via the furniture store than through trying to monitor the whole gamut of electronic transactions.

Some researchers have suggested that a fair and effective way of responding to this situation is to shift from the current system of bottom-up, transaction-based sales taxes to top-down, return-based consumption taxes (similar to the familiar annual income tax returns). Such a fundamental shift in the revenue system might generate a variety of beneficial changes, including the substitution of consumption for income as the basis for taxation[8] (see section, "Taxes on Consumed Income or Expenditures").

TABLE 16.2 Consumption Taxes As a Percentage of Total Taxation
in Selected Countries, 1998

Country	Percentage	Country	Percentage
Australia	8.5	Luxembourg	13.7
Austria	18.7	Mexico	19.4
Belgium	15.3	The Netherlands	16.9
Canada	14.0	New Zealand	26.0
Czech Republic	17.1	Norway	21.3
Denmark	19.6	Poland	20.8
Finland	18.5	Portugal	23.3
France	17.5	Spain	16.6
Germany	17.9	Sweden	13.6
Hungary	23.5	Switzerland	10.0
Iceland	28.9	Turkey	30.0
Ireland	22.2	United Kingdom	18.7
Italy	14.2	United States	7.6
Japan	8.9		
		Average	17.9

Source: Organization for Economic Cooperation and Development.

taxation. The United States uses consumption taxation to a far lesser degree than most other developed Western nations. In 1998, the members of the Organization for Economic Cooperation and Development obtained an average of 18 percent of their revenue from taxes on consumption (see Table 16.2). For the United States, however, the ratio was under 8 percent, less than half of the OECD average.

In recent years, the traditional preference for income-based taxation has eroded. A poll of macroeconomists at 15 U.S. universities reported that 63 percent favored "a fundamental reform of the American tax system towards a consumption tax," with only 37 percent opposed.[9] Tax experts have devised, and criticized, a variety of specific consumption-based taxes. No consensus, however, has been reached on the details. It is likely that two interrelated clusters of issues—the general desirability of a tax on consumption and the specific form that it should take—will receive increased public attention in the years ahead. The following sections of this chapter deal with these matters, which could have substantial impacts on private business firms.

Many analysts believe that taxing people on the portion of society's output that they consume is fairer than taxing them on what they contribute by working and investing. In the nineteenth century, classical economist John Stuart Mill made this point in advocating the exemption of saving as part of a "just" income tax system. In the 1940s, American economist Irving Fisher argued that the income tax involved double taxation of saving and distorted the choice of individuals in favor of consumption. Thus, not only is the income tax unjust, it encourages consumption and leisure at the expense of thrift and enterprise.

The U.S. Treasury actually proposed a "spendings tax" in 1942 as a temporary wartime measure to curb inflation. The proposal was quickly rejected by Congress. A major argument against the expenditure tax—then and now—is that the exemption of saving would favor the rich since they are better able to save large portions of their incomes. Some believe this would lead to greater concentrations of wealth in the hands of a few. Proponents of an expenditure tax respond that it can be made as steeply progressive as desired. Moreover, the trend in income taxation in the United States since 1980 has been away from progressivity and toward a flatter, more proportional revenue structure. The 1981 and 1986 tax statutes are striking cases in point.

Another objection to the consumption base is that it would favor the miser over the spendthrift, even when both have similar spending power or ability to pay. The response offered to this argument is that consumption uses up the resources available to the nation, while saving adds to these resources. Moreover, the fundamental way for an individual to minimize consumption tax liabilities is to consume less; the incentives to work, save, and invest are unimpaired. By contrast, the basic way to minimize the income tax is to earn less, which dampens incentives to work, save, and invest—with deleterious effects on economic growth and living standards.

TAXES ON CONSUMED INCOME OR EXPENDITURES (TOP-DOWN CONSUMPTION TAXES)

In practice, much of the impact of shifting to a consumption tax base would depend on how the tax was structured. The two major categories of alternatives are (1) expenditure (or income) taxes levied on the portion of income not saved (which is conceptually the same as consumption) and (2) sales or value-added taxes collected on individual purchases. In essence, the first category is composed of *top-down* taxes, whereas the latter consists of *bottom-up* taxes. In theory, the base of the two types of taxes is the same—the value of goods and services purchased—and the yields could be very similar. Each of the revised tax systems could be *revenue neutral,* raising as much revenue as the current income tax.

In the top-down category, the two major alternatives are the *flat tax* and the *savings-exempt income tax,* the latter often referred to as the USA tax (for Unlimited Savings Allowance).

The Flat Tax

The key feature of the flat tax is that one rate would be levied on all income above a generous family deduction. In effect, the flat tax would be a form of consumption tax because the returns on saving and investment would not be taxed. The tax would be paid only on wages, salaries, and retirement income. Interest, dividends, and capital gains would be exempt for individual taxpayers based on the justification that adequate taxes had been levied at the business level. Thus, *double taxation* would be avoided. No deductions, however, would be allowed for interest payments, charitable contributions, or state and local taxes.

Companies (and also individuals) would be required to fill out a postcard return form (see Figure 16.2). In its essence, the flat tax would be much simpler than the current income tax. A key reason for the comparative simplicity of the flat tax is the absence of "transition" rules. For example, with the substitution of a flat tax for the current income tax, the holders of municipal bonds (on which the interest is exempt from federal income tax) would experience a substantial reduction in the market value of their portfolios. That is likely because investors buy these low-yielding "munis" for their unique tax-exempt feature—but all interest would be tax-exempt for individuals

Form 2	Business Return (Flat Tax)		2003
Business Name		Employer Identification Number	
Street address		County	
City, state, and ZIP code		Principal product	
1 Gross revenue from sales	1		
2 Allowable costs			
(a) Purchases of goods, services and materials	2a		
(b) Wages, salaries, and retirement benefits	2b		
(c) Purchases of capital equipment, structures, and land	2c		
3 Total allowable costs *(sum of lines 2(a), 2(b), and 2(c))*	3		
4 Taxable income *(line 1 less line 3)*	4		
5 Tax *(19% of line 4)*	5		
6 Carry-forward from 2002	6		
7 Tax due *(line 5 less line 6, if positive)*	7		
8 Carry-forward to 2004 *(line 6 less line 5, if positive)*	8		

FIGURE 16.2   Business Return Under a Flat Tax

under the flat tax. Thus, the loss of this special characteristic would reduce the value of municipal bonds substantially.

Unlike the other variations of consumption taxation, the flat tax on business covers all domestic operations, including domestic sales *and* exports. Likewise, all purchases (including capital equipment) are deducted from taxable revenue *including* imports.[10]

The Savings-Exempt Income Tax

The proposed USA tax (or *consumed income tax,* as technicians often refer to the concept) would be collected much as income taxes now are. The annual taxpayer return would continue to comprise the heart of the collection system, and a rate table accompanying the return could insure as progressive a tax structure as Congress desires. However, one major change would be instituted: The portion of income that is saved would be exempt from taxation—until it was spent.

Figure 16.3 is a hypothetical example of a *short-form* version of a savings-exempt income tax return for an individual taxpayer or family. It shows how the difficult bookkeeping requirement to tally all consumption outlays can be finessed. Basically, it carries out the notion that, if income equals consumption plus saving, consumption can be readily estimated, indirectly but accurately, merely by deducting saving from income.[11]

A companion shift to the adoption of a top-down consumption tax would be the conversion of the corporate income tax to a cash-flow tax on business. A major change—and one that would encourage investment—would be to *expense*, or write off,

---

FIGURE 16.3   A Consumption (or USA) Tax Form

INCOME AND OTHER RECEIPTS	AMOUNTS
1. Wages, salaries, tips, etc.	_____
2. Dividends	_____
3. Interest	_____
4. Rents and royalties	_____
5. Pensions and annuities	_____
6. Net receipts of sole proprietorships	_____
7. Withdrawals from partnerships	_____
8. Receipts from:	_____
a. gifts and bequests	_____
b. insurance	_____
9. Total (add lines 1 through 8)	_____
Saving	
10. Purchases of financial assets	_____
11. Capital contributed to partnerships	_____
12. Net change in bank accounts (plus or minus)	_____
13. Other investments	_____
14. Total (add lines 10 through 13)	_____
15. Gross consumption (subtract line 14 from line 9)	_____
Deductions	
16. a. Itemized deductions	_____
or	
b. Standard deduction	_____
17. Exemptions	_____
18. Total (add lines 16 and 17)	_____
Tax Base	
19. Taxable income (subtract line 18 from line 15)	_____
20. Tax from rate table	_____

all capital investments, such as purchases of production equipment and factories in the year in which they are acquired. At present, these outlays are deductible on the income tax over the useful life of the asset, which is a period of several years or even decades.

In many ways, such a business version of the consumption tax would be simpler than the existing corporate tax. For example, by focusing on cash flows, it would avoid the complicated transfer pricing arrangements under which domestic subsidiaries of foreign corporations minimize their U.S. tax payments (see Table 16.3)

Although these changes may sound quite technical, a top-down consumption tax would be a move toward simplification. In effect, the major substantive change for the individual taxpayer would be to convert the current complicated Individual Retirement Accounts (IRAs) to an unrestricted savings mechanism. The individual taxpayer would decide how much to save and in what form and over what time period.[12] Taxation based on income is by its nature more complicated than extracting revenues from consumption. Income taxation is inherently complex for many reasons. Complicated timing rules are necessary, such as depreciation allowances, capitalization of expenses, and inventory accounting. Inflation distorts the tax base by eroding the value of depreciation allowances and overstating the real value of capital gains. Being based instead on cash flow, taxation of consumption automatically avoids these problems. Of course, simplicity is not inevitable in any tax system. A potentially simple, consumption-based tax can be made complex, just as the present income tax is far more complicated than it needs to be.[13]

In the case of the USA tax, transition rules are provided to avoid taxing consumption that is paid out of income previously taxed. Such a short-term complication—like some others contained in the proposed tax—are designed to maintain fairness among different categories of taxpayers.

Although consumption-based taxation is designed to replace rather than supplement the existing income tax, it could increase federal revenues over a period of time. This would come about from the higher rate of economic growth that could result from the encouragement given to saving and thus to investment. Bottom-up types of sales and value-added tax would likely generate similar effects.

TABLE 16.3   Two Top-Down Reforms of Business Taxation

The Flat Tax	The USA Tax
Allows immediate write-off of all business purchases	Allows immediate write-off of all business purchases
Maintains deduction for employee compensation	Eliminates deduction for employee compensation
Eliminates deductions for employee benefits other than retirement benefits	Eliminates deductions for all employee benefits
Eliminates deduction for employer's share of payroll taxes	Provides tax credit for employer's share of payroll taxes
Interest and dividend income not taxed; interest and dividend expense not deductible	Interest and dividend income not taxed; interest and dividend expense not deductible
"Origin based": exempts imports, taxes exports	"Destination based": exempts exports, taxes imports

SALES AND VALUE-ADDED TAXES
(BOTTOM-UP CONSUMPTION TAXES)

An expenditure or consumption tax, as shown above, can be calculated via a top-down approach, building on the records that are already available to provide the data needed for enforcement of existing corporate and personal income taxes. In contrast, sales and *value-added taxes* (VAT) represent a very different way of collecting a general tax on consumption.

National Sales Tax

On the surface, a national retail sales tax seems like a very simple device for collecting revenues in place of the complicated income tax structure. However, because consumption tends to be a smaller share of income as we go up the income scale, many supporters of the sales tax recognize the need to soften the regressive impact on the poor. The required modifications inevitably introduce complication. The most widely used approach, at the state level, is to exempt categories of purchases on which the poor spend a larger fraction of their income than other citizens, such as food, housing, and medicine. Another proposal is to provide each taxpayer with a "smart card," (similar to a credit card) with credit for sales taxes based on family size. Yet another alternative is to give every taxpayer an automatic standard refund, also based on family size.[14]

A national sales tax levied at the retail level may present special problems for small businesses. Unlike larger companies, which buy from wholesalers or directly from manufacturers, smaller enterprises often make their purchases from the same retailers as do consumers and, therefore, would have to pay the retail sales tax. Problems such as this led France and other Western European nations to move from relatively simple sales taxes to the more sophisticated but complicated VAT.

Because any sales tax (including the VAT) is included in the price of purchases, it registers in all of the price indexes and, hence, exerts an inflationary force on the economy. The counterargument is that this is a one-time effect only, occurring when the tax is enacted or increased and that inflationary impact could be offset by appropriate changes in monetary policy (albeit at times with an adverse effect on the levels of production and employment). A study of 35 countries that introduced a VAT revealed that in only six did the new tax contribute to a faster rate of inflation.[15]

Opponents also charge that either a national sales tax or a VAT would invade the traditional area of sales taxation, that of state and local governments (46 states impose a sales tax). However, most states have come to rely on income taxes, despite heavy use of the same tax base by the federal government.

Turning to administrative aspects, federal imposition of a sales or value-added tax would require establishing a new tax-collection system by the government and new record keeping on the part of taxpayers. However, much of the current tax-collection system could be eliminated (except for the collection of payroll taxes for Social Security and Medicare).

Value-Added Taxes

The VAT is, in effect, a comprehensive sales tax that avoids the double counting otherwise inevitable when the same item moves from manufacturer to wholesaler to retailer. In total, a VAT should be equivalent in yield to a single-stage sales tax levied at

TABLE 16.4   Calculating Value Added in the Production Process

Item	Raw Materials Producer	Manufacturer	Wholesaler	Retailer	Cumulative
Purchases of inputs	—	$100	$500	$800	$1,400
Value added:					
Wages	$60	$275	$200	$100	$635
Rent	10	25	40	50	125
Interest	10	50	25	25	110
Profit	20	50	35	25	130
Total value added	$100	$400	$300	$200	$1,000
Sales of output	$100	$500	$800	$1,000	$2,400

Note: Value added can be estimated in two ways:
1. Deducting purchases from sales of output.
2. Adding inputs by the firm itself (excluding inputs supplied by others).
   Thus, $2,400 − $1,400 = $635 + $125 + $110 + $130 = $1,000.

the retail level. Essentially, a firm's value added is the difference between its sales and its purchases from other firms. As shown in Table 16.4, value added can also be estimated by adding labor and capital inputs supplied by the firm itself—represented by wages and salaries, rent and interest payments, and profit. Although the top-down consumption tax notion remains a theoretical concept, the bottom-up VAT is now an existing tax in many countries.

Proponents of the VAT contend that it is economically neutral because ideally it is levied at a uniform rate on all items of consumption (unless exceptions are made to soften its regressive nature). The VAT does not distort choices among products or methods of production. Thus, shifting to a more capital-intensive and perhaps more profitable method of production does not affect the tax burden. Nor is the allocation of resources across product, market, and industry lines impacted. In these regards, the VAT is superior to the existing array of selective excise taxes.

Advocates of the value-added tax also point out that, in contrast to an income tax, there is no penalty for efficiency and no subsidy for waste. Moreover, the VAT is neutral between incorporated and unincorporated businesses and, theoretically, even between public and private enterprises. By focusing on consumption, it avoids a double tax burden on the returns from capital. This tax starts off with no exclusions or exemptions and thus, at least initially, provides a broader and fairer tax base, one that the underground economy will have more difficulty evading.

Another argument in favor of U.S. adoption of a value-added tax is that so many other nations have adopted this form of revenue.[16] It fits in better than other taxes with the growing international character of production. The VAT has become one of the revenue workhorses of the world. It is a key component of the tax system in over 120 countries, raising about one-fourth of the world's tax revenue. Virtually every important country in Europe imposes this tax, and it has spread throughout the Third World. France has used VAT taxation since 1948, and other members of the European Union have done so since the late 1960s or early 1970s. Canada adopted a 7 percent VAT in 1991.

But, unlike the situation in the United States, the adoption of a tax on value added was true reform in those countries. That is, value-added taxes typically replaced an extremely inefficient form of consumption tax that was already in place: a cascading sales or turnover revenue system. Those latter taxes apply to the total amount of a firm's sales rather than only to its value added. Thus, sales taxes would be paid over and over again on the same items as they moved from firm to firm in various stages of the production process. Cascade-type taxes favor integrated firms (who can legally avoid one or more stages of the tax), but they severely discriminate against independent companies that operate at only one phase of the production process.

An added, widely cited reason for adopting a VAT is the anticipated foreign trade benefits. Unlike an income tax, a sales-based tax can be imposed on goods entering the country and rebated on items leaving—supposedly encouraging exports and discouraging imports. Thus, at first blush, a VAT would seem to help reduce this nation's current large trade deficit. However, most economists believe that fluctuations in exchange rates would largely offset these initial effects and result in little change in the balance of trade.

Opponents of a value-added tax offer an extensive list of shortcomings. They contend that a VAT, as in the case of any consumption-based revenue source, is inherently regressive: Those least able to pay face the highest rates.[17] That regressivity can be softened by exempting food and medicine or by offering refunds to low-income taxpayers, but such variations make the collection of the tax more complicated. They also provide opportunity for people in the underground economy to avoid paying taxes.

A variety of approaches has been suggested for collecting the new tax. The simplest is the credit method (see Table 16.5). Under this approach, the tax is computed initially on a company's total sales, and the firm is given credit for the VAT paid by its suppliers. To a substantial degree, the VAT would be self-enforced. Each company would have a powerful incentive to ensure that its suppliers paid their full share of the tax, because any underpayment would have to be made up by the next firm in the chain of production and distribution.

In practice, the collection of the VAT may not be as simple as outlined here. That would be the case if certain transactions were exempted (such as food) and if nonprofit institutions and government enterprises were treated differently from business firms. Exemptions are no minor matter in terms of the administrative complexity they generate. In France, a long and extensive debate occurred over whether or not Head and

TABLE 16.5 Computing the VAT Using the Credit Method

Item	Raw Materials Producer	Manufacturer	Wholesaler	Retailer
Sales of output	$100	$500	$800	$1,000
Less purchases	0	100	500	800
Value added	$100	$400	$300	$200
Tax on total sales	$10	$50	$80	$100
Credit on purchases	—	10	50	80
Tax liability	$10	$40	$30	$20

Note: Assumes 10 percent VAT on a consumption basis.

TABLE 16.6   Characteristics of Bottom-Up Consumption Taxes

Characteristic	National Sales Tax	Value-Added Tax
Coverage	Retail sales	Sales at every level of business
Tax base	Retail sales price	Value added by each company
Taxpayer	Business	Business
Incidence of tax	Consumer	Consumer

Shoulders antidandruff shampoo was a tax-exempt medicine or a cosmetic subject to the full VAT. (The product is taxable.) Food eaten at a location away from the business at which it was purchased may be tax-exempt. What happens if a McDonald's sets up tables outside of the restaurant?[18]

Contrasting Bottom-Up Taxes

Table 16.6 shows the major differences and similarities between the two major bottom-up consumption taxes. Fundamentally, they are variations on the common theme of focusing taxation at the point that purchases are made.

Conclusions

The four approaches to tax reform analyzed in this chapter—the flat tax, the USA tax, the national sales tax, and the value-added tax—are all variations on the same theme. All would shift the base of federal taxation from income to consumption and also simplify the process of complying with federal tax law. Proponents of consumption taxation believe that, from a macroeconomic viewpoint, each of the four alternatives, by expanding the pool of saving, would increase the rate of capital investment in the economy and thus enhance the prospects for economic growth. In turn, faster economic growth would raise employment opportunities and living standards and also increase the flow of revenues into the U.S. Treasury.

It may not be too surprising that many business leaders advocate a general shift to consumption as the primary tax base, and quite a few endorse one (or more) of the specific approaches to making that fundamental shift. Nevertheless, consumption taxes in general have their critics, especially those concerned about the "distributional" effects. Each of the four approaches would alter the distribution of the federal tax burden by income classes. As noted in this chapter, the bottom-up sales taxes and VAT reforms would require substantial modifications in order to avoid the regressive results that many fear. Also, the allocation of the business tax burden across industries would be different under each of the alternatives. As a general proposition, capital-intensive firms catering to industrial markets tend to favor consumption taxes. Labor-intensive companies, and especially those serving consumer markets, are far less enthusiastic, and many are quite hostile to the entire approach.

The flat tax is the simplest of the top-down reforms of the federal income tax. Its critics are concerned with the potential capital losses to homeowners and investors in state and local bonds that would arise from the absence of transition rules. Also, the reduction in the tax burden on upper incomes (those earning over $100,000 a year) is troublesome to those who give greater weight to "fairness" than to economic performance.

The USA tax, in contrast, maintains the progressive nature of the current federal tax system while shifting the tax base from income to consumption. As a result, however, it is much more complicated than the flat tax. Because all saving is exempt, the top tax brackets on consumption are higher than the current rate table in order to maintain revenue neutrality.

The national sales tax is the simpler of the bottom-up tax reforms. For most individual taxpayers, it would eliminate the need for dealing with the Internal Revenue Service. Responding to the concerns about "regressivity," however, would introduce new complexity. Establishing a separate collection system for this tax raises administrative issues.

The value-added tax, well-known around the world, is the most sophisticated sales-based revenue approach. It would eliminate the worry that small business would be treated less favorably (as in the sales tax case). However, in common with the USA tax, it is a complex concept to explain to the average taxpayer. Like the sales tax, it raises difficult questions about fairness (e.g., regressivity) and would require a new method of collection.

It typically takes several years for Congress to consider and enact a comprehensive tax reform. In the process, numerous changes are usually made in the original proposals on which it holds hearings. Some tax analysts believe that some combination of the four approaches to consumption taxation is likely to emerge—in the form of a tax that is flatter than the current income tax (but not flat), that defers taxation on much saving (but not all), and that is somewhat simpler than the status quo (but still filled with all sorts of complexities).

One of the continuing shortcomings of tax policy is that, like other areas of government, decisions tend to be made in isolation, ignoring the impacts of other governmental policies (see Appendix, "Tax Incentives and Other Promotion of Industry," for a sample of the range of aids to business).

APPENDIX

TAX INCENTIVES AND OTHER PROMOTION OF INDUSTRY

The United States conducts a variety of activities influencing business performance and does so in an uncoordinated manner. There is a long history of government intervention in individual industries rather than a comprehensive generalized policy of aid to business. The typical federal action arose from a specific desire to enhance the performance of a particular part of the economy. Some aids to business reflect the concern over the adequacy of the defense production base; other measures respond to the desire to aid small business; still others are designed to strengthen the nation's maritime position. As shown in Table 16.7, federal support of business presently covers

TABLE 16.7   Types of Federal Support of Business

Industry or Sector Benefited	Type of Federal Support
	Tax incentives
Investment	Liberalized depreciation system
Small business	Lower rates on corporate income
New technology	Expensing of research and development
Energy companies	Tax incentives for new energy sources
Pollution control	Issuance of tax-exempt bonds
Mining	Rapid write-offs of costs
Shipping companies	Deferral of income tax
Pharmaceutical companies	Tax credit for orphan drug research
	Credit subsidies
Exports	Export–Import Bank loans
Small business	Small Business Administration loans
Companies in rural areas	Rural electrification loans
Housing	Credit via Fannie Mae and FHA and VA loan guarantees
Defense contractors	Progress payments and foreign military sales credits
	Direct expenditure subsidies
Aerospace companies	Aeronautical research and technology
Waterborne companies	Coast Guard assistance
Energy companies	Research and development contracts
Mining companies	Stockpile purchases
Companies in urban areas	Community development grants
	Indirect procurement subsidies
Shipbuilders	Prohibition on building navy vessels in foreign shipyards
Ship operators	Bar military from using foreign-owned vessels
Construction companies	Preference for U.S. firms in building overseas diplomatic facilities
Clothing and fiber producers	Limiting Department of Defense to domestic sources
Twine producers	Limiting Forest Service to domestic sources
Companies in "labor-surplus areas"	Providing preference in federal procurement
Small business	Requiring a "fair" portion of government contracts to go to small business
U.S. manufacturers generally	Buy-American Act provides preference to domestic sources in government purchases

a wide variety of tax incentives, credit assistance, expenditure subsidies, and indirect aid, using the powers of the federal government enumerated in Chapter 1.

Because these programs were enacted in isolation, they often work at cross-purposes to other governmental efforts. Export financing promotes overseas business, while export controls inhibit the same activities. Many subsidy programs, notably to mining and other extractive industries, encourage the wasteful use of resources and otherwise degrade the environment, offsetting the hard-earned benefits of EPA regulation.[19]

Although government aid has at times enhanced the international competitiveness of individual American industries, much of it has been provided to achieve other objectives, mainly by responding to the needs of articulate pressure groups. The numerous buy-American statutes are barely disguised efforts to protect powerful economic interests that do little to enhance the competitiveness of the companies that benefit.

Notes

1. Gregory Acs and Eugene Steurle, "The Corporation As a Dispenser of Welfare and Security," in Carl Kaysen, ed., *The American Corporation Today* (New York: Oxford University Press, 1996), p. 373.

2. Arthur P. Hall, "Accounting Costs, Another Tax," *Wall Street Journal,* December 9, 1993, p. A14.

3. Chris Edwards, *Tax Complexity Factbook* (Washington, DC: U.S. Congress, Joint Economic Committee, 2000), pp. 2–4.

4. Bronwyn Hall, *R and D Tax Policy During the Eighties: Success or Failure* (Cambridge, MA: National Bureau of Economic Research, 1992).

5. This may reflect a more general problem for the business community, the tendency for individual companies to free ride "public goods" that benefit business in general and to concentrate their resources on "private goods" (gains limited to their company or industry).

6. Not all of the tax breaks go to business. Other beneficiaries include a "state which ratified the United States Constitution on March 29, 1790," and "a university established by charter granted by King George II of England on October 31, 1754."

7. Rick Wartzman, "Companies Try to Decide Which Version to Support," *Wall Street Journal,* June 28, 1993, p. A10.

8. Stephen J. Entin, *Tax Reform to Handle the E-Tax Controversy* (Washington, DC: Institute for Research on the Economics of Taxation, 2000); Murray Weidenbaum, "The Fundamental Internet Tax Debate," *Washington Quarterly,* Winter 2001, pp. 41–52.

9. "Economists for Clinton," *The Economist,* October 5, 1996, p. 27.

10. Robert Hall and Alvin Rabushka, *Flat Tax* (Stanford, CA: Hoover Institution Press, 1995).

11. David F. Bradford, "An Uncluttered Income Tax: The Next Reform Agenda?" in Gerhard Fels and George Von Furstenberg, eds., *A Supply-Side Agenda for Germany* (Berlin: Springer-Verlag, 1989), pp. 379–398.

12. Murray Weidenbaum, "The Nunn–Domenici USA Tax," in Michael J. Boskin, ed., *Frontiers of Tax Reform* (Stanford, CA: Hoover Institution Press, 1996), pp. 54–69.

13. Charles E. McLure, Jr., and George R. Zodrow, "A Hybrid Approach to the Direct Taxation of Consumption," in Boskin, ed., *Frontiers of Tax Reform,* p. 71.

14. For more esoteric approaches, see Lawrence J. Kotlikoff, "Saving and Consumption Taxation," in Boskin, *Frontiers of Tax Reform,* p. 171.

15. Alan A. Tait, ed., *Value-Added Tax: Administrative and Policy Issues* (Washington, DC: International Monetary Fund, 1992).

16. Liam Ebrill et al., "The Allure of the Value-Added Tax," *Finance and Development,* June 2002, pp. 44–47.

17. Some economists contend that, although the ratio of consumption to income declines with respect to annual income, there is little decline in relation to long-term average income.

18. Gregory Ballentine, "The Administrability of a Value-Added Tax," in Charls E. Walker and Mark A. Bloomfield, eds., *The Consumption Tax* (Cambridge, MA: Ballinger Publishing Co., 1987), p. 297.

19. Murray Weidenbaum, Christopher Douglass, and Michael Orlando, "How to Achieve a Healthier Environment and a Stronger Economy," *Business Horizons,* January–February 1997, pp. 9–16.

PART V

THE BUSINESS RESPONSE

Because so much is at stake, private firms at times devote substantial amounts of resources to influencing the public-policy environment, as well as complying with the many government policies and rules. Part V analyzes the major ways in which businesses respond to government actions that affect them, ranging from making changes in their internal organizations to more actively participating in political campaigns.

17

BUSINESS – GOVERNMENT RELATIONS

Virtually every company has developed some capability to understand current and future developments in government and public policy as they relate to its activities—and to adjust and respond to these developments. Expansions in staff functions, notably human resources and finance, often constitute the most direct company response to the rising role of government in business decision making. Many firms also have increased their resources devoted to other staff activities, especially public relations and government affairs. Many larger companies also establish a Washington office and units to deal with state, local, foreign, and international governments.

REVISED RESPONSIBILITIES AND ORGANIZATIONAL STRUCTURES

Senior executives of the largest corporations are devoting substantial amounts of their time—often one-fourth or more—to problems stemming from external factors. Two or three decades ago, they could focus virtually all of their attention on the nuts and bolts of the business. The emphasis was mainly internal: how to improve efficiency to cut costs while improving quality in order to be more competitive. With a few exceptions, even the outward focus was mainly on the state of competition in the markets for the company's products. Today, these matters are still fundamental, but on occasion they are matched in terms of top management's time by a changing array of forces from outside the company and its markets.

The senior managements of major companies recognize that noneconomic factors can be as potent in fashioning corporate behavior as are economic forces. They generally accept the view that the worst possible strategy is to take positions that would be perceived by the public as unresponsive if not downright opposed to important societal interests. They believe that a strong and viable business system will not exist in a society where a majority of the public view the interests of the business corporation as being in opposition to the social interests of the public. Most large corporations are substantial supporters of the various trade associations, think tanks, and other organizations that are heavily engaged in the public-policy arena.

Senior corporate executives often list four external areas that take substantial shares of their time:

- Meeting with elected officials, say, to discuss specific provisions of a tax bill scheduled for hearings and likely passage—or to oppose a pending reduction in the loans to business by the Export–Import Bank.

- Carrying on a dialogue with regulatory personnel—in the EPA, FDA, OSHA, and so on, depending on the products the company produces and the markets in which it is active.
- Maintaining relations with the corporation's various constituencies—employees, suppliers, shareholders, unions, local civic organizations, and a bewildering variety of public-interest groups.
- Overseeing the company's communications with the public, including a substantial amount of time spent in speech making to business, academic, and professional societies.

In general, the CEO tends to concentrate on external aspects, long-term planning, and basic policy, and the chief operating officer (COO)—usually the president—focuses on day-to-day managerial functions. But the typical pattern is not a clean split. The successful CEO is not divorced from the current management of the company, nor is the COO ignorant of broader corporate and national concerns.

To deal with the increasing array of government involvement, many companies have found it necessary or at least desirable to revamp their organizational structures. Initially, these changes have been modest, such as expanding the Washington office or establishing company interdepartmental committees on job safety, consumer affairs, or environmental compliance. The growth of public-interest groups (often with an antibusiness orientation) is another factor that has encouraged business firms to expand their government liaison staffs (see Table 17.1).

In some cases, more substantial changes have been made. For example, a head-quarters office on government relations is established, with direct ties to each of the operating departments. These offices may be involved in such company actions as introducing new products, making major price changes, and deciding the location of new facilities. The government affairs office frequently works with Washington law firms, public-policy consultants, think tanks, and trade associations.

Traditionally, the strategy of most companies has been to maintain a low profile in public affairs and a predictably negative position against most government initiatives affecting business. The rise of regulation and the simultaneous decline in public confidence in business have convinced a significant portion of corporate executives that such strategies are no longer appropriate. The prevailing approach is often the reverse. It is one of active involvement in the public-policy process and launching new initiatives to communicate with the various publics with which business interacts.

TABLE 17.1   Functions of a Government Relations Department

- Legislative monitoring and analysis (federal, state, and local governments)
- Regulatory agency liaison and response
- International legislative monitoring and analysis (other nations, UN, EU, World Bank)
- Domestic and international market development assistance
- Trade association and coalition liaison
- Government appointment assistance
- Political analysis and response
- Government information services
- Relations with think tanks and public-interest groups

When he was chief executive of General Electric, Reginald Jones stated that the CEO, as designated leader of the corporation, must participate actively in the formation of public policy affecting business. His conclusion was that the time was well spent, not only in alerting the company to economic problems, but also in terms of positive customer, investor, and employee relations. As he put it, "These duties are part and parcel of the CEO's responsibilities for the strategic direction of the company."[1] In the words of John Hoving, a former senior vice president of Federated Department Stores, "Since this is a democracy becoming more participatory all the time, there is no hope at all that government will leave corporations alone. . . . There is no way in which a corporation can say to the political world: 'Stop! I want to get off!' "[2]

In practice, not every large corporation is active in public-policy matters, nor is every smaller enterprise mute in this area of activity. Companies and their senior executives take turns in serving in leadership positions in business associations—although not every CEO of a top corporation may necessarily get or want a turn. In addition, some companies still take an accommodating view toward the rising role of government in business decision making. They prefer to negotiate the best available deal, hoping to convey an image of "social responsibility."[3] The managements merely add compliance responsibilities to the functional jobs of general or line managers. Other firms take a composite position, whereby the senior management assumes a more active role in public policy and the operating managements concentrate on meeting government-imposed requirements.

REPRESENTATIVES TO GOVERNMENT

Many companies—foreign and domestic—find it useful to maintain a continuing presence in Washington, D.C., as well as in other national capitals. One side effect of the global economy is that companies do business in many nations and thus are affected by the public policies in a great variety of governmental jurisdictions. These range from the United Nations (UN) to regional governments, such as the European Union (EU), to individual countries and to states (or provinces) and localities in many geographical areas.

The specialized agencies of the UN take a substantial interest in economic issues and attract lobbying efforts by a variety of interest groups—representing consumers, labor, and business. Examples include the International Labor Organization issuing directives on working conditions, the World Health Organization developing a code on infant nursing formulas, the International Telecommunications Union generating rules governing cross-border communications, the International Maritime Organization dealing with shipping codes, and the World Intellectual Property Organization protecting patents and copyrights across borders.

At the UN agencies, the category of *nongovernmental organization* (NGO) is very specialized, and does not include every organization that is not a part of government. NGO is also a highly desirable designation because a certified NGO can attend many UN meetings and conferences. While it is relatively easy for environmental and consumer groups to become NGOs, few business associations qualify, and as a general rule individual business firms are unable to participate in the process.

In the United States, firms of substantial size generally have full-time Washington offices; smaller companies rely primarily on their trade associations as well as on

Washington-based attorneys and consultants. The permanent Washington representative is no longer limited to the major government contractors (such as aerospace and electronics companies) or the closely regulated industries (such as chemicals and automotive manufacturing).

Most large corporations maintain full-time representation. Major government contractors traditionally have maintained representation in Washington, and many commercially oriented firms, including medium-sized ones, have established a permanent presence in the capital. The expansion of government involvement in business has led to "protective reaction" on the part of companies that historically have had little knowledge of or direct relationship with the federal government.

Over 500 companies currently have on-the-scene Washington representation compared with only about 100 in the 1970s. Their offices vary from one to two people plus a secretary to substantial operations with annual budgets of $1 million or more. Sometimes it takes a painful public-policy experience to get a company to invest in setting up a Washington office. Bridgestone/Firestone had no significant representation in the nation's capital in 2000. A year later, following the costly product recall described in Chapter 3, the company spent over $5 million in lobbying activities. Similarly, Microsoft traditionally boasted of its minimal D.C. representation (one lobbyist)—until the Department of Justice launched a major antitrust case against the company in 1998. Now the company has an annual government affairs budget estimated at "tens of millions" of dollars.[4]

Some companies, however, curtail their governmental representation, especially when under financial pressure. In recent years, J.C. Penney and Lucent Technology closed their Washington offices, while AT&T and Hewlett-Packard reduced the budget for theirs.[5]

The typical corporate office in Washington employs 8 to 12 persons and is headed by an officer at the vice-presidential level. For a variety of reasons (including real estate costs and the locations of key government agencies), not all Washington offices are now located in Washington, D.C., itself. Many have moved to the northern Virginia suburbs, and some have relocated to nearby Maryland.

Activities of Washington offices vary substantially, according to the industry and markets served, the size of the firm, and tradition (see Table 17.2). One company compares its Washington office to an embassy in that it follows and interprets actions of the federal government that have significant impact on it, helps to formulate positions on those actions, and serves as the principal channel for communicating the company's views to the government. Most Washington-based government relations offices are in daily touch with the company's headquarters and other parts of their firms. The world of the larger government relations office goes beyond its own corporate clientele, often extending to suppliers, grassroots organizations, and opinion leaders. Its responsibilities often cover state governments and the international arena.

In general, three primary functions are performed by company offices located in Washington, D.C., and other national capitals:

1. Supplying information to the home office on actions taken or contemplated by government.
2. Assisting in obtaining government contracts.
3. Providing representation before legislative and regulatory bodies.[6]

TABLE 17.2   Factors Affecting Size of Washington Offices

Size of firm (e.g., automobile manufacturers)
- Direct representation by most larger firms
- Economies of scale and variety of interests
- Greater public exposure

Importance of government markets (e.g., aerospace companies)
- Day-to-day contract administration function
- Market intelligence and forecasting
- Support base for sales efforts

Extent of regulation (e.g., chemical firms)
- Day-to-day dealings with regulatory agencies
- Desire to influence regulatory climate—through Congress and the media

Concern of management (e.g., petroleum corporations)
- Level of civic awareness or concern with national policy

Degree of public exposure (e.g., conglomerates)
- Defensive—to counteract adverse media and congressional attention
- Offensive—to obtain great public exposure for government marketing purposes and as institutional advertising

SUPPLYING INFORMATION

Virtually all corporate offices in Washington and other national capitals provide a listening post for the home office. A constant flow of information is supplied to company officials on current government policies and on future plans and actions that might affect the organization's operations. Although trade associations and industry publications are useful, at times a company's unique concerns can be met best by its own personnel on the scene. Some firms refer to this intelligence function as an "early warning" system. It is the most time-consuming activity of the typical corporate office in the nation's capital.

Various communications channels are used. Representatives of some large companies prepare daily newsletters that are sent to senior executives at headquarters and operating divisions. Faxes and e-mail enable the Washington office to contact large portions of the company's managers very quickly when they want to bring an urgent matter to their attention. However, to a large extent information is still passed along by telephone or in person, often to avoid a written record on sensitive matters. The typical Washington office also has day-to-day dealings with members of the government bureaucracy in order to follow up on questions or complaints by company personnel on specific regulatory actions.

A substantial amount of company information and views are also provided to federal agencies. Such a reciprocal relationship helps provide a more cordial welcome to company personnel making inquiries at a federal agency. It can also enhance the weight given to the company's expressed concerns. The more successful governmental representatives also have substantial impacts on company policies and operations. In contrast to the traditional company attitude on public affairs ("If they only saw our side of the story, they would understand"), the representative office can help adapt corporate actions to changing national policies.

Corporate staff members also interact regularly with government and private planning groups and with the numerous public-policy analysis organizations (think tanks) that have been established in the capital cities of most industrialized nations. In the United States, these public-policy research groups range over a wide ideological terrain. On the right, the American Enterprise Institute and the Heritage Foundation represent conservative, free market positions, while the Cato Institute upholds a free market and more libertarian viewpoint. At the center are the Brookings Institution (the granddaddy of Washington think tanks), the Center for Strategic and International Studies, and the Committee for Economic Development. On the left are new organizations, inspired by the successes of the earlier groups, such as the Economic Policy Institute and the Progressive Policy Institute. The Institute for Policy Studies occupies the far left end of the spectrum of D.C.–based policy research organizations. Some of these groups blend research and advocacy.

The success of the major think tanks has encouraged the formation and expansion of a wide variety of more specialized public policy research organizations with which business interacts. These include the Employee Benefits Research Institute, which analyzes fringe benefits; the George Marshall Institute and the Science and Environmental Policy Project, which focus on scientific issues; the Tax Foundation and the Institute for Research and Economics of Taxation, which are devoted to governmental finance; and Citizens for a Sound Economy, which also does grassroots lobbying.

The scope of the government relations function has broadened over the years to include a host of international issues. These range from U.S. government policies on international trade to the treatment of foreign investment by other nations. The change is personified by the experience of a very active Washington business policy analyst: "I remember that when I started out . . . in the 1970s and did corporate briefings on import policy, everyone in the room seemed to get up for a cup of coffee."[7] Today, in contrast, international trade and investment policies are among the key "bread-and-butter" issues of the Washington office.

ASSISTING THE MARKETING FUNCTION

For many company offices in national capitals, marketing is the basic justification of their existence and accounts for the presence of the majority of the personnel assigned to the office. A variety of market research, selling, and contract administration activities are involved. The Washington office often has the responsibility of keeping the company abreast of emerging government product requirements. This information is especially useful in helping engineering departments to get ready to prepare the detailed proposals needed to respond to government invitations to bid on a new product.

Moreover, through such on-the-scene representation, the company often can participate in developing the government specifications for the products that it wants to sell to government agencies. The basic objective is to ensure that the company's products meet government requirements. Such representation also provides advance information on future sales possibilities, as well as the opportunity to qualify company products. In the process, companies learn of and bid on exploratory research and development contracts that the government will be awarding, prior to the actual production phase of a major project. On the more extensive and technical projects, the company will not make the deadline on its submission if it waits until the formal government request for proposals to begin preparing its response.

Although most actual selling is performed by company marketing and engineering personnel assigned to the home office or an operating division, the capital-based staff will often be in a better position to open doors and to maintain day-to-day liaison with governmental research and development and procurement offices and to schedule meetings for company specialists. In addition, by virtue of its location, this office can expedite the numerous and complicated steps involved in government contracting: obtaining the detailed bidding specifications, ensuring attention to company contract proposals, securing the necessary signatures, ensuring company compliance with federal procedural requirements, and expediting payments for work performed.

Some Washington offices also take advantage of their location in developing contacts with the embassies of foreign governments that provide market potential. In turn, those embassies try to open doors in the United States for representatives of business firms in their nations.

REPRESENTATION ("LOBBYING")

The effective Washington office is the focal point of a company's relations with the federal government, serving especially as the principal channel for communicating the company's views on matters of major importance to legislators and executive branch officials. Increasingly, the office keeps in touch with foreign embassies and with international organizations such as the World Bank and the Organization of American States. In good measure, the Washington office is a coordinator, drawing on specialized talents in the company, such as the legal, engineering, and public-affairs staffs. Influencing Washington's largest industry — government — has become the city's second-largest industry. An experienced lobbyist, however, described his function in more negative terms — as a "damage-control operation."

Although many company representatives try to avoid using the term, *lobbying* usually is a primary part of their total function. One experienced company office director, who previously had served as legislative assistant to an influential senator, defines lobbying in very straightforward terms: "Lobbying is a communication with public officials to influence their decisions in a manner harmonious with the interests of the individual or group communicating. . . . A lobbyist's purpose is selfish in the sense that he [or she] seeks to persuade others that his [or her] position is meritorious."[8]

The total lobbying activity includes direct relations with legislative and executive branch officials and, in addition, dealing with the media that abound in national capitals and that influence national agendas. Thus, the Washington office of a large national corporation provides access to key reporters and influential columnists that cannot be readily obtained by senior management located in more remote areas. Similar relationships hold in other national capitals.

Although major public policy issues may dominate the headlines, some of the most effective lobbying focuses on very specialized, relatively minor provisions of laws and regulations. Rather than trying to affect the passage of a major bill or the issuance of a new regulation, much effort is made to exempt a company or industry from a popular new tax or regulation — or to include it in an expenditure program working its way through the legislative process. Thus, ethanol producers wind up supporting (or at least not opposing) a new tax on energy if their industry is exempted from the impact of the statute. In a similar fashion, the Brussels office may try to modify a proposed ruling by the EU to provide the same treatment to European subsidiaries of U.S. firms as is received by European-owned firms.

The Changing Nature of Lobbying

One veteran journalist has remarked, "If all the lobbyists in Washington were crammed into Congress, the lid of the Capitol Dome would pop like a cork."[9] Although their numbers continue to be substantial, the nature of lobbying has changed dramatically from the flamboyant power-play-oriented stereotypes that many people still associate with the term. Today's lobbyist, whether working for a large corporation, a trade association, or a labor union, tends to be a dun-colored organization man or woman who fades easily into the background—and likes it that way. As one highly regarded lobbyist stated, "Visibility is the last thing I need."

The public-policy issues on which companies lobby are increasingly technical in nature and often require high-powered professional analysis in order to obtain serious consideration of their viewpoints. A proposal for reducing the tax rate on capital gains must be bolstered by an examination of the elasticity of federal revenues—to try to show that the revenue loss is minimal or even that total revenues will rise in the period ahead. This type of issue increasingly brings a new set of actors into the lobbying process: accountants, economists, and statisticians.

Thus, a company opposing a higher excise tax on beer or cigarettes will commission a report measuring the high degree of regressivity of such taxes—to demonstrate their unfairness. International trade issues invariably generate a demand for forecasting the macroeconomic impact of increasing (or decreasing) restrictions on foreign commerce—to estimate the effect on jobs and consumer prices.

Proposals for the award of government procurement contracts (for weapon systems, infrastructure, etc.) are bolstered by estimates of the economic impacts on specific regions, especially in terms of the new jobs created. As we have seen, airline mergers have been defended by esoteric theories of antitrust (e.g., by contending that the airline industry operates in "contestable" markets). In the field of regulation, scientists present estimates of the risks present in the environment and the workplace, while economists counter with ranges of the costs of proposals to deal with these matters. As a result, staff-to-staff encounters are far more frequent. It is the rare senator or cabinet secretary who can deal with these technical issues. Typically, the lobbyist's expert will present the findings to the staff experts at the department or congressional committee.

A further complication in analyzing business–government relations is the fact that business is not monolithic in its dealings with the public sector. Some of the roughest battles in government occur between competing industries. Examples in dealing with regulation of financial institutions include investment and brokerage houses versus banks and, within the banking sector, large multistate banks versus small or "country" banks. Similarly, on proposals for federal subsidies, the interests of truckers diverge from those of railroads or companies using the inland waterways. Mutually owned life insurance companies often express very different views on tax legislation than do stockholder-owned life insurance carriers.

On the positive side, business groups often cooperate with nonprofit associations on public-policy matters of mutual interest. For example, high-tech companies join with universities in urging more federal money for research and development. Suppliers of environmental cleanup equipment team up with environmental advocacy groups in supporting stricter clean air and clean water statutes. Nonprofit hospitals and pharmaceutical companies share opposition to proposals to enact price controls on health care.

The limits to the effectiveness of lobbying were dramatically demonstrated in the ramifications of the Enron bankruptcy in late 2001. Despite its earlier successful attraction of the support of political figures (many of whom had received contributions from the company's political action committee), Enron was turned down in all of its requests for help during the period of crisis prior to its bankruptcy.

The related case of Enron's auditor, Arthur Andersen, is also an example of naiveté. Only after it was clear that it was facing scrutiny by the Department of Justice as well as the SEC and congressional committees, did the giant accounting firm hire a bevy of Washington lobbyists and public-relations specialists. That expensive, last-minute spurt of activity did not prevent the government's legal actions, leading to the disintegration of the firm (see Chapter 20 for details).

Variations on the Lobbying Function

Business liaison with the legislative branch can serve both "offensive" and "defensive" functions. The former is designed to get the company's views on pending legislation of special interest across to senators, representatives, their aides, and committee staff members. These efforts often are geared to opposing or amending the flow of government legislation that results in greater public-sector control over business decision making. The defensive function, less widely known, is geared at avoiding embarrassing investigations of and attacks on the company and its executives. This is accomplished by providing additional information, and the "other side of the story," at an early stage of a committee's investigations. Moreover, continuing liaison, although perhaps involving nothing more than an occasional luncheon or cocktail party, helps to soften or even avoid unpleasant encounters by introducing into the situation the natural reluctance to confront one's friends.

When the legislature is actively considering a proposed law vital to the company, the firm's representative office may try to arrange for a corporate officer to be invited to testify, then draft the actual testimony and prepare the officer for hostile questions and public interviews. Much influence on legislative deliberations, however, comes from informal telephone or face-to-face contact in a senator's or representative's office (often with staff members), rather than at a formal committee hearing. *Access* is the most important qualification for a lobbyist—the ability to make contact quickly with key people in government.

Some of the most effective business lobbying occurs with reference to relatively minor provisions of laws or regulations. Thus, the Chemical Specialties Manufacturing Association (CSMA) did not oppose the passage of the Toxic Substances Control Act, but it succeeded in securing special treatment for mixtures of chemicals. Likewise, CSMA, during the deliberations on the Food Quality Protection Act, put its efforts on obtaining special treatment for the special chemicals used by its member firms.

Regulation of Lobbying

Lobbying activities are subject to a modest amount of statutory control in the United States. The basic legal authorization for, and thus protection of, lobbying is found in the First Amendment of the Constitution: "Congress shall make no law . . . abridging . . .

the right of the people . . . to petition the Government for a redress of grievances."
A minimum of restrictive legislation has been enacted since.

Federal regulation of lobbying does not directly restrict the activities of lobbyists but relies primarily on making information on their lobbying activities open to the public. Organizations that solicit or receive money for the principal purpose of lobbying Congress do not have to register. However, they must file quarterly spending reports, detailing how much they devote to influencing legislation. The purposes of lobbying organizations vary from closely focused, such as the groups opposing gun controls, to more general, such as those representing senior citizens favoring higher Social Security and health benefits.

The law requires those hired by someone else for the principal purpose of lobbying Congress to register and to report so that there is public knowledge of their activities. The Lobbying Disclosure Act of 1995 defines a lobbyist very broadly: anyone who is compensated for services that include more than one lobbying contact. Under that law, such individuals are required to register with Congress within 45 days after making a "lobbying contact" with any of a host of federal government officials, including the president, the vice president, heads of departments and agencies, and members of Congress and their staffs.

There are an estimated 17,000 registered lobbyists working in Washington, D.C. Approximately 130 firms receive more than $1 million each in annual lobbying fees.[10] The 1995 law also requires registered lobbyists to disclose semiannually their income, assets, and liabilities and to tell who pays them, how much they are paid, how much they spend on lobbying, and what issues they work on. Inevitably, exceptions are made. In *United States* v. *Harris* (347 U.S. 612, 1954), the Supreme Court held that grassroots lobbying is not subject to federal law. Only direct contact with designated federal officials is covered.

Congress has tried to minimize, if not eliminate, the paperwork burden on people who do very minor amounts of lobbying. Those who spend no more than 20 percent of their time meeting with senior executive branch officials, members of Congress, or their staffs, do not have to disclose the names of their clients and other details on their lobbying activities. Exempt from even having to register as lobbyists are people who are paid $5,000 or less and organizations that use their own employees to lobby and spend no more than $20,000 on those efforts.

Tax-exempt religious organizations also are not subject to the disclosure rules. On the other hand, representatives of U.S. subsidiaries of foreign-owned companies have to register as lobbyists, as do lawyer–lobbyists for foreign entities.[11]

Advising Government

Many companies find it advantageous to provide personnel to serve on governmental advisory committees, although many of these groups are technical rather than policy oriented. Approximately 10,000 business representatives serve on federal advisory committees, far more than any other interest group. Service on these bodies often permits company officials to obtain access to government decision makers.

Representing the corporation to the executive branch of government may involve both attempts to influence future policy and efforts to learn of impending developments and how the company might successfully adjust to them. Viewed in this light, membership on government advisory committees is a desirable form of unpaid public service in that the government becomes aware of a broad array of views prior to taking action.

Advisory committees vary from those dealing with major issues of policy to bodies charged with providing advice on engineering and other technical matters. Virtually all federal agencies have set up one or more public advisory committees. These range from the Department of Defense's prestigious Industry Advisory Council (IAC) to the Business Research Advisory Council (BRAC) of the Bureau of Labor Statistics. The IAC, composed of senior management members of the major defense contractors, advises on Pentagon procurement policy; the BRAC consists of economists, statisticians, and other company specialists who comment on price indexes and other such technical matters. Comparable apparatus exists in other nations and in international agencies (see section, "Lobbying in the Global Marketplace").

Another function of advisory committees is to provide a sounding board or at least a mechanism for the exchange of views by various private-interest groups. The EPA's Clean Air Act Advisory Committee provides a forum for the views of environmental organizations, state and local regulators, business representatives, and academics.

Much depends on the level of representation. In contrast to the staff people who serve on the EPA committee, the Department of Defense has appointed senior management members of major defense contractors and other large industrial corporations to its Industry Advisory Council. That committee provides a major vehicle for the defense industry to present its views to key officials in the Pentagon on such vital questions as changes in departmental regulations and procedures affecting defense contractors.

Lobbying in the Global Marketplace

In lobbying foreign governments, cultural differences can be profound. This was brought home when the author attended an international conference in Tokyo sponsored by Japan's Ministry of Foreign Affairs. Suddenly, all of the Japanese officials at the meeting stood at attention. What could cause that? The prime minister was out of the country and the emperor certainly would not make an appearance. It turns out that the head of the Keidenren, the leading business association, had entered the room! In the United States, the situation tends to be the reverse. Business executives stand when a cabinet officer arrives.

In the case of the European Union (EU), a new type of lobbyist has developed: the EU specialist. More than 3,000 lawyers and other consultants, many of them former EU officials, offer to guide business firms and other organizations through the maze of the Union's bureaus, primarily located in Brussels, the EU's operating headquarters. Social codes differ sharply from those familiar in the United States. Although Americans tend to mix business and pleasure, it is bad form for a European lobbyist to put forward a client's position in a social situation. In another departure from American procedures, the EU regularly subsidizes the lobbying efforts of environmental and consumer groups and other "nongovernmental" organizations. The rationale is that it is important that the NGOs have a voice in the EU decision-making process, even if they lack the financial resources of the companies who maintain regular representation in Brussels.

Over 350 companies have established government affairs offices in Brussels. Of these, 94 are American, the largest number of representatives from any one nation. An indication of the degree of competition present in the public-policy arena is that over 3,000 interest groups are active in the EU's decision-making process. Functioning as a kind of traffic cop, the EU has limited active participation in the meetings of its committees to the companies that have an established European presence. That category includes U.S.–headquartered firms such as Boeing, Ford, IBM, and P&G—as well as the European mainstays of Bayer, Bertelsmann, Ericsson, Olivette, Philips, Siemens, and Unilever.[12]

There is another side to the lobbying coin. Many foreign companies lobby government officials in the United States. Several restrictions are clear. Foreign nationals generally are prohibited from making contributions to U.S. election campaigns. However, the domestic political action committees of U.S. subsidiaries of foreign firms can raise funds from U.S. citizens (and from foreign nationals who are permanent residents of the United States) and donate them to political causes. Registered lobbyists for foreign interests cannot serve on U.S. government advisory committees.

TRADE ASSOCIATIONS

Companies use trade associations to assist them in dealing with government. These associations traditionally have performed services in data collection, education, and other standard and relatively low-profile areas. They also take an active role in public affairs, particularly in the fields of health and safety, consumer affairs, the environment, energy, and foreign trade. (See Table 17.3 for the array of activities carried on.) These business associations range from the 100,000-member National Association of Home Builders to the ten-member Bow Tie Manufacturers Association.

Most U.S. business firms, large or small, belong to one or more trade associations, a majority of which are located in the Washington, D.C., area. (As with private corporations,

---

TABLE 17.3 Key Activities of Associations

Activity

Performed by most associations
- Inform members of legislative developments
- Help members express views to elected officials
- Inform members of government agency actions
- Testify before legislative committees
- Make recommendations on legislation
- Provide data to governments
- Draft legislation
- Lobby and inform government of industry views

Performed by some associations
- Report court decisions
- Train members to become active in politics
- Collect and distribute funds to candidates
- Arrange plant tours for foreign visitors
- Sponsor courses on political participation
- Assist members with trade agreements
- Represent industry in tariff negotiations
- Work with government in participating in foreign trade affairs

Source: American Society of Association Executives.

there has been some movement to the Virginia and Maryland suburbs.) An airline executive was quoted as saying, "If we didn't have the Air Transport Association, I'd need four more people on my staff."[13] Small firms, especially, rely heavily on their associations for a Washington presence especially in heavily regulated industries. As an example, the National Association of Broadcasters has an extensive Washington operation.

Trade associations perform a variety of functions. They keep their members informed of new government regulations and pending legislation. On important issues affecting their industry, the associations develop positions and express them to the government, Congress, and the media. In addition, the trade groups sponsor conferences and other meetings, initiate litigation when necessary, undertake studies and analyses, issue a variety of reports and publications, and conduct many educational programs for the public and industry.

Business associations also provide a way to deal jointly with matters of common concern to an industry without sacrificing independence or violating the antitrust laws. At times, a trade association can act on behalf of individual companies in delicate areas of public policy. The American Electronics Association maintains an office in Japan to help assure "equivalent market access" for U.S. electronics firms. The association office helps firms deal with tariff and nontariff barriers, including complicated requirements for meeting local standards.

The broader the range of products and services a company provides, the more associations it is likely to belong to. A major chemical company may pay dues to the Business Council, the Chamber of Commerce of the United States, the National Association of Manufacturers, the American Chemistry Council, the Fertilizer Institute, the National Paints and Coatings Association, the Society of the Plastics Industry, the Chemical Specialty Manufacturers Association, and the National Petroleum Refiners Association.

A single organization—such as the Polyisocyanurate Insulation Manufacturers Association—may serve such a narrow membership that it cannot cover all the varied interests of a diversified national corporation. Also, the position of a specific association on a given issue may be at variance with a company's. Thus, membership in a variety of trade groups provides management with considerable flexibility on public-policy issues.

GOVERNMENT RELATIONS

Trade associations interpret government actions and attitudes toward business, and vice versa. Some ways in which they accomplish this mission are through testifying at hearings on legislation affecting the industry, appearing in proceedings before government agencies and regulatory bodies, and contributing to precedent-making cases before the courts. They also make available information that the government wants business executives to have. As collectors of statistics for their industries, many trade groups provide government agencies and the public with information not otherwise available.

As government agencies promulgate new regulations, member companies more commonly look to their associations to explain the new rules to them and to take public stands they may not want to take individually. The public sector often fosters this relationship by encouraging companies in a given industry to present their views through a single association rather than scheduling separate sessions with individual companies.

THE UMBRELLA ORGANIZATIONS

In addition to joining specific industry or trade associations, many companies support broader "umbrella" organizations. Of these, the Chamber of Commerce of the United States is the largest and most broadly representative business association in Washington. It is composed of approximately 200,000 members who represent virtually every kind of business, plus 3,000 state and local chambers. The Chamber has approximately 30 standing committees that initiate policy positions in such diverse areas as taxation, antitrust, environmental matters, labor relations, agribusiness, education, and community affairs. The committee members are officials of the companies that belong to the Chamber, and they work with staff experts.

The Chamber attempts to influence the legislative process through congressional testimony. Its lobbyists often work with the Washington representatives of its member companies and through the grassroots contacts of its members.

The National Association of Manufacturers covers a more specialized but fundamentally important grouping of American businesses. Organized in 1895, its membership of over 10,000 industrial firms makes it one of the major voices of private enterprise in the United States. Its policy committees develop stands on such key issues as labor relations, taxation, regulatory reform, and international trade.

Of the broad-based organizations, one of the smallest but most influential is the Business Roundtable. It is composed of 200 chief executives of the nation's largest and most prestigious companies, such as Alcoa, AT&T, Citicorp, DuPont, ExxonMobil, GE, GM, IBM, Procter & Gamble, Sears, and USX. The association is a vehicle for getting members of top management personally involved in presenting business views to Congress and to senior officials in the departments and agencies. Committees are active in areas ranging from accounting principles and antitrust laws to taxation, budget policy, and labor–management relations.

The National Federation of Independent Business is the largest and most influential group representing small business. Its huge membership, in excess of 500,000 business proprietors, gives its representatives access to high places in both the executive and legislative branches. A newer organization of firms of intermediate size is the American Business Conference (ABC), established in 1980 to represent the interest of growth companies. The ABC consists of 100 CEOs of companies whose size ranges between $25 million and $1 billion in revenues and whose sales or earnings have been growing at least 15 percent annually. The organization concentrates on a few key issues, notably capital formation, tax policy, regulatory reform, and international trade. It rarely lobbies for special benefits for member companies, focusing instead on reducing obstacles to business expansion.

The trend toward the formation of more business umbrella organizations in Washington is continuing. Many specialized trade associations find it advantageous to work together on specific items of common interest. In responding to the regulation of food production, for example, the Grocery Manufacturers of America has coordinated efforts with the Food Marketing Institute, the American Frozen Food Institute, and the Potato Chip/Snack Food Association.

A shifting array of trade associations and other organized interest groups bands together on specific issues for limited periods of time. These temporary groups range from the Multilateral Trade Negotiation Coalition to the Energy Tax Coalition.

Euphemisms are frequently used to describe the effort in lofty terms. Thus, the Fiber, Fabric and Apparel Coalition for Trade is the official name of the textile lobby against imports. The group, Citizens for Sensible Control of Acid Rain, is the business coalition that urged less stringent air pollution regulations.

These one-issue efforts are not limited to the business community. The National Committee to Preserve Social Security and Medicare represents a narrow group of senior citizens who constantly advocate more federal benefits for themselves with no interest in how to pay for the increased governmental expenditures.

On occasion, the business community succeeds in reaching out to other important interest groups. For example, the various organizations opposing limits on Medicaid spending for prescription drugs have formed the Coalition for Equal Access to Medicines. In addition to the Pharmaceutical Research and Manufacturers of America, this umbrella group includes the National Medical Association, the National Multiple Sclerosis Society, the National Black Nurses Association, and the California Hispanic-American Medical Association. The common link among all the groups is the concern that poor people get the same access to pharmaceuticals as do other patients.

TRADE ASSOCIATIONS AND THE CONSUMER

Trade associations help deal with consumer complaints against member business firms and reduce the pressure for greater government involvement in business. An effective system for dealing with consumer complaints is the Major Appliance Consumer Action Panel, a joint effort of the Association of Home Appliance Manufacturers, the Gas Appliance Manufacturers Association, and the Retail Merchants Association. This panel, composed of private citizens not associated with the industry, hears complaints that have not been settled by a retailer or manufacturer and makes recommendations that generally result in action.

The advertising industry maintains an ambitious self-regulatory mechanism. The National Advertising Division (NAD) of the Council of Better Business Bureaus acts as the investigatory arm, initiating inquiries, responding to consumer and competitor complaints, and making an initial decision about whether it agrees with the substantiation of the advertising claims being challenged. If it does not, it negotiates with the advertiser to modify or discontinue the advertising. If the NAD cannot resolve the controversy, it appeals to the National Advertising Review Board, a joint creation of the American Advertising Federation, the American Association of Advertising Agencies, and the Association of National Advertisers. It selects an impartial panel to hear each appeal.

RELATIONS WITH FOREIGN GOVERNMENTS

Relatively few American companies have the resources or need to maintain direct representation in foreign countries. With the array of international regulations facing private enterprise, however, companies and their associations maintain liaison with the European Union headquartered in Brussels, the Organization for Economic Cooperation and Development in Paris, and the United Nations and its dozens of specialized agencies and programs in locations ranging from New York to Rome and Geneva. Memberships in organizations such as the U.S. Council for International Business (an affiliate of the International Chamber of Commerce) supplement more domestically oriented associations. The Council interacts with a host of European-based trade groups, ranging from the European Association of Pump Manufacturers to the International Confederation of European Beet Growers.

Two specialized international business associations are the Business and Industry Advisory Committee (BIAC) to the Organization for Economic Cooperation and Development (the OECD consists of the major industrialized nations) and the International Organization of Employers (IOE). The BIAC represents the business community in regular meetings with the Secretary General and other officials of the OECD. The IOE communicates business viewpoints to the UN's International Labor Organization.

A variation on this approach is the formation of the Business Council for Sustainable Development (BCSD), a group of about 40 heads of multinational companies. The group is trying to move private industry to take a more active stance in environmental policy at both the national and international levels. Unlike most other business associations, BCSD acts like a lobby for an outside interest—environmentalism—within the business community.

INTERACTION WITH STATE GOVERNMENTS

Many developments emphasize the role of state governments as regulators of private business. The Clean Air Act delegates the preparation of implementation plans to the individual states. Reduced federal regulation in other areas, such as transportation, has made the state role more conspicuous. Also, substantial reductions in the amount of federal grants-in-aid to states and localities have meant shifting a significant proportion of public-sector responsibility away from the federal government.

The revitalization of state governments often makes a representative in Sacramento or Albany almost as important as the one in Washington. State legislatures operate in a variety of areas of concern to business (see Table 17.4). In addition to the traditional areas of taxes and labor, state governments have established departments and agencies in a variety of areas: hazardous waste, drug abuse, energy conservation, consumer protection, subsidized housing, bilingual education, and mental health. This phenomenon, referred to as "50 little Washingtons," has led many business firms and trade associations to set up formal liaison activities with state legislatures and executive agencies. In some cases, similar offices have been established to work with county and municipal governments.

With most of the nation's governors possessing an item veto on appropriations bills, the executive branch is not to be overlooked either. The well-prepared company representative, with established access to executive offices, is able to offer advice on appointments to advisory commissions, to influence approval or veto of legislation, and to contribute to a more favorable political climate for business.

A study by the Center for Public Integrity, a nonprofit Washington, D.C., research group, reported that lobbyists spent $570 million in 2000 to influence legislators in 34 states—a rise of 91 percent from 1995. Nearly 37,000 businesses, associations, and other interest groups were registered lobbyists in the 50 states.

Although state laws on lobbying differ substantially, several common threads pervade many of them. Every state and the District of Columbia require lobbyists to register, although the precise definition of *lobbying* varies among the states, as do the specific

TABLE 17.4 Major Business Issues at the State Level

General Category	Specific Examples
Tax issues affecting business in general	Corporate income taxes
	Unitary taxes
Other issues affecting business in general	Plant-closing laws
	Corporate officer liability statutes
	Right-to-know legislation
Tax issues affecting selected industries	Gasoline, tobacco, or alcoholic beverage excises
Other issues affecting selected industries	Hazardous waste disposal requirements
	One-way container restrictions
	Clean air and clean water rules
	Food labeling laws
Infrastructure issues	Roads and sewage appropriations
	Power and zoning regulation
Issues affecting business indirectly	Economic development programs
	Regional councils
	Legislative redistricting
Social issues	Education and health
	Housing
	Youth programs

Source: The Conference Board.

reporting requirements. Twenty-two of the states cover grassroots lobbying as well as direct, conventional lobbying activity. The other 28 states and the District of Columbia regulate only direct lobbying. Grassroots efforts may have important effects on voters, but they involve modest amounts of overt funding.

Many states also require the employers of lobbyists to register. In California, Massachusetts, Texas, and Washington, lobbyists before executive branch agencies of state government must also file in addition to those who lobby members of the legislature. All states—except Tennessee, Utah, Wisconsin, and Wyoming—require lobbyists and/or their employers to provide financial reports.

Notes

1. Quoted in George Steiner, *The New CEO* (New York: Macmillan, 1983), p. 29.
2. Quoted in Steiner, p. 36.
3. James Q. Wilson, "The Corporation As a Political Actor," in Carl Kaysen, ed., *The American Corporation Today* (New York: Oxford University Press, 1996), p. 425.
4. Jeffrey H. Birnbaum, "How Microsoft Conquered Washington," *Fortune,* April 29, 2002, pp. 95–96.
5. Shawn Zeller, "Capitol Flight," *CEO Magazine,* February 2002, pp. 7–8.
6. Edwin L. Behrens, "The Five Principal Functions of a Washington Office," *Chemical Trends and Times,* April 1, 1999, pp. 33–36.
7. Selveig B. Spielmann, *Evolution of the Business–Government Relations Function* (Washington, DC: International Business–Government Counsellors, Inc., 1993), p. 5.
8. Richard W. Murphy, "Lobbies As Information Sources for Congress," *Bulletin of the American Society for Information Science,* April 1975, p. 22.

9. Marilyn Wilson, "The New Look at NAM," *Dun's Business Month,* April 1984, p. 44.

10. Mary Hager, "Inside Influence Inc.," *CEO Magazine,* November 2001, p. 53.

11. Jonathan D. Salant, "Bill Would Open Windows on Lobbying Efforts," *Congressional Quarterly,* December 2, 1995, pp. 3631–3633.

12. David Cohen, "Business Lobbying Strategy in Brussels," *Global Focus* 13, no. 2, 2001, pp. 147–156.

13. Quoted in Seymour Lusterman, *Managing Federal Government Relations* (New York: Conference Board, 1988), p. 16.

18

ISSUES MANAGEMENT

The widely used term *issues management* is a misnomer. It does not imply the ability of a firm to "manage" the course of a national policy issue. Rather, the general usage refers to a far more modest and relevant undertaking: managing the company's responses to key public-policy issues affecting its markets, sales, profitability, and internal operations. As shown in earlier chapters, business firms have a great deal at stake in the enactment—or the defeat—of pending legislation.

The development of public policy often goes through a readily identifiable cycle: development of the issue due to public concern; politicization of the issue (frequently as a result of a dramatizing event); enactment of legislation and issuance of regulations; and implementation, often including substantial litigation. Many larger corporations have set up formal procedures to identify, monitor, and respond to issues of public policy that have a substantial impact on their operations.

Great variations occur in the manner in which individual companies set up and operate issues-management systems. Often, the identification of issues and trends is decentralized, while the establishment of company positions is assigned to a high-level management committee. Corporate responses to public-policy issues range from passive to anticipatory to accommodative to active, depending on the nature of the issue and the circumstances of the firm.

THE PUBLIC-POLICY PROCESS

The first step in issues management is to develop an understanding of the process by which items become public-policy issues. Although each policy concern is distinctive, specialists in this area tend to agree that it is useful to consider four stages as constituting the life cycle of a public policy (see Figure 18.1).[1] As a general proposition, the earlier an organization identifies a significant trend, the greater its opportunity to influence the outcome and the larger the number of possible responses.

DEVELOPMENTAL STAGE

The first stage of the public-policy process is the latent or developmental phase. Issues do not usually erupt full-blown. They evolve over time from persistent frictions between important sectors of society or from strong and continuing dissatisfaction on the part of a significant interest group. The individual bits and pieces of a developing issue often come from relatively small numbers of people at the grass roots. However, potential issues that lack broad appeal or effective developmental strategies may never attract widespread public support.

The trigger for developing national attention can come from a dramatic event, such as a major disaster, or something far more basic, such as a change in public expectations or values. For example, the enactment in 1997 of fundamental welfare reform followed several decades of growing public dissatisfaction with the steadily rising

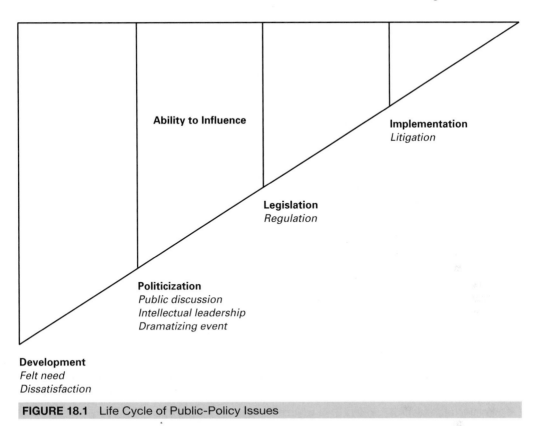

FIGURE 18.1   Life Cycle of Public-Policy Issues

outlays for public assistance. Repeated cycles of poverty within the same family group (often without the formation of a traditional two-parent household) led to a growing disenchantment with the status quo. The formation of a Republican majority in both houses of Congress was the triggering mechanism along with the advent of a presidential election campaign.

POLITICIZATION STAGE

The opinion-formation or politicization phase is the second state of the public-policy process. As a given problem commands more public attention, experts and advocates begin to comment. Organizations may adopt the issue. Such institutionalizing of the cause provides many public-interest groups with a sustained base for advocating changes in public policy.

The issue is now likely to acquire a label: fair housing, truth-in-lending, clean air, welfare reform, and so on. It is discussed in speeches and on television specials, and written up in books, limited-circulation magazines, and professional journals. At this stage, these materials are heard or read by "influentials": academics, writers, clergy, think-tank analysts, columnists, and other idea brokers. With repetition, the message ultimately makes its way into the mass media, where it is popularized. Examples include Rachel Carson's *Silent Spring,* which spurred the environmental movement;

Ralph Nader's *Unsafe at Any Speed,* which led to automobile safety regulation; and Charles Murray's *Losing Ground,* which generated support for moving away from the traditional "transfer payment" approach to alleviating poverty.

Sometimes a dramatizing event occurs, such as Earth Day, which was a staged media "happening." On other occasions, a disaster may occur, such as the explosion at the Union Carbide chemical plant in Bhopal, India, that led to tougher plant-safety regulation. In both cases, attention was suddenly focused on the matter, and it moved quickly into the national spotlight. In these cases, politicians latched onto a promising issue and pursued it with legislative hearings and further publicity.

The *Valdez* oil spill in 1989 gave the entire environmental movement a shot in the arm. The immediate result was the renewal and expansion of the Clean Air Act in 1990, an issue that had been pending since 1981. The spill had very little to do with air pollution, but the accident made the public more environmentally conscious. In a very different policy area, the dramatic bankruptcy of Enron in December 2001 generated unprecedented interest in reforming corporate governance (see Chapter 20).

It is within the developmental and politicization stages that the basic dimensions of a public-policy issue are established. The influence on actions in the next two stages of the policy process may already be decisive. (See Table 18.1 for examples of the historical sequence of issue development.)[2]

TABLE 18.1 Issue Development Phases

Issue	Triggering Event	Politicalization	Legislation	Implementation
Environmental protection	*Silent Spring,* 1963	Included in McCarthy political platform, 1968	EPA established, 1971	Clean air, clean water toxic substance, and many other regulations
Automobile safety	*Unsafe at Any Speed,* 1966	Congressional hearings on auto safety, 1966	NHTSA established, 1966	Mandatory safety features
Discrimination	*Brown* v. *Board of Education,* 1964	Included in Johnson political platform, 1964	Civil Rights Act of 1964	EEOC and affirmative action regulations
Workplace safety	Federal study released in 1970	Congressional hearings, 1970	OSHA established, 1970	Regulations on job safety and health
Energy controls	OPEC embargo, 1973	Congressional hearings, 1973–1975	Energy Policy and Conservation Act, 1975	Energy allocation and price controls terminated in 1981
Growing role of imports in U.S. domestic markets	Rising trade deficit, 1980–1987	Congressional hearings and bills introduced, 1980–1988	Comprehensive trade law passed in 1988	Numerous actions taken against imports of specific products
Shortcomings of corporate governance	Enron bankruptcy, 2001	Congressional hearings and extensive media coverage, 2001–2002	Specific accounting reforms enacted by Congress	Tougher SEC enforcement

LEGISLATIVE STAGE

The third stage of the public-policy process is the institutional action phase, when statutes are enacted and regulations are promulgated. As issues generate widespread interest, pressures develop to resolve the problems. This may take the form of voluntary agreement. The debate on corporate governance in the 1970s mainly resulted in individual corporations voluntarily opening up business decision making by electing more outside directors and establishing public-policy committees of company boards of directors in the 1980s and corporate governance committees in the 1990s. More often, however, the result is legislation and then detailed regulations. The more recent burst of attention to corporate governance may become an example of an issue generating direct governmental response.

It usually takes several years for Congress to write and approve major new laws. Although federal regulation of employee pensions originated in congressional hearings during the 1950s, the first significant bill was not introduced until 1967, and the Employee Retirement Income Security Act was not passed until 1974. In the case of the 1986 explosion in Bhopal, India, job-safety legislation was already on the books in the United States, and the issue moved directly to a period of tougher enforcement.

Sometimes, numerous bills are introduced on a given issue. However, many legislators introduce or cosponsor a bill merely to pacify one or more influential constituents, with no expectation of passage or even hearings on the matter. Yet sometimes events overtake these passive intentions. For example, in the 1981–1982 congressional sessions, 17 energy-conservation bills were presented, but only one passed. By the end of that decade, the issue had become moot—for a while. However, in 1993, President Bill Clinton renewed public interest in the issue by proposing an excise tax on energy. The Congress responded by raising a narrower tax on gasoline. A vigorous debate is now underway on the seriousness of global warming. The most widely suggested policy response is a "carbon" tax to reduce the use of fossil fuel forms of energy, and the entire subject of energy conservation has been revived (see Chapter 13).

IMPLEMENTATION STAGE

The final phase of the public-policy process begins after the enabling legislation has been passed and the rules and procedures have been formulated by the appropriate executive-branch agency. The government agency assigned the new programs begins to organize to carry out its responsibilities. That is when compliance begins. After a while, entrenched interest groups develop, each hoping to receive specific benefits from the program.

Public-interest law firms regularly challenge the execution of the law, either advocating more speed in carrying it out or objecting to some aspect of its regulations. Most of these nonprofit legal organizations are activists, but quite a few are more oriented toward the free market. These actions are encouraged by some environmental statutes that provide for the plaintiff's attorneys to be paid by the government whether they win or lose!

Many companies enter the public-policy process at this late stage. The classic case is the enactment of the Occupational Safety and Health Administration Act in 1970. Most companies ignored the movement of the bill through the legislative process. After all, they reasoned, this was just some technical union matter. But small businesses reacted especially vehemently when they saw the avalanche of onerous, often nit-picking, regulations that was forthcoming. However, as shown in Figure 18.1, the potential for influencing the result is greatest during the early phases of the public-issue development process, before the issue has been framed and attitudes have become entrenched. As an issue moves along the continuum from societal dissatisfaction to public policy, there is less and less opportunity for a business firm to affect the outcome significantly. Although, in its early years, OSHA evoked an unprecedented flow of complaints from business after the enactment of the basic statute, it was too late to make any fundamental changes in the program.

The gestation period for an idea to become public policy can vary substantially. In 1981, William Norris, former CEO of Control Data Corporation, conceived the notion of legislation to authorize cooperative research and development ventures. In 1982, he held the first conference to discuss the idea with other CEOs. The initial bill to exempt such ventures from the antitrust laws was introduced late that year. A statute was enacted in 1984, three years after the effort began.

There is nothing inevitable in the process described here. For example, considerable pressure from consumer groups developed in the late 1970s for congressional enactment of a consumer advocacy agency (also referred to as an agency for consumer protection). The new government unit would intervene in regulatory deliberations on behalf of what it considered the consumer's interest. Many business associations objected to this additional layer of bureaucracy, citing the existing array of regulatory agencies. As the public became increasingly disenchanted with the ability of any group of government officials to determine what is supposedly good for the public, support for the proposal waned. Ultimately, the legislation was defeated. That is one among many examples of the effectiveness of well-organized business involvement in the public-policy arena. The earlier a company gets involved in the public-policy process, the more leverage it can develop. Also, however, the more false starts it will make.

INTERNATIONAL PERSPECTIVE

Viewed in an international context, the United States often has been a follower rather than a leader in public-policy development, especially in the initiation of new governmental programs. For company planners, this relationship provides a useful side effect. Tracking the movement and response to public issues in other nations can provide a forecasting device. A fundamental shortcoming, however, is that no measurable lead or lag pattern emerges from an examination of history. Modern communications does seem to be shortening the lag more recently, and the United States has taken the lead in such areas as deregulation of transportation and communication.

- The United States abolished slavery in 1862, 68 years after France.
- The United States passed a pure food and drug law in 1906, 46 years after the United Kingdom.
- The United States voted old-age assistance in 1889, 46 years after Germany.
- The United States enacted workers' compensation in 1935, 37 years after Germany.
- The United States began unemployment insurance in 1935, 30 years after France.
- The United States gave women suffrage in 1920, 27 years after New Zealand.

However, the United States deregulated airline transportation in 1978 and most nations have not yet followed suit.

ELEMENTS OF AN
ISSUES-MANAGEMENT SYSTEM

Over the years, American companies have been developing increasingly more comprehensive responses to the various policy issues facing private business. Although the position of issues-management director in a given company may be a temporary one, the responsibility for the activity increasingly is lodged with senior management. There is growing recognition that a company's response to major public-policy issues must be a shared responsibility of a constantly changing cast of corporate executives, depending on the issue involved. The responsibility for raising a tax issue, for example, may lodge with the chief financial officer, but the public affairs department may take the lead in the public-policy arena.[3]

Five basic elements provide the framework for the typical corporate issues-management program:

1. Identifying public-policy issues and trends.
2. Evaluating their impact and ranking them by priority to the company.
3. Establishing a company position on the high-priority issues.
4. Designing company actions and responses to help achieve the desired outcome.
5. Carrying out the planned actions.

IDENTIFICATION

Many companies operate early warning systems, employing specialists to deal with trends and emerging issues in which traditional employees lack familiarity. A formal but simple structure can be established for this purpose. Company employees, often volunteers, scan a variety of forward-looking magazines and other sources that reveal early changes in public attitudes. A smaller and more formal group will sort out these issues, focusing on those that are likely to generate the most direct impact on the firm. Senior managers then develop proposed responses to the new trends.

Some corporations retain professional futurists and public-opinion analysts under contract to supplement in-house activities by monitoring social and political change. Two of the most common tools for identifying emerging public policy issues are literature scans and opinion polling. Many firms subscribe to one of several consulting organizations that survey local newspapers for data on social, political, and economic trends. Others assign executives to monitor selected publications systematically.

Most large corporations have been dealing with legislative concerns for many years. To identify and monitor current issues, they often rely on outside sources, such as trade associations, think tanks, and specialized newsletters, to supplement in-house policy analysts (see Chapter 17). Some businesses maintain formal inventories of corporate issues to keep management informed and to help organize their responses.

EVALUATION

A number of companies use a formal methodology to evaluate emerging public-policy trends that affect the company's current planning and future operations. For example, a panel of experts may be commissioned so that a synthesis of disparate individual views is available to corporate decision makers. The most frequently used approach is an interdepartmental public-affairs or issues committee that combines the expertise of key executives in various parts of the organization. Invariably, senior management makes the decisions that involve moving from staff analysis to corporate action.

Table 18.2 is an example of the survey approach, based on a composite of the views of several hundred corporate public-affairs officers.[4] The key issues that emerge from the analysis are taxation, product liability reform, health care costs, environmental cleanup, deregulation, and competitiveness.

At some companies, an issue becomes active simply when a key line manager considers it important enough to bring it to the attention of the public affairs staff. The director of government affairs may then convene a steering group to

TABLE 18.2   Levels of Corporate Involvement in Public-Policy Issues

Issue	Percentage of Firms Actively Involved	Percentage of Firms Closely Monitoring	Percentage of Firms Reporting General Interest
1. Tax reform	70	24	6
2. Product liability reform	47	31	20
3. Health care cost containment	40	34	22
4. Environmental cleanup			
Clean air	32	26	23
Toxic wastes	33	31	21
Other	30	25	27
5. Deregulation	42	25	28
6. Technology and economic competitiveness			
Research support	19	22	45
Copyrights and patents	18	22	42
Science and engineering education	14	20	46
7. Financial disclosure	15	48	30
8. Reregulation	25	33	35
9. Protectionism	26	30	25
10. Employment discrimination	12	45	51
11. Campaign financing reform	13	44	35
12. Budget deficit	16	38	44
13. Employment-at-will	6	42	48
14. Antitrust	10	27	49
15. Family issues	6	29	53
16. Privacy	5	28	59
17. Job creation and retraining	5	26	51
18. Education and business	10	10	50
19. Middle East	4	15	36
20. Farm prices	6	10	30

Source: Conference Board.

develop specific actions and to adjust the company's strategies. As the Public Affairs Council has warned, the biggest problem that companies face in this area is not developing information but deciding which issues to tackle and what action to take.

RESPONSE

In practice, there is great variety in the ways in which companies respond to specific issues of public policy. Table 18.3 presents an analysis of the key issues facing large U.S. industrial companies and the nature of the firms' responses. It is a distillation of internal reports of a variety of corporations.

A company's issues-management action plan—after it has been approved by senior management—typically will involve the headquarters' public-affairs department, the Washington office, and the managements of one or more operating divisions. James Post and his colleagues, in their pioneering research on the corporate public-affairs function, ascertained the key techniques used to achieve company

TABLE 18.3 Responses to High-Priority Issues by Major U.S. Industrial Companies

Identification of the Issue	Nature of the Response
1. Fundamental changes in global-market competition	Emphasize growth markets in which competitors are weak
2. Management of technology; public misgivings about technology	Information program to explain company research to public; formation of expert advisory committee
3. Growing employee demands for changes in quality of life	De-emphasize systems and rules; eliminate levels of supervision; expand involvement in decision making
4. Growth of state and local government influence; increased regulation of manufacturing and marketing	Track developments in all 50 states; state government relations department given principal responsibility for coordinating state lobbying
5. Excess manufacturing capacity, forcing layoffs and plant closings	Consider community impact in determining when and how to close plants
6. Impact of foreign economic trends on company, especially international operations	More active management of foreign exchange operations
7. Resource management to minimize use of materials	Adopt sustainability approach to planning and operations
8. Increasing requests for information about workplace safety and individual health histories	Emphasize preventive health and safety measures; encourage complete, well-grounded disclosures
9. Conflicting demands of employee groups; conflicts among special-interest groups at times of layoffs	Offer alternatives to layoffs, such as redeployment; offer advance notice, severance pay, and job counseling when layoffs occur
10. Management of multinational business	Expand use of foreign nationals, minimizing American overseas employment; involve overseas managers more in decision making

objectives in this area. The responses can be described, in descending order of frequency, as follows:

1. Monitoring emerging issues.
2. Lobbying for legislation within trade associations.
3. Scanning to detect new issues.
4. Updating managers on company positions.
5. Lobbying for legislation at the federal level.
6. Lobbying with state and local governments.
7. Expressing company positions to government agencies.
8. Communicating company positions to employees.
9. Using issues managers.
10. Expanding company information systems.
11. Changing company policies.
12. Setting up public-affairs-issues research committees.
13. Communicating company positions to the general public.
14. Revising company or divisional objectives.
15. Informing stockholders of company positions.
16. Strengthening company reward and penalty systems.[5]

Experienced practitioners warn that an issues-response management system cannot be boilerplated, it must be tailored to the needs and resources of the specific company. Table 18.4 illustrates some of the benefits as well as the inherent limitations of such a system. Generally, issues-management systems help businesses become more aware of the political, social, and economic environment within which they operate. This is especially useful when aspects of that external environment change rapidly.

However, public-policy monitoring programs fail when they overdramatize as immediate threats to company survival such esoteric issues as social responsibility. "I am not suggesting," states one public-affairs official, "that these issues are irrelevant to corporate success over time, but they are seldom jugular concerns to a competently managed corporation."[6]

TABLE 18.4   Benefits and Limitations of an Issues-Management System

Benefits	Limitations
A managed process by which issues are actively dealt with	Cannot predict every issue that will affect the company
An enhanced ability to react rapidly to unexpected or quickly breaking issues	Cannot accurately forecast the environment many years in the future
Greatly increased intelligence about the external environment	Cannot assume that every issue will be resolved according to the corporation's wishes
Involvement of management and enhanced sensitivity to effects of public issues on business	Cannot work as an isolated staff function while the rest of the company continues its traditional routine
Assurance to shareholders, employees, and activist groups that the company's responses are serious and thoughtful	

It is important to know when not to react. Some firms new to the public-policy process are inclined to get involved every time any legislator introduces a bill that could affect the company if it passed. As previously mentioned, most bills do not even get to the stage where a committee hearing is held on it. However, when a large corporation focuses attention on what had been an obscure bill, it can find that the proposal is no longer obscure. Under such circumstances, its early intervention can be counterproductive.

REFLECTIONS ON BUSINESS AND PUBLIC POLICY

Contrary to a widely held notion that the business community maintains a monolithic approach to public policy, most scholars who have analyzed the question quickly conclude that the typical business viewpoint is anything but homogeneous. Some of the differences clearly reflect competitive positions: importers versus domestic producers (on trade policy), thrift institutions versus commercial banks versus investment bankers (on regulation of financial institutions), proprietary drug manufacturers versus prescription drug companies (on pharmaceutical regulation).

Other differences arise because of variations in the impact of government policies: manufacturing versus services (in the case of investment tax incentives), capital-intensive versus labor-intensive firms (for human resources regulation as well as environmental rule making), and high-profit versus low-profit corporations (on reducing tax rates versus maintaining special business incentives).

As pointed out in earlier chapters, business firms are usually far more effective in the public-policy arena when they focus their efforts on specific programs that benefit them (import quotas or tax breaks) than when they attempt to do battle on broad issues of national concern, such as environmental policy.

There is substantial conceptual support for that disparity. In a decentralized political system, general interests shared by large numbers of people tend to fare poorly. In contrast, narrow interests usually do better. The reason is that a broad interest is comparable to a public good, which is available widely, whether the recipient pays for it or not. In such circumstances, it is expected that many individuals (or companies) *free ride,* that is, leave the costs of financing the public good to others. However, if that is a widely held response, an insufficient supply of the public good will be available. In contrast, there are compelling incentives for relatively small groups to organize for their mutual benefit.

An obvious example is the federal budget. Virtually every business firm and trade association pays lip service to the notion of a balanced budget. But, in most cases, their most ambitious public-policy efforts are devoted to advocating increased spending for a specific item benefiting them—or opening (or expanding) a tax loophole with a similar effect on balancing the budget. In the case of the overall budget, any single company or industry would receive extremely small shares of the benefits resulting from lower amounts of deficit financing. However, they obtain very large proportions of specific tax breaks or expenditure subsidies directed to their sector of the economy.

This conceptual approach cannot be carried too far. As noted in the previous chapter, many companies support such umbrella organizations as the Chamber of Commerce of the United States, the National Association of Manufacturers, and the National Federation of Independent Business. At times, these broad-based organizations have obtained the enactment of public policy of general benefit to business. An example is the substantial reduction in the capital gains tax rate, down to 20 percent for most taxpayers (included in a 1997 package of tax changes).

ORGANIZING FOR ISSUES MANAGEMENT

In many companies, formalized programs of issues management were originally assigned to the public-affairs department, which, in turn, was an expansion and strengthening of the traditional public relations staff. Frequently, the formal function remains in the public-affairs area, although the policy decisions are made by executives in the substantive areas. In some cases, the issues-management approach has evolved out of an embryonic social responsibility program. Viewed in that light, issues management is a response to bring company actions into closer alignment with society's expectation of business and—to a far more modest degree—vice versa.

EARLY DEVELOPMENTAL STAGE

Prior to the establishment of formal issues-management efforts, companies reacted to key public-policy initiatives as they occurred. Civil rights legislation and accompanying regulations quickly led to the establishment of equal employment opportunity sections of personnel departments (often renamed *human resources*) and new affirmative action programs. Similarly, legislation and regulation in the ecology area soon led to environmental policy staffs and specific pollution control programs.

In an effort to do more than react to government policy initiatives, companies began establishing formal programs of issues management. Initially, these efforts involved little more than cataloging the pressure points from the public arena so that the company could respond a bit more rapidly. Corporate responses tended to highlight the near-term focus, as would be expected from the public-relations departments that housed many of these efforts.

Some of these early efforts were avowedly straight advocacy programs, helping the company decide which issues to get involved in and then to speak out on them. The initial issues-management programs tended to be short-term, reactive, and traditional examinations of an outside world defined in traditional ways, thus yielding immediate reactions focusing on narrowly defined problems.

ACCEPTANCE AND USE BY MANAGEMENT

Issues management now also encompasses forecasts and evaluations of long-term societal trends, both domestic and international. When the responsibility for the function is transferred from the public-affairs department to the corporate planning department, the opportunity arises to integrate public-policy analysis into the regular planning and decision systems of the company. That enables managers to give more attention to strategic assumptions about external factors in their long-range planning. Probably the most important result of the evolution of issues management and its formal integration into company operations has been the increased sensitivity of the individual manager to nontraditional forces that can affect the bottom line.

Naturally, corporations take varying approaches to issues management. A few companies have full-time staffs of issues managers. Their wide-ranging backgrounds include professionals trained as scientists, engineers, lawyers, marketing specialists, journalists, and social scientists. One corporate issues-management unit identifies between 15 and 20 issues that have potentially significant impact on the company and transmits its analysis to a higher-level, public-affairs committee that sets policy and strategy for dealing with them. The issues range from local matters (for instance, inter-governmental cooperation in the company's headquarters city) to international concerns such as proposed workplace standards in the European Union.

Most companies emphasize legislative and other governmental issues. Some firms, however, use issues managers to spot emerging concerns for their community and philanthropic programs. Many companies do not have formal issues-management programs as such, but rely on traditional staff to perform such functions, including planning, public affairs, and government-relations departments.

FURTHER EXPANSION

Issues-management efforts can also have applications for a company's marketing efforts. One insurance company, for example, devoted the first 19 pages of its annual report to an analysis of public-policy issues affecting business. The graphics dramatized the financial risks and implications for the firm's clients. For example, the report indicated the growing potential for litigation and subsequent losses arising from environmental impairment liability. Key industries likely to be affected were identified, notably food processors, chemical and pharmaceutical firms, and petroleum companies. (See box, "Issues-Management Successes," for examples of positive contributions to company operations.)

ALTERNATIVE STRATEGIES

Individual companies react to changing public policy in a great variety of ways. Nevertheless, four basic patterns of response to threats of government intervention are evident: passive, anticipatory, accommodative, and active. Often, a company will use a blend of these four approaches.

PASSIVE

Some corporate managements simply react to each new or expanded government initiative. The passive approach is the oldest and still the most popular. Before the passage of the Clean Air Act, many capital-intensive firms merely stonewalled when criticized by citizen groups for the large amounts of air pollution they were generating. Those managements criticized the development of a public-sector response and attempted to postpone its effects through litigation and administrative appeals. But ultimately they were forced to gear their operations to meet the new government requirements. Companies in the passive mode typically respond to government regulation by digging in their heels and griping and then going along at the minimum acceptable rate. Inevitably, they are constantly complaining about the government trying to run their businesses.

BOX 18-1

ISSUES-MANAGEMENT SUCCESSES

A staff activity such as issues management can easily deteriorate into a paper-shuffling operation. Although that danger may always be present, it is useful to note some of the genuine successes that have been reported.

- Through its issues-management process, American Express anticipated—well ahead of the event—the pending expiration of a federal law prohibiting merchants from imposing surcharges on consumer use of credit cards. The company realized that as soon as the ban expired retailers would quickly add surcharges, a practice that would discourage the use of credit cards. Such an eventuality never occurred. American Express headed it off by working with consumer groups and legislators to enact laws in many states barring such surcharges.

- ARCO (now a part of BP) credits its issues-management process for identifying—before other petrochemical and chemical companies—hazardous waste cleanup as an issue that would bedevil the industry. Departing from the customary business opposition to new environmental legislation, the company supported the concept of Superfund and worked to

modify the legislation. ARCO maintains that the entire industry subsequently adopted this approach.

- Allstate identified incipient public pressure on insurance companies to provide more affordable homeowner coverage in poorer, more densely populated urban areas in transition. The company formed an Insuring Urban America task force and tailored a new insurance policy to the urban market. Allstate believes that without such action, many state governments would have mandated much more severe action.

- Monsanto credits its issue-identification committee as playing a key role in altering the basic strategy of the company. As part of its environmental scanning process, the committee reported to management that the profit outlook for bulk or commodity chemicals was dim. That advance warning prompted the company to leave the petrochemical and oil businesses and concentrate instead on agricultural chemicals, biotechnology, and pharmaceuticals. In 1997, Monsanto spun off its traditional chemical units so that it could concentrate on the newer fields of business.

ANTICIPATORY

The expanding government role in business decision making has encouraged corporate managements to use their planning capability to forecast likely further changes in government policies that affect business. Such action enables them to adjust their own operations to minimize or obviate the impacts of those external changes. Thus, before congressional enactment of tightened air- or water-pollution controls, some firms incorporate more stringent ecological standards in their own capital projects. The intent is to minimize the likelihood of subsequently running afoul of new federal regulations.

Some companies also take socially responsible actions on a voluntary basis in an effort to reduce the likelihood of government's enacting more stringent controls. An example is the extent to which companies and business associations have adopted standards for advance notification of plant closings, together with private programs to reduce adverse impacts on employees and on the surrounding community. Nonetheless, in 1988 Congress did pass legislation mandating advance notice. Some companies supported the statutory requirement as a way of imposing costs on competitors that did not have voluntary programs.

As corporate executives become more sensitive to evolving social demands, they begin to respond to some of the public's expectations as a normal aspect of conducting business. To the extent that this positive development occurs voluntarily, businesses themselves provide some constraint on the degree of political pressure that social activists can effectively exert against them. Why go to Ralph Nader if someone in the company can handle your complaint? The consumer movement today may seem to lack the dynamism of the 1970s, possibly because business firms have been better able to anticipate consumers' wishes and respond to them. (See box, "Trends in Consumer Activism.") Nevertheless, the consumer movement is far from dead, and on specific issues it can be a formidable force.

BOX 18-2

TRENDS IN CONSUMER ACTIVISM

Citizen groups involved in public policy range from a handful of local residents who are temporarily aroused by an ephemeral local issue to Citizen Action, which is a broad-based federation of groups with approximately 2 million members. With affiliates in 26 states, Citizen Action is one of the most ambitious efforts to date to consolidate the resources of labor, environmentalists, low-income people, and other activist groups. With its state affiliates, Citizen Action boasts a combined staff of 1,500, plus thousands of volunteers.

An activist training center in Chicago was the seedbed for the movement. In the 1970s, the Midwest Academy began to teach members of citizens' organizations the skills required to manage direct-action operations. Groups that had been sending their members to the academy started to do "macro"-organizing. In many states, church leaders formed the initial sponsoring committees.

The Citizen Action platform, *Citizen Action Program for a Working America,* is based on the radical premise that "corporate power has abandoned the well-being of America." The platform advocates a variety of new or expanded government powers over the economy. Specifics include limiting the movement of capital overseas, enacting a special tax on corporate profits, prohibiting agricultural corporations, establishing price controls, and setting up an elaborate system of government planning and direction of the economy.

State affiliates join with outside organizations on specific issues. Examples include the Citizen's Labor Energy Coalition, which delayed natural gas deregulation for several years, and the National Campaign Against Toxic Hazards, which helped pass federal and state Superfund legislation.

Citizen Action has encountered substantial criticism for its direct participation in political activities. The Federal Elections Commission fined the tax-exempt Illinois arm of the organization $5,000 for making illegal contributions to congressional candidates in 1984. In 1997, Citizen Action figured prominently in the investigations of campaign financing. It was accused of illegally funneling money from the Teamsters Union and the AFL-CIO to the campaign coffers of the Teamsters' president. The organization has maintained a much lower profile since that episode.

An older, more conventional activist association is the Consumer Federation of America (CFA), a coalition of some 200 national, state, and regional consumer, labor, cooperative, and other citizens' groups. CFA promotes industry

Continued

responsibility for product liability and the provision of lifeline services by a number of key industries, such as utilities. In comparing CFA to a business lobby, its executive director was quoted as saying, "[W]e do have much better access to the press."

Simultaneously, more narrowly focused citizen or activist groups are continually involved in specific areas, such as environmental and pharmaceutical regulation. Thus, Environmental Defense (ED) urges concerned citizens to press for testing local freshwater fish for dioxin levels and to join ED's "incinerator network" to act as a watchdog to warn of any proposed resource-recovery/solid-waste incinerators.

The Sierra Club Legal Defense Fund promotes citizen action to prevent paper companies from clear-cutting timber in old-growth rain forests. It also sponsors action to halt placer mining in portions of the National Wild and Scenic River System. The fund provides postcards for concerned citizens to send to the Department of the Interior.

Public Citizen's Health Research Group (a Ralph Nader affiliate) urges the Food and Drug Administration to ban or limit the use of some pharmaceutical products and has been active in the effort to have nicotine classified as a drug. The National Resources Defense Council frequently enters environmental disputes, often taking positions opposite to those of business firms.

To some degree, taxpayers directly subsidize activists groups. Under the Superfund Amendments and Reauthorization Act of 1986, the federal government makes funds available to community organizations on a roughly two-for-one basis (65 percent federal money, 35 percent private). The grants are available to groups that can show that they are threatened by sites from a "health, economic, or environmental standpoint." In addition, several environmental statutes provide for the federal government reimbursing activist groups for their legal costs when they institute suits under those laws, even if they lose the cases.

Another trend in consumer activism is the tendency for national groups to form international networks. The International Organization of Consumers Unions (IOCU) is composed of 160 consumer groups in 52 countries. IOCU has official status in many of the UN's specialized agencies. It fosters a variety of issue-oriented networks, such as Health Action International and Pesticide Action Network International, to lobby governments and pressure individual companies. In turn, the Pesticide Action Network consists of 350 consumer, labor, farmer, health care, and other organizations pushing for restrictions on the production and sale of pesticides.

ACCOMMODATIVE

There is one approach to government intervention that companies are reluctant to admit they practice. Many firms try to appease their critics by making generous contributions to them.[7] Thus, some energy companies support the very environmental organizations that regularly attack their industry. Contributions from business firms are reported by such activist organizations as Greenpeace, INFORM, the National Wildlife Federation, the National Resources Defense Council, Operation Push, and the Progressive Policy Institute. The individual businesses hope that the critics will pick on other businesses or at least that they will appear to be more socially minded.

A limitation of the accommodative approach was demonstrated in 2002 when the Sierra Club launched an advertising campaign criticizing the CEO of Ford Motor Company for opposing an effort to legislate higher federal gas mileage standards. The Ford CEO, William Clay Ford, Jr., had been widely perceived as the senior automobile industry executive most sympathetic to the environmental movement. The Sierra Club subsequently acknowledged that was a key reason for singling him out, rather than focusing on the leaders of the other major motor vehicle manufacturers.[8]

Labor unions do not play this dangerous game because it strengthens the people who are attacking the contributor's own interests. The passive, anticipatory, and accommodative approaches to public-policy issues all share a common shortcoming: The companies are always on the defensive in dealing with government and interest groups.

ACTIVE

Still other business executives attempt to head off or shape the character of government intervention by playing a more active role in the development and enactment of public policies. Thus, some companies have strengthened their Washington offices to deal with pending legislation and new regulation or have set up such operations if they did not exist. They join and strongly support trade associations that are active on Capitol Hill. Despite the restrictions on political contributions and practices, many businesspeople, as individuals, attempt to exercise leverage on government decision making by participating more actively in the political process.

Business firms now make extensive use of in-house publications, communications to shareholders, and other media to raise the public awareness of political issues that affect the future of the business community. Businesspeople increasingly participate in public hearings. It is intriguing to note that, of the CEOs who attempt to influence the government, a majority believe their efforts have been successful.

Some firms have developed an outreach effort to open up communications with adversarial groups. Usually that is done after some serious confrontation has occurred. In the case of Nestlé, a variety of such efforts was undertaken after a sustained boycott of its infant formula on the part of a combination of church and activist groups.[9]

An improved knowledge of the public-policy process enables business and its representatives to affect, in entirely legal and legitimate fashion, the formulation of new and revised government policies toward the private sector. Often the most effective form of influence is making available to government decision makers prompt, knowledgeable, and detailed analyses of the various impacts of the proposed legislation. In contrast to the traditional methods of exerting "political" pressure, the information approach may help to reconcile public desires and business reality and to achieve improved public policies.

PUBLIC-RELATIONS EFFORTS

The public-affairs function of the modern corporation has become an important part of the response to the expanding role of government in business decision making. The shift in emphasis to guiding the whole range of management responses to public-policy challenges has been gradual but substantial. The expansion of the role of public-affairs professionals has reflected in good measure the steady and rapid growth in government intervention in traditional business functions. It is also a corporate response to the rise of an array of external pressures and interest groups that can have powerful effects, often quite harmful, on the performance of the business firm.

Companies have moved beyond the initial and largely negative response to this external environment: merely opposing or at least trying to postpone the expanding array of restraints imposed on the discretion of corporate management. Increasingly, business has attempted to respond positively to the concerns that generate government and private pressures for changes in business practices. The entire social responsibility movement is a case in point, although in recent years the charitable aspect has been reduced substantially.

A more entrepreneurial approach is to rely on an expansion of traditional planning and analysis functions in order to understand the urgencies that are arising and to respond to them early enough to reduce the pressures for public intervention. As a result, most businesses—but far from all—have shed the Neanderthal image that much of the public has associated with the corporate sector. Management is learning firsthand that responding promptly to a Senate inquiry can be more timely than calling on a potential new customer. The effective public-affairs function can improve and make less onerous that external environment that impinges on the internal operations of the business firm.

Increasingly, business is turning to the public to exert pressure on government for reforms it believes desirable. Numerous existing channels of communication are available to companies to express their views on public policy. They range from employee newspapers to customer magazines to annual reports to shareholders. In the past, such house organs have tended to be dominated by routine announcements, pictures of employees receiving ten-year pins, and bowling-league scores. Many companies are now including more substantial editorial content in these publications.

Companies can make noncoercive statements to their employees, including soliciting political contributions, expressing political support and corporate philosophy, and urging political and legislative activity. Regulations of the Internal Revenue Service permit deductions for advertising that presents views on economic, social, or other questions of a general nature. But the distinction between tax-deductible, "informational" messages and nondeductible, "persuasional" communications is at best arbitrary.

An important U.S. Supreme Court decision in 1978 (*First National Bank of Boston v. Bellotti*) held that corporations have a constitutional right of free speech to propagate their political and social views. The *Bellotti* case struck down a Massachusetts law that prohibited corporations from making expenditures for the purpose of "influencing or affecting the vote on any question submitted to the voters, other than one materially affecting any of the property, business or assets of the corporation." The First National Bank of Boston had opposed a proposed state graduated individual income tax. The decision held that corporations have a right of free speech.

Rulings by the Internal Revenue Service, however, set limits on tax-deductible grassroots lobbying and related activities. Internal Revenue Ruling 78-111, for example, states that the cost of printing and distributing the text of remarks of a company president on a pending state environmental bill are not deductible, even though the shareholders are not actually requested to contact their representatives. That activity, according to the IRS, is an attempt to influence shareholders to oppose that legislation. In Internal Revenue Ruling 789-112, the IRS holds that the costs of advertisements stating that company's objection to certain proposed land-use legislation and suggesting an alternative program also violates the prohibition on "grassroots lobbying," even if there is no specific request that the reader contact a representative in the legislature.

BUSINESS AND THE MEDIA

One of the areas of greatest contention between business and the rest of society is media coverage. Newspapers, magazines, radio, and television are the principal sources through which the public forms its opinions on issues of public policy. Editors and broadcast executives are the gatekeepers who determine which issues get public attention and hence strongly influence the setting of the public-policy agenda.

There is great variation in media coverage of business. Some journalists have become veritable experts in reporting and analyzing current developments. Their work is relied upon as source information by scholars and government officials alike. Yet many writers on business topics lack a basic comprehension of the activities they are reporting on. No sports desk would assign a baseball game to a reporter who is not familiar with the rules of the sport. Yet, a comparable level of competence is not a general requirement for covering an annual meeting of a major corporation or for reporting on a critique of business by an important interest group.

In recent years, a variety of efforts has been made to enhance the economic and business knowledge of practicing journalists. Several universities sponsor short courses in this area. The Foundation for American Communications (FACS) brings the classroom closer to reporters by holding short courses in many different locations, drawing print- and electronic-media journalists from the surrounding area. FACS courses range from the basics of economics to analyses of key policy areas such as foreign trade and environmental regulation.

The enlightened business executive also learns to accept the fact that much news reporting on business (as well as of other sectors of the economy) does not consist of praise. The late Theodore White, a noted journalist and author, described this problem in fairly colorful language:

> You don't make your reputation as a reporter and I did not make my reputation as a reporter, by praising anybody. You make your reputation as a
> reporter . . . by gouging a chunk of raw and bleeding flesh from this system. . . .
> You gotta be able to prove you can snap your jaws for the kill.[10]

A certain degree of sensationalism, regardless of inaccuracy, does help to get an item into a publication or on the evening news. Fostering the production of such items is the keen competition that exists among reporters on any given newspaper, magazine, or TV or radio station.

On the other hand, experienced journalists present a fairly standard litany of the shortcomings of senior business management in their dealings with the press: They stonewall the media; they live a sheltered life in the corporate cocoon; they are not used to the same give-and-take as the government official or politician; they are defensive and antagonistic—when they answer press calls at all. In any event, a retired managing editor of the *Washington Post* reminds the business community that the First Amendment does not guarantee a competent, fair, and accurate press—but "a free press, which often means a cantankerous, suspicious and inaccurate press."[11]

Conclusions

Identifying and responding to specific public-policy issues that strongly affect private business is a difficult and challenging assignment. Given the increasing globalization of business and the continuing expansion of the range of governmental interests, the likelihood that those challenges will continue, if not accelerate, is very high. As one government affairs executive stated, "Our workload has increased through several presidencies. The next presidency will prove no different."[12]

Notes

1. See W. Howard Chase, *Issue Management* (Stamford, CT: IAP, 1984).
2. See Thomas G. Marx, "Integrating Public Affairs and Strategic Planning," *California Management Review,* Fall 1986, p. 145.
3. Raymond L. Hoewing, *Issues Management Yesterday and Today* (Washington, DC: Public Affairs Council, 1993), p. 7.
4. Catherine Morrison, *Forecasting Public Affairs Priorities* (New York: Conference Board, 1987), pp. 1–15.
5. James E. Post et al., "Public Affairs Officers and Their Functions," *Public Affairs Review* 2, 1981, p. 97.
6. Robert H. Moore, *Monitoring Governmental Regulation,* presentation to the 1983 Strategic Planning Conference, Conference Board, New York City, 1983, p. 5.
7. See Christopher Yablonski, *Patterns of Corporate Philanthropy* (Washington, DC: Capital Research Center, 2001).
8. Danny Hakim, "The Sierra Club Criticizes Ford's Chief in a Campaign for Fuel-Efficient Cars," *New York Times,* June 13, 2002, p. C4.
9. James E. Post, "Assessing the Nestlé Boycott," *California Management Review,* Winter 1985, pp. 113–131.
10. Quoted in John L. Poluszek, *Will the Corporation Survive?* (Reston, VA: Reston, 1977), p. 225.
11. Howard Simons, "The Media and Business," in *Dateline: Washington* (Washington, DC: LTV, Inc., 1979), p. 10.
12. Quoted in Seymour Lusterman, *Managing Federal Government Relations* (New York: Conference Board, 1988), p. 25.

19

BUSINESS PARTICIPATION
IN POLITICS

The extensive impacts of government on business decision making have resulted in expanded interest by business executives in participating directly in the political process. The significant political role of other interest groups, such as labor, environmentalists, and senior citizens, and the antibusiness orientation of many political activists working under the banner of the public interest have encouraged executives in private enterprises to take a more active role in the political arena.

Industry leaders usually attempt to use the political process to slow or shape government intervention in the private sector. However, they frequently tend to be more circumspect in their efforts than are representatives of other interest groups. The glare of national publicity can be intimidating to people who, on a day-to-day basis, operate in a very different environment. Legislation enacted in the 1970s to prevent illegal political contributions by business has been an important factor in changing the nature of business participation in politics. Congressional action in 2002 introduced further complications into political campaigns. Many corporate executives find it necessary to become more knowledgeable of the legal aspects of political participation.

PERMISSIBLE POLITICAL ACTIVITIES

Corporations can participate legally in a wide variety of political activities. Federal law governs only political activities involving candidates for president, vice president, and Congress. (See box, "Limits on Contributions to Federal Election Campaigns.") Involvement in state and local campaigns is covered by varying state statutes and local ordinances.

For example, a corporation may encourage its employees and stockholders to register and vote, but it may not recommend to employees how they should vote. Candidates may tour a company plant or office to meet employees or they may stand at an entrance to greet them, but the company must grant all candidates that right. However, it need not specifically invite every candidate. A corporation may not contribute funds to a candidate or an election campaign at the federal level, but it can sponsor a fund-raising effort on the part of its employees. The federal prohibition against corporations making monetary contributions for campaign financing, which goes back to the Tillman Act of 1907, was extended to labor unions in 1943. In some states, it is entirely legal for companies to contribute directly to state and local election campaigns. However, many states have enacted ceilings on campaign donations, often similar to the federal rules.

The management of a company has a right to state its position on public issues affecting the company's well-being, including legislative proposals before Congress.

BOX 19-1

LIMITS ON CONTRIBUTIONS TO FEDERAL ELECTION CAMPAIGNS

CORPORATIONS AND LABOR UNIONS

- May not directly contribute to candidates for federal offices.
- May sponsor political action committees (PACs).
- May contribute "soft dollars" to state and local political parties, but not to national political parties.
- May not pay for broadcast advertisements that refer to specific candidates and run within 60 days before a general election or 30 days before a primary.

POLITICAL ACTION COMMITTEES

- May contribute $5,000 per candidate for federal office per election.
- May make unlimited "independent expenditures" that do not go directly to a candidate but are intended to benefit or hurt a specific campaign.
- May donate up to $15,000 a year to a party for its campaigns for national offices.
- May make unlimited "soft money" contributions to a party for voter drives, party building, and state and local campaigns (subject to state law).
- May pay for political ads prohibited to corporations and labor unions.

INDIVIDUALS

- May give $2,000 per candidate for federal office per election.
- May give no more than $5,000 a year to any one PAC.
- May give up to $10,000 a year directly to state and local party organizations, depending on state laws.
- May donate up to $95,000 over a two-year period to presidential and congressional campaigns.

GENERAL LIMITATIONS

- No contributions to federal, state, or local election campaigns may be accepted from individuals who are not U.S. citizens or lawful permanent residents.
- Contributions in the name of another person or entity are forbidden.
- Contributions of more than $100 must be by check, not in cash.
- Contributions from children under 18 are forbidden, unless the child controls both the money and the decision to donate. Contributions may not be made from the proceeds of a gift.
- Anonymous cash contributions may not exceed $50.

It also may communicate to its employees and stockholders information on members of Congress and candidates for office, such as voting records. Company-sponsored programs explaining how to be effective in politics are another allowable form of political activity. Moreover, a corporation can provide political education programs for employees, and it can actively promote, on a nonpartisan basis, its employees' voluntary involvement in direct political action on their own time. Employees may be granted leaves of absence without pay to work on political campaigns.

SUPPORTING POLITICAL CANDIDATES VIA PACs

For many years, it was illegal for corporations or unions to solicit political funds from employees or members. At first, unions circumvented the law by forming "educational" groups, such as the AFL-CIO's Committee on Political Education (COPE), as funnels for political contributions. But, initially, businesses and trade groups had no such outlet and were restricted to individual voluntary contributions by executives. Before the reforms to campaign financing laws were enacted in the 1970s, these personal contributions, however, could be made in virtually unlimited amounts.

THE RULES ON PACs

Corporations and associations are prohibited by law from making political contributions or using the organization's resources for federal election campaigns. Since 1971, however, they can use company funds to set up and administer political action committees (PACs), comparable to labor's COPE. Contrary to its name, a PAC does not operate a political campaign; rather, it is a financing mechanism for political activity. PAC managers report that company-financed administrative costs—such as the expense of collecting and disbursing the funds—are 25 to 50 percent of the funds solicited which constitutes substantial indirect support.[1]

Specific statutory provisions contained in the 1971 Federal Election Campaign Act and in later amendments allow business- and union-sponsored PACs to support candidates actively. As separate legal entities organized to solicit and accept voluntary contributions from shareholders and "executive or administrative personnel" and their families, business PACs in turn can make political contributions to candidates for federal office (so-called "hard money"). Twice a year, they can solicit other company employees.

Despite the restrictive rules governing their operation—a PAC must have at least 50 members and give to at least five candidates—the number of PACs is substantial. Approximately 4,500 PACs operated in the 1999–2000 election cycle. About one-half of the *Fortune* 500 firms maintain PACs, as do the larger unions and other important interest groups. Many PACs, however, are small-scale, local operations that contribute only to state or regional candidates and represent small businesses, local labor unions, and political clubs. Table 19.1 lists the ten firms with the largest contributions to federal election campaigns in the 1999–2000 cycle.

Individual contributors to PACs are limited to $2,000 per calendar year. Each PAC is allowed to contribute a maximum of $5,000 per election to each candidate, $20,000 a calendar year to national political parties, and $5,000 a year to other political committees. But there is no limit on total contributions by a PAC.

Some companies permit a PAC contributor to designate which party is to receive the money. More frequently, the PAC is allowed to use the money at its discretion. Decisions about which candidates will obtain PAC funds are usually made by special committees of the corporate PAC. In some cases, rather than establishing a formal committee, the PAC will adopt the recommendations of a special adviser, such as the head of the company's Washington office or the director of government affairs.

TABLE 19.1 Ten Largest Business Election Campaign
Contributors, 1999–2000

Company	Contributions
1. Microsoft	$3,686,781
2. AT&T	3,637,945
3. Goldman, Sachs	3,191,123
4. SBC	2,987,765
5. Philip Morris	2,896,217
6. MBNA	2,291,150
7. Verizon	2,251,644
8. Federal Express	2,249,528
9. Enron	2,248,612
10. BellSouth	$2,234,179

Note: Totals include PAC contributions, corporate soft money, and
individual hard and soft money support.

Source: U.S. Federal Election Commission.

Besides making cash payments directly to candidates, political action groups can provide support in other, often very important, ways. For example, a PAC may pay the salary and expenses of a consultant who goes into a congressional district to counsel a candidate or otherwise work on his or her behalf. The PAC may conduct a target mailing to employees, shareholders, or others in a given congressional district, urging the election or defeat of a candidate. Such in-kind assistance can provide an opportunity for greater interaction with a candidate and staff than do ordinary cash contributions. Also, in-kind contributions can give the PAC greater control over how its help is used.

SOFT MONEY

By the mid-1990s, a major loophole had developed by which corporations (and unions) could make virtually unlimited contributions to election campaigns. So-called "soft money" payments made directly to a political party were exempt from the federal limits on the size of individual contributions because ostensibly the money was not going into the campaign of a specific candidate. In practice, the funds often went to attack the candidate's opponent. The result was both to increase the money devoted to political campaigns and to accentuate the negative style of campaigning that increasingly characterizes political contests in the United States. In the 1999–2000 election cycle, "soft money" contributions financed more than one-half of party campaign spending.[2]

The campaign finance reforms of 2002 prohibit companies from contributing "soft money" to national political parties. The new law also attempts to close the "soft money" loophole by restricting "issue" advertising. Specifically, television or radio broadcast ads that "promote, support, attack or oppose" a specific candidate (even if not overtly urging the viewer to vote for or against the candidate) are banned within 60 days before a general election or 30 days in advance of a primary.

National party committees no longer can accept unlimited amounts of soft money for "party-building" activities. Both major parties had raised substantial amounts in that form. In the 1999–2000 election cycle, Democrats reported contributions of $24 million in soft money from their major business contributors while the Republicans raised $55 million from their large business supporters.

Soft money had its origins in a 1979 campaign finance law (P.L. 96-187) allowing political parties to raise unlimited amounts of money for voter registration drives and get-out-the-vote efforts among their members. Over time, soft money had been used for airing commercials supporting or opposing a particular candidate or issue. The U.S. Supreme Court, in a series of decisions, has ruled that advertisements that did not specifically urge a vote for or against a candidate were not subject to the restrictions imposed by federal election laws. The 2002 law was designed to close that loophole. However, it has not yet been tested in the courts for its constitutionality.

The preliminary regulations of the Federal Election Commission (FEC) carrying out the 2002 law are controversial and are also likely to be challenged in court. The FEC voted to allow national parties to create "independent" groups to continue to raise soft money. Another commission regulation permits national candidates to raise unrestricted funds that will assist in federal election campaigns.

THE DEVELOPMENT OF PACs

In view of the public attention that has been devoted to business-sponsored PACs, it is intriguing to note how relatively few companies have set up such organizations. Not included on the list of corporate sponsors of PACs are such giants of American industry as Exxon Mobil, IBM, Ford, and American Express. Indeed, many corporations consider direct political activity as inappropriate for a business firm. One business equipment manufacturer bluntly stated, "We do not feel we have the right to make political decisions with the money of our employees."[3] Other firms fear that the activity will be misunderstood and that they will be accused of exercising their financial influence in ways that are contrary to the public interest. Following the Enron bankruptcy, energy giant BP announced that it would stop making political contributions "anywhere in the world."

On the basis of Federal Election Commission data, it seems that business in general usually follows a predictable, low-risk pattern in its contributions. The bulk of the money goes to incumbents rather than challengers, in a ratio of more than 9 to 1 (in the case of union support, the ratio is closer to 2 to 1). Business prefers to contribute to general elections rather than primaries or runoffs and helps less frequently in open-seat elections. Business groups are most apt to contribute to the highest-ranking members of congressional committees who have jurisdiction over legislation of concern to the industry or company, regardless of the candidate's political philosophy or need for funds. Thus, many business political donations have the effect of maintaining access to current policy makers rather than attempting to change the actual composition of government decision-making bodies.

Traditionally, Republican candidates have been supported more generously than Democrats, although the pattern has varied in recent years, as a result of the rising financial power of groups other than business. During the 1999–2000 political cycle, however, the major business PACs contributed $120 million to Republican candidates and only $62 million to Democrats. Despite the attention given to PACs, congressional candidates usually raise most of their money from individual citizens. Nevertheless, PAC contributions remain important.[4]

INDIRECT POLITICAL CONTRIBUTIONS

Businesses can legally make indirect contributions to political parties. For example, corporate officers and directors may take positions in political parties, often in connection with fund-raising. Although these officials function in an individual capacity, their corporate affiliations usually are known, and their activities can result in political goodwill for the firm, at least in the case of winning candidates (as discussed below, at times the political involvement can become a liability for the company). Corporations are rarely monolithic in the political sympathies of their individual executives, and frequently some members of a firm's management will actively support one candidate, while others back an opponent.

There are many ways in which corporations can legally finance political involvement. They can advertise in convention and anniversary publications issued by political parties and even in national presidential convention programs—if that cost is deemed reasonable in light of the business the advertiser expects to gain. However, the Federal Election Commission currently prohibits political parties from accepting services, such as free automobiles or buses, that business firms had, at one time, customarily donated for use at national political conventions. On the other hand, companies—and other interest groups—continue to be free to make unlimited contributions to the inaugural celebrations of successful candidates.

Members of Congress and state and local legislators, as well as candidates, may be invited to speak before trade associations, company management clubs, chamber of commerce groups, and similar business-oriented organizations. Until recently, their remuneration could range from merely having a convenient platform to present their views to generous honoraria. However, beginning in 1991, honoraria for members of Congress were prohibited as a result of special reforms enacted by Congress itself.

Any newspaper reader in recent years can readily recall numerous instances of flagrant abuse involving business and political campaigns—and attention to the less savory aspects of the subject is surely warranted. Nevertheless, it is useful to note that, even in politically active years, only a small portion of corporate officers and directors contribute to political parties. Moreover, many experienced political analysts contend that elected officials pay far more attention to the level of group influence within their state or district—and the potential for reprisals if they vote "wrong" in the eyes of a key constituency—than they do to financial contributions. Thus, the major concern of the congressional delegation from centers of defense production, although much attention is devoted to the support given by large defense contractors, is the pleas of the numerous employees and their families who are voters in the district (or state).

Presidential election campaigns are financed primarily by the $3 checkoff on the federal individual income tax return. To be eligible to receive the Treasury funds, the candidates must agree to limit their spending to the amount of the grant and not to accept private contributions for their campaigns. However, George W. Bush succeeded in his expensive bid for the presidency in 2000 without federal financing. Political parties and independent groups—at the state and local levels—may accept contributions for the various campaigns. This is where soft money continues to play a key role.

VIEWS ON BUSINESS IN POLITICS

Corporate political participation can be viewed as a continuum along which individual companies can be placed with regard to both the scope and the magnitude of their operations. Businesses in practice vary in their political efforts, from no conscious participation by company executives to an occasional letter or phone call to a member of Congress or a hundred-dollar campaign contribution to continuous and comprehensive government and electoral activity by political specialists on the company payroll.

Although most corporations engage in some form of participation in the political process, this activity varies substantially with a number of factors. These influences include the size of the firm, the degree of regulation of the enterprise by the government, and the extent to which company business and well-being depend on government decisions. The greater the importance of government to a firm's operations, the greater the likely scope and magnitude of its involvement in political activity. The larger the corporation, the more likely it is to attract the attention of government officials on such issues as taxation, pollution, and antitrust. The larger firm is also likely to have more resources to devote to political participation.

Smaller firms tend to work through the PACs of trade associations; larger companies are more likely to set up their own. Government involvement in business generates the basic pressure for business involvement in politics. Government contractors are more likely to sponsor PACs than companies selling mainly to private markets. Highly regulated firms tend to set up PACs at faster rates than entities less subject to government control. Recipients of special tax benefits and government subsidies are special candidates for political financing. Moreover, companies that face few competitors and operate in highly concentrated markets are more likely to see the benefits of political participation on behalf of their industry than firms in highly competitive markets with greater opportunity for the other firms in the industry to be "free riders."

For example, of the ten largest corporate contributors of "soft money" during the 1999–2000 election campaign cycle, six were in heavily regulated industries such as telecommunications and pharmaceuticals, while two were government-sponsored enterprises with very special ties to the federal government. Of the other two companies, one was the defendant in a major antitrust case. The trend continued into 2001, when the top dozen PACs were sponsored by 11 highly regulated companies plus the same antitrust defendant.[5]

While it is assumed that private donors are interested in a candidate's general philosophy and views on a range of issues, the financial contributions from business sources are often seen as designed to obtain specific advantages. In the words of former Senator Robert Dole, "they expect something in return other than good government."[6] At the very least, substantial political contributions bring the organization access to the elected official. Members of Congress rarely refuse to meet with the representatives of a group that supported their campaigns, although they may not necessarily follow the group's urging in voting. In the words of one CEO, "Talking to politicians is fine, but with a little money they hear you better."[7] A similar sentiment was expressed by a member of Congress to contributors: "My door is always open, but for you folks, it will be open just a little wider."[8]

TABLE 19.2   Campaign Spending for Federal Offices, 2000 Election (Millions of Dollars)

Category	Amount
Presidential campaign	$ 343
Congressional campaigns	1,006
Democratic Party—hard money	275
Democratic Party—soft money	245
Republican Party—hard money	466
Republican Party—soft money	250
Total	$2,585

Source: U.S. Federal Election Commission.

Some statistical perspective is useful on the magnitude of other electioneering spending. The total of political spending for federal candidates in the 1999–2000 election cycle—for presidential and congressional campaigns, hard and soft money combined—came to $2,585 million. That sum was divided among congressional campaigns in all 50 states as well as the efforts for the presidential candidates, and also between the national political party machinery as well as the candidates' own campaign apparatus. (See Table 19.2.) In the private sector, some products backed by huge advertising budgets fail; so do some candidates for public office who outspend their opposition.

Attitudes toward financial contributions to election campaigns fall into two conflicting categories. One view is that these payments constitute a powerful potential for favoritism and corruption. Candidates are seen as changing their positions on public issues in order to attract the huge amounts of financing needed in current campaigns. As they have become larger, political contributions have come under substantial attack. According to one veteran representative, the way to get a member of the House interested in a particular issue is to "let him know you represent a political action committee that is going to be active in the next election." A key industry CEO made a similar point: "Politics is becoming a cash-and-carry game."[9]

The contrasting view sees private financing of election campaigns as a much more benign instrument, bringing more persons into the political process and thereby making government more representative. For example, former Senator David Durenberger (R-MN) was able to hold off wealthy challenger Mark Dayton, who had contributed nearly $7 million to his own campaign, largely by raising more than $1 million in PAC contributions. A different rationale for political contributions has been advanced by Representative Barney Frank (D-MA): "I don't think that votes follow money. I think that money follows votes."[10] Empirical research confirms that point. A study at Bard College demonstrates that campaign money tends to flow to candidates who support the group's position rather than trying to influence the candidate to change a policy position already taken.[11]

PACs are no longer the dominant contributors to presidential campaigns. Government financing (via the voluntary checkoff on the federal personal income tax return) has replaced private funding in the general election period, aside from activities sponsored by soft money. Criticism of the role of money in politics can be tempered by the fact that financial contributions are not monolithic but represent varied and frequently contending interests. Thus, there is competition between business and labor, between liberals and conservatives, and between businesses in competing industries.

The diverging business positions on matters of public policy was summed up by one corporate PAC director: "We don't agree with Mobil Oil, which is in our same business, much less International Paper, which ain't." He notes that their agendas differed and that they often take opposite sides on specific policy issues.[12]

An interesting variation in public attitudes toward business financing of politics occurred following the disclosure of Enron's extensive political activities prior to its bankruptcy. Suddenly, Enron's contributions were a liability to the recipients. The National Republican Congressional Committee returned a $100,000 check the company had sent it. Members of Congress from both parties stated that they would return the campaign contributions they recently had received from the company.[13]

In the 1999–2000 election cycle, Enron's PAC, its soft money donations, and the political contributions from its employees totaled over $2.2 million (its Washington lobbying expenses in 2000 were estimated at over $2 million).[14] Nevertheless, after the election, when Enron sought assistance from various federal officials, they were turned down in every case. One veteran Washington correspondent noted that large and widespread political contributions such as Enron's "may actually make it harder for a CEO to get help from Washington allies."[15]

POLITICAL CONTRIBUTIONS BY OTHER GROUPS

Because of the amount of public attention given to the financial support of politics by business, the public tends to overlook the large efforts by other interest groups. Table 19.3 shows the 20 largest PACs in 1999–2000. It is intriguing to note that 11 unions made the list, but only one company and three business associations. Many individual companies have established sizable PACs. Yet the largest concentrations of financial power are represented by other interests, such as trial lawyers, real estate agents, doctors, unions, and gun owners.

The aggregate amount of financial contributions by business firms to political candidates should not be underestimated, however. Although the funds raised by individual business PACs are, on the average, smaller than those raised by unions, the aggregate amounts raised are larger. For example, in 1999–2000, the contributions of corporate PACs totaled $90 million and those of the labor unions came to $53 million.

Much of labor's election effort does not show up in official reports and hence is not subject to legal limitations. According to a study by the Library of Congress, unions have an infrastructure (phone banks, office space, etc.) and a ready pool of volunteers to make their internal political communications and their voter drives "a significant force."[16] Examples include the virtual full-time assignment of union organizers and clerks to get-out-the-vote duty. The AFL-CIO reports that its state campaign coordinator is usually the principal officer of the AFL-CIO in the state. The details are not

TABLE 19.3 Twenty Largest PACs in the 1999–2000 Election Cycle		
Rank	*Organization*	*Contribution*
1.	National Association of Realtors	$3,423,441
2.	Association of Trial Lawyers of America	2,656,000
3.	State, County & Municipal Employees	2,590,074
4.	National Automobile Dealers Association	2,498,700
5.	Voter Education Fund	2,494,450
6.	International Brotherhood of Electrical Workers	2,455,325
7.	Machinists League	2,181,113
8.	United Auto Workers	2,155,050
9.	American Medical Association	1,942,623
10.	Service Employees International Union	1,887,649
11.	National Beer Wholesalers' Association	1,871,500
12.	National Association of Home Builders	1,822,599
13.	Laborers' International Union	1,792,750
14.	United Parcel Service	1,755,065
15.	United Food & Commercial Workers	1,734,693
16.	National Education Association	1,716,375
17.	United Brotherhood of Carpenters	1,714,200
18.	National Rifle Association	1,583,304
19.	American Federation of Teachers	1,580,355
20.	National Association of Letter Carriers	1,530,650

Source: U.S. Federal Election Commission.

left to chance, as shown by the organization's formal seven-step plan for election campaigning:[17]

Step 1. The campaign coordinator meets with the regional director of the AFL-CIO's Committee on Political Action and other union officials to plan the campaign (120 to 180 days before the election).

Step 2. They recruit helpers and volunteers, including phone bank supervisors, and arrange installations of phones (80 to 90 days before the election).

Step 3. They train and assign phone operations and begin mailings to undecided voters (60 to 70 days before the election).

Step 4. Volunteers begin distributing flyers for candidates and sign up supporters (30 to 40 days before the election).

Step 5. Volunteers call back the undecided voters; more mailings are sent, and handbills are prepared (12 to 20 days before the election).

Step 6. Door-to-door canvassing is conducted using handbills, and more calls are made (4 days before the election).

Step 7. Direct efforts are made to get out the vote of potential supporters of union-endorsed candidates (election day).

Although most of the campaign workers are volunteers, the union effort is quite professional. Volunteers are trained in how to call union members and record their

responses on scanner cards. The undecided voters are asked what issues are most important to them and are sent "persuasion mailings" based on their responses. To encourage
volunteers, incentives are provided by the local unions in the form of tickets to ball
games, plays, and musical events.[18]

In contrast, it is difficult to find companies or trade associations that assign their
executives to full-time campaigning as part of their paid work or that devote their
reports to shareholders and executives to the campaigning in which union publications
openly engage. There is nothing illegal in these union activities per se. But their widespread existence provides further encouragement for business to rely on financial
contributions as a counterweight.

In response to the public concern over improper corporate political activities,
some companies have adopted more open, and at times rather severe, policies on the
subject of campaign contributions. DuPont discloses all U.S. political contributions by
its top executives. In addition, all solicitations for more than $1,000 and responses to
those requests are made public for inspection by reporters, shareholders, and employees. Exxon Mobil prohibits all corporate contributions to political candidates or to
political parties. This policy extends to state, local, and foreign elections, where such
political support by business is often legal.

A more radical approach, recommended by some observers who are unhappy with
all interest group political contributions, is to rely almost entirely on governmental
financing of election campaigns.[19] Such proposals are opposed by those who note the
tendency of government benefits to be accompanied, sooner or later, by government
restrictions on private discretion.

STATE AND LOCAL ELECTION CAMPAIGNS

The 2002 federal election reforms are expected to enhance the role of state and local
political parties because they are not covered by the restrictions that now apply to
national political parties. Subject to the applicable laws and regulations of their own
jurisdictions, state and local parties are allowed to accept up to $10,000 a year in soft
money donations per donor for selected activities, which also affect federal candidates,
such as registration and party building. According to a former chairman of the Federal
Election Commission, corporate and union campaign contributions have been "laun-
dered" through the state parties to avoid federal limits and restrictions.[20]

The role of business (and of other interest groups) in state and local election campaigns is governed by those units of government, and the policies they follow differ
substantially. Most of them are more lenient than the federal government. Many states
allow direct contributions by corporations in their state and local elections. However,
specific restrictions vary as to the size of corporate gifts and whether they can go to
individual candidates, political parties, or both.

Six states allow unlimited company contributions to their political campaigns:
Illinois, Missouri, New Mexico, Oregon, Utah, and Virginia. At the other extreme,
11 states maintain restrictions as tough as those of the federal government, prohibiting
either candidates or parties from accepting financial support from corporations or
unions: Alaska, Arizona, Colorado, Connecticut, North Carolina, North Dakota, Ohio,
Pennsylvania, Rhode Island, Wisconsin, and Wyoming.[21]

Although they do not receive the attention that focuses on national electoral campaigns, state political parties have become important mechanisms for raising campaign funds. In the 1999–2000 election cycle, state parties raised $307 million on their own and received $263 million in transfers from the national parties. Much of that transferred money was spent on advertising, including issue advertisements that attacked federal candidates (this is an activity that the 2002 election reforms attempt to eliminate). According to Charles Lewis, executive director of the Center for Public Integrity, "The states have been the backdoor to American politics for years."[22]

According to a joint study by the Center for Public Integrity and two other watchdog groups, the state-level donations are roughly split evenly between the Democratic and Republican parties. The largest donations to the state Democratic Party come from labor unions and trial lawyers. The major Republican contributions are real estate and securities firms and health professionals.[23]

INTERNATIONAL COMPARISONS

On the surface, it would seem that the U.S. government is at least as generous in providing financing of national elections as are many of the other industrialized nations. For example, presidential candidates who meet statutory requirements for obtaining sufficient financial support from a variety of voters then qualify for generous federal financing. In an effort to provide a level playing field, the law provides that recipients of the federal money not raise any private funds. Such federal government support is limited to the race for president.

In contrast, Japan and the United Kingdom do not provide direct public financing. In the case of Germany, France, and Italy, the government reimburses candidates according to the number of votes received. Denmark provides an allowance to the political parties, based on their strength in the previous election. Some of these countries—the United Kingdom, France, and Japan—also limit the amount of fund-raising or the amount of spending allowed on political campaigns.

Indirectly, however, each of those nations provides very important assistance to political candidates in a way that the United States does not: free time on television (which is the single most expensive election campaign item). Some countries provide that each party gets free and equal time; that is the procedure in France and on public stations in Italy and Denmark. In Britain, the TV time is allocated according to the party's strength in the previous election. Germany also provides free time to candidates on public stations, while Japan gives some free time for speeches by candidates and bars negative advertising.

Conclusions

Business executives, as well as the public, might bear in mind Peter Drucker's thoughts on the subject of business in politics: "If I were to have a criticism of the American businessman, it is that he has made no attempt to understand the political process. He attempts to influence it without understanding it."[24]

Some business organizations attempt to meet Drucker's challenge. Many trade associations regularly sponsor political campaign-management seminars. Designed to be nonpartisan in nature, the seminars typically are aimed at business executives who

TABLE 19.4   Seminar on Political Campaign Management

Program Outline

Research and surveys
Planning strategy
Fund-raising, advertising, and publicity
Direct mail
Campaign organization
Volunteer activities
Graphics and photography
Campaign law
Computers and automated devices
Profile of a successful campaign
Reaching special classifications
   Absentee ballots
   Campus votes
   Rural votes
   Votes in high-rise apartments
Print and electronic advertising

Source: U.S. Chamber of Commerce.

become involved in campaigns for public office at various levels—federal, state, and local. The sessions are aimed at potential candidates, campaign managers, and finance directors, as well as rank-and-file volunteers. Staffed by professional campaign consultants, the seminars show the various steps in developing a campaign, including administrative and financial aspects. Table 19.4 reproduces the program outline of a political campaign management seminar of the Chamber of Commerce of the United States. The sessions are devoted to techniques of political campaigning and avoid advocating positions on specific issues or supporting individual candidates or political parties.

In viewing the entire subject of participation in politics, caution is in order. An unwary management can get into trouble by naively participating in the funding of election campaigns. Contributions to political-action groups are required to be voluntary, without pressure on employees in solicitation. Heavy-handed solicitation on the part of some firms could cause a backlash, both within the company and in the public arena.

Some analysts have pointed to the fundamental pressures for continuing and increasing financial contributions to election campaigns by business and other interest groups: the desire to obtain more of the largesse available from government treasuries and to avoid the restrictions that may result from new government regulations. As the size and power of public-sector departments and agencies continue to increase, it can be expected that more of the private sector's resources will be devoted to influencing the political process. To remind the reader of the obvious, every dollar spent by the federal government ends up in somebody's pocket as a salary, subsidy, purchase, loan, or transfer payment. Also of obvious economic benefit are tax provisions that induce customers to purchase specific products, regulations that favor the "ins" against the "outs," and governmental credit programs that channel funds to favored groups.

Surely, the interactions between campaign financing and politics have been controversial for centuries. In 1750, when George Washington easily won his seat in the Virginia House of Burgesses, opponents criticized the amount disbursed during the campaign. Some attention was paid to the 150 gallons of liquor that Washington distributed among the district's 391 voters in his effort to gain office.[25] Perhaps Will Rogers deserves the last word on the subject: "Politics has got so expensive, it takes lots of money to even get beat with nowadays."

Notes

1. Catherine Morrison, *Managing Corporate Political Action Committees* (New York: Conference Board, 1986), pp. v–vi.
2. Norman J. Ornstein, Thomas E. Mann, and Michael J. Malbin, *Vital Statistics on Congress 2001–2002* (Washington, DC: AEI Press, 2002).
3. Quoted in Morrison, *Managing Corporate PACs,* p. 3.
4. Ornstein et al., *Vital Statistics.*
5. Joshua Green, "PACs and Pols Eye November," *Corporate Board Member,* March/April 2002, p. 13.
6. Quoted in Irwin Ross, "Why PACs Spell Trouble," *Reader's Digest,* July 1983, p. 108.
7. Quoted in Tom Richman, "Picking a PAC," *Inc.,* August 1982, p. 30.
8. Quoted in Morrison, *Managing Corporate PACs,* p. 23.
9. Randy Huwa, "Political Action Committees," *Business Forum,* Winter 1984, p. 13.
10. Quoted in Morrison, *Managing Corporate PACs,* p. 25.
11. Christopher Magee, *Campaign Contributions, Policy Decisions, and Election Outcomes* (Annandale-on-Hudson, NY: Levy Economic Institute of Bard College, 2001).
12. Larry J. Sabato, "PAC-Man Goes to Washington," *Across the Board,* October 1984, p. 25.
13. Tom Hamburger and Greg Hitt, "Lawmakers Return Campaign Contributions From Energy Firm," *Wall Street Journal,* January 14, 2002, p. A6.
14. David E. Sanger, "Laying Low," *CEO Magazine,* February 2002, p. 11.
15. Ibid., p. 11.
16. Joseph E. Cantor, *Political Spending by Organized Labor* (Washington, DC: Library of Congress, Congressional Research Service, 1996), p. 3.
17. Michael Byrne, "Getting Out the Vote," *AFL-CIO News,* June 25, 1992, p. 6.
18. Ibid., p. 7.
19. *Democratically Financed Congressional Elections* (Deerfield, MA: Working Group on Electoral Democracy, 1993).
20. Tom Hamburger, "Soft Money Law Awaits Day in High Court," *Wall Street Journal,* June 24, 2002, p. A4.
21. *Book of the States* (Washington, DC: Council of State Governments, 2002); Thad Kousser and Ray La Raja, *The Effect of Campaign Finance Laws on Electoral Competition* (Washington, DC: Cato Institute, 2002).
22. Richard A. Oppel, Jr., "State Parties Adept at Raising Soft Money, Report Shows," *New York Times,* June 26, 2002, p. A19.
23. Ibid.
24. "Inside Peter Drucker," *Nation's Business,* March 1974, p. 63.
25. Andrea Segedy, "Why We Have PACs," *Business Forum,* Winter 1984, p. 8.

PART VI

THE FUTURE OF THE CORPORATION

Business and government both exist in a society in which a variety of interest groups attempts to impose their ideas on others. To the extent that business voluntarily responds to these other viewpoints, it may reduce the likelihood of additional governmental action. As shown in Part VI, in changing itself by adjusting to and complying with external pressures and desires, the corporation assures its continuance as a vital institution in modern society.

20

CHALLENGES TO
CORPORATE GOVERNANCE
≈*≈

T he governance of corporations in the United States is regulated primarily by the requirements contained in state corporation statutes. While these laws generally provide broad discretion to directors and officers in the normal running of business operations, they vary in the degree of power given to minority shareholders and in the types of company action requiring shareholder approval. Delaware, the state in which most large firms are incorporated, minimizes restrictions on company managements. Some other states, notably California, maintain a policy favoring shareholders at the expense of management discretion.[1]

In addition, the U.S. Securities and Exchange Commission regulates many aspects of corporate reporting as well as the issuance of company stock for interstate sale and, as discussed later, the voting process and related procedures at corporate annual meetings.

The dramatic bankruptcy of the Enron Corporation in late 2001 (see Appendix, "The Collapse of Enron") generated an unprecedented amount of public attention to the hitherto arcane topic of corporate governance. Widespread reports at the same time of specific shortcomings in the conduct of other large companies also set in motion pressures for additional government intervention. However, criticisms of the conduct of private business—and proposals for governmental intervention—are of long standing. The following section provides some historical context for examining the current issues involving public policy toward corporate governance.

THE CRITICS OF THE CORPORATION

To many traditional critics of business, the managements of large corporations are oligarchies, responsible to no one but themselves. Shareholders are seen as largely at the mercy of the management, their only power being to sell their stock in a company when they do not approve of its activities. The typical stockholder is viewed as neither capable of understanding nor interested in the actual business of the company in which he or she owns stock.

Corporate boards of directors are thus characterized as self-perpetuating groups, accountable to themselves or to the chief executives who supposedly select them. Because the critics see corporations as private governments operating under legal constraints that are for the most part irrelevant, over the years they have advocated a variety of changes in the way corporations are governed. Although there is some factual basis for these views, this approach does not take into account the active "market" for corporate control in which dissident shareholders or other large investors attempt, often successfully, to wrest control of major corporations from their managements. Moreover, with top management compensation increasingly geared to the market price of the company's stock, large institutional holders have gained substantial access to management attention.

In 1997, the influential California Public Employees' Retirement System (Calpers) developed a set of proposals to restructure corporate boards that went into greater detail than most earlier suggestions. As a large investor in many companies, Calpers urged strengthening the role of the outside directors in several ways:

- *Adopt a more stringent definition of independent director.* Such a board member would not be allowed to serve more than ten years, hold a personal services contract with the company, or be affiliated with a nonprofit group that receives "significant" contributions from the company.
- *The chairman should be an outside director.* Alternatively, the board should select an independent "lead" director to deal with the chairman. Independent directors should meet alone at least once a year.
- *No director should serve on more than three boards.* Term limits should also be set as well as minimum experience guidelines. Pensions for directors should be eliminated, and no more than 10 percent of a board's directors should be over 70 years old.
- *A formal program, in addition to the annual meeting, should be set for shareholders to communicate with directors.*

In early 2002, following the bankruptcy of Enron, a group of experienced corporate directors proposed additional changes in governance policies:

1. The full board of directors should meet in closed session at each board meeting without the chief executive officer (CEO) or other corporate insiders.
2. Likewise, key committees of the board should meet periodically without management present.
3. Key committees should be authorized to hire outside advisers and their chairmanships should be held in rotation.
4. The assignments to board committees should be made by the board rather than the CEO.
5. Outside directors should not do consulting work for the company nor should their employers provide services to the company.[2]

The common theme of these proposals is to strengthen the authority of the board of directors and thus to enhance its oversight of corporate management. Although no company has adopted all of these reforms, quite a few have voluntarily moved in the direction of enhancing the independence of the corporate board and thus providing a better opportunity for improved internal monitoring of business performance.

EARLIER RESPONSES BY THE CORPORATION

Most past changes in corporate governance have taken place voluntarily, in part to avoid overt action by government (see Table 20.1). A significant voluntary shift has occurred in the composition of the boards of directors of American companies. Outside directors—those who are not members of management—have become a large majority of most boards of public companies in the United States. By 2000, four-fifths of the average corporate board consisted of outside directors.

TABLE 20.1   Key Dates in Voluntary Corporate Governance Policy

1853	New York Stock Exchange (NYSE) enacts first mandate for listed companies, requiring complete statements of shares outstanding and capital resources
1869	NYSE cracks down on issuance of shares in secret ("watering" stock)
1899	All listed companies supply regular financial statements, including balance sheets and income statements
1927	NYSE issues regulations governing solicitation of proxies
1956	NYSE urges listed companies to include at least two outside directors on their boards
1977	NYSE requires audit committees composed of outside directors
1980s	Boards of most larger companies contain a majority of outside directors; audit committees become universal
1999	NYSE sets rules for independence and financial expertise of audit committees
2002	Many companies reduce or eliminate the consulting work they assign to their outside auditors
2002	Some companies begin to treat stock option awards as a current expense of doing business

---

The larger the firm, the more likely the predominance of outside directors. In fact, the biggest companies were the first to name a majority of nonmanagement directors. Simultaneously, the prevalence of formally "dependent" outside directors (those who also provide services to the company) has diminished. In the 1970s, the average board included a commercial banker, an attorney, or both. That is currently true in only a minority of instances. Nevertheless, the true independence of outside directors remains a point of contention.

A broader diversity of backgrounds is also evident in the types of persons serving on corporate boards. Increased numbers of directors have public-service or scientific experience. Boards now also include significant percentages of women, minorities, and academics—as well as directors from other countries (mainly Canada and Western Europe). In 2000, 74 percent of the *Fortune* 500 companies had at least one woman on their board, compared to 69 percent in 1961.[3] Also in 2000, 40 percent of a sample of large corporations had one or more African-Americans on their boards.[4]

The rise of strong board committees is also continuing, mainly on a voluntary basis. As recently as 1973, only one-half of large U.S. corporations had auditing committees. Auditing committees of boards of directors now have become a universal phenomenon. These financial-oversight bodies are usually composed entirely of outside directors. That is an absolute requirement for firms listed on the New York Stock Exchange. The typical audit committee has direct access to both the outside auditing firm that reviews the company's financial records and procedures and the firm's own internal audit staff. This information enables these committees to review the financial aspects of corporate operations in detail and to probe into suspicious situations. As shown by recent experience, the effectiveness of audit committees varies substantially, despite the shift in composition to outside directors.

The boards of directors of most of the larger corporations have set up nominating committees to propose both candidates for the board and the CEO. These committees generally have a large majority of outside directors and frequently contain no members of management. However, the statistics do little to illuminate the continuing powerful role of the CEO in initiating or approving committee selections. In practice, outside directors are often selected by the chairman/CEO and, in virtually all cases, he or she must agree with their appointment.

A recent variation is the transformation of the nominating committee into a broader governance committee. This new body, which has the responsibility for nominating new directors, is also given the primary role in evaluating the work of the CEO and often of the board itself. Given the newness of this development, it seems too early to determine its effectiveness. Nevertheless, merely establishing a process whereby the directors examine the performance of the top management is likely, in the long run, to enhance the role of the board.[5]

In most large companies, compensation committees of the board determine the terms and conditions of the employment of top executives. These committees are composed largely or entirely of outside directors. However, most "comp" committees rely extensively on outside consultants, usually hired by the management. The consultant's surveys of the pay and perks of comparable positions in other companies and industries set the framework for committee deliberations.

Despite the rising number of outside directors and special committees of corporate boards, in most cases the center of power remains with the management. CEOs serve as chairpersons of the board in 90 percent of the larger corporations, and they set the agenda and conduct the board meetings. Many of the directors they choose are CEOs of other companies who tend to be inherently sympathetic in their response to their colleagues' proposals. Nevertheless, in periods of crisis, outside directors typically rise to the occasion and meet their responsibilities. However, it often takes a serious challenge to the future of the company for outside directors to take a strong position independent of the management.

Simultaneously with the expansion of the role of outside directors, a related development has been taking place: the rise of activism on the part of different groups of shareholders. As we will see, the role of the activists has undergone fundamental metamorphoses over the years.

THE RISE OF CORPORATE ACTIVISM

RAISING INVESTOR ISSUES (THE PIONEERING BUSINESS ACTIVISTS)

In the 1930s, two individual shareholders, Lewis and John Gilbert, began attending corporate annual meetings and exercised the dormant right of stockholders to question management. They focused on issues of corporate policy of interest to investors, such as financial disclosure, stock reinvestment plans, and cumulative voting for directors (which would enable minority shareholders to concentrate their votes on one candidate). The Gilberts introduced motions on the floor and otherwise highlighted the power of the stockholders.[6]

In 1942, the Securities and Exchange Commission (SEC) adopted a regulation that promoted the role of the small holder. SEC Rule 14a-8 requires companies to include shareholder resolutions in proxy statements routinely sent to each holder of common stock if the proposals are proper subjects for consideration by all shareholders. Thus, corporate activists were given access to all other shareholders at the company's expense. They also were assured some minimum amount of time at company annual meetings to discuss these issues.

Many corporate practices now considered traditional were pioneered by the Gilberts in the 1930s and 1940s. These include holding annual meetings at sites convenient to large numbers of shareholders, issuing reports on actions taken at the annual meeting, and disclosing substantial amounts of financial data. Because the Gilberts were persistent questioners of the amounts of executive salaries and bonuses, they came to be known as corporate gadflies. Nevertheless, the actions taken by the Gilberts were designed to promote the interests of stockholders as stockholders. Subsequently, however, the enhanced powers of individual shareholders were transformed into mechanisms for achieving very different objectives.

RAISING SOCIAL ISSUES (THE SOCIAL ACTIVISTS)

One of the first efforts to mobilize stockholders to achieve a social objective was launched in 1966 by activist Saul Alinsky. His aim was to convince Eastman Kodak to adopt a preferential hiring plan, whereby the company would train 600 unskilled, unemployed African-Americans over an 18-month period, to qualify for entry-level positions. When negotiations with Kodak broke down, Alinsky brought the battle to the company's 1967 annual meeting.

Buses of demonstrators were met by state troopers and Kodak guards. Most of the session was devoted to the controversy. Kodak's board chairman recognized "that we have a continuing responsibility to you, the shareowners, and to our employees and customers, as well as to the community at large." Two months later, Kodak agreed to a settlement, although much less than Alinsky's demands.[7] The Kodak episode marked an important turn in stockholder activism. The issue raised was irrelevant to traditional shareholders' concerns and was activated by purchasing just ten shares of Kodak stock in order to gain admission to the annual meeting.

In 1968, the Medical Committee for Human Rights (which had received a gift of several Dow Company shares) requested that, as Dow shareholders, they be allowed to ask the board of directors to prohibit sales of napalm for military purposes. The SEC upheld Dow's refusal to include the matter in its proxy statement. But, in 1970, a U.S. Circuit Court of Appeals reversed the agency's decision. Thus, the corporate proxy statement was opened up to social responsibility resolutions by minority shareholders.

Campaign GM, orchestrated by a nonprofit organization called the Project on Corporate Responsibility, was another watershed for shareholder activism. For the first time, it successfully employed the proxy machinery to confront management on social issues. By virtue of its ownership of 12 shares of the company's stock, the campaign succeeded in getting two proposals included in the company's 1970 proxy statement:

1. To add three public-interest representatives to the GM board of directors. The campaign headquarters also named its likely nominees: a consumer advocate, an environmental specialist, and an African-American.
2. To establish a shareholder committee on corporate responsibility, to be composed of 15 to 25 representatives of environmental, civil rights, labor, academic, and

other groups. They would be chosen by a group consisting of a member of GM's board and representatives of the United Auto Workers union and Campaign GM. The shareholder committee would report on the company's efforts to reduce pollution, develop safer products, encourage opportunities for minorities, and facilitate low-cost mass transit.

The SEC upheld the position of Campaign GM. This development opened up corporate proxy machinery to public-interest issues because proposals with a clear social purpose no longer were automatically held to violate SEC Rule 14a-8. Campaign GM dominated the 1970 annual meeting of General Motors, although both of its proposals were overwhelmingly defeated. In the months that followed, however, the company took several steps, although indirect, toward meeting Campaign GM's demands.

General Motors created the first public policy committee of the board of directors of a major U.S. corporation. The committee's charter covered all phases of the corporation's business activities that related to matters of public policy. Many companies have since created board committees with titles such as "public policy," "corporate responsibility," and "public issues." A lasting impact of Campaign GM was to motivate nonprofit institutions to use their corporate holdings to raise social policy questions at corporate annual meetings, especially via the proxy statement.

The volume and variety of public-interest resolutions appearing on corporate proxies has become substantial. By the 1980s, the subjects covered an even wider terrain, ranging from environmental impacts to minority employment to purchasing practices. Nevertheless, most shareholders continue to ignore the agenda of the social activists. At the annual meeting of Exxon Mobil in 2000, shareholders defeated by a vote of 95 percent to 5 percent a proposed requirement that the company issue a special report on drilling in the Alaska wildlife reserve. A proposal for a special report on a pipeline in Africa was turned down by a similar 95 to 5 percent vote. Of seven proposals submitted by minority shareholders, none received as much as 10 percent support.

A statistical analysis of shareholder activism during 1982–1998 reveals the limitations of these efforts. Virtually all of the companies—Enron, Global Crossing, Tyco, Adelphia, WorldCom—whose activities enraged the public in 2001–2002 were ignored by the activists. Instead, their major targets were merely the most visible companies in the nation—General Electric, PepsiCo, and IBM.[8]

However, issues more directly affecting corporate governance are receiving an increasing amount of shareholder support. At the 2002 annual shareholders meeting of Exxon Mobil, a proposal calling for the board to seek shareholder approval before adopting a "poison pill" to deter a takeover bid won 45 percent of the shares cast. Also in 2002, a proposal to eliminate "staggered" board elections (which would limit the election of a director to a year at a time) received support of 69 percent of the votes cast at the annual meeting of Bristol-Myers Squibb. (The company did not take action on the grounds that the positive vote did not represent a majority of the outstanding shares of the company.)[9]

INSTITUTIONAL INVESTORS

A relatively new development is the changed role of a large segment of institutional investors, especially the managers of the pension funds of state and local governments and other large, nonprofit organizations. The justification for their departure from the older

"Wall Street" rule (i.e., if you do not approve of the company's management, sell your stock) is that those large investors are often locked in to the companies whose shares they own. That is, institutional investors own such large blocks of stock that the price of the security would fall sharply if they tried to dispose of their holdings. As a result, institutions often believe that it is more realistic to try to improve the operations of the poorly performing companies than to sell their large blocks of stock. Most of this new type of institutional activism focuses on traditional shareholder concerns rather than social issues.

An important change in the practice of corporate governance in the United States occurred during the 1990s in the case of a few very large and—at times, poorly performing—corporations: General Motors, Sears Roebuck, IBM, Eastman Kodak, and American Express. In each instance, the board responded to the concerns of major institutional investors and took decisive if not belated action, typically replacing the CEO. The directors of GM selected an outside director (the recently retired CEO of Procter & Gamble) to be board chairman during a difficult transition period. IBM also created a new board committee of outside directors to nominate new directors, handle proposals from shareholders, and oversee the board's performance.

THE OUTLOOK FOR FURTHER CHANGES IN CORPORATE GOVERNANCE

As a result of the Enron bankruptcy in late 2001 (see Appendix, "The Collapse of Enron," for details) and dramatic shortcomings in the operations of other large companies, corporate governance in the United States is in a condition of flux. The initial major response was by government officials—stepped-up enforcement of existing laws by the SEC and the Department of Justice and new legislation from Congress. In mid-2002, Congress enacted important reforms of corporate governance. It can be seen in Table 20.2 that most of the changes focus on finance and accounting matters, although the subject of executive stock options also received considerable attention. One of the most specific changes was to require the CEOs and chief financial officers of companies listed on stock exchanges to certify the accuracy and "appropriateness" of financial reports to the public.

Nevertheless, neither the executive branch nor legislative action has dealt effectively with the basic shortcomings of corporate governance that became evident during the rash of bankruptcies and financial writedowns that occurred in 2001 and 2002. Essentially, the problems relate to the structure of individual firms and the judgment exercised by individual business decision makers. These are not matters readily responsive to broad-based governmental laws and regulations.

To a considerable degree, financial markets are exerting a disciplinary force on publicly held corporations. Any significant questioning of the accuracy of a company's financial statements is now likely to generate a decline in the price of its stock. Also, the insurance companies who write the policies on officers' and directors' liabilities are another source of pressure for honesty and accuracy in business reporting. The insurers are demanding more financial data from their clients and the further assurance of high levels of integrity on the part of management and boards of directors.[10]

As noted earlier, to some extent companies are voluntarily responding to current public concerns about the performance of private enterprise.[11] Important questions

TABLE 20.2   Highlights of 2002 Congressional Reforms of Corporate Governance

Company management

1. CEOs and CFOs are required to certify the accuracy of financial reports.
2. They must disclose material changes in company's financial condition "in plain English."
3. CEOs must give up gains from stock options and bonuses based on false reporting.
4. Executives who lie to the SEC face fines and prison.
5. Executives must disclose stock sales within two days.
6. Top managements may not receive personal loans from their company.
7. Companies must allow employees to diversify 401(k) plans away from company stock after three years of service.

Boards of directors

1. Boards must have a majority of independent directors.
2. Audit committee must approve the selection of auditors, auditor consulting contracts, and 401(k) plans.

Shareholders

1. Must vote on approval of stock-option plans.

Investment banking firms

1. May not retaliate against analysts who criticize clients.

Outside auditors

1. Consulting work is limited.
2. Audits subject to new oversight board with power to discipline.
3. Required to rotate lead partners of company audits every five years.

Securities and Exchange Commission

1. Must make rules on conflicts of interest of stock market analysts.

Source: Sarbanes–Oxley Act of 2002, "To protect investors by improving the accuracy and reliability of corporate disclosures made pursuant to the securities laws, and for other purposes," August 2002.

continue to face the senior members of corporate management as well as their boards of directors. The multiplicity of governance issues that have arisen fall into four major categories: management, boards of directors, outside auditors, and other specialists (including attorneys, credit-rating analysts, and securities analysts).

THE ROLE OF TOP MANAGEMENT

Under established law, the board of directors is elected by the shareholders to exercise the basic authority over the corporation. This includes selecting the CEO and establishing the policies under which management carries out its functions.[12] As a practical matter, CEOs and their key associates exercise the basic decision-making authority over contemporary corporations. The ramifications of that reality are numerous. Most fundamentally, it means that the management, although nominally the "agent" of the shareholders, really makes the major decisions affecting the future of the organization.

Viewed in this light, excesses of compensation and other discretionary shortcomings are mainly a reflection of the reality of the location of corporate authority. It is clear that the public has been aroused by reports of abuses of that authority, such as individual CEOs receiving annual compensation in excess of $100 million. Investors are outraged when they juxtapose such extremely generous rewards with the company's mediocre or even poor performance. For example, senior management of Bankers Trust Company received $1.1 billion in bonuses for 1998, even though the company lost $6 million that year.

Efforts by government to limit compensation of management have been unsuccessful and even counterproductive. In 1993, Congress responded to an earlier wave of public concern about high management salaries by limiting to $1 million the amount of compensation per individual that could be deducted on federal tax returns as an acceptable business expense ($1 million seemed to be a generous cap back then). An analysis of 1,400 publicly traded corporations revealed no effect of the legislation on company pay decisions.[13]

However, under the 1993 law, no limit on deductibility would apply to income received under an incentive compensation plan. Not surprisingly, the enactment of the statute was followed by a burst of new management incentive plans. These plans frequently included options to purchase the company's stock in the future at a fixed price (typically, the price at the time the options were issued).

If the price of the stock rose, the executives could purchase shares from the company at the low guaranteed price. The justification was that they would be motivated to take actions that would raise the market price of the company's shares. On the other hand, if the stock price fell, the executives would not purchase the stock at the higher option price. In some cases where the stock price declined, the board "rebased" the options at a lower price. Under those circumstances, the executives would still have the opportunity for financial rewards—without delivering the expected improvement in the company's stock.[14]

A recurring controversy is whether companies should be required to treat the issuance of stock under an option plan as a deductible expense—and hence to reduce reported earnings. Those who favor this approach believe that it is necessary to demonstrate that issuing such shares is a real cost to the companies and thus they should be given an incentive to economize on this cost—and to restrain the generous issuance of stock options in recent years. Those who oppose such a change in accounting policy note that no cash is expended by the company in connection with stock options and that such incentives are necessary because of the limited ability of some companies, especially new high-tech firms, to offer compensation as cash. In response to widespread criticism, some corporations, led by Coca-Cola, announced in 2002 that they will voluntarily expense executive stock options.

Other aspects of questionable management compensation relate to such matters as the range of personal expenditures to be reimbursed by the company as well as retirement benefits. These specific issues lead to examining the role of the corporate board of directors, which has the authority to approve or reject these benefits.

THE ROLE OF THE BOARD OF DIRECTORS

In practice, the board is not as all-powerful as would appear from a simple reading of corporate law. In the great majority of cases (90 percent for the larger firms), the CEO also serves as chairman of the board. Thus, this senior member of management sets the agenda for the board and presides over its meetings. The members of the board themselves are often selected by the CEO or at least subject to his or her approval.

As noted earlier, in recent years the effectiveness of the board has been enhanced by strengthening the key committees—audit, compensation, and nominations (the latter often has been expanded into a governance committee). It has become standard practice for these committees to consist entirely of outside (nonmanagement) directors. However, this nominal independence has not prevented the occurrence of numerous shortcomings in corporate governance.

Few legislative proposals have been offered to improve the effectiveness of boards of directors. In the main, the suggestions that have been made involve voluntary changes in corporate governance to be adopted at the company level. The most frequent proposal is to appoint an outside director as board chairman. Although American CEOs strongly object to this dilution of their customary authority, the separation of the management from the board chairmanship is common practice in the United Kingdom. For example, Alexander Trotman, retired CEO of Ford Motor Company and now Lord Trotman, serves as the chairman of the board of Britain's Imperial Chemical Industries. The separation of CEO and chairmanship is close to universal in the case of nonprofit institutions in the United States. The California State Employee Pension Fund (Calpers) suggests that separating the chairmanship from the CEO position should be considered when the board is selecting a new CEO—rather than attempting to "demote" an individual who holds both positions.

The views of John G. Smale are quite instructive. He is a retired CEO/chairman of Procter & Gamble and subsequently served as the outside chairman of the board of General Motors. Smale notes that, as a CEO/chairman, he would not have welcomed a diminution of his authority and that he viewed his outside chairmanship at the time as merely a transitional appointment. However, on reflection, he now believes that the board should be chaired by an outside director:

> If the purpose of a board is to represent the shareholders in overseeing management's conduct of the business, such a structure [an outside director serving as chairman] seems considerably more logical than having the board chaired by a manager who is also the subject of such oversight.[15]

An increasingly popular compromise is for the outside directors to select a "lead" director to represent their views in private meetings with the CEO and, at least once a year, to chair a board meeting consisting entirely of outside directors. By 2000, 32 percent of the larger companies had appointed lead directors, up from 27 percent in 1996.

The 2002 corporate reform statute (the Sarbanes–Oxley Act) specifies that the audit committee of the board, rather than the management, is directly responsible for the appointment, compensation, and oversight of the accounting firm selected to serve as outside auditor. The audit committee is also charged with resolving disagreements between the management and the outside auditor on financial reporting.

It has been proposed that similar authority be given to the board's compensation committee to select the consulting firm that provides the analysis on which the top management compensation program is based. Where the management is the client of the compensation consultant, it is difficult for the board to make a truly independent assessment of executive compensation.

In addition, the developing role of the governance committee may become another important way of enhancing the effectiveness of the board of directors. Boards are experimenting with methods of evaluating the performance of the CEO without assuming the prerogatives of management. Simultaneously, many boards of directors (about 40 percent) also evaluate the effectiveness of the board itself, although relatively few review the work of individual directors.[16]

THE ROLE OF THE OUTSIDE AUDITORS

Disclosures of inadequate controls over corporate financial reporting have highlighted the role of the accounting firms that conduct the external audit. These firms assess the accounting principles used in the preparation of the company's financial statements and audit the details supporting those statements so that they can state that the company's financial reports are "in conformity with generally accepted accounting principles."

Congress legislated in 2002 a variety of restrictions on the operations of the firms conducting audits of corporations listed on U.S. stock exchanges (see Table 20.2). The outside auditors are specifically prevented from performing a long list of nonaudit tasks for their audit clients. These prohibited services range from bookkeeping and internal auditing to providing legal or investment banking services. Other nonaudit services, such as providing assistance on tax returns, must be approved in advance by the board's audit committee.

In addition, the work of outside auditors is subject to review by a new nonprofit nongovernmental organization chartered by Congress—the Public Company Accounting Oversight Board. The SEC appoints the five members of the Oversight Board and exercises oversight of and enforcement authority over it. The companies being audited are required to provide the bulk of the financing of the Oversight Board, based on their relative capitalization. Creating a nonprofit organization to carry out responsibilities designated by the Congress is an unusual but not unique compromise between public-sector and private-sector responsibilities (see Chapter 14 for an analysis of government-sponsored credit enterprises).

THE ROLE OF OTHER SPECIALISTS

Numerous other professionals participate in the corporate practices that have received widespread criticism. So far, none has received the attention that has been directed to the accountants, and Congress has responded in the case of some professions and not others. For example, although credit rating analysts have maintained favorable reports on the bonds of firms on the edge of bankruptcy, reform is left to private-sector discretion. On the other hand, in the case of the stock analysts whose favorable reports on poorly performing companies have been subject to considerable criticism, several brokerages and investment banking firms have taken steps to provide more independence for these analysts. The Sarbanes–Oxley Act of 2002 prohibits investment banking firms from punishing analysts who write reports critical of the firm's clients.

Although not to the detailed extent to which the accounting profession is subject to new regulation, the 2002 statute does extend to the work of lawyers who practice before the SEC. Specifically, these attorneys are required to report evidence of any "material" violation of securities law or breach of fiduciary duty to the CEO of the company or to its chief legal counsel. The chairman of the SEC at the time, Harvey L.

Pitt, offered a broader interpretation in a speech to the American Bar Association shortly after the passage of the 2002 law:

> Lawyers for public companies represent the company as a whole and its shareholder-owners, not the managers who hire and fire them.[17]

Conclusions

There are many changes now occurring in corporate governance, both on a compulsory and on a voluntary basis. The evolutionary pattern, which has been the experience in the United States over the years, also mirrors the status of the common law that governs much of business activity in the United States and the United Kingdom. It is likely that the reforms that were adopted in 2002 will not be the last word on the subject. The accompanying box, "New York Stock Exchange Proposals on Corporate Governance," provides some indication of the future direction of voluntary changes in corporate governance.

BOX 20-1

NEW YORK STOCK EXCHANGE PROPOSALS ON CORPORATE GOVERNANCE

In 2002, the New York Stock Exchange (NYSE) issued a report urging new rules to strengthen the role of member-company boards of directors. Although violations of the rules are not a legal offense, the consequences are not trivial. The NYSE can publicly reprimand first-time violators—a potential source of considerable embarrassment—with negative potentials for investor interest in the company's stock. Companies who repeatedly or flagrantly violated rules can be delisted—their stock could not be traded on the exchange.

The NYSE report sets forth the following key rules (and many detailed restrictions):

1. A majority of each board should consist of independent directors.

2. The definition of *independent* director should exclude any individual with "material relationship" to the company or someone who has worked there during the last five years.

3. All members of the audit, compensation, and nominating committees should be independent directors.

4. The audit committee should have sole authority to hire and fire independent auditors and to approve nonaudit work.

5. The nonmanagement directors should hold regular executive sessions. They should appoint a lead director to chair these meetings. They should be able to communicate directly with employees and shareholders.

6. Shareholder approval should be required for all equity-based (stock option) pay plans.

7. The CEO must certify each year that the information provided to the shareholders is accurate and complete.

8. Each listed company should adopt and publish corporate governance guidelines and a code of business conduct and ethics. Any waiver of ethics or business codes for executives and directors must be disclosed promptly.

APPENDIX

THE COLLAPSE OF ENRON

The dramatic December 2001 bankruptcy of Enron Corporation, previously one of the nation's most admired enterprises, was the single most important contributing factor to the current wave of criticism of American business. The collapse of Enron occurred almost as rapidly as its rise.[18]

CEO and chairman Kenneth Lay had led the transformation of Enron from a traditional operator of gas pipelines to a pioneer in energy trading. In the late 1990s, Enron reinvented itself again, at times under the leadership of President and, for a while, CEO Jeffrey Skilling. The new Enron downplayed the role of traditional fixed assets and emphasized brokering a wide variety of activities, ranging from broadband Internet capacity to water contracts, matching buyers and sellers in the same fashion of exchanges that provide the mechanism for buying and selling stocks or commodities.

As measured by sales, Enron was the seventh-largest company in the United States in 2001. This achievement occurred in part because Enron included in its reported revenues not just the commissions it earned from its trades, but the total amount of trades that it arranged. If an investment banking firm such as Merrill Lynch followed that practice in connection with the stocks and bonds bought and sold for its clients, it would be listed as a global behemoth!

Enron further exaggerated its revenues and hid much of its debt through dealings with hundreds of subsidiaries and ostensibly independent offshore partnerships. (An Enron submission to the SEC in 2000 contained a 49-page list of subsidiaries.) The "special purpose entities" were, in fact, controlled by company insiders. The chief financial officer, Andrew Fastow, acted as general partner of the supposedly independent partnerships. The financing of these special-purpose entities was so complex as to be termed "arcane," although a more accurate description might be "sham." When President Skilling resigned unexpectedly in the summer of 2001, these arrangements began to unravel. Although it was not brought to light until 2002, it turns out that several members of Enron's middle management questioned very seriously the sustainability of the company's unusual financial arrangements. Ultimately, Enron was forced to conclude that its off-balance-sheet partnerships were not truly independent. The poor results of their operations were reluctantly consolidated into the company's financial reports.

As a result, in October 2001 the company announced an unprecedented loss of $618 million for the third quarter of the year. A follow-on conference call with financial analysts only worsened the situation. During the call, CEO Lay mentioned in passing that the company's value had declined by $1.2 billion, as a result of deals with the special partnerships. Enron's liquidity came under stress. Its situation became more precarious when, in November, the company reported that it had overstated its profits by almost $600 million during the previous five years. Investors in Enron, who had been unaware of the impact of its unusual financial arrangements, accelerated their sales of the company's stock. Efforts to merge with another energy company failed. In December 2001, Enron filed for bankruptcy.

The announcement of Enron's collapse dominated media coverage and public discussions for weeks. Reports surfaced of other questionable activities conducted by Enron management. It turned out that, during the fall of 2001, senior company officials repeatedly called upon the White House and on individual cabinet officers for help in avoiding bankruptcy. During the presidential campaign of 2000, Lay and other senior company officials had been very generous contributors to the successful effort in behalf of George W. Bush. The company contributed substantial amounts of "soft money" to the Republican election effort and also to the January 2001 presidential inaugural (for details on "soft" money and other financing techniques, see Chapter 19).

Nevertheless, Enron was turned down by every member of the Bush administration that it approached for help and so proceeded into bankruptcy. The repercussions were particularly severe on the rank-and-file employees. Many of them had invested the bulk of their retirement savings in the form of company stock held in their 401(k) accounts. Enron had supplemented voluntary employee payroll savings with generous amounts of company stock, which employees could not sell until they reached the age of 50. In early 2001, shares in Enron represented 62 percent of all investments in Enron employees' 401(k) accounts.

Thus, when the company declared bankruptcy, many of its employees lost both their jobs and the bulk of their retirement money. Their anger toward the company was exacerbated by the memory that, as recently as September 2001, Lay, during an online chat, urged employees to buy Enron stock, calling it "incredibly cheap." Subsequently, reports surfaced that senior officials cashed in over $1 billion of their Enron stockholdings during an extended period prior to the bankruptcy.[19]

For apparently technical reasons related to a change in administrators of Enron's retirement plan, employees were prevented from selling any stock in their 401(k) accounts in late October and early November 2001. That was the time when the market price of Enron stock was declining rapidly.

A series of congressional investigations, begun in January 2002, revealed a variety of unusual if not downright suspicious activities. Employees of Enron's outside auditors, Arthur Andersen LLP, destroyed thousands of e-mails and paper documents related to the audit of the company. Apparently, a request to Enron from the SEC for information about its financial accounting had led to an expedited effort at the accounting firm to eliminate many of the audit-related documents. Considerable controversy arose as to who specifically directed the destruction of the files and, also, how important or unique the destroyed papers actually were. An October 2001 e-mail from an attorney at Andersen had advised the auditors to follow company procedures that allowed for the disposal of many documents. Opinions at the firm differ as to whether this communication was a disguised message to eliminate much of the "paper trail" related to the audit of Enron.[20]

During the congressional investigations, quite a bit of illuminating information surfaced about the prior conduct of key Enron and Andersen personnel. For example, when Andersen's Professional Standards Group (its internal watchdog) objected to Enron's "creative" accounting approach, it was overruled by Andersen's line management.

Subsequently, the Department of Justice initiated an unusual criminal indictment of the entire firm.[21] This legal action, in turn, led to the loss of most of its clients and to the loss of partners to other accounting firms. Andersen, a major worldwide organization in the field of accounting, rapidly disintegrated.

It is likely that it will take a variety of legal proceedings and governmental investigations to uncover the details underlying the events surrounding the Enron bankruptcy, especially concerning the role and responsibility of key officials. Yet, some basic facts about Enron's top management are clear.

Chairman and erstwhile CEO Kenneth Lay, and Jeffrey Skilling, when he was CEO and president, both signed the letters to shareholders in Enron annual reports and approved the section, "Management's Discussion and Analysis of Financial Condition and Results of Operation." Nevertheless, both later claimed ignorance of the problems that led to the company's collapse, claiming that they relied on their legal and financial advisers for the information contained in the annual report.

Skilling insisted in congressional hearings that he thought the company was in good shape when he resigned in the summer of 2001. (He never offered a convincing explanation for why he suddenly left such an important and rewarding position.) A number of red flags subsequently were made public, notably a letter to Lay from Enron official Sherron Watkins charging serious accounting misdeeds. She wrote, "I am incredibly nervous that we will implode in a wave of accounting scandals."[22]

Yet Lay maintained that he was ignorant of the details of the partnership structures and related problems. It was later learned that both Lay and Skilling signed off on the controversial partnerships. Both had been effectively deputized by the Enron board of directors to oversee them.[23] A belated investigation by the Enron board, chaired by the dean of the University of Texas Law School, concluded that the responsibility for Enron's inadequate financial disclosures "is shared by Enron management, the Audit and Compliance Committee of the Board, Enron's in-house counsel, Vinson & Elkins [the company's outside law firm], and Andersen [the outside auditors]."[24]

A cogent and short summary of the Enron episode was provided by Frank G. Zarb, an experienced senior official in business and government: Enron "mixed aggressive accounting, reckless financing, and a touch of greed. . . ."[25]

Notes

1. Ira M. Millstein and Salem M. Katsch, *The Limits of Corporate Power* (New York: Macmillan, 1981), pp. 3–4.
2. "Boardrooms in a Post-Enron World" (New York: *Director's Alert,* 2002).
3. *28th Annual Board of Directors Study* (Los Angeles: Korn/Ferry International, 2001).
4. *Directors' Compensation and Board Practice in 2000* (New York: Conference Board, 2000).
5. Murray Weidenbaum, "Proceed Cautiously with This Innovation," *Directors & Boards,* Fall 1997, p. 21.
6. Lauren Talner, *The Origins of Shareholder Activism* (Washington, DC: Investor Responsibility Research Center, 1983), pp. 1–4.
7. David Vogel, *Lobbying the Corporation* (New York: Basic Books, 1978), p. 35.
8. Samuel B. Graves, Kathleen Rehbein, and Sandra Waddock, "Fad and Fashion in Shareholder Activism," *Business and Society Review* 106, no. 4, Winter 2001, pp. 300–302.
9. Louis Lavelle, "How Shareholder Votes Are Legally Rigged," *Business Week,* May 20, 2002, p. 48.

10. Diane Brady, "If You Don't Open Your Books, We'll Cancel Your Policy," *Business Week,* August 26, 2002, p. 38.
11. See *Principles of Corporate Governance* (Washington, DC: Business Roundtable, 2002).
12. Benjamin E. Hermalin and Michael S. Weisbach, "Endogenously Chosen Boards of Directors and Their Monitoring of the CEO," *American Economic Review,* March 1998, p. 96.
13. Nancy L. Rose and Catherine Wolfram, *Regulating Executive Pay: Using the Tax Code to Influence CEO Compensation* (Cambridge, MA: National Bureau of Economic Research, 2000).
14. Lucian Bebchick, Jesse Fried, and David Walker, "Managerial Power and Rent Extraction in the Design of Executive Compensation," *University of Chicago Law Review* (forthcoming).
15. John G. Smale, "Where Was the Board?" *Across the Board,* May/June 2002, pp. 11–12.
16. John T. Gardner, "Building Better Boards," *Business Week,* August 26, 2002, p. 163.
17. "Pitt Says Lawyers Will Be Held Accountable to Directors," *New York Times,* August 13, 2002, p. C2.
18. For details, see Joel Seligman, "No One Can Serve Two Masters: Corporate and Securities Law After Enron," *Washington University Law Quarterly* (forthcoming).
19. "The Enron Hearings: Cleaning Up After the Debacle," *New York Times,* January 20, 2002, p. 12W.
20. "Andersen Fires Partner It Says Led Shredding of Enron Documents," *Wall Street Journal,* January 16, 2002, p. A1 et ff.
21. Mike McNamee with Amy Borus, "Out of Control at Andersen," *Business Week,* April 8, 2002, pp. 32–33.
22. Michael Schroeder and John Emshwiller, "Letter to Lay Prompts Queries to Enron," *Wall Street Journal,* January 15, 2002, p. A3.
23. "Boardrooms in a Post-Enron World," p. 11.
24. Cited in Seligman, "No One Can Serve Two Masters."
25. Frank G. Zarb, "It's the Soul, Stupid: New Lessons from Enron," *Simon Business,* Spring 2002, p. 13.

21

THE FUTURE OF
THE BUSINESS FIRM
━━◦∘◦━━

The demonstrated ability of the business corporation to gradually adapt to shifting political, social, and economic forces is the key to its continuing strength and resilience. In responding to public-policy demands and interest-group influences in a practical and nondogmatic manner, the corporation is likely to continue to be the dominant way of organizing economic activity in the developed world through the twenty-first century.

Responding to a variety of new influences, the business corporation has gone through three stages of development: from the simple, competitive classical model of the nineteenth century to the managerial model of the first half of the twentieth century to the social environment model characteristic of the second half of the twentieth century. The major changes related to the increased attention required on the part of management to a host of forces external to the corporation, both domestic and international.

In this vein, we may speculate about the future of the private enterprise system in the United States. What will be its relationships with governments at all levels? And with various private forces? We may obtain some useful insights by contemplating how American business has adjusted to past threats and opportunities. If any common theme emerges from examining the transition of seventeenth-century colonial business to the early twenty-first century global American enterprise, it is the gradual nature of the changes. This characteristic is borne out by an old clichè of historical analysis, "Every period is an age of transition."

Thus, it is altogether likely that the quintessential colonial businessman Benjamin Franklin, after the briefest period of adjustment, would feel comfortable at board meetings of a large modern multinational enterprise. Of course, not all of today's management has the wide range of interests and capabilities of Dr. Franklin.

The United States is in the midst of several important transitions that affect business–government relations in powerful ways. The most obvious is away from the Cold War competition with the former Soviet Union (and the emphasis on awesome nuclear armaments) to a period where threats to the national security are less conventional and arise from far more diverse and unexpected sources (and the responses are equally innovative). Simultaneously, we are witnessing a shift from less government involvement in business during the last quarter of the twentieth century to more regulation of the private sector—but not a simple return to the earlier policy framework.

Within the private economy, Americans have been experiencing a very different and relatively benign type of business cycle—long periods of growth interrupted by short and modest downturns. Substantial and widespread, but not universal, prosperity has encouraged large portions of the American public to become direct owners of business. They may not think of themselves as capitalists, but they have taken a direct ownership in the private-enterprise system—above and beyond their customary roles as employees and customers.

Nevertheless, some observers of the American corporation have produced rather negative evaluations of its long-term prospects. They see the larger companies as too muscle bound to compete successfully against newer and smaller enterprises. Also, because of their high visibility, the large corporations are especially attractive targets for increased government involvement in private business. The critics also cite the gradual reduction over the years in the discretion of managers to conduct day-to-day operations—a development they attribute to the joining of forces of politicians and all sorts of special-interest groups. As shown in many earlier chapters, these concerns are bolstered by a substantial factual foundation.

Yet this negative view likely has excessively discounted the powerful adaptive capability of private enterprise. Viewed from a positive standpoint, we can state with considerable confidence that the corporation, albeit with substantial modifications, is likely to continue to be the dominant institution in the economy of developed countries such as the United States through the twenty-first century. Such optimism has a firm basis, for the modern corporation never has been a static or inflexible entity, and there is no reason to expect that it will become one. The typical corporation has become more aware and, in many ways, more responsive to the social needs of the society of which it is inescapably a part. This is an important aspect of its protective feedback mechanism. Here is a pertinent example. In 1988, when Richard J. Mahoney, then the chief executive of Monsanto, saw the large numbers on the emissions of pollution by the various factories of his company, he unilaterally and voluntarily ordered the company to reduce its total air emissions of toxic chemicals by 90 percent by the end of 1992. To the surprise of many, the company achieved this ambitious objective on schedule.[1]

Even a strong critic of American capitalism like Robert Heilbroner concedes that history has shown capitalism to be an "extraordinarily resilient, persisting and tenacious system." He cites as a key reason the fact that the driving force is so widely dispersed rather than being concentrated in a governing elite. Heilbroner also notes that the propelling force of profits has yielded a capacity for change that Karl Marx did not anticipate.[2]

TOWARD GREATER SOCIAL RESPONSIVENESS

We can develop some useful conceptualizations of the successive shifts toward greater business responsiveness to its external environment—a change that is basic to the public's continued acceptance and support of the private enterprise system.

In reality, of course, corporations—especially the larger and publicly owned ones—have always departed substantially from the narrow confines of the profit-maximizing model of classical economics. Essentially, the departures have been a matter of degree and, in the past half century, those departures have been increasingly large. Thus, we can define three basic points on the continuum of change: the classical market model of the business firm, the modern managerial model of the business firm, and the contemporary social environmental model.[3]

THREE MODELS OF BUSINESS ORGANIZATION

The *classical market model,* in large measure the original concept of business organization, was based primarily on the British economy of the nineteenth century.[4] It was a period characterized by many small companies producing fairly standard products. Competition was effective and centered mainly on price. The modest scale of most industrial enterprises forced businesses to focus on short-run profit maximization. The owner-manager style of business operation, which fits the classical model, continues to characterize many of the smaller and newer entrepreneurial firms of the present.

The *managerial model* was the next major development in terms of the fundamental approach to the organization and functioning of the business firm. It was the dominant business mode in the first half of the twentieth century and it has not disappeared from the business scene. Its basic identifying characteristic is the acknowledgment of the effective separation of ownership from management.[5] The key goals of the enterprise are modified in the process, reflecting the importance of satisfying the desires of professional managers. The latter tend to emphasize growth in size, market share, and profitability, as well as the security of their position in the community and in society generally. As a consequence, market concentration becomes common, resulting from heavy investments in technology, product differentiation, and expanded advertising efforts.

A late variation on the managerial model focuses on the manager as trustee for various groups, including shareholders, employees, the community, customers, and other interests. To some degree, each of the "stakeholders" makes a type of investment in the corporation.

- Employees invest their own human capital—the education they have received and the skills they have acquired. Much of this knowledge is specific to the firm and cannot readily be transferred to other employers.
- Suppliers of goods and services often invest in designing and producing the specific components they sell to the company.
- Customers often come to rely on the company for a steady flow of products. This is exemplified by firms who have adopted "just-in-time" inventory policies.
- Suppliers of capital include the shareholders in a very fundamental way. They are the legal owners of the corporation. However, other important sources of financial resources include bondholders who supply long-term capital and banks that finance working capital.
- Local communities often provide special infrastructure support to the company such as roads to the factory and new schools and other expanded local services for the families of company employees.

Because the broader social purpose of the corporation is seen as creating wealth, society may have a moral as well as economic interest in business taking account of all the firm-specific investments. Nevertheless, shareholders retain a special status—as residual claimants in the enterprise.[6] This alternate view, it will be recognized, is a transition phase to the third approach. Yet both variations of the managerial model share a key assumption that the behavior of the business firm is determined in large part by the discretionary power of its management. The conduct of the corporation continues to be constrained by competition, but the constraints allow management considerable discretion within broad limits.

A way of reconciling the different viewpoints on the purpose of the corporation is contained in a statement offered by a firm that invests large sums in corporate securities.

According to Hermes Pensions Management Ltd., which is responsible for $80 billion of pension funds in the United Kingdom:

> The overriding objective of the corporation should be to optimize over time its return to its shareholders. . . . To achieve this objective, the corporation should endeavor to ensure the long-term viability of its business, and to manage effectively the relationships with its stakeholders.[7]

In theory, the management remains the agent of the owners (the shareholders). In practice, management has the difficult but strategic task of balancing the desires of the different stakeholders, including the stockholders. Many CEOs in their heart of hearts believe that they know what is truly in the corporation's long-term interest. As they see it, board members only spend a few hours a month on company business, while investors, suppliers, customers, and employees come and go. Accurate or not, it is not surprising that CEOs who have devoted much of their professional lives to a company believe that they best represent the spirit of the enterprise.

All sorts of variations occur in terms of the locus of power. The interests of employees may dominate for a while as the result of a successful strike. Customer concerns are fundamental during a highly publicized product "scare" (such as the expensive recall and repackaging of Tylenol). Failure to meet bond covenants may force companies to slash capital budgets and abandon expansion plans in order to satisfy financial institutions. And, of course, stockholders may replace the management in a takeover battle.

The *social environment model* is the most recent of the three approaches to business behavior. Under this concept, the enterprise reacts to the total socioeconomic environment, not merely to markets.[8] Corporate behavior responds to political forces, public opinion, and government pressures, regardless of whether those factors are welcome. It is widely understood that both market and nonmarket forces can affect the firm's costs, sales, and profits. At times, these two forces can become intertwined. For example, consumer or civil rights groups can launch a boycott of a company's products in order to force changes in its internal policies. On the positive side, private interest groups can sponsor "affinity" credit cards encouraging their members to make purchases from a specific enterprise.

Another—and related—way of looking at the modern corporation is to see beyond the firm as a bundle of assets owned by the shareholders. In this view, the corporation is an institutional arrangement for governing. Corporate governance covers a set of contracts and relationships among a group of participants in the enterprise.[9]

The modern corporation does not behave either like the simple profit-maximizing firm or the traditional monopolist. It innovates, and at times its profit rates may be above average. For it, competition has expanded in new dimensions and involves many nonprice variables. Management is very much concerned about shareholders—as a group. To underscore that relationship, a large portion of the compensation of senior executives is frequently tied to the firm's profitability or to the performance of its shares in the stock market. As we have seen, that incentive system in practice can become quite complicated and generate unforeseen results.

Although the role of the individual investor remains quite nominal, the power of the shareholders as a group is enhanced by the activities of institutional investors (banks, life insurance companies, mutual funds, and pension funds) that hold large blocks of stock in individual firms (often one-half or more in the case of the largest corporations). Thus, the decisions of these financial intermediaries to buy or sell their substantial holdings can severely affect the compensation if not the future of a company's management. The many corporate takeovers that occurred via stock purchases in the open market during the 1980s and 1990s underscored the point that the power of stockholders, albeit often latent, is not trivial.

THE VARIETY OF CORPORATE CONCERNS

According to many analysts, the contemporary giant corporation cannot be sensibly thought of as merely a private entity owned by its shareholders. Nor is it an agency of the state. Instead, in this alternative view, the large private firm is seen as a servant of multiple interests.

Most of those interests have both some plausible social claim to the attention of the corporation and some power to pursue that claim—through stockholder initiatives, collective bargaining, taxation, regulation, private litigation, public pressure, and marketplace influence.[10] How can the large corporation be governed so as to allow appropriate consideration of multiple interests without becoming a political body in which governance becomes an end to itself? That is a difficult question to answer, and no specific response is likely to be adopted universally or to hold for long periods of time. As noted in Chapter 20, critics of the private corporation advocate a variety of reforms, ranging from specifying changes in the membership and role of boards of directors to imposing expensive new accounting and financial reporting requirements.

Given the continued pressures for greater governmental involvement in business decision making, no company can afford to ignore public attitudes and expectations for long. In the current environment, to do so could result directly in loss of sales and customer goodwill or indirectly in increased costs—to the extent that public pressures lead to new and expensive government impositions on business. The knowledge that they can elicit such voluntary business responses, firmly motivated by enlightened self-interest, is a factor that some interest groups and government decision makers take into account before proposing or implementing additional government involvement in the activities of the private sector of the economy. The point is not that business should be expected to agree to each new demand of every interest group, but that such external forces are important enough to warrant considered and significant responses.

There are many forces at work in American society; few if any have achieved all of their objectives. Moreover, neither consumer groups nor labor unions nor corporations have monolithic views on all issues. As we have seen in earlier chapters, changing alliances among them make for great variation in the development of public policy in the United States.

THE CONTINUING DEBATE OVER GOVERNMENT AUTHORITY AND PRIVATE POWER

In the broad sweep of American history, the transcendent ideological debate has been between the Jeffersonian and Hamiltonian approaches to democracy: centralizing or decentralizing the location of power in society. To update that debate, the more pertinent and frequent question now is how to allocate power between, on the one hand, individuals and voluntary institutions in the private sector and, on the other, the sovereign authority of government at all levels in the public sector.

This dichotomy between centralization and decentralization of political and economic power is oversimplified, of course. Nevertheless, such a construction is useful in examining the ebbs and flows of public-policy changes affecting the business system. Over the years, the public-policy pendulum has continued to swing from one alternative position to the other—and often back again. In the United States, national administrations from Franklin D. Roosevelt to Lyndon B. Johnson engaged in extremely ambitious efforts to expand the role of the federal government. Yet, every president since—Democratic and Republican—has made some attempt to reduce the power of Washington, although their levels of enthusiasm and effectiveness have varied.

Because so many of the government's policies are carried out through the business firm and thus are hidden from general view, the public is not always aware of how far down the path of government involvement the American economy has gone. As a point of reference, we can note that, in 1965, Adolph Berle (coauthor of his seminal work, *The Modern Corporation and Private Property*) described the extent to which government had at that time limited the ability of business to use its "productive property." But, he added, the state "has not attempted (aside from policy limitations) to tell a man what or how he should consume—that would constitute an intolerable invasion of his private life."[11] Obviously, Berle wrote before the compulsory installation of seat belts in private automobiles or efforts to curtail smoking or attempts by regulatory agencies to get the public to reduce the amount of sugar, salt, or calories in its diet.

Yet some swings of the policy pendulum toward lesser involvement of government also have been visible. In recent years, the disenchantment with large-scale government in general has grown. At times it has taken the practical form of limits on state government spending and taxing voted by aroused taxpayers or simply the rejection of proposed local tax and bond issues. To some extent, this attitude is being translated into a slowdown in the growth of federal expenditures and the reluctance to embark on new government programs financed by general taxation—invariably with exceptions for urgent new priorities. Also, as we have seen, government has attempted to be responsive to the numerous pleas to reform the array of regulation of private activity or at least to reduce some of the avoidably burdensome aspects.

Within the public sector, cutbacks of traditional welfare benefits have occurred simultaneously with efforts to introduce competition in the provision of electricity and telecommunications. However, some countermoves are also visible, ranging from second thoughts on economic deregulation to increased political activity on the part of the labor union movement.

In Western Europe, numerous barriers to the adoption of a more efficient operation of industrial facilities have been cited repeatedly as a key reason for the slower growth of employment and economic activity than have occurred in the United States in recent decades. The reluctance to rely fully on market-oriented policies can be seen in a report, *The Company in the 21st Century,* issued by a progressive group of 2,300 young French business executives. Stating that "the greatest misery in our society is social and spiritual rather than material," the report urged that companies be judged on their contribution to the well-being of society and their employees. In their rather advanced view, enterprises that harm society, ecologically or otherwise, should be closed down.[12]

However, for the most part, today's European governments have made their peace with the world of business. They rarely think of themselves as defenders of unions or champions of large, public-sector initiatives. Words such as *enterprise* and *opportunity* have become part of their everyday vocabulary.[13]

In part, a more limited or perhaps more positive approach to public policy toward business is encouraged by a growing understanding of the international dimensions of private enterprise. The typical worker in every industrialized nation is learning, often from sad personal experience, that domestic companies compete with increasingly powerful foreign firms in both domestic and overseas markets. Many of those foreign corporations, rather than being restricted by their governments, are often encouraged or subsidized by them.

In any event, virtually every broad-based analysis of public opinion in the United States reports continuing and overwhelming support for the private enterprise system. One such survey shows that two-thirds of the sample surveyed agree that capitalism provides people with the highest living standard in the world; it also affords all individuals the opportunity to develop their own special abilities; moreover, capitalists are entitled to the reward of profits because they assume the risk of loss. Nevertheless, these and other surveys also show substantial dissatisfaction with specific aspects of business performance, including the quality of products (too low) and the prices charged and rewards to top management (too high)—and thus endorsement of continuing external pressure on business.[14]

Viewed in that light, we can gain some insight into the changing nature of the large multinational enterprise by examining an increasingly common example. A U.S. producer of electronics equipment, for example, may generate more than half of its revenues from overseas sources. Its products and services may be sold in 50 or even 100 nations, located throughout Europe, Asia, and the Western Hemisphere. This prototypical multinational enterprise may use components that are produced in the United States as well as in the major nations in which it sells its output. Likewise, its financing is worldwide, provided by a shifting consortium of 20 to 40 international banks. Its shares may be listed on the world's major stock exchanges and held by investors in every continent, except Antarctica. The company's intellectual capital and property rights are also highly moveable. It is both a customer of and a supplier to the other major electronics companies. Together, these corporations engage in joint ventures, coproduce, serve as sources for each other, share output, and compete.

Advances in technology have fundamentally altered—and basically strengthened—the way contemporary corporations now do business. These technological and organizational changes also have exerted an important effect on the government's ability and desire to influence company decision making. In an increasing competitive global marketplace, at times government becomes an observer on the sidelines—but retaining its power to take a more active role in business policy should its priorities or circumstances change.

Undoubtedly, the corporation will continue to be a central institution of American society in the twenty-first century. The conclusion of the late Neil Jacoby is still pertinent: "There is simply no promising alternative way of organizing and carrying out most of the tasks of production."[15] How well U.S.–based corporations perform those tasks will depend, of course, on myriad future decisions in both the public and private sectors. Thus, as an astute observer has noted, "One of the requirements of an effective business manager is the ability to live with ambiguity."[16]

A NEW POLICY CLIMATE

On the basis of the public reaction to developments in government during the 1980s and 1990s, a new policy climate for business may be taking shape in the early twenty-first century. It is an external environment less hospitable than that existing during the administration of Ronald Reagan. However, this changed business climate is not a return to the 1970s, when business was almost uniformly portrayed as the villain and subjected to a pattern of constantly new or expanding government restrictions and regulations. But we are seeing a step away from a relatively uncritically pro-business environment to a somewhat more ambivalent position.

This equivocal attitude reflects the dual views that many Americans hold about the private enterprise system. On the one hand, they view it positively, as the most important and effective way of providing jobs and income as well as goods and services. But on the other hand, they see all sorts of shortcomings, ranging from selfish or shortsighted actions on the part of insulated managements to the truly venal and illegal acts on the part of a relatively small but conspicuous number of executives.

In an attempt to please conservative and liberal critics simultaneously, government leaders have been seeking more effective and less burdensome ways of carrying out the government's desires. Thus, environmental statutes have been revised to reduce the adverse impacts of acid rain while simultaneously minimizing the economic costs by creating a market in which air pollution credits can be traded.

What the new policy background makes possible is another and perhaps different wave of government and public involvement in internal business decision making. Potential areas for deeper government involvement are numerous:

- The rising concern over the threats from international terrorist groups and the difficulty of reconciling specific responses with traditional notions of freedom and privacy. Many business firms see mainly increased government involvement in the private sector, while other firms focus on the new opportunities in the homeland security market.

- Renewed emphasis on environmental protection and fairness in the treatment of employees. The newer issues range from global warming and species diversity to concerns over diversity in the workplace. Each of these potentially involves substantial private action along lines determined or strongly influenced by government officials.

- Reducing the sale of illegal drugs and dealing with the adverse impacts of widespread use of various "chemical substances" (including alcohol, etc.). This includes wider testing of employees. A related area is the effort to reduce very substantially the purchase of cigarettes, especially by teenagers, and also to discourage consumers from buying other products that may contribute to health problems.

- Better education of the workforce so that American business can compete more effectively in an increasingly global market. This desire often gets translated into the odd position of business leading drives for higher school taxes and bond issues and supporting other extensions of government involvement in an effort to promote productivity and competitiveness. Perhaps not too surprisingly, some of the public interest groups that earlier saw strong business opposition to most extensions of government regulation are suspicious of the current corporate efforts to become "good guys." This is apparent in the less than universal acceptance by environmental groups of company offers to participate in and finance annual Earth Day celebrations.

• A continued tendency of government to achieve new priorities while minimizing its own expenditures by imposing social costs on business. These range from tougher ecological standards to broader requirements for employee leave for a variety of family and personal purposes.

• Attention to new forms of governmental revenue such as a national sales tax or a flat tax to replace the traditional income taxes. Such fundamental reform of the tax system is driven by the domestic concern to reduce the economic burdens of raising increasing amounts of government revenues and the international pressures to finance a larger share of domestic investment by domestic saving—rather than seeing the United States become even more dependent on the continued import of huge amounts of foreign capital.

• Rethinking the role of the antitrust laws in an increasingly global marketplace. Complicating the policy process is the contention by some sectors of the economy that the traditional way of enforcing domestic antitrust laws may unwittingly generate trade barriers.

• Renewal of protectionist forces in those segments of the population that believe they do not benefit from globalization, but feel the downside impacts.

Political and economic change in the United States has been a gradual, evolving process. Dramatic departures have been few and infrequent. It is reasonable to predict, therefore, that the future of business–government relationships in the United States will be a continuing reconciliation of conflicting forces, rather than an inevitable movement to a polar alternative.

Contemporary business has come a long way from the pristine world of small traders and skilled workers in which buyers and sellers could meet and satisfy their needs with scarcely little more coordination than that provided by the "invisible hand" of the free market. The corporation has become the fundamental organizing unit of the capitalist economy. Its most important attribute is its unique capacity for managing large-scale processes required for converting labor, raw materials, and energy into mass-produced and widely distributed goods and services.

With the demise of the communist regimes of Eastern Europe, it has become more apparent than ever that the American model of capitalism is just one variety—albeit a very important and unusual one—in a continuum of types of private enterprise systems. In countries such as Germany, France, Italy, Japan, Brazil, South Korea, and China, much greater emphasis is placed on government policies to more directly influence the anticipated contributions of business to the welfare of the nation. Simultaneously and reciprocally, these other countries manifest less of the adversarial nature of business–government relations so characteristic of the United States.[17]

In many other countries, government plays a measurably larger role than it does in the United States, and business institutions have adjusted to that reality. As shown in Table 21.1, in several Western European nations government spending (a useful but

TABLE 21.1 Variations in the Importance of Government Spending, 2000

Country	Percent of GDP
Sweden	55.4
France	52.8
Italy	48.2
Belgium	46.7
The Netherlands	46.3
United Kingdom	39.7
Russia	35.1
Norway	34.4
New Zealand	33.7
Germany	33.2
Czech Republic	33.1
Austria	27.6
Australia	26.0
Japan	23.7
Ireland	23.6
Poland	22.0
Canada	21.0
United States	18.4
Switzerland	14.6

Source: U.S. Department of Commerce.

incomplete proxy for the total government role) equals more than one-third of the gross domestic product.

Cogent examples of the fundamental difference in the scope of governmental influence in the economies of industrialized nations range from Sweden and France (over 52 percent) to the United States (18 percent) and Switzerland (15 percent). However, these relationships can change substantially over time. As recently as 1960, in none of the countries shown in Table 21.1 did government spending equal as much as 35 percent of GDP. Much of the expansion has been in transfer payments redistributing income within the societies, rather than in the expansion of public production or even purchase of goods and services from the private sector.

As in the past, the business system of the future will continue to be a developing institution characterized by dynamic responses to a constantly developing external environment, especially the powerful role of government.[18]

Notes

1. *Environmental Annual Review, 1996* (St. Louis, MO: Monsanto Company, 1997).

2. Robert L. Heilbroner, *Beyond Boom and Crash* (New York: W. W. Norton, 1978), p. 89.

3. Neil H. Jacoby, *Corporate Power and Social Responsibility* (New York: Macmillan, 1973), pp. 192–195.

4. See Alfred Marshall, *Principles of Economics,* 8th ed. (New York: Macmillan, 1949), pp. 240–313.

5. The classical work in this area is Adolph A. Berle and Gardner C. Means, *The Modern Corporation and Private Property* (New Brunswick, NJ: Transaction Publishers, 1991).

6. Margaret Blair, *Ownership and Control* (Washington, D.C.: The Brookings Institution, 1995); Michael Novak, *Business As a Calling* (New York: Free Press, 1996).

7. Cited in *The Global Investor and Corporate Governance* (New York: Conference Board, 2001), p. 27.

8. See *Social Responsibilities of Business Corporations* (New York: Committee for Economic Development, 1971).

9. Ronald H. Coase, "The Nature of the Firm," *Economica* 4, no. 16, 1937, pp. 386–405.

10. Lee E. Preston, *Social Issues and Public Policy in Business and Management* (College Park: University of Maryland, Center for Business and Public Policy, 1986), pp. 25–26.

11. Adolph A. Berle, "Property, Production and Revolution," *Columbia Law Review,* January 1965, p. 12.

12. Barry James, "Executives' Warning on Raw Capitalism," *International Herald Tribune,* October 5, 1996, p. 23.

13. "The Future of the State," *The Economist,* September 20, 1997, p. S7.

14. Robert A. Peterson et al., "The Public's Attitude Toward Capitalism," *Business Horizons,* September/October 1991, pp. 59–63; Philip Angelides and Amy Domini, "Open Proxy Balloting," *Barron's,* May 13, 2002, p. 32.

15. Jacoby, *Corporate Power,* p. 269.

16. William E. Schlender, "Counter-Vailing Values in Business Decision-Making," in Donald G. Jones, ed., *Business, Religion, and Ethics* (Cambridge, MA: Gelgeschlager, Gunn & Hain, 1982), p. 183.

17. George David Smith and Davis Dyer, "The Rise and Transformation of the American Corporation," in Carl Kaysen, ed., *The American Corporation Today* (New York: Oxford University Press, 1996), pp. 28, 65.

18. Peter Drucker, "The Next Society," *The Economist,* November 3, 2001, pp. 3–20.

INDEX

WITHDRAWN

WITHDRAWN

WITHDRAWN